Theory and Practice in Epicurean Political Philosophy

Also available from Bloomsbury

Anaximander, Andrew Gregory
Early Greek Philosophies of Nature, Andrew Gregory
Ecology and Theology in the Ancient World, edited by Ailsa Hunt and Hilary F. Marlow
The Origins of Music Theory in the Age of Plato, Sean Alexander Gurd

Theory and Practice in Epicurean Political Philosophy

Security, Justice and Tranquility

Javier Aoiz and Marcelo D. Boeri

BLOOMSBURY ACADEMIC
LONDON • NEW YORK • OXFORD • NEW DELHI • SYDNEY

BLOOMSBURY ACADEMIC
Bloomsbury Publishing Plc
50 Bedford Square, London, WC1B 3DP, UK
1385 Broadway, New York, NY 10018, USA
29 Earlsfort Terrace, Dublin 2, Ireland

BLOOMSBURY, BLOOMSBURY ACADEMIC and the Diana logo are trademarks of
Bloomsbury Publishing Plc

First published in Great Britain 2023
Paperback edition published 2024

Copyright © Javier Aoiz and Marcelo D. Boeri, 2023

Javier Aoiz and Marcelo D. Boeri have asserted their right under the Copyright,
Designs and Patents Act, 1988, to be identified as Authors of this work.

For legal purposes the Acknowledgements on p. vi constitute an extension
of this copyright page.

Cover design: Terry Woodley
Cover image © The philosopher's garden at Athens. Coloured engraving.
19th century. Lanmas / Alamy Stock Photo.

All rights reserved. No part of this publication may be reproduced or transmitted
in any form or by any means, electronic or mechanical, including photocopying,
recording, or any information storage or retrieval system, without prior
permission in writing from the publishers.

Bloomsbury Publishing Plc does not have any control over, or responsibility for, any
third-party websites referred to or in this book. All internet addresses given
in this book were correct at the time of going to press. The author and publisher
regret any inconvenience caused if addresses have changed or sites have
ceased to exist, but can accept no responsibility for any such changes.

A catalogue record for this book is available from the British Library.

Library of Congress Cataloging-in-Publication Data
Names: Aoiz, Javier, author. | Boeri, Marcelo D., author.
Title: Theory and practice in Epicurean political philosophy : security,
justice and tranquility / Javier Aoiz, and Marcelo D. Boeri.
Description: London : Bloomsbury Academic, 2023. |
Includes bibliographical references and index.
Identifiers: LCCN 2022030742 | ISBN 9781350346543 (hardback) |
ISBN 9781350346581 (paperback) | ISBN 9781350346550 (ebook) |
ISBN 9781350346567 (epub) | ISBN 9781350346574
Subjects: LCSH: Epicureans (Greek philosophy) | Political science--Philosophy. |
Philosophy, Ancient.
Classification: LCC B512 .A55 2023 | DDC 187—dc23/eng/20220824
LC record available at https://lccn.loc.gov/2022030742

ISBN: HB: 978-1-3503-4654-3
PB: 978-1-3503-4658-1
ePDF: 978-1-3503-4655-0
eBook: 978-1-3503-4656-7

Typeset by RefineCatch Limited, Bungay, Suffolk

To find out more about our authors and books visit www.bloomsbury.com
and sign up for our newsletters.

Contents

Acknowledgements		vi
Notes on the Texts and Translations		vii
List of Abbreviations		viii
	Introduction	1
1	The Genealogy of Justice and Laws in Epicureanism	15
2	The City, the Natural Good and the Epicurean Promise of Security	33
3	Preconception, Justice and Usefulness in the Epicurean Contractual Political Model	59
4	Cicero, Plutarch and Lactantius as Readers of Epicureanism	79
5	The Epicurean Sage, the Issue of Justice and the Laws	105
6	The Greek Poleis, Rome and Its Illustrious Epicurean Citizens	131
7	Conclusions. Friendship, Law and Justice: The Epicureans and their Interest in Interpersonal Relations	159
Notes		167
References		207
General Index		225
Index Locorum		233

Acknowledgements

This book began life almost four years ago, when we started to have frequent Epicurean conversations in which we discovered many affinities of approach in our understanding of Epicureanism. From then on, we met every week to discuss some Epicurean text or to assess an interpretation of a specific topic until we decided to embark on writing a volume, the result of which is this book.

We have incurred many debts in the preparation of this volume. First and foremost, we are grateful to Michael Erler and David Konstan, who read drafts of a couple of chapters of this work. Their comments (on form and content) offered highly constructive criticism and led to significant improvements. Special thanks also go to Ronald Polansky for his constructive suggestions and critiques regarding chapter 1. We would also like to express our deep gratitude to Anna Angelli, Laurent Anglade, Dino De Sanctis, Matthias Haake, Jürgen Hammerstaedt, Bernard Ludwig, Riet Van Bremen and Francesco Verde. They were kind enough to send us their books and papers on topics relevant to our project. Our reading of their texts helped us consider the results of their research and produce a better-quality manuscript. Also, we would like to thank Bloomsbury (and especially Alice Wright and Lily Mac Mahon) for a straightforward and professional process of reviewing and publication. The critical remarks and suggestions of the reviewers for the press were invaluable. Marcelo D. Boeri acknowledges the support provided by the Agencia Nacional de Investigación y Desarrollo (ANID), Chile, through his Fondecy Project 1200213 (some aspects of this book are a partial result of that project).

Several sections of this book appeared recently as papers in scientific journals: a slightly different version of chapter 1 ('The Genealogy of Justice and Laws in Epicureanism') was published with the same title in *Ancient Philosophy* 42, 1, 2022. A different version of two sections of chapter 6 was published in *Transformação. Revista de Filosofia* 45, 2, 2022, as '¿Cuán apolíticos fueron Epicuro y los epicúreos? La polis griega y sus ilustres ciudadanos epicúreos'. Finally, a rather distinct version of sections of chapters 4 and 5 appeared in *Ciceroniana on line. A Journal of Roman Thought* VI, 1, 2022, as 'Cicero and his clamorous silences: Was he fair enough with the Epicureans and their Ethical and Political Views?'. We are grateful to the editors of the mentioned journals for allowing us to use this material for our book.

Notes on the Texts and Translations

Most of the Greek text of Epicurus' letters and sayings as well as the fragments of passages about Epicureanism were contrasted with the still masterpiece by Graziano Arrighetti's compilation *Epicuro, Opere* (1973). All the translations of the main Epicurus' letters (*Letter to Herodotus*, *Letter to Menoeceus* and *Letter to Pythocles*), *Vatican Sayings* and *Principal Doctrines* follow Inwood and Gerson (1994) and sometimes A. A. Long and D. Sedley (1987), unless otherwise stated. Translations of Lucretius' *De Rerum Natura* are those of Martin Ferguson Smith (2001). When we deviate from these translations, we indicate it in the text (for the most part, those deviations are only slight modifications or different emphases). Translations of the other writers that quote and discuss Epicurean doctrines and arguments (such as Cicero, Plutarch, Athenaeus, Porphyry, Lactantius, etc.) are conveniently indicated in the References. The Greek and Latin texts we have considered are listed in the References. When citing a passage from Cicero, Plutarch, Lactantius (or any other ancient writer) that is included in Hermann Usener's compilation (*Epicurea* 1887), we cite Us. followed by the passage number (e.g. Plutarch, *A Pleasant Life* 1090C-D; Us. 532). The Greek texts of all Platonic works are from J. Burnet's Oxford editions (1900–7) except for the Greek text of the *Republic*, which is from S. R. Slings' Oxford edition (2003). For Aristotle's *Nicomachean Ethics* and *Politics*, we have used Reeve's translations (1983), and the Greek text from J. Bywater's edition (1894) and Ross' edition (1957), respectively.

Abbreviations

Abst.	Porphyry, *De Abstinentia*
Acad.	Cicero, *Academica*
An. Post.	Aristotle, *Analytica Posteriora*
Aristog.	Demosthenes, *In Aristogitonem*
Col.	Plutarch, *Contra Colotes*
Comm.	Plutarch, *De communis notitiis*
Contempt	Polystratus, *On the Irrational Contempt of Popular Opinions*
DA	Aristotle, *De anima*
De Re.	Cicero, *De Re Pvblica*
Diss.	Epictetus, *Dissertationes*
Div. Inst.	Lactantius, *Divinae Institutiones*
DK	Diels & Kranz, *Die Fragmente der Vorsokratiker*
DL	Diogenes Laertius, *Lives of the Eminent Philosophers*
EE	Aristotle, *Ethica Eudemia*
EN	Aristotle, *Ethica Nicomachea*
Ep.	Seneca, *Epistulae Morales ad Lucilium*
Fin.	Cicero, *De Finibus*
Gorg.	Plato, *Gorgias*
Leg.	Cicero, *De legibus*
LH	Epicurus, *Letter to Herodotus*
LM	Epicurus, *Letter to Menoeceus*
LP	Epicurus, *Letter to Pythocles*
LS	Long & Sedley, *The Hellenisitc Philosophers*
M	Sextus Empiricus, *Adversus Mathematicos*
ND	Cicero, *De Natura Deorum*
Noc. Att.	Aulus Gellius, *Noctes Atticae*
Off.	Cicero, *De Officiis*
PD	Epicurus, *Principal Doctrines*
PH	Sextus Empiricus, *Pyrrhoniae Hypotyposeis*
Phaed.	Plato, *Phaedrus*
Phd.	Plato, *Phaedo*
Phy.	Aristotle, *Physics*

Pleasant Life	Plutarch, *That Epicurus actually makes a Pleasant Life Impossible*
Phl.	Plato, *Philebus*
Prot.	Plato, *Protagoras*
Resp.	Plato, *Respublica*
Rh.	Aristotle, *Rhetorica*
RN	Lucretius, *De Rerum Natura*
Stoic. Rep.	Plutarch, *De Stoicorum Repugnantiis*
Stat.	Plato, *Statesman*
Strom.	Clement, *Stromateis*
SV	Aristotle, *De Somno et Vigilia*
SVF	von Arnim, *Stoicorum Veterum Fragmenta*
Tht.	Plato, *Theaetetus*
Tim.	Plato, *Timaeus*
Tusc.	Cicero, *Tusculanae Disputationes*
Us.	Usener, *Epicurea*
VS	Epicurus, *Vatican Sayings*

Introduction

The opponents of Epicureanism in antiquity successfully established a cliché that has remained to this day: the theoretical and practical disinterest of Epicurus and the Epicureans in political communities. The best proof of their success is the transformation of the expressions 'live unnoticed' [λάθε βιώσας] and 'do not participate in politics' [μὴ πολιτεύσεσθαι] into famous Epicurean slogans. It is worthwhile, however, to note two well-known facts that cast doubt on this cliché. On the one hand, the Epicurean Lucretius' poem *On the Nature of Things* constitutes, as Strauss has underlined,[1] one of the best documents of the conventionalist theory of justice. On the other hand, Epicureanism underpins one of the foundational works of modern political philosophy, Hobbes' *Leviathan*. Before Hobbes, Pierre Gassendi also viewed Epicurus' philosophical project with sympathy. In fact, Hobbes and Gassendi had at their disposal the same Epicurean texts as did opponents of Epicureanism such as Cicero, Epictetus and Plutarch (though the ancients also had access to works that have not been preserved). But while Hobbes and Gassendi found valuable considerations of political philosophy in Epicureanism, neither Cicero, Epictetus nor Plutarch refer to these ideas in their anti-Epicurean writings. Hobbes' interest in Epicureanism was not doxographical, nor did he seek to reproduce Epicurean political theory scrupulously and show what place it occupied in the Epicurean philosophy and way of life. He appropriated elements of this theory and reformulated them for the sake of incorporating them into his theory of the state, implying that there was some convergence between the two theories.[2] Nor was the treatment by Cicero, Epictetus or Plutarch of Epicureanism doxographical. Their framework was the ancient genre of philosophical diatribe. These undoubtedly included relevant testimonies and criticisms, but the omission of the adversary's views, simplification, exaggeration and even melodramatic tone were also some of their usual resources. It is therefore more than reasonable to question the portrait of Epicureanism conveyed by the famous slogans 'live unnoticed' and 'do not participate in politics'.

The purpose of this book is to shed light on how political reflection was integrated into Epicurean philosophy and how it influenced the actions and lifestyle of those who subscribed to it. As is well known, no treatise by the Hellenistic philosophers has come down to us. In the catalogues of their works in Diogenes Laertius' *Lives of eminent philosophers*, the magnitude and thematic heterogeneity of the lost works can be appreciated. These include several works by Epicurus related to the subject of this book: *On Choice and Avoidance*, *On Piety*, *On Ways of Life*, *On Justice and the Other Virtues*, *On Kingship* (DL 10.28). Fortunately, research on Epicureanism in the last decades has considerably expanded the documentary base available for the twofold task at hand. Relevant texts have been recovered from the papyri of Herculaneum of particular significance to our understanding of Epicurean political theory and its doctrinal role in the lives and actions of the Epicureans. Furthermore, the remains of Greek epigraphy and the prosopography of the Roman Epicureans has provided interesting testimonies of the public activities of the Epicureans.

Epicurus' remarks on political theory are contained in the so-called *Principal Doctrines*. Almost a third of them refer to the Epicurean lifestyle and society. The gnomic and condensed style of *Principal Doctrines* combines elaborate accounts of the Epicurean view on different matters with an implicit dialogue with the philosophical tradition. Fortunately, in addition to the letters of Epicurus and the testimonies transmitted by Diogenes Laertius, we can count on the *Vatican Sayings*, discovered in 1888, and on two other texts from early Epicureanism. The first is a fragment belonging to Hermarchus, the successor of Epicurus as head of the school, devoted to the genealogy of justice and the laws. It is preserved in Porphyry's treatise *On abstinence from animal food* (*De abstinentia*). The other is part of a treatise belonging to the successor of Hermarchus, Polystratus, the third head of the Epicurean school, which was found among the papyri from Herculaneum. Titled *On the irrational contempt of popular opinions* (*De contemptu*), it contains important debates related to the nature of justice and the laws. Lucretius' *On the Nature of Things* (especially book 5) also provides significant indications, theses and arguments that are particularly relevant to this book. The same is true of the fragments recovered from the treatises of Philodemus (*On Piety*, *On Rhetoric*, *On the Good King According to Homer*, *Against the Sophists*, *On Property Management*, and so on), from the *Vita Philonidis* (PHerc. 1044), as well as from letters of Epicurus and his followers. Through the analysis of these texts and documents, and by means of a cautious reading of the hostile testimonies of Cicero, Plutarch and Epictetus, we hold that it is possible to reconstruct the main aspects of the political reflection of Epicureanism and its role in the doctrine and activities of the Epicureans.

This book is structured around two key questions: what, according to Epicureanism, are political communities; and what are the connections between the way of life that Epicureanism espouses and its understanding of the nature of political communities? Both questions are entirely in the tradition of Greek philosophy. Cicero excludes Epicureanism from 'the true and elegant philosophy' [*verae elegantisque philosophiae*; *Tusc.* 4.6] which originated with Socrates and was preserved by the Peripatetics, the Stoics and the Academics. However, Epicurus and the Epicureans, despite their intemperate rhetorical references to the philosophers of the past and to their contemporary rivals, answer these questions through an ongoing dialogue with the Greek philosophical tradition. Such a tradition is clearly not reducible to 'the true and elegant philosophy' Cicero mentions, even though there is no doubt that Epicurus and the Epicureans often have Plato and Aristotle in mind. It is in this sense that we argue that the presence of Plato in Epicurus is more powerful than has usually been recognized. It is true that Epicurus spits upon [προσπτύω] what is noble whenever it does not yield any pleasure (Us. 512), and that he consequently appears to deny Plato's Forms an effective role in the good life. However, Epicurus also rejects the pleasures of extravagance due to the difficulties that follow from them (Us. 181). This remark advances his thesis that if some pleasures finally turn out to be painful – as profligate ones do – they must not be pursued (*LM* 131). If this connection is reasonable, one should assume that Epicurus was probably reacting to some of Plato's tenets and was sensitive to Socrates' criticism of Protarchus' crude hedonism when formulating aspects of his own hedonist agenda. Epicurus considered the Platonic analysis in the *Philebus* not only uncontroversial, but also highly advantageous in incorporating them to his own view. In Epicurean political theory there is both dialogue and polemics with Plato. Epicurus even uses – as we shall show – ingenious reformulations of Plato's expressions to refer to crucial aspects of his own philosophy.

In *Laws* 10 Plato presents the physicalist cosmogony and the contractual theory as two faces of the same disease (*Laws* 888b8) and condemns its harmful fusion as impious and subversive, perhaps with Archelaus the disciple of Anaxagoras in mind. The Epicureans understand philosophy as a study of nature [a 'physiology': φυσιολογία], from which they raise the question 'what are political communities?' Epicurus may have been inspired by Archelaus, whom according to Diogenes Laertius he valued positively (DL 10.12). In any case, the response of Epicureanism is consistent with the fusion of physicalist cosmogony and contractualism that Plato emphatically condemned. In *On the Nature of Things* 5, Lucretius explains the origin of life and the survival and extinction of species without resorting to divine or teleological explanations. The formation of human groupings subject to covenants of justice constitutes the final point in a sequence of processes that Lucretius posits to explain the survival of the human species and the origin of civilized life. This application of the Epicurean study of nature to the analysis of political communities is translated into a genealogical approach to justice and laws. Such a genealogical approach would seem to be far from the foundation of the Epicurean way of life and from the imperturbability [ἀταραξία] it advocates. In the first three chapters we try to show that this genealogical approach brings, on the contrary, a substantial benefit: the category of security [ἀσφάλεια].

We will now focus on the argumentative structure of the book (something we will revisit later in the summaries of the chapters). Contractualist theories include descriptions of the agents of the pact. Epicurean texts offer two, because they differentiate the covenants that establish justice from the later ones that required laws and sanctions to fulfil the purposes implied by the former. This purpose is expressed in the doctrinal formula 'neither harming one another nor being harmed' (*PD* 33) and its achievement is the security which, as Hermarchus and Lucretius stress, made possible the survival of human beings. In Epicureanism security means the satisfaction of natural desires and confidence regarding their future satisfaction and 'the danger of violent death'. Thus, justice is for Epicureans a modality of the useful, as can be seen especially in the above-mentioned excerpt from Hermarchus. The typology of the actors in the two pacts differs. Laws and sanctions are established among actors who, unlike their predecessors, hold false views about the gods and death while also experiencing fears that trigger unlimited desire for wealth and power as ways of achieving security. The Epicurean genealogy of laws is consequently accompanied by a genealogy of fears and vain desires, as well as of the security to which human beings aspire. Security is, in our view, a key concept for analysing how Epicureanism understands itself concerning both the genealogy of justice and law and that of irrational fears and unlimited desires. The security provided by the city is a necessary condition of the *vita epicurea*, and this is recognized in Epicurean texts. However, Epicureanism postulates 'the purest security' (*PD* 14), i.e. a way of life freed from irrational fears and unlimited desires that make human beings unhappy and anxious for spurious securities, despite the valuable security provided by the polis. The fusion of physicalist cosmogony and contractualism in no way makes Epicureans subversive and impious. On the contrary, as we shall show, Epicureanism emphatically vindicates the value of laws and security, and also links true piety with justice. Hence, Epicureans oppose those who deny the existence of justice, maintain a crude relativism, or defend a cynical way of life.

Like any other political model, the Epicurean paradigm has a compelling normative or regulative character. The Epicurean genealogical approach to justice and laws, we hold, is also the theoretical framework from which this normative component is derived. The normative or regulative function of the Epicurean political model is embodied in the preconception [πρόληψις] of the just. Cicero (*ND* 1.43–4) ascribes to Epicurus the achievement of having coined the term πρόληψις and his testimony is now widely accepted. At the risk of being repetitive, it is worth noting that although Epicurus' two most extensive *Principal Doctrines* (*PD* 37 and 38) deal precisely with the preconception of the just, the opponents of the Epicureans in antiquity do not even mention them. *PD* 37 and 38 discuss the dynamics arising from the relationship between the just and the legal in political communities. The prolepsis of the just operates as a canon of the usefulness of the laws; that is, of their suitability to the purpose of the pact ('neither harming one another nor being harmed'). The Epicureans embedded the collective ownership of the preconception of the just in language and explains their acquisition and continuity through the world's conceptualization, involving the transmission and learning of language.

The documentary basis of the first three chapters consists mainly of Epicurean texts. The anti-Epicurean literature of antiquity provides neither testimonies nor considerations of the elements of Epicureanism's political reflection that we have indicated. Consequently, nor does it deal with their contribution to the treatment of the Epicurean way of life. This is undoubtedly a very significant fact that underlines the relevance of examining the interpretative procedures of the opponents of Epicureanism. For this reason, the purpose of chapter 4 is to examine the interpretative strategies followed by Cicero, Plutarch and Lactantius to disqualify Epicureanism. Above all, we are interested in pointing out the contributions of Cicero, Plutarch and Lactantius to the formation of a certain *forma mentis*, already present in antiquity, that has determined how Epicurus and his doctrines are read and understood. Our examination of them as readers of Epicureanism, we suggest, might eventually shed some light on how the philosophical diatribes of antiquity influenced the transmission of Greek philosophy (especially of Epicureanism) to posterity. The cliché of the theoretical and practical disinterest of Epicurus and the Epicureans in political communities stems from this kind of philosophical literature. If these anti-Epicurean diatribes, as we have indicated, omit the political reflections of Epicureanism, it is entirely reasonable to wonder about the apoliticism that they attribute to Epicurus and the Epicureans. We consider that this question can be answered on two complementary levels. On the one hand, by reconstructing the model of the Epicurean sage derived from the literature of antiquity and, on the other, through the collection of testimonies and documents about the social interaction of Epicurus and the Epicureans. We deal with these tasks in chapters 5 and 6, respectively. Both converge in a picture of Epicurus' and the Epicureans' interaction with their political communities that is far more complex, varied and interesting than the anti-Epicurean tradition has allowed.

The general approach outlined above is articulated as follows in the six chapters of the book. In the first chapter we consider the Epicurean genealogy of justice and the laws. First of all, we analyse what the conception of justice involves. We show that, contrary to what might be expected, such a genealogical pattern does not lead to conventionalist and relativistic views like those of the Sophists. The Epicureans examine the just as a modality of the useful, making use of the Hellenistic category of the relative [τὸ πρός τι]. The just is not conventional, being constrained by conformity to the purpose established in the first pacts of human communities (pacts based on the basic agreement 'neither harming one another nor being harmed'). This conformity is always determined by circumstances. In the Epicureans' view, the geographical diversity and temporal variability of justice pertains precisely to its unconventional character. Secondly, we explore the stages and actors of the Epicurean genealogy of justice and law. We emphasize its continuity with the rationalistic attempts to explain the origin of living beings and civilized life in society and stress that the traditional opposition between disordered and bestial primitive life and civilized human life receives an interesting reformulation in Epicureanism. This is so, we argue, because Epicureans did not view pre-social primitive life as 'Hobbesian'; they rather contrasted this primitive state of human beings not only with the arrival of human groups and justice, but also with the subsequent stage in which it became necessary to establish laws and sanctions due to the complexity of societies, the weakening of the awareness of the usefulness of the pacts, and the dissolution of the bonds that had made pacts possible in the first place. According to Lucretius, the gradual 'softening', or humanization, of human beings makes possible the birth of a pact amongst what he terms neighbours [*finitimi*], people immersed not in a state of 'war of all against all' due to vain and irrational desires but in affective relations such as friendship and pity for the weak. The utility and the relations of friendship (established between individuals humanized by the use of fire, housing and family life) are the two causes through which Lucretius explained the origin of human associations capable of forming pacts of justice. Finally, against those who argue that it is incoherent to appeal to friendship as the essential cause of the origin of justice within a hedonistic theory, we maintain that such readings presuppose a too sharp distinction between altruism and selfishness, a view that does not seem applicable to the way in which interpersonal relations were conceived in the ancient world.

We argue that the Epicurean programme of philosophy includes a remarkable naturalistic genealogy that attributes the survival of human beings to the security derived from the creation of justice and laws. Chapter 2 aims to show how Epicureanism develops the category of security to conceptualize the philosophical life it proposes. We emphasize the continuity between the recognition that Epicureans give to the security provided by political communities and the discussions that ancient literature dedicates to security [ἀσφάλεια], safety or preservation [σωτηρία], and freedom from fear [ἄδεια, ἀφοβία] in texts concerned with the genealogy of civilized life, the 'civil strife' [στάσις] and the good order [εὐνομία]. As we have indicated, in Epicureanism security means satisfaction of natural desires, but also confidence regarding their future satisfaction and the danger of violent death. Security, both physical and psychological, is recognized in ancient literature as a constituent element of the polis. Epicurus extends this approach and presents security as the good of nature [τὸ τῆς φύσεως ἀγαθόν] and as an end according to what is naturally congenial (κατὰ τὸ τῆς φύσεως οἰκεῖον; *PD* 7), which establishes an interesting consistency between our nature and the purpose of pacts, justice and laws. Epicureanism bases this consistency on the natural desires which are limited and have generic objects that are easy to satisfy. We then consider some of the approaches that Epicureanism has to understanding the genealogy of false beliefs that give rise to irrational fears of gods and death. This genealogy seems to have been of special interest to the Epicureans due to the doctrinal contrast that they establish between the true piety, based on the preconception [πρόληψις] of the gods, and common or popular assumptions about the gods. One of the most interesting contributions of Epicureanism, the link between the fear of death and ambition for power, is also framed in this genealogy. Finally, we examine the Epicurean idea of security, that is, 'the purest security' [εἰλικρινεστάτη ἀσφάλεια; *PD* 14] that Epicureanism advocates. To be sure, the Epicureans assume the positive attributes that recognize contractual security. Thus, unlike the Cynics, they claim that care without anguish for one's property is a legitimate means of strengthening tranquillity and minimizing fear. The limitation of natural desires, friendship and philanthropy are, in the Epicureans' view, the main factors that give the purest security to the Epicurean way of life. Their fusion reinforces the liberation from irrational fears and desires and establishes an attitude of gratitude towards the past, satisfaction towards the present and confidence in the future, which gives unity and stability to Epicurean life, properties that are highlighted in the two most representative figures of the Greek political imagery: the ship and the body.

In chapter 3 we deal with the preconception of the just. The term πρόληψις ('preconception', 'prolepsis') was coined by Epicurus and, as we have indicated, the two most extensive *Principal Doctrines* (*PD* 37 and 38) treat the preconception of the just. Firstly, we provide some general clarifications regarding what Epicurus calls 'the just of nature' (*PD* 31) to explain the connections between justice and usefulness. Next, we set out to clarify our claim that, within the domain of the Epicurean contractual model, justice can be considered a 'modality of utility' and the prolepsis of the just a canon which validates the just. Secondly, we examine how the criteria of truth work in Epicurean epistemology and show that in the practical domain confirmation has specific features that *PD* 37 and 38 underline. Opinions are not properly contrasted with bodies or properties of bodies, but by an examination of their practical consequences, that is, the advantageousness or disadvantageousness of the actions that are based on determined opinions. In our view, the preconception of the just possesses a functional or 'operative' nature, as it were, which makes it a criterion to evaluate empirically the 'truth' of certain convictions about justice, embodied in the laws, out of their adequacy for the sake of not harming one another nor being harmed (*PD* 31 to 33; 35). Due to the variation in the circumstances, the validation itself is temporary: what has been confirmed or counter-witnessed in the present as just, may not have been confirmed or counter-witnessed in the same terms in the past or may not be confirmed or counter-witnessed in the future. Finally, we explore where Epicureanism locates the ownership of the preconception of the just. We reject interpretations that locate the prolepsis of the just in the constitution that rules over the life of a community or which distinguish a hierarchical and historical plurality of preconceptions of the just; in this way we attempt to show that the Epicureans embedded the collective ownership of the preconception of the just in language. We underline the relevance of an ingredient of experience that is not usually considered when dealing with Epicurean preconception's empirical genesis: the transmission and acquisition of language.

As aforementioned, chapters 4, 5 and 6 are more 'informative' and 'doxographical' in character, although, as will be seen, they provide historical and doctrinal data that help reinforce our view that the Epicureans were not indeed averse to political life. Chapter 4 faces a well-known subject: how Epicurus and Epicureanism were received already in antiquity. There we dispute the reading that three prominent ancient writers made of Epicurus and his followers. Our struggle is against the interpretive procedures employed by Cicero, Plutarch and Lactantius – who were very hostile to Epicureanism – while examining Epicurean views. Our purpose is to show how decisive these ancient writers were in forging the traditional negative image of Epicureanism, as well as how their version of Epicureanism contributed to demoting Epicurean political reflection. These writers share several characteristics that demonstrate clearly their destructive intentions as well as the harmfulness of their account of Epicurus: (i) the reconstruction of Epicurean views drawing from the absolutization of decontextualized or mutilated slogans, or through the omission of certain views; (ii) the consideration of Epicurean assertions based on the supposed 'germs of danger' they contain and their repercussions at the level of social practice; and (iii) the banalization of Epicurus' hedonism. Indeed, these are the three interpretive resources most frequently used by Cicero, Plutarch and Lactantius when disparaging Epicureanism. At any rate, the important point in chapter 4 is that if our knowledge of Epicurean philosophy depended *exclusively* on people like Cicero or Plutarch, we would practically be unaware of the political component of the Epicurean study of nature, and of its contribution to the grounds of the Epicurean way of life.

Both the philosophers of the classical Greek period (Plato and Aristotle) and those of the Hellenistic era (Stoics, Epicureans and Sceptics) put forward their own version of a proverbial motif from ancient culture: the image of the sage. In chapter 5 we present the model of the Epicurean wise man and we investigate how it delineates the social interaction of the sage. We contrast Epicurean and Stoic sages and suggest that, contrary to what is claimed in several indirect sources, the Epicurean sage was interested in having a link with his polis. An Epicurean sage lives in and contributes to the development and well-being of the political community in which he lives as a citizen. In this characterization of the Epicurean sage, respect for laws and institutions, as well as a friendly attitude towards his homeland, play an important role. In order to deepen this characterization, we analyse an issue that Epicurus raised in his *Puzzles* [Διαπορίαι]: whether the wise Epicurean, knowing that he will not be discovered, will carry out actions contrary to the laws. In our view, this passage evokes the story of the Ring of Gyges in Plato's *Republic*, but yet the figure of Gyges represents neither a challenge nor a fascination for the Epicureans. We stress the biased reading of Cicero in *On Duty* (*Off*. 3.38-39) of the Epicurean view regarding the story of Gyges and Plutarch's mischievous interpretation of Epicurus' reply to the above-mentioned passage from the *Puzzles*. We note that both omit the role of the study of nature [φυσιολογία] and prudence [φρόνησις] in the motivations and decisions of the Epicurean sage when analysing the topics mentioned. Both suggest that the reason Epicureans refrain from crime is the fear of being discovered and punished. The Epicurean sage, we argue, does not act out of fear of punishment, but, on the contrary, disregards behaviours authorized by the law and goes beyond what is required by law in social relations, cultivating friendship, philanthropy and gratitude. We also note the importance of self-sufficiency for the Epicurean sage and state that, far from being an egoistic property of the sage, self-sufficiency involves a social dimension and thereby an engagement with the law. Finally, we show how two communal ingredients of life, friendship and justice, occupy a central place in two fundamental doctrinal resources of the picture of Epicurean sage: the biographical tradition of the 'imitation of Epicurus' [*imitatio Epicurei*] and 'becoming like god' [ὁμοίωσις θεῷ].

In chapter 6 we endeavour to answer the question as to how apolitical Epicurus and the Epicureans actually were. We use the term 'apolitical' in a broad sense to refer to political participation and social interaction. Our purpose in this chapter is twofold: on the one hand, we are concerned with examining the various tenets by which the adversaries of the Epicureans ascribe to them a kind of apoliticism and hostility to political communities. On the other hand, the chapter attempts to highlight various aspects of the interaction between Epicurus and the Epicureans and the societies in which they developed their philosophy. We first show how Cicero, Epictetus and Plutarch ground the apoliticism of the Epicureans on their refusal of the premise that human beings are naturally sociable. Their argumentation is highly rhetorical, as is usual in the philosophical diatribes of antiquity and they ignore the political approaches of the Epicureans and downgrade the Epicurean assessment of motivations and ambitions in politics which, at least since Socrates, had been inherent to the process of philosophical self-definition in Greece. The polemical strategy of these adversaries to Epicureanism, we state, involves historical levity since they were not interested in scrupulously reporting details of their lifestyle but rather in discounting their philosophical status. In sections 3, 4 and 5 of this chapter we are concerned precisely with presenting heterogeneous testimonies of the lifestyle of Epicurus and of numerous Epicureans that refute the apoliticism that has traditionally been attributed to them. We show how the testimonies about

Epicurus' life and his testament do not paint a picture of a person shut away in Epicurus' school (the Garden) and isolated from the life of Athens, but of someone who, while refusing to participate actively in politics, respected the laws and institutions of the city, participated in its worship and piety, integrated family relationships into the exercise of philosophy, and cultivated numerous and heterogeneous friendships, including with influential politicians. Furthermore, on the basis of Epicurean texts and epigraphic documents from various Greek cities, we show how numerous Epicureans belonging to the upper classes served as advisers to kings, distinguished diplomats, ambassadors, priests of the imperial and local cult, and even as prophets, without their status as Epicureans being perceived as a problem. Finally, we present several examples of illustrious Roman Epicureans who were involved in the most important political events in Rome in the first century BC; we highlight that Philodemus in *On the Good King According to Homer* is concerned with showing how the Epicurean philosopher can be useful and advise the ruler. In sum, the testimonies analysed paint a much more complex and fascinating picture of the theoretical and practical relationship between Epicurus (and the Epicureans) and their political communities than is present in the writings of the anti-Epicurean tradition.

To conclude: all Epicurean scholars know that Epicurus has been venerated and reviled as a philosopher since ancient times. A significant example of veneration is the philosopher-poet Lucretius (one of the main protagonists of this book) who holds that it was Athens, with its illustrious name, that gave the wheat-producing seed to wretched mortals that restored life and fixed the laws. It was also Athens that gave them 'the sweet relief of life' when she gave birth to 'that man of such great talent, from whose true lips everything was spread, and from whom, even after his death, his divine discoveries have carried his glory, which has been revealed since ancient times' (Lucretius, *RN* 6.1-8). Epicurus also received very bad press in antiquity: Cicero disapproves of his physics because he maintains that it is only a kind of deformation of Democritus's ideas (*Fin.* 1.17). Later in the same work, Cicero complains that Epicurus' doctrines are attractive because the crowd thinks that he maintains that actions correct and honest in themselves produce joy [*laetitia*], that is, pleasure (*voluptas*; *Fin.* 1.25). But as already indicated above, likely the most illustrative example of this approach is the Christian apologist Lactantius: he states disparagingly that, although Epicurus' doctrine was always more famous than that of others, this was not because it revealed some truth, but because the word pleasure, 'which is so popular', attracts many. Besides, as Lactantius continues, no one is immune to vices. The apologist says that all Epicurus cared about was attracting a large number of people to his cause and making them all happy: the lazy person is forbidden to learn the letters, the greedy man is allowed not to give alms, the indolent person is forbidden to hold public office, the obese one to exercise, the fearful man is forbidden to join the army, and the irreligious are satisfied when they hear Epicurus say that the gods do not care about anything. This is so, Lactantius concludes, because the wise man does everything in his own interest (*Div. Inst.* 3.17, 2-5).

These three descriptions of Epicurus are surely overemphasized and probably inaccurate: the 'sweet reliefs of human life' did not appear with Epicurus nor were his physics so trivial as to be a mere paraphrase of that of Democritus. Additionally, Epicurus was not interested in gaining adherents to his cause by justifying any action at any cost. If one reads his texts and tries to understand them, one quickly notices that, no matter how objectionable the Epicurean project may have seemed to various ancient writers, no one remained indifferent to his theses and arguments. Although in the popular imagination Epicurus is generally remembered for his ethical doctrines, we know he tried to formulate an explanation of reality that covered all of its aspects. He built up a philosophical system in which the different parts of philosophy (canonical, physical and ethical; DL 10.29-30) were interrelated, and in which all of them had a *raison d'être*. Political reflection also occupied an important place in this system. It is distressing to recognize the pitiful state in which Epicurus' work came down to us and the fragmentary material through which we must reconstruct the theories and arguments of Epicureanism about human society and the Epicurean way of life. Nevertheless, as can be seen, the few surviving texts of Epicurus and the Epicureans offer enough material to justify this study of their political reflections. One of its main attractions is that it constitutes the best evidence we have of the naturalistic approach of the ancients to the treatment of polis, justice and laws, a perspective that the great works of political reflection written by Plato and Aristotle overshadowed. The naturalistic approaches of Epicureanism do not entail primitivism or crude relativism. Nor do they imply 'presentism' (i.e. the philosophical view that only present things exist). The Epicureans recognize in the political community a reality which, to paraphrase Aristotle's words, is not restricted to the vicissitudes of the day (*Pol.* 1252b16), nor to what is convenient in the present. The political community looks at life as a whole (*EN* 1160a21-22; Porphyry, *Abst.* 1.7 2) and provides human beings with security, one of whose elements, as the Epicureans repeatedly emphasize, is confidence regarding the future satisfaction of natural desires and the danger of violent death.

In her magisterial 1994 book *The Therapy of Desire*, M. C. Nussbaum observes that when one discusses the issue of politics regarding the Epicureans, 'things are already more complicated. Epicurus himself strongly discourages active involvement in the political community and treats justice as merely instrumental to one's freedom from disturbance'. According to Nussbaum, Epicurus is 'very much concerned with the body and its needs, ... with structures of community, and the ways in which these can help human beings meet their needs.'[3] We do not think, though, that Epicurus was concerned with 'structures of community' *solely* because they help humans meet their needs. Indeed, the satisfaction of human needs was an important part of Epicurus' worries, but he did not reduce such needs to their physico-biological aspects. Even though a body with its soul is a body, human beings have interests that go beyond the bodily needs associated with their desire and the satisfaction of those desires. The interaction of Epicurus and the Epicureans with their political communities was not restricted to the space of satisfying needs. As indicated above, the testimonies about Epicurus paint a picture of someone who was involved in the laws and institutions of his city. According to Epicurus, pleasant living not only implies living prudently and justly [φρονίμως καὶ δικαίως], but also honourably (καλῶς; *LM* 132; *PD* 5). Nonetheless, Epicurus' interaction with Athens, and that of the Epicureans with their political communities more generally, was not restricted to actions dictated by living prudently and justly but was also related to the desire to live honourably, a way of life that their doctrine advocated through friendship and philanthropy.

1

The Genealogy of Justice and Laws in Epicureanism

The Epicureans understand philosophy as a study of nature [φυσιολογία] aimed at dissolving empty opinions, along with the vain desires and fears grounded on them, and at attaining imperturbability [ἀταραξία]. At first glance, their programme seems to suggest – or, more precisely, to call for – a move away from society and politics, as suggested by the two famous Epicurean slogans 'live unnoticed' [λάθε βιώσας] and 'do not participate in politics' [μὴ πολιτεύσεσθαι]. This is how the adversaries of the Epicureans (mainly Cicero and Plutarch) presented their views in antiquity. But to distance oneself from contingent politics and society does not necessarily mean a solitary way of life or a lack of interest in society, the existence of which it certainly presupposes (or so we shall argue). At the beginning of *On the Nature of Things* 6, Lucretius praises the work of Epicurus for its critique of societies that have achieved the security to satisfy necessary natural desires, since paradoxically such societies foster in human beings both the vain desires and the fears that prevent them from being happy. Moreover, few philosophies have exalted friendship as the noblest of all relationships in the same manner as Epicureanism. We hold that a philosophy that extols friendship and understands itself in the terms indicated by Lucretius cannot lack interest in the 'communal ingredient' of life. In fact, consideration of the nature of human communities, justice and laws was a crucial part of Epicurean philosophy. That this has been missed is due largely to the vicissitudes of the transmission of Epicureanism to posterity, and to the silence of Cicero and Plutarch regarding the specific approaches of the Epicureans to political philosophy. The core of this chapter focuses on discussing how the application of the Epicurean study of nature to the analysis of justice and laws is translated into a genealogical approach to these realities. We proceed as follows. In section 1 we show that, contrary to what might be expected, such an interpretative pattern does not presuppose a conventionalist view of justice. The Epicureans analyse the just as a modality of the useful, and for that they make use of the Hellenistic category of the relative [τὸ πρός τι]. The just is not conventional because it is constrained by conformity to the purpose established in the first pacts of human communities (pacts based on the basic agreement encapsulated in the principle 'neither harming one another nor being harmed'). This conformity is always determined by circumstances, these circumstances constituting an inexorable factor. In the Epicureans' view, the geographical diversity and temporal variability of justice pertains to its unconventional character. In section 2 we emphasize that the genealogical pattern that underpins the Epicurean investigation of nature extends the rationalistic attempts to explain the origin of living beings and of civilized, social life. We stress that the traditional opposition between disordered and bestial primitive life and human civilization receives an interesting reformulation in Epicureanism. This is so, we hold, because in their view the pre-social primitive life is not 'Hobbesian'; the Epicureans contrast the primitive state of human beings not only with the arrival of human groups and justice, but also with the subsequent stage in which it became necessary to establish laws and sanctions. The utility of the pacts and the relations of friendship (established between individuals humanized by the use of fire, housing and family life) are the two causes through which Lucretius explained the origin of human associations capable of forming pacts and of justice. In section 3, against interpretations stressing the incoherence of appealing within a hedonistic theory to friendship as the essential cause of the origin of justice, we maintain that such interpretations presuppose a too sharp distinction between altruism and selfishness. Such an approach misconstrues the way in which interpersonal relations were conceived in the ancient world and by the Epicureans. For the Epicureans, the origin of laws and sanctions is precisely the result of the weakening of friendly community relations and the forgetting of the usefulness of justice for the survival of the individual and the contractual community. Finally, in section 4 we summarize and indicate some conclusions.

1 Empty opinions about the just

For the most part, those who refer to the political philosophy of the Epicureans start by quoting *PD* 33, in which Epicurus claims, apparently against Plato:

> (i) Justice was not a thing in its own right, (ii) but [exists] in mutual dealings in places of any size whenever there [is] a pact about neither harming one another nor being harmed.
>
> trans. Inwood and Gerson modified

Οὐκ ἦν τι καθ' ἑαυτὸ δικαιοσύνη, ἀλλ' ἐν ταῖς μετ' ἀλλήλων συστροφαῖς καθ' ὁπηλίκους δήποτε ἀεὶ τόπους συνθήκη τις ὑπὲρ τοῦ μὴ βλάπτειν ἢ βλάπτεσθαι.[1]

Nevertheless, the presence of the expression 'a thing in its own right' [τι καθ' ἑαυτό] in proposition (i) of *PD* 33 does not oblige us to focus exclusively on Plato's idea of justice. Epicurus himself uses the expression 'in its own right' [καθ' ἑαυτό] in other passages (such as in *PD* 8 and *LH* 68, 71), without its understanding requiring, at least directly, an appeal to Plato's Forms. In the passages from *LH*, Epicurus distinguishes the way of being of bodies and their properties [συμβεβηκότα], whether permanent or accidental. Epicurus calls bodies '[existing] natures in themselves' [φύσεις καθ' ἑαυτάς] and their accidental properties συμπτώματα (*LH* 40). Lucretius calls permanent properties *coniuncta* and accidental properties *eventa* and insists that nothing exists beyond the entities existing by themselves – bodies and void – and the permanent and accidental properties.[2] Slavery, freedom, poverty, wealth, war and peace do not have the same type of existence as bodies, but represent, according to Lucretius, mere *eventa* of these (*RN* 1.455-456). Lucretius states that these things can be called *eventa*, accidents, or 'accidental properties' of matter and of space in which all things happen (*corporis atque loci, res in quo quaeque gerantur, RN* 1.482).

Now, the exclusion of justice from the category of existing natures in themselves presented by proposition (i) of *PD* 33 could lead one to think that Epicurus assimilates justice to the properties of bodies. Lucretius' emphasis on the space-time instantiation of the *eventa* (*RN* 1.482) and the examples he offers (*RN* 1.455-456) suggest that justice should be included among the accidental properties.[3] However, the presence of the word 'conglomeration' [συστροφή], a technical term in Epicurean physics (see *LH* 73, 77, and Diogenes of Oenoanda; fr.14 Smith) in proposition (ii) of *PD* 33 could also suggest that justice possesses the status of permanent properties [*coniuncta*].[4] Both attempts at classification face the same interpretative problem: of which body is justice the permanent or accidental property?[5] Proposition (ii) of *PD* 33 states that justice exists in the mutual dealings in territories where a particular pact takes place. This statement does not seem to refer to a bodily property but rather to something like the 'property of properties' of a body that is certainly not easy to specify.

The only mention of something similar in the Epicurean literature is the contention in the definition of time (attributed to Demetrius of Laconia; see Sextus *M* 10.219-220) as an accidental property of accidental properties. Nothing similar is found regarding justice. In fact, the Epicurean literature contains no analysis dedicated to specifying whether justice is a permanent or an accidental property. Yet Epicurus, Hermarchus, the successor of Epicurus as head of the school, and Polystratus, the third head of the Epicurean school, do all write about a topic which reveals the status they attribute to justice, since they all argue against those who deny that justice exists or claim that it is merely conventional. Polystratus' *On the Irrational Contempt of Popular Opinions* contains the most detailed argument in this vein. He directs the Epicurean study of nature toward dissipating the confusion generated by what he takes to be a vain impression of the non-existence of the noble and shameful (τὰ καλὰ καὶ τὰ αἰσχρά; col. xxii 23-24, xxiv 3-5, xxv 9-10, xxvi 22-5, xxviii 10). This vain impression, he asserts, is caused by the geographical and historical variability of the noble and shameful, and by the fact that animals do not possess a notion of 'what is noble and shameful'.[6] This confusion about the noble and shameful seems to be a matter with which the Epicureans were concerned. Hermarchus refers to those people who state that all that is noble and just [πᾶν τὸ καλὸν καὶ δίκαιον] exists according to certain individual beliefs [κατὰ τὰς ἰδίας ὑπολήψεις]; such beliefs or suppositions, he thinks, are full of a most profound stupidity (ἠλιβάτου τινὸς γέμειν εὐηθείας; Porphyry, *Abst.* 1.12, 2). At the end of *PD* 37, Epicurus also stresses that the existence and temporality of the just are manifest for those who do not allow themselves to be disturbed by empty assertions but who keep strictly to the facts.

On his part, Polystratus refers to a Hellenistic reformulation of the traditional theories of the categories which is different to the physicalist reformulation developed by Epicurus [φύσεις καθ᾽ ἑαυτάς/συμβεβηκότα].[7] In such a reformulation, the distinction between what exists by itself and what is relative [τὰ πρός τι κατηγορούμενα] takes on an epistemological orientation and a sceptical perspective. In fact, such a distinction is intended to emphasize that what really is everywhere and for everyone, while the relative instances, because they are not the same everywhere and for everyone, are not.[8] Polystratus seeks to refute those who deny the existence of relative properties because they do not satisfy the same predicates as the existing entities by themselves. Stone or gold, they claim, is everywhere and for everyone the same, while a relative property 'producing health' does not satisfy these predicates. In Polystratus' view, one can only conclude from this argument that the mode of existence of things such as stone or gold is not identical to that of relative entities (and vice versa), not that some exist and others do not. Likewise, from the fact that the relative properties do not constitute natures in themselves, it does not follow that their existence is conventional, since they represent real properties of the bodies and not mere opinions.

Although Polystratus does not include the just among his examples of relatives, his list incorporates the traditional expression 'the noble and the shameful' (τὰ καλὰ καὶ τὰ αἰσχρά; col. xxii 23-24, xxiv 3-5, xxv 9-10, xxvi 22-5, xxviii 10) and concludes with the indefinite expression τὰ ὅμοια τούτοις (xxii 6). As a matter of fact, the just could be taken to be implicit there. There is an additional argument for its inclusion: among the relational properties that Polystratus considers are 'producing health' and 'being useful'.[9] Hermarchus refers to both in criticizing those who claim that justice exists according to individual beliefs. In Hermarchus' view, it is not possible that what is noble and just can take place in any other way than that in which the other modalities of usefulness such as matters of health and thousands of others exist (ἐπὶ τῶν λοιπῶν συμφερόντων, οἷον ὑγιεινῶν τε καὶ ἑτέρων μυρίων εἰδῶν, Porphyry, *Abst.* 1.12, 2).[10] Hermarchus and Polystratus reiterate Epicurus' conception of what is just. In the *Principal Doctrines* the just [τὸ δίκαιον] is presented as the useful (or 'the advantageous', τὸ συμφέρον) in mutual associations, i.e. what contributes to neither harming one another nor being harmed (*PD* 31, 33, 36-38).

Polystratus' remarks (in addition to helping clarify *PD* 33) show that the consideration of the ontological status of the just is not necessarily oriented to the questioning of the laws through their confrontation with nature, as had already happened many times in the Greek tradition. Demetrius of Laconia, apparently a meticulous connoisseur of Epicurus' work,[11] underlines a semantic connection between nature and utility that complements Epicurus', Hermarchus' and Polystratus' remarks about what is useful and what is just. In *Pap. Herc.* 1012 (col. lxvi-lxviii), Demetrius attributes three possible meanings to the adverbial dative φύσει: ἀδιαστρόφως, κατηναγκασμένως, and συμφερόντως. These adverbs can be translated respectively as 'without distortion' (in the sense of 'by natural instinct'), 'by necessity', and 'by usefulness'.[12] Despite holding that the just, which constitutes a modality of the useful, does not possess the mode of existence proper to physical bodies (the only entities that exist in themselves), the Epicureans do not therefore argue that the just is conventional. On the contrary, they stress that the just is not conventional because it is constrained by conformity to the purpose established in human communities' first pacts ('neither harming one another nor being harmed'). Indeed, these pacts make possible the security and survival of human beings. The fact that these pacts are inexorably concretized in determined circumstances secures their unwavering conformity to serving the just purpose of the pacts. Demetrius of Laconia seems to refer to the inexorable nature of these circumstances when he notes that one of the meanings of the adverbial dative φύσει is συμφερόντως.

Since the means of accumulating and conserving food in the ancient city were rudimentary, we can imagine a situation somewhat akin to the following. If a drought led to a poor harvest and consequent poor health amongst livestock, the situation in the community would require reduced food consumption; it would therefore be fair to consume smaller rations, since this would prevent harm and being harmed. This simple example allows us to see that, in a desperate situation of food shortages, no member of the community could claim to have privileges over another and consume more food than was permitted. That would be the same as damaging others, and it would follow that the others would also feel that they had the right to harm the one who had ruined the rest of the community, in turn destroying the pact and the wider community that is grounded on it. Anyone who breaks the agreement based on not harming or being harmed would be threatening the security of the other individuals as well as their own freedom. If in this situation of food scarcity, the State, or the wise people of whom Hermarchus speaks, determines the quantities of food to be ingested per day, and a person ingests more than he is allowed, he threatens not only the preservation of other citizens but also their freedom to continue being persons. This example helps point out that justice, understood as a modality of what is useful, is valid for the specific time and circumstances in which the law is established for the preservation of the community and, at the same time, the integrity of its citizens. The relevance of circumstances is especially stressed by Epicurus in *PD* 38-39.

2 From the rustic, lonely and primitive people to the first human groupings

The link between what is just and what is useful is by no means an idea that originates with Epicurus. To focus on philosophical discussion, it is present in Thrasymachus' contentions in Plato's *Republic* (also in the *Theaetetus* and the *Gorgias*), as well as in several passages of Aristotle's practical philosophy (*Rh.* 1375b3-4; *EN* 1159a10-13). The link between justice and agreement is also traditional; proof of this is that Aristotle deals with it as a commonplace in the *Rhetoric* and the *Nicomachean Ethics*. The formula *not to harm or be harmed* (used by Epicurus to refer to the purpose of the pact in *PD* 33) repeats a similar expression employed by Plato (*Resp.* 359a) that would seem to come from an earlier source.[13] What the Epicureans take up in these 'traditional' topics is, (i) the link between what is just and useful, (ii) the link between the just and the pact, and, finally, (iii) the purpose of the pact understood as neither harming nor being harmed. The Epicurean study of nature reworks these traditional topics of Greek thought in a way that returns to its origins. Thus, the Epicureans develop the fundamentally theoretical rationalist constructs of Ionian natural philosophy to explain the origin of living beings and of civilized life in society.[14] One of the best testimonies of this rationalist tradition (and the significance of the pact in the origin of justice) is Lucretius' *On the Nature of Things* 5. By contrast, the Sophists and Plato represent two faces of the belligerent handling that this rationalist tradition of the genealogy of justice and the laws underwent in later philosophy. The Sophists question laws and customs through their confrontation with nature; Plato, particularly at the beginning of *Laws* 10, rejects this questioning as impious, subversive and nihilistic, and presents the physical theory and the contractual theory as two faces of the same coin or, to use his own words, 'of the same disease' (*Laws* 888b8). Plato does not specify to what philosophers he attributes this harmful fusion of physicalist cosmogony and contractualism.[15] Perhaps he had Archelaus in mind. In any case, the testimony transmitted by Diogenes Laertius is very significant since he states that, according to Diocles, Epicurus recognized Anaxagoras above all of the ancient philosophers (although he contradicted him on some points) and Archelaus (DL 10.12; Us. 240).

Apparently, Epicurus dealt with the origin of civilization in *On Nature* 12.[16] The epitome of Epicurean philosophy contained in the *Letter to Herodotus* picks up on a subject that the Epicureans seem to have considered especially appropriate to their theory of the beginnings of civilization: the origin of language. In the compressed lines that Epicurus dedicates to this topic, two fundamental explanatory guidelines stand out: the rejection of the figure of a divine or human legislator [νομοθέτης] or of an inventor [πρῶτος εὑρετής] of language,[17] and the recognition of two causes for the formation of language, i.e. the constraints of nature and the application of human ingenuity (*LH* 75-76). One of the traditional arguments for defending the conventional character of language was the diversity of languages. Epicurus reverses this argument by contending that this diversity is precisely due to the natural origin of language. In each instance, according to Epicurus, the constraints of nature are concretized in a specific 'environment'. This causes similar natural reactions in the human groups that are part of specific linguistic communities and thus gives rise to particular linguistic codes.[18] Unfortunately, Epicurus' preserved texts do not analyse the relationship between the origins of language and justice.[19] Perhaps this kind of analysis would include references to the formation of the preconception [πρόληψις] of the just mentioned in *PD* 37 and 38 (see chapter 3). Our knowledge of the Epicurean genealogy of justice and laws primarily derives from the extract of Hermarchus in Porphyry and from Lucretius' *On the Nature of Things* 5 (which also refers to language). In these verses (*RN* 5.1020-23) Lucretius highlights the cohesive function of language for the strengthening of pacts and justice. This approach is focused in turn on the persuasive function of language, a connection which is already underlined in the references to the origin of laws that populate Greek fifth-century literature.[20] The decisive contribution of language in the formation of human associations and pacts was a common topic in ancient literature. This idea is found at the beginning of Aristotle's *Pol.* 1253a7-18, as well as in Cicero's *On the Republic* (*De Re.* 1.25, 40). Hermarchus and Lucretius, despite some differences, coincide in their approaches to the genealogy of human groupings, justice and laws. Both take human groupings and justice to predate the existence of laws and sanctions.

The traditional contrast between primitive bestial life without order [ἄτακτος καὶ θηριώδης βίος] and civilized ways of life thus receives an interesting reformulation in Lucretius.[21] He does not describe a Hobbesian bestial and warlike 'prehistoric' life of human beings. In his opinion, early humans were stronger than modern humans and led a solitary and wandering existence in the manner of beasts (*more ferarum*; *RN* 5.931-932, 948); violence was sporadic. Lucretius contrasts this primitive state of human beings not only with the arrival of human groups and justice, but also with the subsequent stage in which it became necessary to establish laws and sanctions. As is the case today, ancient reconstructions of humankind's earliest times function primarily as expressions of their authors' theories and ideals. Throughout *On the Nature of Things* 5 the Epicurean Lucretius does not fail to point out the absence of superstitions about gods and death in primitive pre-social human beings, and the easy satisfaction of their natural desires. Lucretius also emphasizes the emergence of pacts of justice, framed in friendly relations, without the need for laws and sanctions. He thus finds a sort of 'authentication' of Epicurean ethics in prehistoric humankind and also reveals its genealogical superiority over rival philosophical schools. In this way the story of the primitive discovery of justice takes on paradigmatic status for the Epicureans in their reflections on justice, and comes to represent a symbol of an Epicurean utopia in which laws, sanctions and boundaries would vanish. For the Epicureans, the universalization of their philosophy would imply the disappearance of the causes that produce the vain desires and fears that trigger political ambition and the greed that makes laws and sanctions necessary. For the adversaries of the Epicureans (mainly Cicero and Plutarch), however, its universalization would mean the impossibility of all concord among men. One of the fragments of the Epicurean from the second century AD Diogenes of Oenoanda (fr. 56 Smith) seems to refer to just utopian societies that function without laws or sanctions. Therein, a singular community version of the traditional topic of the assimilation to god [ὁμοίωσις θεῷ] is presented, a theme to which, as Erler shows, Epicureanism was in no way foreign.[22] In both societies (the primitive and the utopian of Diogenes of Oenoanda), there is pact and justice, but *no laws*.

The rationalist treatments of prehistory in antiquity appropriately dismiss the intervention of gods or providential individuals and bring natural causes into play. However, the repeated reference to the steps as very gradual, the anonymity of the actors, and the spatial and temporal indeterminations show that these are fundamental attempts at reconstruction through analogies, extrapolations and so on. Thus, at the end of book 5, Lucretius indicates that our age cannot know anything of what happened previously except for the vestiges discovered by reason (*nisi qua ratio vestigia monstrat*, RN 5.1447).[23] In his reconstruction of the origin of justice, Lucretius stresses that the just is based on a pact resulting from a gradual process of softening [*mollescere*], physical and psychological, that affected the rustic, solitary and self-focused primitive man. Through this humanization,[24] primitive men began to establish relations of friendship [*amicities*] and pacts [*foedera*] with neighbours [*finitimi*], so as to neither harm nor be harmed (*RN* 5.1020):

> Next, they provided themselves with huts and skins and fire, and woman, united to man, went to live in one [place with him. The advantages of cohabitation] were learned, and they saw the birth of their own offspring. It was then that human beings first began to lose their toughness [*mollescere*]: the use of fire rendered their shivering bodies less able to endure the cold beneath the pavilion of the sky; Venus sapped their strength; and the children with their charming ways easily broke down the stern disposition of their parents. It was then, too, that neighbors [*finitimi*], in their eagerness neither to harm nor be harmed, began to form mutual pacts [*foedera*] of friendship [*amicitiem*], and claimed protection for their children and womenfolk, indicating by means of inarticulate cries and gestures that everyone ought to have compassion on the weak [*imbecillorum esse aequum misererier omnis*]. Although it was not possible for concord to be achieved universally, the great majority kept their compacts loyally. Otherwise, the human race would have been entirely extinguished at that early stage and could not have propagated and preserved itself to the present day.
>
> *RN* 5.1011-1027

Lucretius reconstructs the transition from the life of primitive man *more ferarum* to the beginnings of civilized life, and compresses into a few lines processes that give rise to knowledge, capacities and relationships of various kinds between human beings. Interpreters have generally focused on one of the processes mentioned: the birth of justice through pacts of friendship. The scarcity of Epicurean texts on the origin of justice and the significance of friendship in Epicureanism explain this focus and the prevailing doctrinal approach to the passage. Before referring to discussions about the 'orthodoxy' of the passage, it is important to remember its place in the plot of Lucretius' poem. The arrival of justice constitutes the final moment in the sequence of processes that Lucretius postulates as an explanation of the survival of the human species and the origin of civilized life. It is a task framed by the overall purpose of *On the Nature of Things* 5 to explain the origin of life and the survival and extinction of the species without resorting to god or teleological explanations. Lucretius highlights the difference between the explanations required in the case of the human species and those of other species (except for the animals under the care of man), dramatically contrasting the endowments with which animals come into the world with the perilous condition of human infants. The child, Lucretius emphasizes, is thrown into the world as a castaway, naked, speechless, and lacking any help for life (*RN* 5.218-227).[25]

This poetic image dramatizes the idea that nature has not been created by divinity in the interest of human beings (*RN* 5.195-200) and that, consequently, their survival and propagation is due to creations, inventions and strategies established by human beings themselves. The establishment of life by couples and the recognition of children by their parents represent, for Lucretius, fundamental causes of the survival and propagation of the human species.[26] Lucretius seems ingeniously to adapt the traditional idea of the family as the seed of the polis to his reconstruction of the processes of prehistory that made possible the arrival of pacts of friendship and justice.[27] According to Lucretius, a psychological softening of the human being takes place first within the family, which seems to make possible the neighbourhood relations from which the first human groupings were established. Certainly, those who come to such covenants are not rough and lonely primitive men, but rather parents who experience pity for the weak (women and children) and recognize the convenience of protecting them, along with themselves, so that all should survive. The recognition of children by their parents as their own creations should also have contributed to the genesis of the parents' awareness of their own weakness.[28] Thus, the pact of justice seems to extend the experiences that arise from establishing the family.

Maybe the development of emotions favoured by the *mollescere* of the primitive man also contributed, in Lucretius' view, to the evolution of language.[29] Several ancient authors emphasized the contribution of friendship and piety to the establishment and preservation of human groupings. The distinctive feature of Lucretius' treatment of this topic is his evolutionist and rationalist approach. In contrast to authors such as Polybius, who relates friendship and sociability in a primarily historical manner (*Histories* 6.5 9-10; 6.6 2-5), or Lactantius, who points out that God bestowed piety on human beings for the mutual protection of their lives (*Epitome* 55 1, 60 2; *Div. Inst.* 5.7 1; 6.10 2), Lucretius presents friendship and piety as the results of evolutionary transformations of prehistoric human beings due to strictly human processes.

Lucretius points out that concord was not universal, but that the vast majority kept their pacts faithfully. Without this broad agreement, Lucretius insists, the human race would have perished entirely (*RN* 5.1024-1027). Hermarchus also emphasizes that if human beings had not united to defend themselves from the beasts and other human beings, they would not have survived (Porphyry, *Abs.* 1.10, 1). Regardless of the meaning given to the term *amicities*,[30] there is no doubt that Lucretius speaks of pacts, which are made between subjects who already possess and share techniques (fire, clothing, dwellings) and modes of socialization (coupling, offspring, neighbourhood) and who come to these civilizational techniques out of, and for the sake of, their own benefit. In other words, they are not beings who, like the rustic primitive people, fend only for themselves and live as they please (*RN* 5. 960-961) in the way of wild beasts (*more ferarum*; *RN* 5.932). Rather, they are individuals whose use of fire and life alongside couples, children and neighbours in sheltered dwellings has softened them, configuring them properly as a socialized 'I' immersed in mutually helpful and affective relationships.

3 *Amicities*, pacts and the just: Unorthodox epicureanism?

As usual, Lactantius refers to Epicurus in polemical terms. In a memorable and inaccurate passage (if one compares what Lactantius declares to the Epicurean textual evidence) of his *Divine Institutions*, he claims that, since for Epicurus the supreme good is pleasure, human society does not exist for the Epicurean. He also adds that 'each person consults his own interest, no one loves his neighbour except for his own purposes' (*Div. Inst.* 3.17, 42; Bowen and Garnsey trans.). Lactantius' statements express the standard interpretation (within a specific interpretive domain) of how the Epicureans conceive interpersonal relationships: in Epicurus' view, Lactantius appears to suggest, relationships with others would always be mediated by benefit and self-interest. But Lucretius' verses (*RN* 5.1011-1027) about early pacts [*foedera*], in which he appeals to friendship and piety, do not seem to be reconcilable with this kind of standard interpretation. Lucretius, according to several interpretations, inserts in the rationalist and evolutionist explanations a sentimental ingredient alien to hedonism, on which, according to the Epicureans, friendship would be based.[31] Thus, those scholars argue, Lucretius is heterodox in not regarding the possible 'theory of the origin of culture' of the Epicureans but, rather, concerning Epicurean hedonism and its 'utilitarianism' (that is, the sense in which the just can be considered as a modality of the useful). This kind of remark seems to presuppose that, for Lucretius, the members of the first human groupings were, to varying degrees, Epicurean. This is not true. On the contrary, the objectors themselves, we argue, apply to Lucretius' account their own convictions about the Epicurean conceptualization of friendship and the modern idea of the pact and thereby declare these verses heterodox. However, it is not only possible to reconcile Lucretius's approaches to *amicities* and the pacts of the early communities with the Epicurean notion of friendship and interpersonal relations, but such a reconciliation also allows us to understand the Epicurean filiation of his theory of culture's origins.

In actual fact, it is not easy to ignore these verses of Lucretius; this is so because, in several Epicurus' texts, as we will show, friendship is presented in such generous terms that, at first glance, it is not easy to understand how those Epicurus' passages could be reconciled with the supposed Epicurean orthodoxy on hedonism and the utilitarianism of relations with others. The *Vatican Sayings*, found and edited by Wotke (in *Wiener Studien* 1888), with remarks by Hartel, Gomperz and Usener, include one sentence on *friendship* that produced Usener's perplexity. According to the reading proposed by Usener, *VS* 23 runs as follows: 'Every friendship is worth choosing for its own sake, though it takes its origin from the benefits [it confers on us]'.[32] In Usener's view, this sentence showed that Epicurus had modified his utilitarian standpoint.[33] However, it is not the only text in Epicureanism in which friendship is exalted. *VS* 78 qualifies friendship as an 'immortal good' (see also Epicurus' *PD* 27 and 28). *VS* 52 is even more striking, since it extols friendship through the expressions of mystical cults: 'Friendship dances around the world announcing to all of us that we must wake up to blessedness.'[34] Neither Hartel nor Usener accepted that such a disproportionate exaltation could refer to friendship. The former proposed the correction ἡ φιλοσοφία instead of ἡ φιλία, while Usener suggested reading ἡλίου σφαίρα ('sphere of the sun') instead of ἡ φιλία ('friendship'). For both of them it was inadmissible that Epicurus was referring to friendship in *VS* 52. But there are other striking texts in Epicureanism about friendship. Plutarch notes in *Col.* 1111B the statement by Epicurus to the effect that one will face the most severe sufferings for the sake of friends. Diogenes Laertius, for his part, points out that the wise person, according to Epicurus, will sometimes die for a friend (DL 10. 120).

Like Usener, some contemporary interpreters have also highlighted that Epicurus' statements about friendship reflect tensions and inconsistencies in his ethical theory. This is due to the attempt to integrate friendship into hedonism as an ingredient of happiness (thus increasing the vulnerability of man that Epicureanism seeks to minimize).[35] Other interpreters have tried to show that Epicurus' statements about friendship are reconcilable with Epicurean egoism and that it does not provoke inconsistencies in Epicurean ethics.[36] These antagonistic interpretations share a noteworthy common ground regarding the concept of friendship. They tackle friendship from the selfishness–altruism disjunction. Yet this dichotomy presupposes a conception of what is understood by the 'self' and by 'the other' or 'others' that is not straightforwardly applicable to the Greek world. In the ancient concept of φιλία and in the ordinary use of expressions such as κοινωνία, οἰκειότης, συγγένεια, ὁμόνοια and so on, a model is visible for comprehending interpersonal relations in which the selfishness–altruism disjunction is not useful. In fact, sharp borders between the self and the other are consistently blurred in the ancient understanding of friendship, so that as a result the idea of reciprocity and of a community of interests and purposes (understood in differing degrees of intensity) forms a fundamental part of the sphere of the self.[37]

Both Gill and Algra[38] find an example of this traditional model in Aristotle's discussion of friendship. It is significant that when Aristotle clarifies (in a modal sense) the object of deliberation, he underlines that it is possible for us to do both what we ourselves can do and what we can do through our friends, as its realization is *somehow* our own [τὰ γὰρ διὰ τῶν φίλων δι' ἡμῶν πως ἐστίν]: this is so because the principle (surely of action) is in us (1112b27-28. See also *EN* 1166a31-32: 'since a friend is another himself'). Moreover, the son is, for Aristotle, 'another himself' of the father (*EN* 1166a31-32). However, when Aristotle comes to discuss the nature of self-love, he explains it through an analogy of love for others rather than the reverse, 'since we rejoice and condole with ourselves, just as we do with friends, it follows that we are, in some sense, friends to ourselves as well'.[39] The Epicureans and the Stoics were inspired by Aristotle and it is not difficult to recognize his influence on the Stoic theory of familiarization [οἰκείωσις]. There are also clear terminological traces of the Aristotelian model in Epicurus' *Principal Doctrines,* in the *Vatican Sayings* and in the excerpt of Hermarchus. In *PD* 39, the terms ὁμόφυλα and οὐκ ἀλλόφυλα appear; in *PD* 40, one can read πληρεστάτην οἰκειότητα, while in the *VS* 61, the expression τῆς πρώτης συγγενήσεως ὁμονοούσης is found. These expressions are part of some truly contentious statements that have generated much disagreement among scholars,[40] though all of them – explicitly (*PD* 39, see also Hermarchus in Porphyry, *Abst.* 1.10, 1) or implicitly (*PD* 40, *VS* 61) – contain reference to a community of interests in interpersonal relations, but not to a selfish/altruistic disjunction such as we often find in the philosophical Greek tradition and especially in Aristotle.

In the exposition that Torquatus devotes to friendship, Cicero points out that some Epicureans believe that the first human meetings, contacts and the will to establish close relationships came about due to pleasure. But when the progressive treatment or the frequency of association leads to familiarity or a certain kind of intimacy [*cum autem usus progrediens familiaritatem effecerit*], such a great love flourishes that, although no usefulness comes from friendship [*etiamsi nulla sit utilitas ex amicitia*], friends are loved in themselves (*Fin.* 1.69). Torquatus argues that if this is how it usually happens to us with places and animals, it is reasonable to think that treatment and custom make us fond of our fellow men. In the face of objections to the Epicurean considerations of friendship, Torquatus regards these Epicureans as *timidiores*. In reply to Torquatus' exposition developed in *Fin.* 2, Cicero points out that they are more recent Epicureans [*recentiores*], i.e. people introducing a more human view [*humanius*] than that expressed by Epicurus, who (in Cicero's view) hold that friendship cannot be dissociated from pleasure and should be cultivated with it in mind (*Fin.* 2.82). Cicero does not provide data to identify the Epicurean *timidiores*. Perhaps, as in the case of the other two Epicurean theories of friendship contained in *On Ends*, Cicero does not expound the theses of certain particular Epicureans but, rather, extracts and combines relevant arguments from works of Epicurus or his followers that we do not possess.[41]

It is not difficult to recognize that the remarks of the Epicurean *recentiores* on friendship contain the combination of the two issues that Lucretius highlighted when referring to the pacts of the first human groupings: both the utility and the familiar treatment producing *amicities*. The very expression συστροφαί in *PD* 33 (see also Hermarchus' expression συντρεφομένους μετ' ἀλλήλων in Porphyry, *Abst.* 1.10, 1) could designate a sense of familiarity and habituation.[42] It is worth noting that Mitsis has argued (i) that this 'associative' genealogy of altruism and friendship attributed to the Epicurean *recentiores* was simply the recognition of a psychological *factum* that could not be derived from a utilitarian justification of altruism and friendship.[43] He adds (ii) that the Epicurean theory of friendship was inconsistent, for if Epicureanism established hedonistic calculation in sober reasoning (*LM* 132) that subjected all desire and inclination to rational evaluation, the same should be done with the supposed tendency to altruism and friendship arising from utility [*usus*] and familiarity [*familiaritas*].[44]

The consideration of Mitsis' statements (i) and (ii) allows us to reaffirm the Epicurean orthodoxy of the reference to *amicities* in Lucretius, *RN* 5.1019. With regard to Mitsis' affirmation (i), we would like to recall that Lucretius *does not* intend to justify altruism and friendship. Lucretius' appeal to the role of fire, utility and familiarity as sources of the *mollescere* and the *amicities* that make possible pacts amongst the first human groupings corresponds precisely to his attempt to construct an account of the origin of culture in naturalist and rationalist terms. This means that this process occurs to the exclusion of any explanatory supernatural causes – and the psychological *factum* of compassion for the weak and friendship are certainly not supernatural causes. In fact, it cannot even be affirmed that it is a matter of a set of completely original theses. In describing the physical and psychological softening [*mollescere*] of the rough primitive man, the use of fire and experience of familial relations along with the recognition of friendship (as arising from utility and custom) are all presented as socializing elements to explain the emergence of the human groupings in texts of diverse filiation.[45]

Mitsis' remark (ii), we hold, disregards the prudential tradition behind the Epicurean reference of all choice to 'sober reasoning' (νήφων λογισμός; *LM* 132). This is not something that is strictly specified in the form of axiomatic prescriptions for hedonistic calculation; rather, faithful to the prudential tradition to which Epicurus belongs (and which Aubenque so brilliantly discusses),[46] it also assumes and weighs up singularities and individual facts and leaves evidence of this in the repeated recognition of the relevance of contexts, exceptions and alternatives. The fact that the famous slogans attributed to the Epicureans – 'live unnoticed' and 'do not participate in politics' – do not even appear in the *Principal Doctrines* proves that the hedonistic calculation is not specified in absolute prescriptions. This being so, Roskam seems to be right when he characterizes Epicureanism as a moral philosophy of 'conditional qualifying'.[47] Fish has also referred to the flexibility of Epicureanism regarding one's lifestyle choices.[48] Inherited status and the condition of *homo novus*, for example, are facts that the Epicureans seem to have considered when assessing dedication to politics (we examine these approaches in detail in chapter 6).[49] The preceding considerations demonstrate that the Lucretian verses which focused on the way that primitive relations of *amicities* and the pacts between neighbours [*finitimi*] give rise to justice did not constitute approaches foreign to Epicureanism. Additional proof of this is provided by its concordance with a thesis highlighted in the *excerptum* on the genealogy of justice and the laws by Epicurus' successor, Hermarchus, as transmitted by Porphyry. As we have already indicated, the establishment of laws and sanctions is regarded (by both Hermarchus and Lucretius) as not only posterior to the human groupings that were aware of the utility of the just for survival ('neither harming one another nor being harmed'), but also as a response to new social realities.

In Porphyry's excerpt, when referring to the original establishment of laws by outstanding people (not by force of their bodies, but by wisdom of their souls), the Epicurean Hermarchus indicates that such an establishment was preceded by an irrational perception (or awareness) of what is useful [ἀλόγως αὐτοῦ – sc. τοῦ χρησίμου – πρότερον αἰσθανομένους], but one that operated without reason and which was often forgotten. These wise people induced those who held these irrational perceptions to a comparative appreciation of what is useful [εἰς ἐπιλογισμὸν τοῦ χρησίμου].[50] The others they frightened through the severity of the punishments (*Abst.* 1.8, 1-2) and the instigation of an irrational fear of being impure for the crime committed (1.9, 4). Presumably, this was a ploy involving fear of the gods. Hermarchus states that laws would be unnecessary if everyone could see what was useful and hold it in their memory. The 'contemplation' (or simply 'the vision', θεωρία) of the useful and the harmful would be sufficient to bring about the choice of what is useful and the avoidance of what is harmful (*Abst.* 1.8, 19-20). Hermarchus suggests that the event of forgetting the non-rational perception (or awareness) of what is useful is the result of population increase (and the presumable mitigation of social bonds) as well as the diminution of dangers such as the threat of wild beasts which in the (distant) past made the advantage of group solidarity obvious (see Porphyry, *Abst.* 1.8, 4; 1.10, 4). Thus, Hermarchus attributes the need to introduce laws and sanctions to the dissipation of the two causes to which Lucretius ascribes the advent of the pacts in the first human groupings: neighbourhood relations and *amicities*, and the recognition of the usefulness of justice for the survival of the community as well as the individual.

For his part, Lucretius links the establishment of laws and sanctions to a double process: after the formation of the first groups, some men became kings, founded cities, and built fortresses for their defence and shelter. The kings distributed cattle and fields 'according to the beauty', strength and ingenuity – until wealth took precedence over all else. Then, according to Lucretius, the vain and greedy desires emerged that gave rise to the search for security through power, wealth and fame. The kings were murdered, and the human race was immersed in wars and violence until, tired of anarchy, people voluntarily submitted to the laws that magistrates taught them. Lucretius also stresses that the introduction of penalties represented a bitter milestone in history: 'Ever since that time fear of punishment has poisoned the blessings of life' (*RN* 5.1115).

Thus, the pacts that sustained increasingly extensive societies with laws, sanctions and magistracies were fundamentally the result of calculation and utility. However, when explaining the pacts of justice among later human groups in relation to the experience of primitive, lone and wandering men (that is, a person that had yet to establish familiar bonds and pacts), the Epicureans seem to have combined an explanation of utility with approaches similar to the Stoic theory of familiarization [οἰκείωσις]. Such views, though, would be different from Stoic familiarization because of their not-strictly natural character. Ultimately, Lucretius refers to pacts between *finitimi*, people who are immersed in affective relations that do not emerge against the backdrop of a Hobbesian war of all against all and in which vain and irrational desires do not seem to prevail. On the contrary, according to Lucretius, the establishment of magistracies, of a sense of the right and of the laws obeyed the desire to end the general state of dissension and violence that emerged after the original pacts had broken down.

4 Summary and concluding remarks

In the introduction, we recalled that Epicureans understand philosophy as a 'physiology' aimed at dissolving empty opinions and the vain desires and fears grounded in them, with the ultimate goal of attaining peace of mind. Among such empty opinions are those that can concern justice. Epicurus (*PD* 37), Hermarchus (Porphyry, *Abst.* 1.12, 3), and Polystratus do not have in mind – or, at least, not primarily – the Platonic idea of justice. Instead, they write in debate with those who derive the conventionality or non-existence of justice from the geographical diversity and temporal variability of what is just. The Epicureans are not opposed to a view of justice that minimizes its variability; on the contrary, they recognize that this is inherent in its peculiar ontological status. On the one hand, the Epicureans analyse the just as a modality of the useful and employ the Hellenistic category of the relative [τὸ πρός τι]; on the other hand, they maintain that the just represents conformity with a collective purpose established by human beings as a result of their evolution, as is language, family or technology.

At first sight, the combination of these explanatory schemas seems to play out in favour of the conventionality of what is fair. For the Epicureans, the opposite is true. The just is not conventional because it is constrained by conformity to the purpose established in the first pacts of human communities ('neither harming one another nor being harmed'), which, as Hermarchus and Lucretius emphasize, enabled the survival of the human species. However, as such conformity is always operative in determined circumstances, these circumstances constitute an inexorable and thus natural prerequisite for conformity. As a result, the geographical diversity and temporal variability of the just coheres, in the Epicureans' view, with the unconventional nature of what is just.

Another result of the genealogical approach to the just and to the laws is the capacity to distinguish between these concepts. For the Epicureans, the just precedes the laws, both logically and chronologically. What is just is established as that which is in accordance with the purpose of the pacts in the first human groupings. It possesses a foundational and paradigmatic character. The Epicureans believe that the introduction of laws and sanctions only became necessary due to the complexity of societies, the weakening of the awareness of the usefulness of the original pacts, and the dissolution of the bonds that made pacts possible. The Epicureans do not describe the pre-social human beings or the first human groupings subject to pact as warlike or savage. Only the stage of culture in which the introduction of laws and sanctions becomes necessary has Hobbesian features. According to Lucretius, violence is sporadic in the solitary wandering of primitive pre-social beings. The gradual 'softening' or humanization of said beings makes possible the birth of a pact between *finitimi*, people immersed in affective relations [*amicities*], and not in a state of 'war of all against all' due to vain and irrational desires. The role of friendship in this benevolent image of the first groups submitted to pact is, for some interpreters, inconsistent with the Epicurean conception of friendship. In section 3, we have attempted to dismiss these arguments by showing that they do not adhere to the purpose of Lucretius' theory of the origin of culture. They approach friendship from the selfishness–altruism disjunction. But this way of treating friendship neither corresponds to the Epicurean approach to friendship nor to the way of understanding interpersonal relations in the ancient world which inspires the Epicureans.

2

The City, the Natural Good and the Epicurean Promise of Security

Imperturbability or peace of mind [ἀταραξία], unlike security [ἀσφάλεια], is one of the central concepts that are immediately associated with Epicureanism. It symbolizes the exceptional character of the Epicurean way of life; by contrast, the word 'security' (a term that is vertiginously ubiquitous today, as observed by Hamilton)[1] sounds prosaic and general. Nevertheless, seven of the forty *Principal Doctrines* refer to security, and one of them (*PD* 14) equates the Epicurean style of life to the 'purest security' [εἰλικρινεστάτη ἀσφάλεια]. *PD* 40 closes the series of *Principal Doctrines* with several superlative expressions focused on the security of Epicurean life. Security is therefore one of the main doctrinal issues of Epicureanism as condensed in the *Principal Doctrines*. But Epicurus does not coin the word ἀσφάλεια; when he employed it to qualify the way of life that he posits, the use of this term already had a long tradition of characterizing the life made possible by the existence of political communities. If we add to the *Principal Doctrines* concerned with security those that refer to the Epicurean contractual justice, it can be said that almost a third of the *Principal Doctrines* refer to the topic of the Epicurean life and society. It is striking that this theme is a major presence in the doctrine of a philosophy to which has been attributed, since antiquity, a contempt for laws and the polis.

Epicurean philosophy includes, as we have discussed in chapter 1, a remarkable naturalistic genealogy of the human groupings that attributes the survival of the species to the security derived from the creation of justice and laws. This chapter aims to show how Epicureanism develops the category of security to conceptualize the philosophical life it proposes. Firstly, in section 1, we emphasize the continuity that exists between the recognition that Epicureans give to the security provided by political communities and the considerations that ancient literature dedicates to security [ἀσφάλεια], safety [σωτηρία] and freedom from fear [ἄδεια, ἀφοβία] when dealing with the origin of culture, civil war [στάσις] and good order [εὐνομία]. Such continuity makes it evident that Epicurean philosophy understands itself as a curious historical phenomenon (the analysis of which occupies section 2 of this chapter). Indeed, Epicurean philosophy recognizes the security provided by the polis as a necessary condition of its possibility on the one hand, and on the other attributes to the polis the promotion of the vain fears and limitless desires that it seeks to dissipate through 'physiology' or the study of nature in order to attain Epicurean security. The Epicurean genealogy of justice and law is thus complemented by a genealogy of these fears and desires and, additionally, of the security to which human beings moved by them aspire. In both cases, the genealogical explanation is oriented towards the understanding of the present time. Next, in section 3, we focus on studying the Epicurean conception of security. After again emphasizing the dependence of the Epicurean way of life on the security provided by justice and law, we show that attention to necessary natural desires, friendship and philanthropy are, in the Epicureans' view, the main factors that give the purest security to the Epicurean way of life. Their conflation reinforces the liberation from irrational fears and desires. Further, it establishes in human beings a permanent articulation of the pleasant memory of the past with the satisfaction of the present and the reliable expectation of the future. This disposition is the basis of the unity and stability of the Epicurean life from which its exceptional security results. Finally, in section 4, we summarize and indicate some conclusions.

1 Political organization and ἀσφάλεια: Why does there need to be security for a political organization to exist?

The two most representative figures of the Greek political imagery – the ship and the body – highlight the complex unity of the polis, its dependence on the satisfaction of needs as well as its exposure to external and internal dangers.[2] This vision of the polis is framed by the presence of the terms security [ἀσφάλεια] and safety [σωτηρία], and other related terms such as freedom from fear [ἄδεια, ἀφοβία], in texts of various kinds which, with greater or lesser theoretical pretension, refer to the nature of the polis.[3] These concepts play an especially central role in genealogies of civilized life and the considerations of speakers and philosophers around the ideas of civil war and good order.[4] We will offer some examples that demonstrate the continuity between these considerations and the recognition that the Epicureans give to the security that the political groupings provide. In our opinion, this is the first step towards the clarification of Epicurean security.

In Plato's *Protagoras*, one can find one of the most famous genealogies of civilized life in antiquity. According to Plato, political associations arose to protect people from wild animals and other people. In the framework of the myth, Prometheus stole 'artisanal wisdom' from Hephaestus and Athena since he was desperate to find some means of survival for the human race, the only species devoid of the suitable equipment for survival [σωτηρία]. However, human beings did not yet have wisdom for living together in society, 'political wisdom' which was in the keeping of Zeus (Plato, *Prot*. 321c7-d5). After the machinations of Prometheus and his theft from the gods for the sake of preserving humanity, human beings invented houses and produced clothes, shoes and blankets; they also were nourished by food from the earth. But even though they were thus equipped, they continued to live in scattered isolation because there were not yet any cities (*Prot*. 322a-b). Thus, even though their technical resources were appropriate for getting food, they were inappropriate for fighting wild animals, and these nascent groupings were consequently destroyed by wild beasts. Plato concludes that this was the case because human beings did not yet possess the art of politics (322b5: πολιτικὴ τέχνη), part of which is the art of war.[5] So, they tried to gather together and preserve themselves by founding cities. But when they met, they wronged each other, scattered, and perished. Once again, help came from the gods: Zeus was afraid that the human race might be wiped out, so he sent Hermes to bring justice and a sense of respect to humans so that they could live in cities; thus, the human race survived (*Prot*. 322c).

Aristotle's view that the polis is the highest of all political associations is well known; in fact, to Aristotle, the polis embraces all other such structures, like the household and village. In addition, the polis aims at good to a greater degree than any other, and at the highest good (*Pol*. 1252a6-8); the polis is also the best-developed form of political association insofar as it can provide better security for its members than a household or village. While Aristotle underlines that the purpose of the polis is to facilitate living well [εὖ ζῆν], he never loses sight of the demand for security that the polis involves. Polis security and self-sufficiency require different constitutive elements, which imply the risk of conflicts and polarizations that can lead to civil war (*Pol*. 1261a10-b15).[6] Aristotle, like Thucydides and Plato, understood στάσις as one of the fundamental challenges to political theory. In Cohen's opinion,[7] none of these authors attribute political instability to the machinations of particular political groupings, but rather to underlying moral-psychological dispositions whose genealogy and consequences, as we shall see, were of profound interest to the Epicureans. Thucydides stresses that the love of power, operating through greed and rivalry for honour, was the prime cause of civil war (3.82). For Aristotle, in Cohen's words, 'the moral psychology of *stasis* essentially has two prongs: that which men want either to acquire or to avoid losing (i.e. honour and gain) and envy of what others have'.[8]

Aristotle applies the twofold use of the term 'preservation' [σωτηρία] in politics and psychobiology to the traditional analogy of the polis and the body. On the one hand, understanding the aetiology of preservation and corruption in terms of political regimes, oriented to the design of 'the best political regimen', constitutes a fundamental task in Aristotle's *Politics*; on the other hand, the aetiology of preservation and corruption of living beings is a central concern of his treatise *On the Soul* and the biological treatises. In both cases, necessities, threats and dangers evince the fragile ontological condition of preservation; as observed by Rashed, in such an ontological condition the hypothetical necessity and contingency are combined.[9]

Within the framework of the topic of 'good order' [εὐνομία], the last fragment of *Anonymous Iamblichus* offers, in a contractualist background which assigns praises to virtue and condemnation to 'advantage' [πλεονεξία], one of the most interesting recognitions of the benefits of the security furnished by laws and the polis. Without laws, it can be read in the fragment, any form of life in common between human beings would be impossible; the absence of laws would turn out to be a greater chastisement than that of a primitive lonely life (100, 13-15). The *Anonymous Iamblichus* makes trust [πίστις] the key achievement of 'good order' in both the public and private spheres. Trust promotes the circulation of goods, benefits relations among social classes, reduces the time citizens must devote to public affairs, and lessens the risks of civil or non-civil war. Trust also lets citizens immerse themselves in sleep without fear [ἄφοβος]; when they wake up, it permits them to pleasantly and painlessly take on [ἡδέως φροντίδας μὲν ἀλύπους] the tasks of life. In 'good order' citizens are not constantly assaulted by bad memories, but live confidently and with proper expectations (ἐλπίσιν εὐπίστοις καὶ εὐπροσδοκήτοις; 102, 8–17). The state of 'absence of law' [ἀνομία], on the other hand, makes human life fearful; due to distrust [ἀπιστία], it also compels human beings to accumulate goods that always seem to be insufficient (103, 1-3). Consequently, ἀνομία opens the way to tyranny (103, 20–21).

Demosthenes' *Against Meidias* also provides interesting insights regarding these issues. A crucial argument of Demosthenes against the rich and violent Meidias is that, though there are citizens (like Meidias himself) who have more strength and wealth than many, freedom from fear [ἄδεια] is a common patrimony provided by the laws (τὴν ἄδειαν, ἣν ἡμῖν κοινὴν οὐσίαν οἱ νόμοι παρέχουσι; 210, 6). In order for the judges to condemn Meidias, Demosthenes says to them:

> **T1** Look: immediately after the court recesses, each of you will go back home, one more quickly perhaps, another more leisurely, without worrying or turning around, not afraid about [οὐδὲ φοβούμενος] whether he will encounter a friend or a foe, a man who is big or small, strong or weak, or anything like this. Why in the world is this so? Because he knows in his own mind, is confident, and trusts in our form of government [ὅτι τῇ ψυχῇ τοῦτ' οἶδε καὶ θαρρεῖ καὶ πεπίστευκε τῇ πολιτείᾳ] that no one will drag him off or abuse him or beat him. And so, you yourselves walk around in complete security [ἀδείας] ...
>
> *Against Meidias* 221; trans. Harris 2008

Demosthenes argues that Meidias' insolence (or even 'violence': ὕβρις) and impiety [ἀσέβεια] must be punished,[10] since otherwise the freedom from fear that is made possible by laws will be snatched away by him and other citizens like him. The violence Meidias has inflicted on him, Demosthenes emphasizes, is therefore violence against the community. If it remains unpunished, the common heritage represented in the state of 'freedom from fear' [ἄδεια] suffers. In fact, as noted by Cohen, Demosthenes emphasizes the fact that the punishment of an offender is a real benefit for the polis.[11] The citizen's duty is to be solicitous for what is best in the sense of what is 'commonly best', i.e. in a communal way [ὑπὲρ τοῦ κοινῇ βελτίστου δεῖ μέλειν ὑμῖν]. In fact, Demosthenes contends that the many crimes that do occur are due to the failure to punish the offenders; therefore, the only way to prevent such crimes (which are taken to be real outrages or atrocities; ὑβρίζειν) is to adequately punish every offender who is caught. The offender, then, not only insults the individual who receives the offense but also, through the experience of the individual, outrages the political community. This remarkable passage shows that, in the fourth century BC, a statesman and orator like Demosthenes believed that just punishment of the criminal contributes to the security of both the individual and the political community. It also shows that the view that the Epicureans were interested in the issue of security because the polis, as a form of political organization, was disappearing or had almost disappeared cannot be right. Like their illustrious predecessors in the fifth and fourth centuries BC, the Epicureans still believed that, even if the State cannot guarantee that a citizen will not suffer a criminal attack, it must ensure a certain level of individual and collective security. Individual and collective security must be backed up by justice, and justice (if it is really just) must punish the criminal. This is so because when a citizen is attacked, at the same time and in a certain way, the political community is attacked as well.

Coming back to Epicurus and his theory of harm, it is interesting to examine his use of the verb 'to harm' [βλάπτειν]. Goldschmidt highlights the repeated use of the verb in the active and passive voices in the *Principal Doctrines* where the significance of the pact is stressed.[12] In fact, regarding the actions that the pacts intend to avoid, these *Principal Doctrines* never use the verb ἀδικεῖν ('to commit injustice', 'to injure'; in the passive voice 'to suffer injustice', 'to be injured'), nor do they enter into distinctions about voluntary and involuntary actions. The meaning of this lack of distinction is clearly understood when one reads a passage from Hermarchus' genealogy of laws, transmitted by Porphyry, which, as we will show in what follows, helps clarify one of Aristotle's observations. Hermarchus points out:

> **T2** The legislators did not exclude even *unintentional homicide* from any punishment, so as not to concede any excuse to those who intentionally [ἑκουσίως] choose to imitate the deeds of those who act *unintentionally* [ἀκουσίως], and also to prevent many genuinely unintended killings happening through negligence or inattention.... Since they wanted to prevent the negligence which harms our neighbours, they laid down that not even unintentional acts were exempt from penalty and they more or less eradicated this fault through fear of punishment [φόβῳ τῶν ἐπιτιμίων].
>
> Porphyry, *Abst.* 1.9, 1-16, trans. G. Clark, slightly modified, which is based on Bouffartigue's 1977 text

At the end of *Politics* Book 2, Aristotle refers to several legislators, including Pittacus, one of the seven sages. Aristotle attributes to him the law that says if a drunken person commits a crime, she must be punished more severely than a sober one. Aristotle comments on this thus:

> **T3** For since more drunken people than sober ones commit more acts of arrogance, [Pittacus] paid attention not to the greater indulgence [πρὸς τὴν συγγνώμην] one should show to those who are drunk, but to what is convenient [πρὸς τὸ συμφέρον].
>
> *Pol.* 1274b 19-23; transl. Reeve, slightly modified[13]

Aristotle observes that indulgence and compassion are reactions sometimes produced by more or less involuntary actions (*EN* 1109b31-32). Pittacus, like Hermarchus, seems to pay attention to the damage produced by the crime and its frequency, and subordinates indulgence to the usefulness of laws and punishments. It is not irrelevant that considerations on justice and the usefulness of pacts and laws are fundamentally attached to homicide here, because they show that the fundamental meaning and validity that the Epicureans ascribe to pacts, justice and laws is the security [ἀσφάλεια] of human life and the elementary resources it requires.

As a matter of fact, there cannot be a political community if there is no security, but just a set of individuals which would be adequately characterized as a 'herd of wild beasts' (or beasts that live 'scattered about' to use Aristotle's terminology; *Pol.* 1256a23: σποραδικά), trying to destroy each other. This does not need to be proven insofar as Epicurus himself explicitly says that justice or injustice is impossible regarding those animals which are unable to make pacts about neither harming one another nor being harmed. In this vein, the Epicurean Hermarchus argues that if animals had been able to make pacts with other animals in the same manner as do human beings, then neither should we kill them nor they us, and it would be well to extend the concept of justice to cover animals too. Indeed, it would have been a 'safety prescription'. Unfortunately, because animals cannot participate with us in law due to their lack of reason, then usefulness [τὸ συμφέρον] cannot be provided more by security.[14] That explains why human beings are authorized, so to speak, to kill irrational animals; otherwise, we cannot have security (Porphyry, *Abst.* 1.12, 23-25). Justice or injustice is also impossible, Epicurus states (in Goldschmidt's view, polemicizing against Stoic cosmopolitanism),[15] regarding 'those nations (τῶν ἐθνῶν ὅσα) which were unable or unwilling to make pacts about neither harming one another nor being harmed' (*PD* 32). Thus, there seems to be a sense in which Epicurus suggests that security provides pacts with their 'real character of pacts', as it were; otherwise, if those pacts are not real agreements but merely nominal accords, there cannot be a political association. So, security endows pacts, justice and laws with 'reality'. If individuals do not have security regarding their possessions and lives, the 'social pact' that constitutes the state disappears, and they no longer have any reason to obey the basic rule that regulates life in the Epicurean conception of society: 'neither harming one another nor being harmed'. To some extent, we argue, this is in line with Epicurus' tenet that human beings do everything for the sake of being neither in pain nor in terror; in fact, as soon as we are able to remove these disturbances, 'every storm in the soul is dispelled' (*LM* 128). As is clear in these passages (and as was clear to both Plato and Aristotle), although certain issues can be analysed in a particularly ethical context, they may certainly have an impact upon, or be closely related to, the political domain.[16]

Security, both physical and psychological, is widely recognized in ancient literature as a constituent element of political associations. This convergence suggests it is necessary to reconsider the Hermarchus extract from a broader perspective than the strictly genealogical and Epicurean one to which it is usually confined. As we showed in chapter 1 and have just repeated, the Hermarchus fragment represents a valuable testimony of the Epicurean genealogy of justice and law. The interpreters insist on this and so, for example, Roskam notes that the absence of references to the famous Epicurean slogan 'live unnoticed' is due to the fact that, in the first human groupings (the subject of the fragment) this slogan is meaningless.[17] This suggestion by Roskam can be challenged; probably Porphyry selected from Hermarchus the sections relevant to the purpose of his treatise *De abstinentia*, and the theme of 'live unnoticed' is certainly not relevant for that purpose. It could also be objected that the Hermarchus fragment is not *merely* genealogical because it explicitly and implicitly offers repeated allusions to the present. This emphasis of the fragment is not detached from genealogy but transitively applies the aetiology of the constitutions of the first human groupings to the societies of the present.[18] A passage from Colotes, preserved by Plutarch, agrees with the complementary interpretation of Hermarchus' fragment that we propose:

> T4 He says that 'those who appointed laws and usages and established the government of cities by kings and magistrates brought human life into a state of great security and peace [εἰς πολλὴν ἀσφάλειαν καὶ ἡσυχίαν ἔθεντο] and delivered it from turmoil [θορύβων ἀπήλλαξαν].[19] But if anyone takes all this away, we shall live a life of brutes, and anyone who chances upon another will all but devour him'.
>
> Plutarch, *Col*. 1124D; trans. Einarson and De Lacy

As can be seen, Colotes, like Hermarchus, extrapolates the achievements of the first legislators to the present, to which he refers implicitly, in the same manner as Hermarchus, by using the personal pronoun 'we'. In this passage from Colotes, which picks up on the same themes discussed above in the *Anonymous Iamblichus* and Demosthenes' *Against Meidias*, the psychological benefit of the security provided by the laws is emphasized to a greater extent than in the Hermarchus excerpt. Nevertheless, Hermarchus notes tangentially that in the first human associations the merciless killing of harmful animals and the preservation of useful ones contributed to fearless (ἀφοβία; *Abst*. 11.2).[20] Lucretius adds 'the voice of Epicurus' to these considerations regarding security by Hermarchus and Colotes. In the eulogy to Athens and Epicurus that begins book 6, Lucretius writes:

T5 It was Athens of glorious name that in former days first imparted the knowledge of corn-producing crops to suffering mortals and remodelled their lives and established laws ... He [Epicurus] saw that almost everything that necessity demands for subsistence had been already provided for mortals, and that their life was, so far as possible, established in security.

RN 6.1-11

On the Nature of Things, book 6, closes with a description of the plague of Athens, inspired by the account in Thucydides. Its beginning, in our opinion, also evokes Thucydides, as when in the so-called 'Archaeology' he underlines that Athens was the first city in Greece that represented a stable refuge for those fleeing from war or rivalries (1.2, 6). The Athenians, according to Thucydides, were the first to stop carrying weapons due to their more relaxed way of life (1.6, 3). The interpretation of the dramatic end of Lucretius' *On the Nature of Things* has given rise, as is well-known, to an extensive literature. Perhaps the crude scenes of the end represent a confirmation of the caution with which Lucretius refers, at the beginning of book 6, to the security that a city like Athens was able to achieve ('their life was, so far as possible, established in security'; *RN* 6.10-11; *US*. 396). Certainly, Lucretius reiterates (in a quasi-Heraclitean way) that time transforms the nature of the whole world, and everything passes on from one condition to another with nothing remaining constant and everything in permanent flux (*nec manet ulla sui similis res: omnia migrant, omnia commutat natura et vertere cogit*; *RN* 5.830-831). The human world is not exempt from this kind of process: humans are subject, like the rest of living creatures, to change and eventual destruction.[21]

If war, especially civil war, is one of the great threats to the security of the polis, the plague is no less so, although, as Gardner has recently suggested, it may also represent a metaphor for the illness of the body politic brought on by destructive competitions undertaken for individual glory, a phenomenon which Lucretius also observed in his time.[22] In any case, for Lucretius the plague seems to show that, as we read in Epicurus' *VS* 31, one can attain security against many things; but when it comes to death, all men live in a city without walls. Lucretius, as Erler points out, uses the story of Thucydides as a starting point to introduce his contemporaries to the doctrine of Epicurus.[23] While Epicurus recognizes the need for the security of the polis, he starts from the premise of *VS* 31 and therefore puts forward the purest security (see *PD* 14: εἰλικρινεστάτη ἀσφάλεια)[24]: 'nothing is more blissful', writes Lucretius, 'than to occupy the heights effectively fortified by the teaching of the wise' (*RN* 2.7-8).[25]

2 The security of the Polis and the vain fears and desires

We do not know the precise context of the passage from Colotes (see **T4** above) extracted by Plutarch who, as Kechagia notes,[26] seems to use it to complete his presentation of Epicurean philosophy, after referring to and opposing logic and physics (thus going beyond the traditional Hellenistic division of philosophy and subjecting the ethical-political part of Colotes' approaches to criticism). Indeed, in its simplicity, and in its connection to the cliché of the contrast between bestial, primitive life and civilized life, the passage contains important indications as to how to approach the Epicurean concept of security, although Plutarch, as we will emphasize later (see chapter 4), does not approach the passage from this perspective. This evinces his lack of insight, or even perhaps slander, insofar as he interprets it as a sign of the hypocrisy of the Epicureans in the face of the laws.

Plutarch may also have been focused on rejecting the limitations imposed upon the meaning of the polis in the Platonic and Aristotelian tradition, as Colotes does not exalt security, tranquillity and the release from disturbances as achievements leading to other higher ends belonging to the polis, such as living well [εὖ ζῆν]. This is a view especially underlined by Aristotelian political theory and opposed precisely to the ethical minimization of the polis that represented, for Aristotle, the approach of Lycophron; according to Aristotle, this thinker turns the community of the polis into a mere alliance and makes the law a pact and a reciprocal guarantee of what is right (*Pol.* 1280b5-12).

Consequently, one might ask whether the achievements of the polis which Colotes praises constitute, for him, the desirable status of human life or, rather, a necessary condition for other modes full of security, tranquillity and liberation from disturbances. Epicureanism is inclined towards the latter, as Epicurean 'physiology' aims at providing 'modes full of security', as it were, tranquillity and release of disturbance. This means that Epicurean philosophy understands itself as a curious historical phenomenon. On the one hand, it recognizes security provided by the polis as a necessary condition of its possibility.[27] On the other hand, it attributes to the polis the promotion of vain fears and limitless desires that it seeks to dissipate through physiology to attain the state of Epicurean security. The Epicurean genealogy of justice and law is therefore complemented by a genealogy of vain fears and limitless desires. This double programme corresponds to the Epicurean distinction between natural desires (both necessary and unnecessary) and unnatural and unnecessary desires (*PD* 30); the Epicureans also maintained an analogous distinction regarding fears.

For the Epicureans, the security of political groupings represents a human achievement in terms of satisfying natural desires and reducing the fear of aggression and violent death. Lucretius, as we have shown above, frames the establishment of pacts and justice with his explanation of the emergence, extinction and survival of animal species, developed in *On the Nature of Things* Book 5. Certain capacities such as strength, cunning and agility, in his opinion, protected and preserved other species from extinction (*RN* 5.857-859). The establishment and observance of pacts, made without the intervention of the gods, saved the human species from extinction (*RN* 5.1026-1027). Hermarchus also stresses that if people had not gathered together to carry out their common existence, they would not have survived (*Abst.* 1.10 1).

When Colotes praises laws, cities and magistracies, he has in mind, as evidenced by his reference to the primitive bestial life, the evolutionist perspective witnessed by the verses of Lucretius and the fragment of Hermarchus. The *Principal Doctrines* do not deny this view: *PD* 7 presents security as the good of nature [τὸ τῆς φύσεως ἀγαθόν] and as an end according to what is naturally congenial [κατὰ τὸ τῆς φύσεως οἰκεῖον], which establishes an interesting consistency between nature (understood as our nature)[28] and the purpose of pacts, justice and laws. This is so because Epicureanism bases this consistency on the necessary natural desires which, unlike unnecessary and vain desires, are limited and have objects that are generic and easy to satisfy. This appreciation seems to endorse the primitivism[29] which some interpreters have attributed to the Epicureans. However, it also points to the recognition that only civilized life based on pacts of justice provides human beings with security, for while primitive men are exempt from vain and unnecessary desires, they lack, in turn, instruments to guarantee the satisfaction of necessary natural desires. In fact, as Lucretius emphasizes, they are subject to famines and poisonings and are prey to wild beasts and other men. From this perspective, Lucretius does not hesitate to consider them 'miserable' (*miseri*; *RN* 5.983), a qualification that shows that, for the Epicureans, security [ἀσφάλεια] implies a clear satisfaction of the necessary natural desires and a state of confidence [θαρρεῖν], or as Hermarchus puts it, of lack of fear (ἀφοβία; *Abst.* 1.11, 2; ἡσυχία in **T4** above) with respect to its future satisfaction and to the danger of a violent death. The 'presentism' usually linked to the notion of natural desires and to vulnerability regarding the future leads to a dismissal of the role of confidence in the Epicureans' considerations regarding security. However, the consideration of the future constitutes an essential element of the Epicurean analysis of security, as in the *Anonymous Iamblichus* and in *Against Meidias*, and highlights that the Epicureans recognize a reality in the community founded on pact which, to paraphrase Aristotle's words, is not restricted to the vicissitudes of the day (ἕνεκεν μὴ ἐφημέρου; *Pol.* 1252b16), nor to what is convenient in the present. It instead looks at life as a whole (*EN* 1160a21-22; Porphyry, *Abst.* 1.7, 2: εἰς τὴν ὅλην τοῦ βίου σύστασιν) and offers human beings confidence in the future satisfaction of their needs. The dramatic contrast between civilized and primitive life included in the quoted passage from Colotes shows, as does Porphyry's excerpt from Hermarchus, that such confidence also concerns fears about aggression and violent death.

The Epicurean analyses of the negative consequences of an irrational fear of death constitute one of their most significant contributions to philosophy. However, they also considered the fear of violent death[30] from a prudential perspective which, as Aristotle observes in his study of fear, leads to the recognition that fear makes human beings deliberate in view of their salvation (*Rh.* 1383a5-8). Polystratus stresses that humans, unlike irrational animals, can take precautions in anticipation of suffering ailments [εὐλαβεῖσθαι πρὸ τοῦ παθεῖν] and thereby provide beneficial or useful things (τὰ συμφέροντα πορίζεσθαι; *Contempt* 3.5-11). In fact, the strengthening of the satisfaction of natural desires and the reduction of the fear of the threat of violent death are, in both Lucretius and Hermarchus, factors that explain the Epicurean genealogy of the first human groupings and the pacts of justice. The security of the political community is a useful instrument to mitigate the fear of violent death, and, according to the Epicureans, the fear of violent death itself seems to have contributed to the creation of such a community. The polis can generate security, and, as we have previously argued, such security is a necessary condition for actual political organizations. However, that does not mean that all fears have been eliminated. No polis can guarantee complete security, although everyone usually assumes that, in a real political association, the members of that association must enjoy some security (with respect to their goods and especially their persons). Paradoxically, the polis can also generate insecurity; think, for example, of political factions organized for the sake of achieving political power – a power that implies subjugating all those who do not share the purposes of those factions. The Epicurean formula for neutralizing this type of phenomenon (which, of course, has a dissolving potential within any political community) is the fundamental rule of its contractual approach: 'neither harming one another nor being harmed'. This simple but at the same time powerful injunction explains why Epicurus rejects the idea that justice is a thing in its own right (*PD* 33) and why the just can be understood as a 'modality' of usefulness. To use Epicurus' words, it is this slogan which explains why 'the justice of nature [presumably of human nature] is a pledge of reciprocal usefulness' (*PD* 31).

There are, however, fears that neutralize and undermine the usefulness of the security that political communities provide. These are, in the Epicurean view, fears based on false beliefs about death and the gods. Such fears give rise to unnatural and unnecessary desires, the main characteristic of which is to be unlimited and impossible to satisfy. The most representative examples are greed and ambition.[31] Both, as we have indicated, are considered by Thucydides and Aristotle to be the main causes of civil war.

The preserved Epicurean literature makes it possible to reconstruct some approaches of Epicureanism towards the genealogy of false beliefs that give rise to irrational fears of gods and death and their connection to greed and ambition for power. Hermarchus points out that, in the past, to induce ordinary people to not commit murder, some shrewd legislators instilled, in addition to the fear of punishment, an irrational fear [ἕτερον φόβον ἄλογον] of being impure because of the crime (*Abst.* 1.11). Presumably, this is a ploy involving fear of the gods. Lucretius also stresses that the introduction of penalties represented a bitter milestone in history: 'Ever since that time fear of punishment has poisoned the blessings of life' (*RN* 5.1115).

Hermarchus' statement recalls the fragment of the sophist Critias (or Euripides),[32] in which he maintains that the ancient lawmakers invented the gods so that no one would commit injustice in secret for fear of divine punishment (Sextus Empiricus, *M* 9.54). Gigante has detected echoes of the fragment of Critias in Lucretius.[33] According to Philodemus (*On piety* 519-541, ed. Obbink), Epicurus in *On Nature* 12 described as madmen those who, like Prodicus, Diagoras and Critias, denied the existence of the gods and generated confusion. Epicurus pointed out that they eliminate what is commonly accepted and even suggest (like Critias) that belief in the gods is due to a deception early in the history of culture. Philodemus (*On piety* 2145-2174, ed. Obbink) seems to distinguish two stages in the shaping of irrational beliefs about gods: at first, fear of the gods serves to ensure the preservation or safety of state, but ultimately it is not successful and, in time, lies about the gods become dissociated from the purpose of community security and become simply inconsistent and irrational claims.[34] Also, one of the inscriptions of Diogenes of Oenoanda (Hammerstaedt and Smith fr. 167, and Smith fr. 126) insists on the ineffectiveness of fear of the gods in promoting justice.[35] Plutarch, naturally, objects to these Epicurean theories; in his view, the ancestral faith in the gods, which includes hopes and fears, is the foundation of the city and, because of that, belief in the gods is the first and most important disposition of the laws (*Col.* 1125E-F; *Pleasant Life* 1104B, Us. 534; 1105B).

The thesis of Critias and, in general, the language, myths, literature[36] and ideas of the philosophers about the gods seem to have been of special interest to the Epicureans due to the doctrinal contrast that they establish between the preconception [πρόληψις] of the gods and the common or popular suppositions about them. What the many say about the gods is not based on preconceptions, but on false suppositions (ὑπολήψεις ψευδεῖς; Epicurus, *LM* 123-124). Epicurus argues that to live well, certain practices should be carried out. First, following the general conception of what god is, one must believe that it is an indestructible and blessed living being [ζῷον ἄφθαρτον καὶ μακάριον], thus avoiding ascribing anything foreign to its characteristics (i.e. blessedness and indestructibility). This is a significant argument that Epicurus provides to remove the fear of god; what follows is the well-known Epicurean view that death is nothing to us (the chief reason being that good and bad consist in perception, and given that death is the privation of perception, when one is dead, perception is gone, so death is nothing to us). These are two good examples of how two significant fears can be removed; they are chiefly fears that usually torment people in their inner mental states and, as is clear, the procedures described to eliminate them are highly dependent on a rational exercise that the agent can perform.

The fear of death evokes a sense of insecurity that prompts people to break the law and destroy the pacts that allow them to live without harming one another nor being harmed. This is, in fact, what Lucretius has in mind when arguing that 'avarice and blind lust for status, which drive wretched people to encroach beyond the boundaries of right and sometimes ... to strive night and day with prodigious effort to scale the summit of wealth these sores of life are nourished in no small degree by dread of death'. He adds that 'the ignominy of humble position and the sting of penury are considered to be incompatible with a life of enjoyment and security' (*RN* 3.60-71).

For Lucretius, the reason for the belief in such incompatibility is that poverty and anonymity are perceived as anticipations of death (*RN* 3.67; see also Porphyry, Us. 478). To avoid death, human beings therefore seek wealth and fame at any price. As Fowler notes, men desire life because they fear death, and reify life as wealth and power.[37] The purpose is as vain as greed and ambition. Both are desires, whose object is undefined and impossible to satisfy, as is the object of the irrational fear of death that gives rise to them. From this perspective, the security that is sought through wealth and power is spurious: it cannot escape death, nor does it free those who pursue it from suspicion and the irrational fear of death. Epicurean physiology, on the other hand, teaches its adherents how to face death and dispels such suspicions and irrational fears.

However, wealth and power can provide security regarding the satisfaction of natural desires and 'the danger of violent death' (see *PD* 6, 7, and 14). As we mentioned above, Epicurus states that if those who aspired to fame gained security, then they achieved the good of nature [τὸ τῆς φύσεως ἀγαθόν] and an end according to what is naturally congenial [κατὰ τὸ τῆς φύσεως οἰκεῖον]. The formulation of *PD* 7 is careful, and suggests that the quest for power and fame is an uncertain, though not impossible, way to achieve security. It is easy to imagine the reasons that the Epicureans might give: the search for and preservation of wealth and power gives rise to envy, violence, restlessness and anguish. Often, far from being a cause of security, it means greater risk and insecurity for human beings, and can even lead to death.

Lucretius, as we indicated above, insists on the damaging effect that the search for security through wealth and power has for contractual security. His assessment evidences a relationship that is worth highlighting. For the most part, interpreters rightly contrast the partial security obtained through wealth and power with the total security of an Epicurean life based on physiology. However, the polis' security is not a result of the pursuit of wealth or power, nor of the practice of Epicurean study of nature. The activity of the avaricious, as Epicurus points out, presupposes the security of the polis and can, of course, be conducted justly or unjustly.[38] For the Epicurean, even the just activity of the greedy turns out to be shameful. However, even Epicurean life, like that of the greedy, presupposes the security of the polis. It is precisely in this sense that a passage of Stobaeus (Us. 530) may be interpreted; it points out that the laws are established for the sake of the wise [χάριν τῶν σοφῶν], not so that they will not commit injustice, but so that they will not suffer it.[39]

3 Epicurean security

Although Epictetus rebukes Epicurus for denying the natural sociability among human beings (*Diss.* 1. 23), some interesting parallels can be drawn between Epictetus' treatment of imperturbability [ἀταραξία] and Epicurus' analysis of the same topic (in addition to the examination one can make regarding the connections between imperturbability and the issue of security). Of course, imperturbability is a stable (or 'katastematic') pleasure for Epicurus, but it sometimes also plays an important role in late Stoicism. In *Diss.* 2.2, when discussing the issue of ἀταραξία, Epictetus states that when someone goes into court then that person will have every security and facility and no troubles if she wishes to maintain a will conformable to nature. The secret to doing this is to keep to what is up to oneself and is therefore naturally free; if one is happy with that, what else does one need to watch out for? Epictetus says that this is enough and that one does not need anything else since no one can take these things away from oneself. In the same vein, in his *Handbook* chap. 38, Epictetus argues that the only real concern one should have is with her 'commanding principle' [τὸ ἡγεμονικόν]; more precisely, one should be careful not to damage her guiding ruling principle. Otherwise, one will not be able to engage in affairs with greater security [ἀσφαλέστερον]. These passages show an interesting difference between late Stoicism and Epicurus: unlike the way in which Epicurus and the Epicureans seem to have posed the problem of security (i.e. both at the level of the inner state of one's soul and at a socio-political level, which would guarantee one's preservation), Epictetus anchors the issue of security solely in the agent's internal state. As is evident, for Epictetus one's security is attained when one admits that her well-being is entirely independent of external things. In the case of the Epicurean, her internal psychological state is undoubtedly highly relevant, too. Certainly, in *PD* 14 Epicurus argues that the purest security [εἰλικρινεστάτη ἀσφάλεια] is that which comes from tranquillity and withdrawal from the many; as we have already pointed out, though, he also recognizes that a certain degree of security from other people comes by means of power and prosperity [εὐπορία]. There is a sense in which the adequately established political organization, based on the golden principle of 'neither harming one another nor being harmed', guarantees the survival and physical conservation of the agent. To be sure, for the Epicurean, this 'guarantee' is not trivial; in a way, it seems to be a necessary condition to allow the agent to work on her psychological states and achieve the purest security of Epicurean life.

The Epicureans consider security from three perspectives: the contractual security provided by the polis; the security achievable by wealth, power and fame; and the security attributable to Epicurean life. The first is a necessary condition for the other two; the second is not a necessary condition of the third since greed and ambition are incompatible with Epicurean life, though that does not mean that wealth and fame are also incompatible. It would certainly be absurd for Epicureans to subtract from the purest security that they postulate positive attributes that recognize contractual security. As we have shown, the contractual security provided by the polis makes possible the satisfaction of the necessary natural desires and a state of confidence [θαρρεῖν, ἀφοβία, ἡσυχία] with respect to future satisfaction and to the danger of violent death. The Epicureans recognize in the community a reality which is not restricted to what is useful for the present, but which looks at life as a whole and offers human beings confidence in the future satisfaction of their needs and ways to avoid a violent death.

It might be interesting to point out that in the *Symposium* (200b-e), Plato indicates that desire is always prospective because it is inherent to its nature to want to achieve its object in the future. Epicurus, conscious like few philosophers of the disturbing effects of fear, assumes the application of this principle to the necessary natural desires and maintains that their full satisfaction is not exempt from prospective components. In *VS* 33 Epicurus presents this idea in an exaggerated or deliberately provocative tone,[40] which is not unusual: 'The cry of the flesh: not to be hungry, not to be thirsty, not to be cold. For if someone has these things and is confident [ἐλπίζων] of having them in the future, he might contend even with ‹Zeus› for happiness'.[41] One can also notice the provocative tone in a parallel fragment apparently coming from the work *On the end* (Plutarch, *Pleasant Life* 1089D; Us. 68): 'For the stable condition of the flesh [τὸ γὰρ εὐσταθὲς σαρκὸς κατάστημα] and the reliable expectation [τὸ πιστὸν ἔλπισμα] concerning this contains the highest and most secure joy, for those who are able to reason [τοῖς ἐπιλογίζεσθαι δυναμένοις]'. Epicurus' adversaries in antiquity cited this statement to show the baseness of the Epicurean's ultimate end and its inconsistencies.[42] But, like Epicurus in *VS* 33, such a statement does not seem to propose a definition of the ultimate end, but rather underlines the pleasant attitude towards the present and the future that is derived from the Epicurean 'comparative appreciation' [ἐπιλογίζεσθαι],[43] which makes such an attitude possible by welcoming the necessary natural desires. On the one hand, it implies rejecting procrastination (μελλησμός; see *VS* 14). Moreover, it shapes a confident disposition towards the future[44] which constitutes an essential element of Epicurean security.[45] Epicurus emphasizes that what will happen is neither unconditionally within our power nor unconditionally outside our control (*LH* 127). The satisfaction of necessary natural desires, as Epicurus and the doxography (especially Porphyry; Us. 464, 466, 470) state, is easy to obtain εὐπόριστος; *PD* 15, 21; *LM* 130). For this reason, it is in some way in our power; that is, it concerns the future in a way that can be trusted (*LH* 127; *LM* 131). *VS* 33 and the fragment of *On the end* already quoted express this idea. A confident disposition towards the future implies a concern for the future that seems to cloud peace of mind. It is precisely this objection that derives from the position of the Cynics, whose daily living, lack of foresight, shamelessness, wandering life, and begging Epicurus strongly rejected (DL 10.119).[46] Philodemus reports (*On Property Management* xii 25-14.9) that Metrodorus quarrelled with the Cynics, who claimed to have chosen a way of life that was by far the lightest and easiest, and, in general, the most devoid of disturbances. Metrodorus objected to them that whoever has to worry permanently and on a day-to-day basis about their subsistence is subject to greater penalties and disturbances than those generated by the possession of the property that insures it. In *On the Stoics*, Philodemus tries to assimilate Cynics and Stoics and, by taking advantage of Zeno's *Republic*, insists that both approaches imply losing the condition of Greeks in general and thereby excluding humanity from civilized life.[47] The Stoics, however, included wealth and good reputation among the preferred indifferents (DL 7.105-107). The Epicureans claim that concern for good reputation and care without anguish for one's heritage and future is a legitimate means of strengthening tranquillity and minimizing fear (DL 10.120; *VS* 41). This treatment of goods, which looks at life as a whole [πρὸς ὅλον βίον] and is not limited to the present day, constitutes one of the central ideas of Philodemus' *On Property Management* (Col. xiii 36-38, xxv 1-14).[48]

At this point, Epicurus' position also unexpectedly aligns with Aristotelian approaches; he uses the expression 'wealth of nature' (ὁ τῆς φύσεως πλοῦτος; *PD* 15) and suggests that 'natural wealth' is required to satisfy the necessary natural desires, so it must be limited. Vain desires, on the other hand, lead to an endless path (ἀπέραντος ὁδός; DL 10.12; *PD* 15). In *Politics* Book 1, Aristotle distinguishes the management of goods required in the domestic and political administration from the chrematistics directed to the accumulation and increase of goods, and especially of money. The first has a limit, as it is directed at the provision of the needs of the house and the city. Aristotle talks about 'real wealth' (ὅ γ' ἀληθινὸς πλοῦτος: *Pol.* I 1256b30-31) and 'natural wealth' (ὁ κατὰ φύσιν πλοῦτος; *Pol.* 1257b19-20).[49] The latter has its goal in accumulation and increase, which makes it unlimited and insatiable. It shows an unlimited desire to live and presupposes excessive pleasures that unnaturally turn all the faculties of man into chrematistics, as if the end of all of them was the accumulation of money (*Pol.* 1258a12-14; *EN* 1096a5-7). Aristotle sees an unnatural, forced character in the life dedicated to profit (βίαιος; *EN* 1096a6); though, like Plato in the *Republic*, he links it to the search for pleasure, he does not consider it specifically among the ways of life in relation to which the philosophical tradition used to consider happiness. As can be seen, the Epicureans' approach to security and wealth is similar to that of Aristotle,[50] although they adopt two different treatments of the relationship between security (ἀσφάλεια; or 'preservation', σωτηρία, in usual

Aristotelian terminology) and political community, whose meaning for Aristotle is to live well [εὖ ζῆν]. At any rate, they are an example of the continuity of Epicureanism with 'the discourses of the ancients' which, as we will show later, Plutarch (*Col.* 1107D) opposed so rhetorically and forcefully to the Epicureans.

Although the possession and care of assets contribute to security, Epicurus considers that by far the most significant endowment that wisdom procures for the blessedness of one's whole life is the possession of friendship (*PD* 27). Once again, the focus is on confidence in the future: 'We do not need utility from our friends so much as we need confidence [ἐλπίς] concerning that utility' (*VS* 34). The benefit of friendship is not only about trust regarding the satisfaction of the necessary natural desires,[51] but also about irrational fears. At this point, Epicurus argues that there is no eternal or ever-lasting terrible or bad thing to fear.[52] We can have confidence about that since our mind has also realized that security is most easily achieved through friendship (*PD* 28).[53]

This *Principal Doctrine* is rarely cited, though it qualifies the security provided by friendship [ἡ ἀσφάλεια φιλίας] as security achieved to the highest possible degree [μάλιστα συντελουμένη], especially concerning such fears. This interpretation, we hold, helps clarify the meaning of the adjective 'pure' [εἰλικρινές] in the *PD* 14 expression 'the purest security' [εἰλικρινεστάτη ἀσφάλεια], apparently referring to the Epicurean life. This adjective, in a superlative degree, seems to underline security free from suspicions and irrational fears. Epicurus maintains, in effect, that irrational suspicions and fears neutralize security (*PD* 13), just as they make it impossible to receive unmixed pleasures (ἀκέραιοι; *PD* 12). As Cicero witnesses, Epicurus' view is that 'of all the things which wisdom procures to enable us to live happily, there is none greater, richer or sweeter than friendship' (*Fin.* 1.65, 80; Us. 539). In *On Ends* (*Fin.* 2.82; Us. 541), Cicero is even more emphatic about the close relationship between friendship and security: while friendship cannot be divorced from pleasure, it deserves to be cultivated, as people cannot live secure and free from fear without it, and therefore cannot live pleasantly. In other words, friendship guarantees the security of people as well as the preservation and attainment of the ultimate end of human life: pleasure. Seen from a slightly different perspective, one could argue that friendship, understood as a means to obtain and preserve security, contributes additionally to the elimination of fear and all those affective states that plunge human beings into turmoil and cause their lives to cease to be truly human. This certainly helps us understand why Epicurus would have held that friendship is pursued for the sake of usefulness; in fact, friends are a form of mutual protection for people, and that is why 'friendship is sought for utility' (*utilitatis causa amicitia est quaesita*; Cicero, *Fin*. 2.84). Thus, friends are helpful for providing protection and, thereby, security. But of course, this must be a reciprocal feeling: everyone in the Epicurean community must make an effort to strengthen their feelings of friendship towards their fellow citizens. This must be the meaning of Cicero's argument when he ascribes to 'some Epicureans' the view that the wise make a pact among themselves in order 'to adopt the same attitude towards their friends as they have towards themselves' (*Fin*. 2.83). Interestingly, within the dramatic context in which this tenet is recorded, Cicero reminds us (through one of his characters) that 'this is possible and has actually occurred'. Maybe his intention (or the intention of his Epicurean sources) is to emphasize that this proposal was not utopian or entirely absurd (at least not for Epicurus and Epicureans, though no evidence is provided for that). But, of course, Cicero does not miss the opportunity to present an objection to the Epicurean approach to friendship: if it is for utility or advantage that the Epicureans cultivate friendship, and no bond of affection exists to make friendship desirable in its own right, then we should prefer land and buildings to friends. No doubt the objection is not unreasonable. Since friendship is only a means to something else but never something choice-worthy by itself, why should it be preferred to anything else? The Epicurean, though, might reply that although it is a means to something else (that other thing being, say, a 'greater good'), friendship is not necessarily a feeling or disposition towards other people that is completely lacking affection or value. Friendship is highly relevant to strengthening trust, or, as put by the Epicureans, 'if there is mistrust there is no friendship' (DL 10.11; Us. 543).

Moreover, if, as Epicurus states, the greatest blessedness by far of one's whole life is friendship (*PD* 37), it cannot merely be a means whose importance should be understood in a basic instrumental character. Finally, there is some evidence to think that Epicurus would actually accept a kind of objection such as Cicero's. Epicurus argues that 'every friendship is worth choosing for its own sake' (δι'ἑαυτὴν αἱρετή; *VS* 23); although this statement seems to be at odds with the view that friendship is sought for the sake of utility, he clarifies that friendship takes its origin from the benefits it eventually confers on us (Epicurus appears to suggest that this is actually the way 'utility' should be taken). Furthermore, the merely instrumental character of friendship is, to a certain extent, neutralized by Epicurus himself when he argues that a friend is not in every case one who searches for utility, nor one who never links friendship to utility. The former becomes a merchant of favours, while the latter 'cuts off all good hope for the future' (ἀποκόπτει τὴν περὶ τοῦ μέλλοντος εὐελπιστίαν; *VS* 29). This being so,

Epicurus envisages friendship not just as a mutual and utilitarian exchange of favours but as a risk; however, as he states in *VS* 28, it is a risk that the wise person is willing to take. Ultimately it is, as Armstrong affirms, a risk inherent in our mortal condition, which is in need of mutual support and defence. Friendship, as Philodemus recalls (*On the Gods* 3), also belongs to the lives of the gods.[54] In this aspect, too, the example of divine life inspires the sage to assimilation to god. *PD* 40 states that those who could have the greatest confidence [τὸ θαρρεῖν μάλιστα] from those around them lived together most pleasantly with the surest guarantee [τὸ βεβαιότατον πίστωμα ἔχοντες] and experienced the fullest sense of belonging. Security, usefulness, friendship, trust, pleasure and affection are realities that, in the opinion of the Epicureans, are combined in the optimal condition described at the end of the *Principal Doctrines*.

Although Epicurus and the Epicureans, unlike the Stoics, do not explicitly assume that their society should be a 'society of wise people', some of their texts seem to suggest a similar position.[55] Epicurus emphatically states that 'the purest security' stems from a quiet life and withdrawal from the many (*PD* 14), with this 'many' being those who have not yet been able to practice and internalize the Epicurean prescriptions for a good life. The Epicurean requirement of living prudently, honourably and justly (*LM* 132; *PD* 5) does not respond to the fear of the punishment of laws, as happens to the 'many', but results from his abiding by natural desires that not only do not promote unjust actions but may not even endorse the performance of actions that the law authorizes (see *VS* 43). This is so because their origin is in vain desires that are disregarded by Epicureans. The combination of the adverbs prudently, honourably and justly (*LM* 132; *PD* 5) qualifies the life of the Epicureans in more restrictive terms than those dictated by attachment to laws. The life of the Epicureans requires the security provided by 'contractual' justice, but also promotes the reduction of the causes of harm and being harmed (*VS* 79), to the avoidance of which, as is known, the pact and justice is oriented (*PD* 33).

However, contempt, envy and hatred are permanent causes of damage for human beings (theses damages stem from 'men', Epicurus states, these men presumably being 'the many' see DL 10.117, Us. 536; *VS* 67). The Epicureans certainly count on the laws and penalties of the city against these threats. Still, they also recognize good reputation, wealth and proximity to power (on this see chapter 6) as a means to minimize them. Although Plutarch accused Epicurus of being incapable of philanthropy (*Pleasant Life* 1098D), philanthropy seems to have been integrated into the Epicurean conception of a pleasant life (see DL 10.9 and Philodemus, *On Property Management* xxiv 29-31).

The Epicureans understood the development and propagation of their philosophy as a task that provided pleasure, affection and utility while offering serenity to human beings. As De Sanctis has shown, Epicurus' philanthropic vocation is evident in his letters; the personalized tone is intertwined with a clear intention of universality that Epicurus assumes to be a presupposition of his mission as a sage.[56] Centuries later, the same philanthropic disposition can be seen in the monumental Epicurean inscriptions that the wealthy Epicurean Diogenes of Oenoanda placed at the service of his fellow citizens and outsiders. Philodemus explicitly includes living with goodwill to the whole human race [φιλανθρώπως] among the people who live pleasantly (*On Choices and Avoidances* xiv 1-4). In Epicurean philanthropy, as in friendship, the goods, utility, security, pleasure and affection are combined. Donation is pleasant (Us. 544), just as it is pleasant to experience the recipient's benevolence. In addition, minimizing the causes of damage from human beings strengthens and increases the personal security of those who act philanthropically.[57]

Restricting oneself to the necessary natural desires, friendship and philanthropy are fundamental elements of the Epicurean security. Since security and contingency go hand in hand, the relationship between security and temporality appears, as we have shown, to be explicitly focused on the temporal modes of the present and the future. However, various considerations of Epicurus about the past, centred on memory and gratitude, converge with those collected around the present and the future in underscoring the link between the unity and stability of the Epicurean way of life and the purest security that Epicurus attributes to it.

Diogenes Laertius collects some well-known and commented-on lines from the letter that Epicurus sends to Idomeneus as he is about to die. After referring to what is happening as a 'blessedly happy day', he tells him that he is suffering from very acute pain and adds: 'But against all these things are ranged [ἀντιπαρετάττετο] the joy in my soul [τὸ κατὰ ψυχὴν χαῖρον] produced by the recollection of the discussions we have had' (ἐπὶ τῇ τῶν γεγονότων ἡμῖν διαλογισμῶν μνήμῃ; DL 10.22). The scene, as Erler interestingly underlines, responds to the topic of the death of the sage and evokes the death of Socrates. It is exemplary and contributes to the genre of Epicurean commemorative texts.[58] The day is unique: the last day of Epicurus; the conflation of 'scenographic' elements is also unique: it is a 'blessedly happy' day, as the pleasant memory of past conversations is opposed to intense, excruciating pains. The scene elicited Cicero's biting irony (*Fin.* 2.94-95), while Plutarch commented on it with disbelief (*Pleasant life* 1099D). But perhaps the singularity of Epicurus' personality prevents us from seeing that it represents a picture of the Epicurean way of life. In fact, the passage does not speak of the memory of a conversation, but of the memory of conversations – presumably, conversations about Epicurean philosophy.[59] As is known, Epicurus recommended the practice of recollecting the principles of his philosophy on all occasions. Attitudes towards pain and death are two of its fundamental areas of application. There is nothing exceptional, therefore, in the fact that Epicurus kept his philosophy in mind and applied it with pleasure (a natural upshot of the exercise of philosophy and his memory; see VS 27)[60] to the circumstances described in the letter to Idomeneus. Furthermore, as we shall now show, the attitude regarding the past and the present of the Epicurean old man who is close to death constitutes a specific theme of the Epicurus texts.

Lucretius describes the figure of an old man who precisely reflects the antithesis of this attitude: he fears death, he laments, he has always lived discontented with the present and with constant thoughts of the future. He feels that his life has been incomplete, and that death comes prematurely and will deprive him of what he could still yet obtain (*RN* 3.955-963; see also 3.931-942 and 1003-1010). Lucretius highlights a fundamental feature of such an attitude: ingratitude towards the past. One might perhaps think that this idea represents a contribution of Lucretius to Epicureanism. Surprisingly, gratitude and ingratitude towards the past have a notable presence in the Epicurus texts.[61] The first characterizes the Epicurean old person. Gratitude anchors him in a safe harbour. But the old man has let down anchor in old age as though in a harbour, since he has secured the goods about which he was previously not confident by means of his secure sense of gratitude (see Epicurus, *VS* 17: τῶν ἀγαθῶν ἀσφαλεῖ κατακλείσας χάριτι). The old man who cultivates philosophy, notes Epicurus, may stay young in good things owing to gratitude for what has occurred (διὰ τὴν χάριν τῶν γεγονότων; *LM* 122).

However, gratitude or ungratefulness to the past is not an issue that Epicurus restricts to old age. It concerns both the young and old because, in his opinion, the attitude towards the past is a mirror of the attitude towards the present and the future. If gratitude keeps young the one who becomes old, ingratitude can also make one old (*VS* 19). Furthermore, as Epicurus points out, the misfortunes that occur in life must be cured by a sense of gratitude for what has been (τῇ τῶν ἀπολλυμένων χάριτι; *VS* 55). Epicurus, like Lucretius, links ingratitude towards the past, discontent towards the present, and anxious expectations of the future to the prevalence of unlimited desires (*VS* 69; Us. 491).[62] Aristotle had indicated that memories and expectations of good people are pleasant because they harmonize with their moral character and their desires (*EN* 1166a23-29; see also Cicero, *Fin.* 2.57). It is not difficult to note that the Epicurean wise person can nourish grateful and pleasant memories concerning the past by restricting himself to the necessary natural desires, friendship and philanthropy, to which his philosophy exhorts.

The grateful memory of the past, satisfaction regarding the present, and the reliable expectation regarding the future harmonize and endow Epicurean life with unity and stability.[63] Its security is based on these two properties, which are not alien to the traditional imagery of the polis.

4 Summary and concluding remarks

Epicureanism, as already discussed in chapter 1, attributes the survival of the species to the security derived from the creation of justice and laws. In this chapter, we have shown how Epicureanism develops the category of security to conceptualize the philosophical life it proposes. The first step of this task was to highlight the continuity that exists between the recognition that Epicureans give to the security provided by political communities and the considerations of *Anonymus Iamblichus*, Plato, Aristotle and Demosthenes around security [ἀσφάλεια], safety [σωτηρία] and freedom from fear [ἄδεια, ἀφοβία]. Next, we have shown that such continuity makes it evident that Epicurean philosophy understands itself as a curious historical phenomenon. Epicurus both recognizes the security provided by the polis as a necessary condition of its possibility and also attributes to the polis the promotion of vain fears and limitless desires that Epicureanism seeks to dissipate through the investigation of nature (i.e. the Epicurean 'physiology') to attain security. The Epicureans develop a genealogy of such fears and desires and of the security to which human beings moved by them aspire. The analysis of these issues allowed us to advance towards the clarification of the Epicurean conception of security and its relationship to the security that the polis provides. Another important detail that we have emphasized in this chapter is that necessary natural desires, friendship and philanthropy are the main factors that give the Epicurean way of life the 'purest security'. Their combination reinforces the liberation from irrational fears and desires. Furthermore, it establishes a permanent attitude of gratitude, satisfaction and trust in human beings with regard to the past, present and future. This permanent temporal disposition enhances the unity and stability of the Epicurean life. Interpreters of Epicureanism have not regarded security as a main topic of focus. However, its study contributes significantly to the clarification of aspects of the Garden's philosophy that may be subsumed under the name of the Epicurean life and approach to society. Security is the key concept for analysing how Epicureanism understands itself concerning both the genealogy of justice and law and of irrational fears and unrealistic desires. Consideration of both relationships sheds light on the intersection of central aspects of the Epicurean way of life, such as the observance of necessary natural desires, friendship and philanthropy, with the way of life made possible by political communities. Two elements of this interest, which are generally not very prominent, are particularly illuminated: the role of property in Epicurean life and the contribution of attitudes towards the past, present and future to the unity and stability of the Epicurean way of life.

3

Preconception, Justice and Usefulness in the Epicurean Contractual Political Model

Scholars usually quote a well-known passage from Cicero's *On the Nature of the Gods* 1.43-44, where the Roman ascribes to Epicurus the achievement of having coined the term πρόληψις ('preconception').[1] The Epicurean neologism 'preconception' gained an undeniable success in antiquity. The Stoics seem to have appropriated the term early, but at the end of antiquity it appears to have been used by all philosophical schools. As is evident, such versatility can only be the result of numerous reworkings of the Epicurean neologism. Some inflections are clear, although they are hard to date, such as the conjunction of the term πρόληψις with the adjectives 'innate' [ἔμφυτος] and 'natural' [φυσική] and their connection with another important expression of the Hellenistic philosophy, the notion of 'common conceptions' [κοιναὶ ἔννοιαι]. These brief remarks allow us to see that the term 'preconception' focused on the Hellenistic controversies around the origin and foundation of knowledge, the development of a *consensus omnium* theory, the gods, justice and universals. The preserved texts of Epicurus contain few considerations about the notion of preconception. Still, two of Epicurus' most extensive *Principal Doctrines* (*PD* 37 and 38) deal precisely with the preconception of the just. These two passages discuss the historical dynamics that were engendered by the relationship between the just and the legal in political communities.

Like any other political model, the Epicurean one has a compelling normative or regulative character. The two main perspectives on the nature of political organizations in the ancient world are, on the one hand, the 'naturalistic' account (two of whose most relevant representatives were Aristotle and the Stoics), and, on the other hand, the 'contractualistic' view.[2] Epicurus and the Epicureans supported the latter and rejected the former. As observed by A. A. Long, some of the principles an Epicurean should adopt (regarding satisfaction of desires, self-sufficiency and freedom) have much in common with Cynic precepts.[3] But the contractual Epicurean view regarding society cannot be anarchist at all.

In fact, a pact implicitly establishes a pattern of conduct, said pattern being an implicitly or explicitly coercive principle. The normative or regulative function of the Epicurean political model is embodied in the preconception of the just.

Now, if Epicurus and the Epicureans defended a contractual theory (as they did), one could cast doubts on the notion of the 'just' insofar they hold that the just is the object of a 'preconception' (πρόληψις; see *PD* 37, 38). The function of the preconception of justice in a contractual framework, we hold, turns out to be clear within a genealogical account of what justice is. Certainly, such a preconception can only be conceived within the domain of a social or 'communal' context where there is an already established language. Indeed, (i) if Epicurean justice can only be understood as something related to what is useful or convenient, and (ii) if the establishment of the pact depends on the 'discretion' of those who establish it, (iii) it seems that the preconception of justice (which, after all, is a kind of concept) does not have the 'objective character' that we tend to ascribe to concepts in general. But this is not necessarily so: although language does not have the same fixed or unchanging character as mathematics (since any language is a dynamic entity that changes over time), once a language is established in a linguistic community it comes to feature elements of stability that allow people to communicate with each other. Thus, the previous character of a preconception must be related to the previously fixed uses of language (or so we shall argue). Moreover, if the just is a modality of what is useful for a given community, it is not merely conventional. The fact that a community decides that *x* is just does not make *x* useful to fulfil the purpose of not harming or being harmed that Epicureanism attributes to the pacts of justice (*PD* 31, 32, 33). Usefulness is constrained by the facts (τὰ πράγματα; *PD* 37. τῶν περιεστώτων πραγμάτων; *PD* 38). For the same reason, what is just, that is, useful, for one community, may not be useful for another (*PD* 36, 37). And even what is useful for one community in certain circumstances may not be useful later or in different circumstances (*PD* 37, 38).

This chapter proceeds thus: first (section 1) we provide some general clarifications regarding what Epicurus calls 'the just of nature' (*PD* 31 = **T1**, below). There we also explain the connections between justice and usefulness and set out to clarify our statement that, within the domain of the Epicurean contractual model, justice can be considered a 'modality of utility' and the prolepsis of the just as a canon that validates the just. In section 2, we refer to Epicurean epistemology and analyse the specific characteristics of the confirmation [ἐπιμαρτύρησις] of the just. Finally, in section 3, we reject interpretations that (i) instantiate the prolepsis of the just in the constitution that rules over the life of a community or (ii) distinguish a hierarchical and historical plurality of preconceptions of the just, and we try to show that the Epicureans embedded the prolepsis of the just in language. To do that, we study the relationship between the origin and development of language and the establishment of the pacts of justice. We argue against Philippson's view that the Epicureans supported the idea of natural law in the supposed parallelism between the origin and development of language and that of justice and laws. If our textual evidence is to be trusted (mainly Epicurus' texts, Lucretius' testimony, Hermarcus, and so on), Philippson's suggestion cannot be accurate and introduces severe confusion. Next, we underline the relevance of an ingredient of experience that is not usually considered when dealing with Epicurean preconception's empirical genesis: language learning.

1 Justice, utility and the 'Justice of Nature'

The extant texts of Epicurus contain few considerations about the notion of preconception.[4] The three most noteworthy passages refer to the preconception of the gods (*LM* 123-124), to that of the just (*PD* 37 and 38), and to the recommendation stating that we should not investigate time by referring to the preconception that we have in ourselves. What we have to do, Epicurus contends, is to pay attention to the 'clear datum of experience' [αὐτὸ τὸ ἐνάργημα], according to which we utter expressions such as 'for a long time', 'for a short time', that is, interpreting the issue in a way closely related to our experience (*LH* 72). Moreover, one should add the preconception of cause or rather of 'responsibility' (Epicurus, *On Nature* 34, 26-30).[5] The remaining references are highly controversial.[6] The testimonies in the doxography are not abundant either; they are also burdened by subsequent non-Epicurean reworkings. In our view, therefore, Epicurus' considerations about the just in *PD* 37 and 38 turn out to be particularly valuable since, despite having been the least studied by those interested in the Epicurean neologism πρόληψις, they provide two illustrative references. As a matter of fact, in these passages they play the role of criteria to determine what is really just. Diogenes Laertius reports that in his *Canon*, Epicurus stated that preconceptions (along with 'affections' or 'feelings' and perceptions) are the criteria of truth (DL 10.31). This is particularly clear in *PD* 38, where Epicurus reminds us of the fact that things taken to be just must be in accordance with the preconception of justice.

As already observed, the presence of the term πρόληψις is rather scanty in the Epicurean texts. We do not intend to suggest that it had a secondary role in the Epicurean theory of justice, but rather to emphasize that its clarification must begin by considering the precise aspect of the theory within which the term appears. The analysis of *PD* 31 allows us to begin our journey on that path; the expression 'the wealth of nature' [ὁ τῆς φύσεως πλοῦτος] in *PD* 15 has a certain paradoxical character that is even more evident in a similar expression, 'the just of nature' [τὸ τῆς φύσεως δίκαιον], contained in *PD* 31:

> **T1** The just of nature [τὸ τῆς φύσεως δίκαιον] is a pledge of usefulness [σύμβολον τοῦ συμφέροντος], to neither harm one another nor be harmed.
>
> trans. Inwood and Gerson, modified

As we have already pointed out, some of the principles that an Epicurean should adopt regarding the satisfaction of desires, self-sufficiency and freedom have much in common with Cynic precepts. Nevertheless, unlike the Stoics, Epicurus explicitly denied that an Epicurean wise man should practice Cynicism (DL 10.119; Us. 14). Moreover, the Epicurean Philodemus, following Metrodorus, rejected the Cynic lifestyle and, especially, Cynic poverty (on this point see chapter 2, section 3). Of course, this does not mean that he is in favour of wealth (as if it were something good in the strict sense); instead, he is in favour of limited wealth.[7] Thus every possession is wealth when it can satisfy nature (i.e. a natural desire) and the greatest wealth is poverty when it comes to unlimited desires.[8] The correct use of wealth must be what Philodemus calls 'natural wealth' (ὁ φυσικὸς πλοῦτος; col. xiv 19) and what Epicurus calls (in *PD* 15) 'the wealth of nature' [ὁ τῆς φύσεως πλοῦτος], (on this see also Porphyry, *To Marcella* 27; Us. 202). In this *Principal Doctrine*, Epicurus contrasts 'the wealth of nature' with the wealth defined by groundless opinions [ὁ δὲ τῶν κενῶν δοξῶν]. As we are going to show, both Epicurus and the Epicureans develop a similar contrast between 'the just of nature', on the one hand, and justice such as it is defined by 'foolish wisdom' and 'vain and stupid' opinions, on the other.

But let us return to *PD* 31, where the meaning of 'nature' in the expression 'the just of nature' is undoubtedly decisive. Although what we have argued so far (chapter 2, section 3) should suffice to show how we think that phrase ought to be understood, allow us to present a general account of why this sentence cannot be read from a 'naturalistic' approach.[9] First of all, it must be recalled that the expression 'the just of nature' is not an Epicurus innovation. As we show and discuss below, it is already found in a remarkable passage from Plato's *Gorgias*. But before we focus on that passage, let us briefly consider how the Epicureans understand nature. There is good reason to suspect that the expression 'the just of nature' must be seen in a primary and easily understandable sense of what human nature is. To be more precise: if, in fact, for Epicurus the just should be conceived only along with the notion of usefulness (such usefulness being the one that guarantees that people neither harm one another nor are harmed in political organizations), the word 'nature' in the expression 'the just of nature' must refer to human nature. As indicated in chapter 1, section 1, Demetrius of Laconia underlines a semantic connection between nature and utility that complements the remarks of Epicurus, Hermarchus and Polystratus about what is useful and just. According to Demetrius, one of the meanings of the adverbial dative φύσει is συμφερόντως, which might be rendered 'by usefulness' (*PHerc.* 1012, col. lxvi-lxviii). Moreover, unlike what the Stoics believe, Epicurus maintains that there is no finality or providence in nature.[10] Therefore, nature cannot be understood as an entity that deliberates or acts in any understandable sense of acting or deliberating.

Let us now turn to the remarkable passage of Plato's *Gorgias* mentioned above. Here, the character Callicles employs expressions such as 'according to the law *of* nature' (κατὰ νόμον τὸν τῆς φύσεως; 483e3), and 'the just *of* nature' (τὸ τῆς φύσεως δίκαιον; 484b1) with the explicit intention of underlining, as Dodds observes in his commentary on the dialogue, the paradox that represented linkage through the expression 'of nature' opposed concepts such as 'nature' and 'law'.[11] We do not know whether Epicurus knew the *Gorgias*, a dialogue against which his disciple Metrodorus seems to have dedicated a text. However, we know that Epicurus reformulated proverbs of traditional wisdom, as well as Democritus' and Solon's expressions, to develop his doctrine and thus facilitate its reception and memory.[12] It therefore cannot be ruled out that in *PD* 31 Epicurus had the shocking expressions of Callicles in mind, and that he presented his own doctrine through a reformulation (no less surprising, incidentally) of their content.[13]

Epicurus does not introduce the expression 'the just of nature' to oppose it, like Callicles, to the laws, nor does he maintain that 'taking advantage' (Plato, *Gorg.* 483c3-4: τὸ πλεονεκτεῖν), inherent to human nature in Callicles' view, is the foundation of the supposed law of nature, i.e. the law of the strongest.[14] Nor does Epicurus cite in his support, like Callicles, the actions of human groups in international relations, or animal behaviour. In Epicurus' view, it is not possible to speak of justice with regard to irrational animals since they cannot make pacts. The same applies to peoples who were unable or unwilling to establish such agreements (*PD* 32).[15] Some interpreters, such as Philippson 1910: 292–5, proposed to include Epicurus' expression as a form of iusnaturalism. However, as we have shown, in Epicureanism justice implies a pact, a contract, which rules out both the iusnaturalistic link (between nature and justice) and Calliclean immoralism. It is clear to us that the genitive τῆς φύσεως, 'of nature', is not orientated to highlight, as in Callicles' immoralism or in iusnaturalism, a normativity of nature, but to qualify the effective ontological status of a phenomenon such as justice and, implicitly, the methodology that must be followed in its explanation. Epicurus and the Epicureans certainly oppose empty substantive formulations revealing 'foolish wisdom' (μωροσοφία; *POxy.* 5077col. 2, fr. 2, l. 9), such as those represented by expressions like 'justice in itself' (*PD* 33) or 'natural law.' However, they also reject the 'vain and stupid' opinions of those who claim that there is no such thing as the just (Polystratus, *Contempt* col. xxii 23-24, xxiv 3-5, xxv 9-10, xxvi 22-5, xxvii 10) or that it only exists according to individual assumptions (κατὰ τὰς ἰδίας ὑπολήψεις; *Abs.* 1.12,2). The heterogeneity of the views that the Epicureans oppose offers a critical clue to analysis of the expression 'the just of nature' (*PD* 31). Indeed, 'the just' does not possess the substantial mode of existence characteristic of things like a piece of gold, for instance (called καθ' ἑαυτάς φύσεις by Epicurus and the Epicureans; Epicurus, *LH* 68; Polystratus *Contempt* col. xxv 18-24: καθ' αὑτά, κατὰ τὴν ἰδίαν φύσιν λεγόμενα). It does not follow, though, that its existence is conventional; the just (like other modalities of usefulness, such as 'producing health'; *Contempt* col. xxiv 24-xxv 16. *Abst.* 1.12 2) represents, as we have shown in chapter 1, real properties and not mere opinions.

Thus, when Epicurus talks about 'the just of nature', he does not refer to what nature prescribes as just; the expression seems to point to the ontological and epistemological reference of the phenomenon constituted by justice *to our nature*, for which the security, the purpose of the pact that founds justice, is, in accordance with *PD* 7, the good of nature [τὸ τῆς φύσεως ἀγαθόν] and 'what is naturally congenial' [τὸ τῆς φύσεως οἰκεῖον]. This being so, 'the just of nature' must be framed in the liberating investigation of nature that Epicurus often advocates (*LH* 37; *PD* 1).[16] Therefore, it is not wrong to make it equivalent, as Strauss and Goldschmidt[17] suggested, to the expression 'the nature of the just', used by Epicurus in *PD* 37 as opposed to representations of the just grounded in empty words that, unlike the 'science of nature' [φυσιολογία], deeply disturb those who try to give an account of reality through them.

Plato makes the character Glaucon say (with evident irony) 'the nature of justice' (ἡ φύσις δικαιοσύνης; *Resp.* 359b6) to refer to the conventionalist genealogy of justice. Such a conventionalist genealogy of justice is exposed as an expression of a merely instrumental assessment of justice, which, according to Plato, would make it impossible to speak of the 'nature of justice'. One of the fragments of a 'doctrinal' letter of Epicurus contained in the *POxy.* 5077 (col. ii, fr. 2, l) includes the same expression of Glaucon [ἡ φύσις δικαιοσύνης]. According to the interpretation proposed by Angelli,[18] Epicurus is developing in the fragment an antithesis between the hypostatization of an absolute and universally justice (perhaps the mathematical–geometrical resolution of justice developed by the Pythagoreans as well as by Plato) and the several forms of justice dependent on the geographical, historical and ethnic setting. Epicurus states in the fragment that the nature of justice corresponds to the clear datum of experience regarding its forms (κατὰ τὸ ἐπὶ τῶν σχημάτων ἐνάργημα; *POxy.* 5077 col. 2 of fr. 2, l.), i.e. to the evidence of the diversity already indicated.

One of the tasks of Epicurean 'physiology' is precisely to clarify the ontological status of instances such as justice. *PD* 31 contains compelling indications to start the analysis of the notion of the preconception of what is just, and through it to clarify the ontological and epistemological status of the just. Indeed, it recognizes a regulatory imprint in the phenomenon of justice. Such an imprint neither derives from the idea of natural right (as shown by the examination of **T1** above) nor from the reduction of justice to legality, but through the proper predicate 'pledge of usefulness for the sake of neither harming one another nor being harmed'. In fact, even though justice and usefulness are not directly linked to each other in the text, they are connected through the notion of σύμβολον, 'pledge', which allows us to glimpse the view – so clearly expressed through the use of the preposition εἰς plus τὸ μὴ βλάπτειν . . . βλάπτεσθαι – that suggests understanding the whole expression as a distinction between guideline and realization or formal determination and content. The two *Principal Doctrines* that introduce the term πρόληψις confirm this distinction:

> **T2** *PD* 37: Of what is sanctioned as just [τῶν νομισθέντων εἶναι δικαίων], that which is confirmed [τὸ μὲν ἐπιμαρτυρούμενον] to be useful in the necessities of mutual associations [ἐν ταῖς χρείαις τῆς πρὸς ἀλλήλους κοινωνίας] has its existence in the domain of the just [ἔχει τὸ ἐν τοῦ δικαίου χώρᾳ εἶναι], whether it is the same for everyone or not. And if someone establishes a law and it does not turn out to be in accord with what is advantageous [κατὰ τὸ συμφέρον] in mutual associations, this no longer possesses the nature of what is just [οὐκέτι . . . τὴν τοῦ δικαίου φύσιν ἔχει]. And if what is advantageous in the sense of being just changes, but for a while fits our preconception [of justice] [εἰς τὴν πρόληψιν ἐναρμόττῃ], nevertheless it was just for that length of time, [at least]

for those who do not disturb themselves with empty words [φωναῖς κεναῖς] but simply look to the facts.

transl. Inwood & Gerson, modified and adapted to Dorandi's text 2013[19]

T3 *PD* 38: If new circumstantial facts did not arise [μὴ καινῶν γενομένων τῶν περιεστώτων πραγμάτων], it was evident [ἀνεφάνη] that the things sanctioned as just [τὰ νομισθέντα δίκαια], while not matching [μὴ ἁρμόττοντα] anymore in the fact themselves with the preconception [i.e. of what is just], these things are no longer just [οὐκ ἦν ταῦτα δίκαια]. But if circumstantial facts are new and the same things established as just are no longer advantageous [οὐκέτι συνέφερε], they were just at that moment, when they were advantageous for the mutual associations of fellow citizens, but later, when they were no longer just [ὕστερον δ' οὐκ ἦν ἔτι δίκαια], they were not advantageous [μὴ συνέφερεν].

our translation

It is not hard to see that in the two mentions of preconception included in these passages, preconceptions work as criteria of truth. The Epicurean passages conveyed by Diogenes Laertius (10.31; Us. 36) do not deny this statement. Each of these instances is said to be 'evident' or 'clear'[20] [ἐναργής], and consequently they are a canon of truth insofar as such evidence constitutes a manifest truth that does not require proof and which allows for the further verification of opinions. Sextus Empiricus seems to ascribe the introduction of the technical term ἐνάργεια, 'evidence', to Theophrastus (*M* 7.218). Several late testimonies reveal that Theophrastus would have made ἐνάργεια and its correlate, conviction, [πίστις], the fundamental ground of his philosophical expositions. Indeed, he recognized the foundation of knowledge in the evidence of perception and the first principles.[21]

Sextus Empiricus also maintains that Theophrastus referred evidence to the sensible and the intelligible (or rather, Sextus ascribes to Aristotle, Theophrastus and the Peripatetics in general that the criterion is twofold, sense perception and thought, but common to both, he says, is τὸ ἐναργές; *M* 7.218).[22] However, even accepting that such testimonies are reliable, it is almost impossible to determine to what extent Theophrastus' expositions about evidence influenced the Hellenistic philosophers. Thus, today we tend to accept instead that it was Epicurus who introduced the technical term ἐνάργεια, since his writings and the doxography manifestly prove that he not only used the term frequently (sometimes even as a synonym of perception), but that he also explicitly made ἐνάργεια the cornerstone of his philosophy, which represented an innovative approach in Greek philosophy. Epicurus thus witnesses the beginning of a linkage between evidence, truth and praxis that the Hellenistic culture will cover from multiple perspectives.[23]

2 The confirmation of the just

The presence of the Epicurean technicality 'to confirm' (or 'to witness in favour of': ἐπιμαρτυρεῖν)[24] in the first line of *PD* 37, referring to what is taken to be just, certainly suggests a similarity between the validation of what is just and the confirmation procedures recognized by Epicurean epistemology. Sextus Empiricus, reporting Epicurus' view, defines confirmation [ἐπιμαρτύρησις] as a grasp [κατάληψις] through evidence of the fact that the subject on which the opinion (or conjecture) is held is such as the opinion (or conjecture) held it to be (*M* 7.212; Us. 247).[25] For Epicurus, perception works as a criterion and implies that we can deliberately direct our attention to carry out processes of confirmation. The question arises as to what makes it possible to trigger such processes of confirmation or verification. In Epicurus' view, human perceptions are related to an internal movement that gives rise to opinions, suppositions and conjectures (DL 9.34: *LH* 50. Sextus Empiricus, *M* 7.203; 7.212, 215, Us. 247). The epistemic agent has the possibility of considering the truth of these opinions, suppositions and conjectures as 'waiting' [προσμένον], since it is a truth that future perceptions will either confirm [ἐπιμαρτυρεῖται] or not disprove [οὐκ ἀντιμαρτυρεῖται], or not confirm [οὐκ ἐπιμαρτυρεῖται] or disprove [ἀντιμαρτυρεῖται]. Unfortunately, the extant texts of Epicurus are extremely sparse at this point, where prudential tradition also seems to be present in Epicurean epistemology. However, it appears that, when speaking of opinions, suppositions or conjectures as 'that which awaits' (i.e. which awaits *confirmation*), Epicurus attributes to this movement (which combines perception and opinion) a sort of recognition, and a certain sketch of the conditions of confirmation. Such recognition and sketch of confirmation conditions is tantamount to a certain recognition of the best conditions of the exercise of perception. We can only highlight the general relevance of this topic in Hellenistic philosophy by saying that it is enough to point out that one of the most significant results of the bitter disputes between the Stoics and the Academic Sceptics was that it forced both schools to try to limit the best conditions of the perceptive exercise, as is clearly witnessed by Sextus Empiricus (*M* 7.166-189, 253-260, 424-425).

In ancient tradition, there are two examples of the 'waiting for' confirmation regarding opinions and conjectures (DL 10.33; Sextus Empiricus *M* 7.212, 215), where what is subject to confirmation is the form of an object seen from far away (the repeated example of the tower)[26] or the identity of a person who is seen in the distance (Plato, in Sextus' example). Under this aspect, the verification or confirmation moves in a restricted area: the world of objects located in an accessible space. Not every opinion matters to this field since opinions and conjectures are also concerned with the non-manifest [ἄδηλον]. Epicurus distinguishes two domains of the non-manifest: objects that can only be observed from far away, such as astronomical and atmospheric phenomena, and unobservable objects, such as atoms and void. In both cases, it is only possible for opinions or conjectures to be 'counter-witnessed' (ἀντιμαρτυρεῖται)[27] or not 'counter-witnessed' [οὐκ ἀντιμαρτυρεῖται]. In his brief treatise on 'meteorology' in the *Letter to Pythocles*, Epicurus refers to astronomical and atmospheric phenomena and stresses that they can be explained differently (*LP* 85-87). In his opinion, to seek unique explanations in this domain not only corresponds to a life of irrationality and empty opinion [οὐ γὰρ ἀλογίας καὶ κενῆς δόξης ὁ βίος], but also to an abandonment of physical inquiry (in the sense of a 'scientific treatment of nature'). In this case, one ends up having to resort to a mythical account that offers no real explanation (*LP* 86-87; 113).[28]

Finally, it could be said that, in the complex articulation existing between perceiving and supposing, lies the possibility of using perception as a criterion of truth. To clarify this relationship, the Epicureans tried to accurately delimit perception through an exhaustive explanation of its cognitive content. This task demanded a supposedly 'phenomenological' conception of perception, accompanied at all times by the corresponding physical explanations of the theory of 'images' [εἴδωλα] or rather '*simulacra*' (as Lucretius says, surely thinking of Epicurean εἴδωλα, 'the mind is deceived by "images" – *simulacra* – in sleep when we have a vision of one whom life has deserted'; *RN* 5.62-63).

In the practical domain, confirmation [ἐπιμαρτύρησις], as Epicurus himself seems to have pointed out in his treatise *On Nature*,[29] has specific features that are underlined by *PD* 37 and 38. This is so because in the practical domain opinions are not properly contrasted with bodies or properties of bodies, but by an examination of their practical consequences, that is, the advantageousness or disadvantageousness of the actions that are based on the opinions.[30] The practical consequences of certain convictions about justice, embodied in the laws, are actually examined as to whether they are convenient or useful as a result of not harming each other or being harmed.[31] The language of *PD* 37 and 38 clearly reflects the confirmation process [ἐπιμαρτύρησις] specific to the domain of praxis. *PD* 37 uses the verb ἀποβαίνειν ('to turn out') to refer to the practical consequences that derive from the establishment of a law. *PD* 38 refers to the practical consequences of what is sanctioned as just through the proposition 'it was evident … in the facts themselves' [ἀνεφάνη … ἐπ' αὐτῶν τῶν ἔργων]. Consequently, the process of validation or confirmation mentioned in *PD* 37 and 38 obeys, rather, the dynamic that is established in the relationship between means and ends, or instruments and functions.[32] Ends and functions sketch the suitable means: a plasticine hammer, for example, is an absurd tool, as are laws whose consequences would be collective starvation and the disappearance of the community. In this sense, ends and functions ('neither harming one another nor being harmed', *PD* 33) constrain means and instruments. But circumstances also constitute another unavoidable factor to be considered in the validation of the conformity of means to ends. This implies, of course, that the validation itself is temporary: what has been confirmed or counter-witnessed in the present as just, may not have been confirmed or counter-witnessed in the same terms in the past or may not be confirmed or counter-witnessed in the future (this epistemological procedure is not alien to Epicurus; see *LH* 51-52).

In our opinion, this detail explains in a clear way the sense in which it can be said that Epicurean justice is a sort of 'modality of usefulness'.[33] It also explains why Epicurus holds that justice is not something by itself, but instead a certain kind of pact [συνθήκη τις] that refers to neither harming nor receiving harm, which is always the case in reciprocal relationships in specific places and times (*PD* 33). In other words, justice is not something entirely invariable and immutable by itself: according to the circumstances, so too is what is just. However, this does not mean that justice is something 'relative' (in the sense of a crude relativism), but rather that the law must be flexible enough to adapt itself to the concrete situation in which people are living. This approach also helps to understand why, even though Epicurus states that justice is not a thing in its own right (*PD* 33; see also Lucretius, *RN* 5.855-877), it is nevertheless generally the same for everyone since it is something useful in association with one another (συμφέρον . . . ἐν τῇ πρὸς ἀλλήλους κοινωνίᾳ; *PD* 36). For example, suppose that food reserves in a city are low because of a poor harvest; it may be fair and reasonable to pass a law requiring the citizens to consume smaller rations of grain (at least while the food emergency lasts). Of course, that law should be identical for everyone: if a person received any privileges connected with the distribution of food, anyone else could claim the same privilege, which eventually would lead to the destruction of the city. Thus, the pact would not be kept, which is the same as saying that the political community would be dissolved. Indeed, if the agreement is annulled according to which harming and being harmed is avoided, then there will be no pact. This trivial example is helpful since it shows how justice must be considered as a modality of usefulness. Furthermore, it shows the sense in which what is just is valid for the time and circumstances in which that law is reasonable as a means of preserving the political community (*PD* 37).

As already stated, the relevance of a specific time and circumstance mostly depends upon Epicurean contractualism.[34] However, once again, there is an interesting remark in Plato regarding the time and circumstance in which laws have their legal power. In the *Statesman* (294a7-8), he underlines the tension existing between the establishment of laws and the infinite variability of the circumstances related to specific actions. This topic is also reflected in Aristotle's debates on the universality of the law and the singular character of actions (this is especially evident in the recognition that the 'situational' nature of praxis has in his ethical investigations; see *EN* 1141b14-21). Plato had no doubts that human goods and the good are not the same thing. Even though the highest standard of what is good is the Form of the Good (*Resp.* 6), he reminds us that the just person will be just in the usual sense of keeping an oath, not committing robberies, thefts, or betrayals of friends, and avoiding adultery, disrespect for parents, and neglect of the gods (*Resp.* 442e-443b). More importantly, Plato explicitly notes that the legal norm is in various ways subordinated to the person knowing what justice means for the city.[35] Of course, the person who actually knows what is right is the Platonic philosopher; but what is relevant here is that Epicurus, probably inspired by this remarkable Platonic passage, reminds us that the law cannot be universal in scope always and everywhere regardless of the circumstances and the person applying it. Circumstances are relevant, but so is the sober calculation of the person who can discern the specific circumstance in which a rule should be applied.

The epistemological aspects discussed above and related to the issue of justice, as well as its confirmation or validation as discussed in *PD* 37 and 38, concern the 'truth' of things instituted by people and not the substantial objects of the world that they find before themselves. Some of its elements, as we have indicated, are present in the philosophical tradition, but perhaps the most interesting parallel is Aristotle's attempts to clarify the specificity of practical truth and, of course, the assumption of modern philosophies about the notion of truth as an active constitution on the part of the subject.[36] The aforementioned *Principal Doctrines* allow us to understand how the Epicureans dealt with the nature of the 'truth' of that which the human beings had established.

3 The development of language, the origin of justice and law, and the preconception of the just

In the discussion put forward by *PD* 37 and 38, what is just appears as object of preconception. The practical effects of what is held to be just, the circumstances, and the preconception of what is just are, indeed, the factors involved in the previously mentioned discussion. According to the above considerations regarding what is just, the correlate of this preconception is the sense of something that is 'advantageous because of not harming one another or being harmed'. It is enough to look at the terms of this expression to understand the formal and operative nature of the preconception of what is just, which forces one to ask oneself to whom one should attribute the belonging of preconception in the debate presented by the passages under review. The *Principal Doctrines* 37 and 38 differ from the other *Principal Doctrines* concerning justice because of their greater concreteness. They oppose to the indeterminacy of the gnomic style of these other *Principal Doctrines* specific approaches that can be exemplified in the practice of Athenian law.[37] The *Principal Doctrines* 37 and 38 do not mention pacts, nor do they refer explicitly, as do Hermarchus and Lucretius, to the origin of justice and the causes of the subsequent need to establish laws and sanctions. They do not refer to the origin of the preconception of the just, either. They consider societies with the preconception of just, laws and magistracies and, from them and concerning them, they examine what is held to be just and the nature that the just should possess. If this is so (and we think it is), the Epicurean political model must have been designed not only to provide guidelines for what a society of 'Epicurean friends' should look like (a society Epicurus must certainly have been thinking of), but also to describe the political organization understood as a polis, in which not necessarily everyone was an Epicurean. Like any other political model, the Epicurean one has a compelling normative character which may have shortcomings. Moreover, it is not entirely idealistic, and is intended for human beings capable of understanding the normative principles that are supposed to guarantee a healthy social community.

In this spirit, Goldschmidt (one of the few scholars who, like Müller, has investigated where the Epicureans locate the preconception of the just) maintains that in *PD* 37 and 38, the preconception of the just *is* the political community. Goldschmidt also distinguishes this preconception from the universal or philosophical preconception of the just which, according to him, would not allow for the validation of what is taken to be just due to its generality. The preconception mentioned in *PD* 37 and 38 is the idea that citizens make of the common interest and thus embody in their constitution and their legal system. The validation they present would primarily concern the conformity of legal provisions with the constitution.[38] Changes to the constitution (that is, the redefinitions of the public interest)[39] would raise this conformity in new terms, but would not imply any denial of the just while the abolished constitution and the legal provisions adjusted to it were still in force. In the history of Athens, the constitution of the ancestors would represent a principle of permanence and continuity regarding the changes of a regime similar to that which, in general terms, performs the philosophical preconception of the just. Goldschmidt also maintains that, if we consider these maxims in relation to the Hellenistic era in which Epicurus lived, it becomes necessary to grant to the issue of security the role of permanence and continuity that he attributes to the ancestral constitution.[40]

The first interpretative framework suggested by Goldschmidt is very appealing: while highlighting the continuity of laws and justice, it has the merit of agreeing with one of the fundamental purposes of the Epicurean political theory: the apology for the security and tranquillity of civilized life governed by laws and magistracies. It also makes clear the collective belonging of the preconception of justice. However, apart from relying on readings that do not enjoy consensus, such as the aforementioned interpretation of μεταπίπτειν in *PD* 37, it introduces a hierarchical plurality of preconceptions of the just that, at least from the evidence of *PD* 37 and 38, is hard to sustain.

Principal Doctrines 37 and 38, as we have already noted, consider societies and the place of justice in them as a backdrop to the preconception of the just, laws and magistracies. They do not refer, like Hermarchus and Lucretius, to the genealogy of justice and laws. Müller posits different modalities of preconception of the just, taking as his standpoint the extract of Hermarchus where he argues that the original establishment of laws and sanctions by outstanding men (not by force of their body, but by the wisdom of their soul) was preceded by an irrational perception of what is useful [ἀλόγως αὐτοῦ –sc., τοῦ χρησίμου– πρότερον αἰσθανομένους]; that is, one that operated without using reason and often went unnoticed. These wise people, who were aware of usefulness, instigated a reflection on such usefulness [εἰς ἐπιλογισμὸν τοῦ χρησίμου].[41] Further, they frightened the others by the severity of the punishments (*Abst.* 1.8 1-2). In Müller's view, these two moments in the conceptualization of the useful in human groups correspond to two levels of the preconception of the just. The lower or simpler level is the result of the irrational memory of what is useful (ἄλογος μνήμη τοῦ συμφέροντος; *Abst.* 1.10, 4); the higher level is reached through 'comparative appreciation' of the useful (ἐπιλογισμὸν τοῦ χρησίμου; *Abst.* 1.8, 2).[42] Interestingly, Müller also states that the modalities of the preconception of the just correspond to distinct stages of language development. Although we do not have a systematic discussion in Epicurus' texts about the origin of language, we do possess clear statements that (i) names did not come into being from the beginning by convention, but by the constraint of nature,[43] and (ii) that later, in order that the meanings of words might be less ambiguous and more concise, such names were established by a general convention in each tribe (Epicurus, *LH* 75-76). This being so, language is something natural, but it can be 'perfectioned' through its use and thereby by a sort of convention. In Müller's opinion, the inferior modality of the preconception of the just would be inscribed in the natural stage of language; the superior modality of preconception of the just takes place, on the contrary, in a third stage of language development,[44] in which some individuals establish words to express unobserved (or rather 'non-understood') facts (οὐ συνορώμενα πράγματα; *LH* 76), which he, like other interpreters, identifies with abstract entities.[45] Goldschmidt also relies on this extract of Hermarchus to argue that the preconception of the just implies a comparative appreciation [ἐπιλογισμός] and is the most advanced stage of language development.[46]

As can be seen, in Müller's and Goldschmidt's remarks three obscure 'genealogical' themes are interwoven: the origin and development of language, that of justice and laws, and that of preconceptions. It is natural that the result is speculative and has not given rise to consensus. Unlike Goldschmidt's position, *PD* 37 and 38 seem to link the preconception of the just with the nature of the just without intermediation, as evidenced by the formal and operative nature of its content, which can also be assimilated to what Epicurus presents as the just according to what is common and similar for all (*PD* 36). From this reading, we can maintain the collective belonging of the preconception of the just no longer, as Goldschmidt suggests, due to its incarnation in the constitutions (in which the communities define public utility), but through another more general reality that represents a more significant and denser continuity than the constitutions for the communities. This 'denser continuity' is also intertwined with the history of justice and with another realm of experience which the Epicureans deemed to be equally crucial for the survival of the human species: language.

The decisive contribution of language in the formation of human associations and pacts was a topic of ancient literature that Isocrates used skilfully in his discourses.[47] The idea is found at the beginning of Aristotle's *Politics* 1253a7-18, as well as in Cicero's *Republic* (1.25, 40) and Lucretius (*RN* 5.1021-1023). There were fathers in neighbourhood relations, who, according to Lucretius (as we stressed in chapter 1), eager not to harm or be harmed, began to make friends [*amicities*], (*RN* 5.1019-1020). Lucretius proceeds in a rather dramatic tone, stating that those neighbours started claiming protection for their children and women, indicating by means of clumsily articulated sounds and gestures [*vocibus et gestu cum balbe signarent*] that it was right to have compassion for the weak (*imbecillorum esse aequum misererier*; RN 5.1021-1023). Those who make the pact were not the prehistoric and rude people, whose wandering and solitary life 'in the manner of beasts' (*more ferarum*; RN 5.931-932) Lucretius had described earlier in the poem. They are beings humanized through physical and psychological 'processes of softening' [*mollescere*] brought on by the use of fire and clothing, life in dwellings with a partner, and the recognition of children (RN 5.1011-1027). Their language is not in the manner of beasts; it has the essential characteristics of human language: an articulated system of words with conceptual meaning and objective reference. Therefore, it constitutes a collective phenomenon and not something private.[48]

For the Epicureans, the origin and development of language represented a central issue in their rational and naturalistic reconstruction of human history. So was, as we have shown, the origin of justice and laws. Philippson held that the Epicureans defended the idea of natural law in the supposed parallelism existing between the origin and development of language and that of justice and laws.[49] But as we have already advanced, if Epicurean contractualism is so strong that justice is not possible without such a contract (based on the fundamental rule 'neither harming nor being harmed'), the iusnaturalistic approach is untenable as a likely reading of the Epicurean theory of law. As a matter of fact, Epicurean justice depends on a pact (in addition to the fact that, as Epicurus himself stresses, justice is not incontrovertible; PD 38). Neither the texts of Epicurus nor the verses of Lucretius' *On the Nature of Things* book 5 (describing the emergence of pact and justice of the first human groups) endorse the Philippson interpretation.[50] At any rate, the interesting point in Philippson's suggestion lies in the fact that the origin and development of language is, to some extent, associated with the problem of justice. These last lines allow us to turn to the issue of language and the preconception of what is just.

The 'most accurate' way to understand the preconception of justice, we hold, is through a reference to the issue of language. Among interpreters, there is a certain consensus in believing that Epicurus held that there is a *natural* connection between things and words.[51] By the time Epicurus focuses on whether names are natural or conventional, that issue had already been largely debated by the preceding philosophical tradition. As pointed out above, language appears naturally for Epicureans, but it can be 'perfectioned' through its use and thereby by a sort of convention.

Moreover, if language is not something private (but rather a collective phenomenon that is shared by every member of a 'linguistic community'), it must be the basic fact from which *our* conceptualization of the world (and likely that of Lucretius' neighbours [*finitimi*], who are 'eager not to harm or be harmed') is derived. Further, if Epicurus recommends that we must grasp *first* what is 'subordinated' to our words (τὰ ὑποτεταγμένα τοῖς φθόγγοις; *LH* 37-38),[52] language should have a founding character in the concept formation and, of course, in the preconception of what is just. The Epicureans rejected the value of definitions and insisted that the ordinary use of words is more helpful than that of definitions.[53] Hirzel conjectured that the antecedent of this ingredient in the Epicurean notion of prolepsis was already present in Democritus, as various recent works have also pointed out.[54] Thus the Epicurean preconceptions appear to constitute 'schemes' or 'sketches' (ὑπογραφαί or ὑποτυπώσεις in Hellenistic terminology) rather than definitions, which enable the identification of objects and the beginnings of research. Galen underlines that such schemes and sketches do not express more than what everyone knows.[55]

As is well known, the explanation of an Epicurean preconception (and of how it is acquired) as put forward in DL 10.32-33 suggests that a concept arrives at one's mind through *the repetition* of sensory impressions stemming from the corresponding representations or images of things. Thus, the preconception of the just (such as that of god or usefulness) should derive from the external environment. This kind of explanation works relatively well when it refers to empirical concepts, such as 'man' and 'horse' (which are the examples provided by DL 10.32-33); it is more difficult to uphold when it refers to the preconception of what is just since, as Konstan (2011, 70) has acutely remarked, there is no physical object to which the preconception of justice corresponds. One might think, however, that the same occurs in the case of the preconception of god (although if Sextus Empiricus is to be trusted,[56] Epicurus believed that people get the notion of god [ἔννοια θεοῦ] from the representations they have in dreams); therefore, if people have representations of divinities, then, they must be bodily entities and, from that perspective, they are no different from other corporeal things. But what of the preconception of justice, which has no physical object linked to it? Following the empirical explanatory framework of Epicurus, one might suggest that the external physical object impressing upon one's mind must be a just action, in which case the problem is how to determine what action *is* just, *apparently* just, *likely* just, and so forth. Once again, the relevance of language arises, and especially of how a speaker incorporates that language. Parents can teach their children from a very young age what kind of actions are either just or unjust; if a child asks why an individual action is unjust, their parents can answer: because if you perform that action, you will harm another person, and you do not wish to harm anyone, because if you do, that person will also wish to harm you (here again the connection between justice and usefulness can be seen). A father or a teacher can show in a very concrete way the sense in which individual acts are either unjust or just (those are the 'external or extramental bodily objects' that provide the sensory data to the subject). And in that 'exemplification process,' so to speak, the teacher or parent can say 'this act is just, this one is unjust'. In fact, Philodemus seems to refer to this kind of 'exemplification process' in the teaching of the just. According to Philodemus, it is necessary to teach children never to touch injustice, just as they are taught never to touch fire, since both injustice and fire are destructive by nature (ὀλέθριοι φύσει; see *On Rhetoric*, PHerc. 1078/1080, fr. 13.9–22, 2.155 Sudhaus).

The character Alcibiades says to Socrates that he learned the just and the unjust in the same way that he learned to speak Greek (ἑλληνίζειν; *Alcibiades I* 111a). Socrates, of course, uses this statement to try to show him that those who taught him 'the many' [οἱ πολλοί] lack, just like him, knowledge about what is just. To do that, as observed by Denyer, Socrates assumes a minimal interpretation of the meaning of 'to speak Greek' [ἑλληνίζειν].[57] For Alcibiades, to speak Greek involves moral implications that reflect clichés of Greek culture. To speak Greek means to possess a way of being distinct from and superior to those who do not speak Greek, i.e. the barbarians. The Greeks' moral superiority over the barbarians consists primarily in their sense of justice and readiness to obey the law.[58] The Epicureans were not admirers of Socrates and ascribed great importance to the ordinary use of language. Philodemus, for example, in *On the Management of Property*, attributes to Socrates a frivolous attitude towards the regular use of language (Frag. 2, col. v lines 1-4). In his view, when Socrates distinguishes the rich from the poor, he does so in a way that depends on opinion, not on preconception in accordance with ordinary usage [δοξαστικῶς, οὐ προληπτικῶς κατὰ συνήθειαν]. Clearly, what Philodemus wishes to point out is that this kind of Socratic procedure is impracticable and is at odds with reason (ἄπορον τῷ ἔργῳ καὶ τῷ νῷ μαχόμενον; Frag. 2, col. v, 13-14). Indeed, when Philodemus says this, he is not innovating but evoking Epicurus' primary teaching. For an Epicurean, when one examines a problem (such as whether or not gods exist), one should do so not according to a vain opinion but according to a preconception. That is the reason why, if someone denies 'the gods of the many' he is not impious, since what the many say about the gods are not preconceptions but false suppositions (Epicurus, *LM* 123-124). As is obvious from the context, Philodemus believes that this procedure can also be applied to cases which are seemingly more pedestrian cases but no less important, having to do with the relevance of showing how to cover basic needs through 'actually existing money', which, strictly speaking, is the only thing that can perform this function.[59]

To be sure, Epicurus and the Epicureans offer an assessment of the world's conceptualization that involves the transmission and learning of (especially Greek) language that is very different from that of the Socrates of *Alcibiades I*. As we have tried to show, the prolepsis of the just is a good example of the recognition they give to the conceptualization that involves the transmission and learning of language.

4 Summary and concluding remarks

Like any other political model, the Epicurean one has a compelling normative or regulative character. This function of the Epicurean political model is embodied in the preconception of the just. We have provided some general considerations regarding what Epicurus calls 'the just of nature' for the sake of explaining the connections between justice and usefulness. Our purpose was also to clarify what we mean when we state that, within the domain of the Epicurean contractual model, justice can be considered a 'modality of utility' and that the prolepsis of the just is a canon that validates the just. The expression 'the just of nature' does not aim, as in Callicles' immoralism or in iusnaturalism, at upholding the normativity of nature. Its framework is Epicurean 'physiology', and it responds to the attempt to qualify the effective ontological status of human phenomena such as justice, and, implicitly, the methodology that its explanation must follow. So, it is not wrong to make it equivalent to the expression 'the nature of the just', employed by Epicurus in *PD* 37, as opposed to representations of the just grounded in empty words. For Epicurus, the just should be conceived only along with the notion of usefulness, such usefulness being the one that guarantees that in the political community people neither harm one another nor are harmed. The preconception of the just is the 'regulative' instrument that political communities possess to assess whether laws serve the purpose of the pact on which they are founded. It functions as a criterion to evaluate empirically through its results the 'truth' of certain convictions about justice embodied in the laws, out of their adequacy for achieving the end of not harming one another nor being harmed. Due to variation in circumstances, the validation itself is temporary. What has been confirmed or counter-witnessed as just in the present may not have been confirmed or counter-witnessed in the same terms in the past, or may not be confirmed or counter-witnessed in the future. We reject the interpretations that locate the prolepsis of the just in the constitution that rules over the life of a community or which distinguish a hierarchical and historical plurality of preconceptions of the just. The Epicureans embed the collective ownership of the preconception of the just in language. We underline the relevance of an ingredient of experience that is not usually considered when dealing with Epicurean preconception's empirical genesis: the transmission and learning of language.

4

Cicero, Plutarch and Lactantius as Readers of Epicureanism

The Epicureans recognize that the polis offers security [ἀσφάλεια], but that it can also encourage models of life that produce unhappiness. The study of nature that they advocate (the Epicurean 'physiology': φυσιολογία] frames their argument for security in naturalist and evolutionist explanations of the origin of justice, and tries to diagnose and respond to the paradoxical unhappiness that exists in the midst of living conditions in which people have achieved security (see Lucretius, *RN* 6.1-40). The influential philosophical historiography of the nineteenth century saw in this claim an expression of the decadence of the polis and emphasized the reaction to extremely convulsed times that led to focus the philosophical activity of Hellenistic schools on the formulation of personal salvation ethics. It is undeniable, however, that in the last five decades or so there has been a change of appreciation.

One of the major achievements in the modern study of Epicureanism has been the recovery of a balanced and respectful tone of analysis, one that has rejected the imprint made on the interpretative tradition by the aggression and contempt of Cicero, Plutarch and the Christian apologists. The works of historians of the Hellenistic world in recent decades have also contributed to a balanced tone of analysis. They have highlighted the vitality of the polis in the Hellenistic period, the persistence of its social relations and its mental world, and have also argued against the thesis of an exacerbated consciousness of the turbulence of the times which is often used to draw a sharp distinction between this period and other moments in the history of Greece.[1]

These new approaches have been favourable to a legitimate treatment of Epicureanism and to the recognition of both its connection with the traditional problems of Greek philosophy and of the particular interpretive guidelines and procedures, from which the main adversaries of antiquity, especially Cicero and Plutarch, refer to the political considerations of Epicureanism.

It is true that both Cicero and Plutarch are very important sources for our knowledge of Epicureanism; however, they certainly had their own agenda and hence sometimes avoided details in Epicurus' tenets, treated them superficially, or introduced biases that compel us to read some issues from a very partial perspective. The same can obviously be said of Lactantius, who, in addition to having his own agenda, is a Christian writer belonging to a completely different ideological world. Moreover, he is located in a historical-ideological framework where he wishes to show that 'true wisdom' cannot be found in pagan philosophy, but only in the revealed word. This can at times make his testimony and assessment of Epicurean philosophy particularly virulent and negative.

The core of this chapter is focused on how Cicero, Plutarch, and Lactantius considered Epicurus and Epicureanism in general, and in particular their political views. We argue that Cicero's, Plutarch's and Lactantius' analyses, albeit partial and biased, are relevant because the traditional portrait of Epicureanism was forged to a great extent through their hostile testimonies. Our examination of these figures as readers of Epicureanism, we suggest, might eventually shed some light on the modes of transmission of Greek philosophy (and especially of Epicureanism) to posterity. Although we will focus mostly on the controversial aspects of these writers in their transmission of Epicureanism, thus pointing out their shortcomings as testimonies of that philosophical movement, we will also highlight some more interesting aspects of their readings of Epicurus' philosophy. Above all, we are interested in pointing out the relevance of Cicero, Plutarch and Lactantius in the formation of a certain *forma mentis*, already present in antiquity, that influenced the reading and understanding of Epicurus and his doctrines.

To illustrate this: Epicurus himself vividly describes the last hours of his own life, hours that he refers to as 'a blessedly happy day'. It is not difficult to imagine the terrible pains he would have suffered when he spoke of the urinary blockages and dysenteric discomforts that were affecting him (DL 10.22; Us. 138). But when Cicero reminds us of this episode, he states, while ascribing his reading of the event to 'the sinister interpretation of the Stoics', that the urinary blockages and gastritis that afflicted Epicurus were due to gluttony, in the latter case, and, in the former, to a 'still baser kind of self-indulgence' (*Letters to Friends* 7.26, 1). Perhaps Cicero was being honest and did believe that this biased reading of Epicureanism belonged to the Stoics, and thus he did not actually support it. But this kind of passage led many people in ancient times to associate Epicurean hedonism with a life of mere sensual pleasure and excess. Of course, Plutarch also contributes to the idea that Epicurean hedonism is nothing new, merely another form of crude hedonism. He provocatively suggests that, if someone removes the light of knowledge at 'the symposium of life' [ἐκ τοῦ βίου καθάπερ ἐκ συμποσίου], so that people could do anything they choose for pleasure without being noticed, such a person can indeed say 'live unnoticed' (λάθε βιώσας; *Live Unnoticed* 1129A-B). Or again, Plutarch polemically remarks that, if one proposes to live with his mistress, or if one ends days with Leontion, 'spits on what is honourable',[2] and says the good consists of 'the flesh and its titillation',[3] one would like to live unnoticed (*Live Unnoticed* 1129B). This is clearly nothing more than a crude presentation of Epicurean hedonism, though, as we will show, Plutarch was entirely aware of the sophistication of the hedonistic position defended by Epicureanism.

In section 1, we discuss some details of Cicero's reading of Epicureanism. First, we will present some of Cicero's considerations about Epicurean terminology and his defence of Latin as an appropriate language for discussing philosophical or literary topics. Next, we shall examine some passages where Cicero's readings of Epicurean theology turn out to be debatable, inasmuch as they often overlook relevant details of Epicurean doctrine or are formulated against the backdrop of his own agenda. Finally, we argue that Cicero deliberately omits important details of Epicurean arguments on ethics and politics and includes some silences that are 'clamorous'. In fact, Cicero omits the entire, crucial Epicurean interconnection between the study of nature and political theory. While he does include passing reference to Epicurean contractualism, he does not set out the Epicurean theoretical framework in which it is inscribed. Consequently, Cicero ignores its specific features.

Section 2 of the chapter is devoted to examining how Plutarch deals with Epicurus. Starting from his Platonic premises, we claim, Plutarch argues that Epicurus' thesis that there is no providence or teleology in the cosmos is absurd, but does not provide a sound argument to show clearly that a world without providence is absurd. We also stress that Plutarch attempts to ridicule Epicurus by pointing out some elemental logical mistakes he would have committed. In this framework, we show that the effort to discredit some Epicurean views was noted already in antiquity (notably by the Roman jurist Aulus Gellius). We also underline the fact that Plutarch accuses the Epicureans of banishing laws and forms of government and so of banishing human life. However, his remark turns out to be a mischievous rhetorical exaggeration which, strictly speaking, evinces an eloquent silence: Plutarch, like Cicero, omits the rich Epicurean themes focused on security, justice and law and does not provide any testimonies or considerations on the elements of Epicureanism's political reflection that we have discussed in the first three chapters.

Section 3 of this chapter is devoted to Lactantius, who believed himself to have the mission to free people from the absurdities derived from pagan religion and philosophy. His objections, we claim, are based on the view that Christianity, insofar it is the only belief system that has set out to unite wisdom with religion, is the best doctrine both religiously and philosophically. But, of course, that was not part of the Epicurean project; therefore, we argue that it is clear that Lactantius' starting point is full of biases and inaccuracies, and that this determines the way he reads (and makes others read) Epicurus' hedonism. In section 4 we offer an overview of Cicero's, Plutarch's and Lactantius' testimonies. Finally, in section 5, we provide some brief concluding remarks.

1 Cicero: The biased reading of a Roman rhetorician and politician

That Cicero did not generally agree with Epicurus is stated by Cicero himself and is thus not a point to be proved. This could be due to the fact that, unlike Epicurus, Cicero 'passionately admires Plato';[4] but there is ample textual evidence in Cicero's writings demonstrating he had deep reasons to disagree with Epicurus in almost every aspect of his philosophy.[5] At the beginning of *Fin.* (1.13) Cicero says that his presentation of the Epicurean stances is no less accurate than that given by the school's own members[6] (maybe this preliminary warning is addressed against those who were objecting to Cicero's shortcomings regarding Epicurus). After this, he immediately introduces the Epicurean Torquatus, who is said to be learned in *every* philosophical doctrine. But the reason why Cicero is usually annoyed with the Epicureans is that they allege that their adversaries do not understand what they are arguing when they make an argument; for example, that pleasure is the final end. Thus, Cicero states that what he means by *voluptas* is the same as what Epicurus means by ἡδονή and, even though Latin writers frequently must search for a Latin equivalent to a Greek term, no search is necessary in this case (Cicero, *Fin.* 1.15, and especially 2.12-13). In fact, there are several passages in the Ciceronian *corpus* in which Cicero defends the use of Latin as an appropriate language for discussing philosophical and literary topics (cf. *Acad.* 1.9-10; 25-27); although he is aware that Latin (or, in general, Latin literary culture) has a certain dependence on Greek (*Fin.* 1.1-4), he is interested in showing that, lest Latin writers be reduced to working as mere translators of Greek works, there is no reason for preferring the Greek language 'to that which is written with brilliance and is not a translation from Greek' (*Fin.* 1.6).

In Cicero's opinion, some turn away from the Latin texts because 'they have tended to come across certain rough and unpolished works which have been translated from bad Greek into worse Latin' (*Fin.* 1.8; of course, the same could apply to texts originally written in Greek; the issue is not whether the texts are written in Greek or Latin, but whether they are well written). However, Cicero argues that this does not mean that one could not profitably read good works originally written in Latin, so long as such works are 'written with well-chosen words, with dignity and style' (*Fin.* 1.8: *verbis electis graviter ornateque dictas*). Cicero is determined to try to prove that Latin is not only not poor [*inops*], as is usually thought, but also richer [*locupletiorem*] than Greek (*Fin.* 1.10).

Further, it is arguable that, even though Cicero apparently took pleasure to be an easy topic that anyone can relate to (*Fin.* 2.15), it is obvious that Epicurus did not consider it so straightforward. Cicero maintains in his own defence that the problem is not his misunderstanding of what Epicurus means when he says that he offers not to remove wickedness, but to rest content with a moderate degree of vice; he despises elegance in his speech [*contemnit enim disserendi elegantiam*], Cicero insists, and speaks in a confused manner (*confuse loquitur*; *Fin.* 2.27).[7]

Most of the time in contemporary scholarship, Cicero's testimony regarding Epicurus and Epicureanism has been taken to be unfair and hence not very reliable.[8] In what follows we shall examine some passages where Cicero's readings of Epicurus and Epicureanism turn out to be debatable, inasmuch as his remarks overlook relevant details of Epicurean doctrine or are formulated against the backdrop of his own agenda. Of course, there is a sense in which no one can tackle a problem discussed by another person without reflecting on one's own assumptions. But if one is engaged in striving as much as possible to invest energy and effort into improving his countrymen's learning, like Cicero explicitly declares (*Fin.* 1.10), one is obliged to examine one's own biases and assumptions to provide a more believable explanation of the doctrine under discussion. This is what, we submit, Cicero often does not do; since the Ciceronian influence on the transmission of Epicurean philosophy has been so powerful, it is worth making the effort to highlight Cicero's shortcomings (and sometimes errors) in his understanding of Epicureanism.

Cicero starts by observing that Epicurus' system is the easiest one to understand, and that most people are familiar with it (*Fin.* 1.13). Cicero sets out to show that the identification of good with pleasure is a view taken for granted by anyone, which means that his exposition of it cannot be less accurate than that given by the Epicureans themselves. In a very well-known passage of *Fin.* 2.88, Cicero presents Epicurus' tenet that pleasure should be tantamount to the supreme good. However, as Cicero notes, Epicurus claims that time adds nothing to the supreme good insofar as there is no greater pleasure in an infinite period of time than in a brief, limited one. But this, Cicero contends, is said in an extremely inconsistent way, since what Epicurus holds is that pleasure is the supreme good while at the same time claiming that pleasure does not increase with duration; it is the same pleasure in an infinite time as in a brief and limited one, which seems absurd. If this were the case, the same would apply to pain, which does not appear reasonable.

Cicero's attack against Epicurean theology is finely elaborated; he imagines a dialogue between Velleius and the Academic Cotta. Interestingly, Velleius observes that Epicurus 'has freed us from superstitious terrors and has brought us back to freedom, so that we don't feel any fear towards some beings that ... do not cause any discomfort to themselves and try not to cause any to others'. This, of course, does not depict anything strange in the dialogue between Velleius and Cotta, since the former is a supporter of the Epicureans. Cotta, on the contrary, presents a demolishing set of arguments against Epicurus and finally suggests that the Epicurean view is an enemy of religion (*ND* 1.57-115). The way in which Cicero presents Cotta is particularly interesting: he intervenes in the debate with his usual kindness (*Cotta comiter, ut solebat*; *ND* 1.57); Cicero adds that the reasons why a tenet should be true do not present themselves to Cotta's mind so readily as the reasons why it should be false. This is a way of saying that Cotta is a serious and unbiased arguer (his way of arguing is 'kind'), even though he stresses that it is easier for him to conceive an argument to show that a thesis is false, which seems to anticipate the fact that his argument will try to show that Epicurean theology is false. The dramatic background in which Cicero presents the debate between Cotta and Velleius is also relevant: Cotta states that Velleius has discussed 'an obscure and difficult matter clearly' [*de re obscura atque difficili ... dilucide*], and that he has done so not only with fullness of expression, but also with more elegance of diction than is usual in the Epicurean school (*ND* 1.58-59).

This last remark corresponds relatively closely to Cicero's view that Epicurean language sometimes is twisted (through his spokesman Cotta, Cicero remarks elsewhere that the Epicurean Zeno did not speak as most Epicureans do, but like Velleius did: clearly, weightily, and elegantly: *distincte, graviter, ornate*). At the beginning of his argument, Cotta describes the Epicurean statements as 'vain and foolish' (*tam leves, ne dicam in tam ineptas sententias*; 1.59). Cicero has Epicurus say (through Cotta) that it is hard to deny that the gods exist if the question is debated in a public assembly, since through their adherence to common opinions almost everyone and, in particular, Epicurus himself (even though he is sometimes of the opinion that they do not exist) seems to endorse the view that the gods exist; by contrast, it is perfectly easy to make the denial in a conversation. Cotta reasonably complains that the simple evidence that people of all races and nations are of the view that the gods exist is not enough to warrant us acknowledging the existence of the gods. In the first instance this is so because it is difficult to know that different peoples do hold the belief that there are gods, and Cotta adds that he suspects that there are many races so barbarously savage as to be without any suspicion about the existence of the gods (*nulla suspicio deorum sit*; 1.62).

Up to this point, one might argue, Cicero behaves philosophically by presenting a respectable objection to a set of central points defended by Epicurus.[9] To be sure, he would have a reasonable reply to this kind of objection: 'let's take a look at the objection concerning the existence of the gods'. The way in which Cicero presents Epicurus' view on the gods leaves this argument highly vulnerable, and the Epicurean point certainly looks trivial and foolish. But if one focuses on the texts of Epicurus that have come down to us, it seems that his argument was more robust and sophisticated. First of all, when Philodemus says in the fourfold remedy, surely inspired by what Epicurus states in the *LM* 123, that 'god is not to be feared' (ἄφοβον ὁ θεός; Philodemus, *Against the Sophists* 4.7-14), this cannot mean that there is no god. What Epicurus and the Epicureans believe is that god is an indestructible and blessed living being [ζῷον ἄφθαρτον καὶ μακάριον], and that this is so due to the common notion of god [κοινὴ τοῦ θεοῦ νόησις], or rather due to the notion of god commonly held by everyone and even by those who do not believe in god: if an *x* in the world is god, such an *x* must be an indestructible and blessed living being. If it is indestructible, it must be entirely happy. This is a relatively simple (and non-technical) way of saying that god is a 'preconception' (this is what Cicero reiterates when he says that through the *communia* almost everyone thinks that the gods exist). Moreover, Epicurus is willing to claim straightforwardly that the gods do exist, although they do not exist as the many understands them to exist (*LM* 123; 134). This explains why Philodemus, certainly evoking this Epicurus passage, states that god is without fear. If god were an entity worthy of being feared, what one would be doing is transferring to god certain human attributes that, by its very nature, god cannot have. What is impious, Epicurus contends, is not to deny the gods of the many, but to ascribe to the gods what the many thinks about them, beliefs certainly based on false assumptions [ὑπολήψεις ψευδεῖς] and not on preconceptions (προλήψεις; Epicurus, *LM* 124).

As is obvious, this conceptualization of divinity depends heavily upon Epicurean epistemology, and Epicurus' argument is certainly more sophisticated than the one presented by Cicero in *ND* 1.57-62. However, Cicero declares his awareness that some people believe that Epicurus, while in theory retaining the gods (to avoid the hostility of the Athenians), in practice did away with them (1.85). To prove his point, Cicero refers to Epicurus' *Principal Doctrines* and cites the first lines of *PD* 1.[10] But what is striking is the way in which Cicero understands this passage: Epicurus' goal was to produce *deliberately* [*consulto*] an impression which is explained due to his awkwardness of style [*plane loquendi*]. It is likely that Cicero is referring either to Epicurus' unrhetorical language or to his lack of attention to logic or dialectics. But *PD* 1 can be regarded as an additional argument for the position that god cannot be what most people think him to be.

In what follows, we would like to develop another point focusing on the way Cicero discussed some central Epicurean stances that were not irrelevant to the way in which he regarded the role of politics in the Epicurean project. As argued by Catherine Steel, Cicero's central motivation in his writings on this topic was often a concern for the nature of his public profile.[11] This, we hold, is an attractive approach for considering Cicero's philosophical interests and developments, as well as the manner in which he responds to the arguments of other philosophers. In this vein, we suggest that the 'political profile' of Epicurus and the Epicureans was crucial as well. Epicurus (and other philosophers such as Plato, Aristotle and even the Stoics) had political interests, and though Epicurus himself was a philosopher and not a 'professional politician' especially interested in his political profile as Cicero was, one of his main interests was providing a normative model of what a just society should be. Certainly, Epicurus' discussions of what law or justice are, were not merely descriptive of an actual situation, but also normative (as is the case in any other political and social model). To some extent, this is a truism, but it is helpful to turn to Cicero's *De Finibus* to better explain our point. In *Fin*. 4, 4-6 he discusses the Stoic division of philosophy into three parts; one of these is focused on shaping our character, he upholds (it is this section that deals with the highest good or what is truly good). Cicero announces that he will shortly be considering this part of philosophy as treated by the Stoics, but that for now he is concerned with mentioning the topic which, according to him, is correctly named 'related to citizenry' (*civilem recte appellaturi*), what the Greeks call πολιτικόν. As usual, Cicero is translating from the Greek into Latin, and adds that both the Peripatetics and the Academics dealt with this topic carefully and fully (*graviter et copiose*; *Fin*. 4.5).

This comment is important to our purposes because, as is obvious, Cicero straightforwardly links the treatment of the ethical part of philosophy with politics or, more appropriately, with what affects (our fellow) citizens [*civile*]. Interestingly, when Cicero refers to the 'account of nature' (*de explicatione naturae*; *Fin.* 4.11) developed by the Peripatetics, the Stoics and Epicurus, he stresses the fact that the latter recommended pursuing such a study 'to drive out fear of the gods and religious superstition'. It is true that in these pages Cicero concentrates especially on the Stoics, but he also mentions Epicurus and his view that his 'physiology' allows people to drive out fear of the gods and any form of superstition. For the sake of our argument, the most relevant point here is that Cicero is aware of the 'interconnection', as it were, among the different parts of philosophy in view of our practical life, which naturally encompasses the political life.[12]

As just mentioned, Cicero acknowledges that in Epicureanism this interconnection concerns liberation from fear of the gods and religious superstition. In the case of the Peripatetics, the Stoics, and Cicero himself, from the 'account of nature', he states, 'we gain a sense of justice when we understand the will, the design and the purpose of the supreme guide and lord to whose nature philosophers tell us that true reason and the highest law are perfectly matched' (*Fin.* 4.11). He reiterates in *On the Laws* that the root of justice and law is nature, and, as Annas emphasizes, he draws primarily on the Stoic view of natural law in order to endorse the doctrine of the natural basis of justice.[13] Cicero passionately admired Plato (in fact, he believes him to be the 'god of philosophers' and 'prince of philosophers'; *ND* 2.32; *Fin.* 5.7).[14] He knew his work very well and writes *On the Laws* with Plato's work of the same name in mind. In *Laws* 10 Plato refers to the harmful fusion of the physicalist cosmogony and the contractual theory (*Laws* 888b8), and condemns it as impious and subversive, perhaps with Archelaus, the disciple of Anaxagoras, in mind. Epicurus may have been inspired by Archelaus, whom, according to Diogenes Laertius, he valued positively (DL 10.12). In any case, Epicureanism's response to the question 'what are political communities, justice and the laws?' concurs with the fusion of physicalist cosmogony and contractualism that Plato emphatically condemned. The application of the Epicurean study of nature to the analysis of political communities is translated into a rationalistic genealogical approach of justice and laws. In this way the interconnection between the study of nature and political philosophy forms, as we have shown, a crucial part of Epicurean philosophy, and constitutes the framework of the *Principal Doctrines* focused on security, justice and the laws. The same thing applies to the genealogy of

Hermarchus' extract, the treatise by Polystratus, and Lucretius' *On the Nature of Things* Book 5. In these Epicurean texts the just is presented as a modality of usefulness, specifically as the useful for the sake of the pact and its basic rule ('neither harming one another nor being harmed'; Epicurus, *PD* 33) for human groupings. Interestingly, in *On the Laws* Cicero criticizes the link between justice and utility defended by the Epicureans. He implies that the Epicureans equate utility with merely selfish gain. This is undoubtedly a mischievous interpretation, for in reality the Epicureans reiterate the traditional link between justice and common utility. The 'common advantage' [τὸ κοινῇ συμφέρον] is already for Aristotle the proximate end of law and serves as a criterion for assessing the correctness of constitutions and laws. The common advantage is a normative reason, identifiable with political justice.[15] Justice and common interest (*utilitas*), as Wood highlights, are also the two crucial characteristics of Cicero's definition of the state.[16] Wood suggests that, for Cicero, the reason for the existence of the state is the common interest of those concerned (*De Re.* 1, 39: *utilitatis communione sociatus*), interest defined here in terms of security, protection and well-being.[17]

Like Aristotle and Cicero, Epicurus, through his famous formula 'neither harming one another nor being harmed', conceptualizes the just with reference to a dimension common to the idea of utility. In fact, Hermarchus uses the expression 'common utility' (τὰ κοινὴν ἔχοντα τὴν ὠφέλειαν; Porphyry, *Abst.* 1.12, 19). In Epicureanism the just has a compelling normative or regulative character embodied in the preconception of the just (*PD* 37-38). Surprisingly, neither the sophisticated reflections of Epicureanism on the ontological status of the just nor the preconception of the just finds any articulation in Cicero's work. Perhaps it could be argued that these are very distant themes from the foundation of the Epicurean way of life and from the imperturbability [ἀταραξία] it advocates. In fact, like the genealogical approach in which they are embedded, they form significant elements of the Epicurean way of life, such as the category of security and the genealogy of vain desires. Cicero does not comment on Epicureanism's rich reflection on security and vain desires. But such pertinent details, we hold, cannot have escaped Cicero, an attentive and critical reader of his philosophical and cultural past.

Cicero asserts that the 'commonwealth' [*res publica*] is that which belongs to the people [*res publica res populi*]; but 'people' in this formulation are not simply any group of persons gathered together in any which way. Rather, they are an assemblage of people associated by one and the same right [*coetus multitudinis iuris consensu et utilitatis communione sociatus*], serving all equally.[18] Cicero seems to be implicitly referring to the Epicurean contractual doctrine, and also departing from it (Cicero, *De Re.* 1.39; 3.23). But Cicero's objection is clearly based on the bias that human beings are political or social beings *by nature*. When we say that the view that humans are political by nature is a 'biased approach', we are not implying that this tenet is biased in itself, but instead that Cicero's *way* of presenting it to argue against Epicurean contractualism looks like a shortcoming. On the one hand, the argument provided by Cicero to convince himself that political naturalism is better or more reasonable than contractualism is not clear. When he endorses naturalism, that position already had a long philosophical pedigree; but unlike Aristotle in *Politics* 1 and what the Stoics had written in support not only of political naturalism but also the existence of a universal natural law, Cicero seems to assume that this is the best approach. Sometimes he qualifies himself to say that nature has produced and shaped us for better things, or so it seems to him (*Fin.* 1.23). On the other hand, Cicero merely *refers* to Epicurean contractualism, i.e. he does not set out the Epicurean theoretical framework in which it is inscribed. Consequently, its specific features are ignored.

2 Plutarch and his effort to reject (and even ridicule) Epicurus and the Epicureans

Aulus Gellius (the second century AD Roman lawyer and grammarian) turns out to be a helpful starting point for exploring the role of Plutarch in the transmission of Epicureanism. When citing Plutarch, Gellius ascribes to him the view that Epicurus uses 'an inappropriate word and gives it foreign meaning' [*verbo usus sit parum proprio et alienae significationis*; interestingly, a terminological problem already indicated by Cicero reappears in Gellius]. Immediately Plutarch (through Aulus Gellius) cites Epicurus *PD* 3, according to which 'the removal of all feeling of pain is the limit of the magnitude of pleasures', and objects that he should not have said 'of all feeling of pain' but rather 'of everything that is painful' since it is the removal of pain that should be invoked, not of that which feels pain (Aulus Gellius, *Noc. Att.* 2.9, 1-4).

Sagaciously, Gellius notes that when Plutarch makes this objection to Epicurus he is 'word-chasing' with excessive nit-picking and almost with frigidity (*Nimis minute ac prope etiam subfrigide Plutarchus in Epicuro accusando* λεξιθηρεῖ'; *Noc. Att.* 2.9, 4-5). The chapter where this Gellius passage is included is titled 'Plutarch criticized with obvious bad faith a phrase of Epicurus'. In a previous passage, Gellius recalls that Plutarch (in book 2 of his *Commentaries on Homer*) says that Epicurus formulated a syllogism in a wrong and clumsy way (*Noc. Att.* 2.8, 1). According to Gellius, Plutarch quotes Epicurus verbatim [*verbaque ipsa Epicuri*]: 'Death is nothing to us, for what has been dissolved has no sensation and what has no sensation is nothing to us'.[19] According to Plutarch (as cited by Gellius), Epicurus forgot to include the premise 'death is the separation of the body and of the soul'; otherwise, the conclusion does not follow. In this instance, Gellius concurs with Plutarch that such a premise is required (*Noc. Att.* 2.8, 5); but beyond the agreements and disagreements between Gellius and Plutarch, what is especially interesting is that in antiquity Plutarch was already taken to be a 'polemic reader' of Epicurus and, in general, of Epicurean tenets. But Gellius' testimony, is also remarkable because he notes that he cannot suppose that Epicurus, 'being the man he was' [*cuiusmodi homost*], omitted such a premise through ignorance; such an omission, Gellius contends, is due to the fact that, since the separation of body and soul by death is evident, he did not consider it necessary to call attention to what was entirely obvious to everyone (*quod omnibus prosus erat obvium*; *Noc. Att.* 2.8, 8; the premise according to which death is the separation of the soul from the body can be traced to Plato; see *Gorg.* 524b; *Phd.* 67d4-10). This is how Gellius says that one must be charitable with Epicurus; one might argue that it is a way to neutralize Plutarch's vigorous hostility against Epicurus. Gellius' reference to Plutarch is therefore accurate insofar as he recognizes that Plutarch is right in noting that a premise is missed in Epicurus' argument, but at the same time Gellius attempts to balance the impact of Plutarch's critique by suggesting that such an omission cannot be due to Epicurus' ignorance or stupidity.

Of course, Plutarch's agenda is always present in his objections to the Epicurean philosophy: Epicurus, since he was not a Platonist, did not endorse the tenet that providence and teleology have any role in the explanation of the cosmos.[20] In his brief essay *Live Unknown*, Plutarch's purpose is to show that the Epicurean 'live unnoticed', which is supposed to advocate a certain kind of tranquillity and absence from public life, is false, and that the person who originally said this had no wish to live unknown but 'was seeking undeserved fame from the advice to avoid fame' (1128A-B; transl. D. Russell). From Plutarch's treatises, it is clear that he thinks of Epicurus as an atheist, since he denies divine providence (for the accusation of atheism see also Cicero, *ND* 2.76).[21] One might wonder how effective this kind of remark is as a real argument (in the context Plutarch is clearly objecting to Epicurus' famous saying 'live unnoticed', and he is taking it to be a recommendation for an absence from public life). More importantly, in *On the Pythian Oracles* (399 D-E) Plutarch openly argues against Epicurus' view that there is no providence in the cosmos. He starts by mentioning a series of historical events (the Romans defeated Hannibal and overcame the Carthaginians; Philip met the Aetolians and Romans in battle and was defeated, and so on). In Plutarch's view, it is without doubt that no one could say that all these events occurred *at once* by chance [κατὰ τύχην] and spontaneously [αὐτομάτως]; in fact, all the events mentioned display a certain order, one that shows foreknowledge (ἡ τάξις ἐμφαίνει τὴν πρόγνωσιν; 399D7). The text is unfortunately corrupted in the following lines; but from the context and, as far as the text can be reconstructed, the passage seems to suggest that what Plutarch is intent on arguing is that (i) there is order in the cosmos, (ii) that such an order is not due to chance, and (iii) that the cosmic order is nothing baffling [ἀτέκμαρτον] and blind [τυφλόν]. On the contrary, there is a certain inner rationality [λόγος] in experience, a rationality that provides many guarantees of experience [πολλὰ τῆς πείρας ἐνέχυρα] and 'shows the road through which fate [τὸ πεπρωμένον] advances'. In other words, the cosmos as designed by reason points out the road on which fate is to advance; that is, if there is destiny without providence (*quod non*, in Plutarch's view), teleology is prior to a mechanically fated world. Plutarch concludes by stating that he does not believe that anyone can find these things to occur by chance.[22] In order to reinforce his argument, Plutarch adds that if this was not the case then nothing would prevent one from saying that Epicurus did not write the *Principal Doctrines*, but that the letters came together by chance and spontaneously.

This is, so to speak, a typical 'rhetorical argument' against the view that a cosmology without teleology is possible. But the Epicurean passages from which such an idea is argued are more complex than that. Once again, it is frustrating that the clearest Epicurean writings against a teleological-providential cosmos are reported only by the indirect tradition (mainly Lucretius and Cicero) and not found in Epicurus' texts themselves. Lucretius, for example, is willing to argue against any teleological component in the cosmos while warning that one should avoid supposing 'the clear lights of the eyes to have been created in order that we might see' (*RN* 4.823-824; transl. Long and Sedley; it occurs similarly with the other parts of one's body). Lucretius attributes this to a 'distorted reasoning', contending that nothing has been produced in our body in order that we might be able to use it. It is the fact of its being engendered that creates its use. This seems to be addressed against a Stoic argument for proving the existence of teleology in the cosmos (see especially DL 7.85-86 – reporting the Stoic Chrysippus' view –, Cicero, *Fin.* 3.67 – where, ascribed to the Stoic philosopher is the view that animals are born for the sake of human beings and the gods –[23] and Hierocles, *Elementa Ethica* 1.44-50; 3.5-45 *et passim*). Seeing did not exist before the lights of the eyes were engendered, Lucretius goes on to argue, nor was there pleading with words before the tongue was created. If this is so, neither the eyes nor the tongue can have grown for the sake of their use. The presumably providentialist argument according to which the cosmos was created by the gods is also rejected by Lucretius, this time on the grounds that imperishable and blessed beings such as the gods could gain no profit at all from our gratitude (on this, see again Epicurus, *PD* 1).[24] Besides, the gods have no need to interrupt their tranquil lifestyle to focus on a task for our sake (*RN* 5.156-170). Moreover, had the gods decided to create the cosmos (*quod non* in Lucretius' opinion), they would have had no model for such a creation (*RN* 5.181) and it is hard to know how they would have arrived at the preconception of human beings and thus know and perceive in their minds what they wished to create. Further, if the gods did decide to create the cosmos, it is unclear how they recognized the capacity of the primary particles and the effect of their different arrangements, if nature herself did not furnish them with a pattern for creation. This is so, Lucretius states, because so many primary particles have been propelled in manifold ways by impacts and by their own weight for an infinity of time past, and have combined in all possible ways, that it is not surprising if they have also fallen into arrangements, and arrived at patterns of motion, like those repeatedly enacted by this present world.

This is a concise and general description of some arguments provided by Lucretius against providentialism (we omit the rest of them for the sake of brevity); what should be noted here is that these arguments do not correspond to any passage in Epicurus' texts, although the last example of Lucretian reasoning evokes Epicurus' *Letter to Herodotus* 45. Here, it is argued that atoms, being infinitely many, travel any distance and, because of being of a suitable nature to be constituents of a world *or responsible for its production*, have not been exhausted on one world or on any finite number of worlds. The clear conclusion, in Epicurus' view, is that there must be both an infinite number of worlds and that the world has not been created (or rather 'produced') by an intelligent being that has foreseen everything, but by the atoms that, due to their nature and permanent movement, suitably arrange their combinations in order to produce the different worlds.

Thus, no matter how relevant Plutarch's work is to a reconstruction of Epicurean philosophy, the fact is that he was not sympathetic to Epicurus and Epicureanism (a detail already recognized by Aulus Gellius) and that he constantly attempts to reject or ridicule the Epicurean tenets.[25] For example, Plutarch accuses the Epicureans of banishing laws and forms of government [οἱ νόμους καὶ πολιτείας ἀναιροῦντες], and therefore of banishing the possibility of human life. This is what he infers from the fact that Epicurus and Metrodorus dissuade their disciples from practising what is common to all people [ἀποτρέποντες τοῦ τὰ κοινὰ πράττειν; presumably this is politics in the sense of 'public life' understood as what must concern everyone who shares mutual interests in a social environmente and dispute with those engaged in it (*Col.* 1127D-E; 1125C). But this must be taken as a personal reading by Plutarch (based on his own Platonic agenda), since if it were true, it would not be possible to account for what Epicurus meant when he argued that someone can pass a law in order to check if the law is in accord with what is useful in mutual associations, and that if such a law is not in agreement with what is useful then it can no longer possess the nature of justice (*PD* 37).

If this kind of Epicurean passage is taken seriously, it is hard to understand Plutarch's position that Epicurus and the Epicureans banish, without qualification, both laws and the various forms of government. It would not be possible either to explain how the Epicurean wise person 'will not have intercourse with a woman in a manner forbidden by the laws' (DL 10.118; transl. Inwood and Gerson). The same goes for those stances which claim that the Epicureans maintain that the one who breaks the law and commits injustice lives in fear and misery (interestingly, this tenet is reported by Plutarch himself, *Pleasant Life* 1090C-D; Us. 532). In other words, it cannot be possible that Epicurus and the Epicureans banish laws; what they did was to furnish a different view of what law *should* be. Their suggestion should have been that a real law is that prescription which can be in agreement with what is useful in mutual associations, and that such an agreement must be the outcome of a rational deliberation concerned with what is convenient for the social community. Otherwise, the alleged law would only be a law in a nominal sense, not in a real one, since it would have no real 'force of law', and one could raise fundamental questions regarding the nature of the force underlying legal authority. For this reason, Epicurus states that 'the justice of nature is a pledge of reciprocal usefulness' (a usefulness consisting of neither harming one another nor being harmed; *PD* 31), and that justice is not a thing in its own right but exists in mutual dealings where there is a pact (such a pact focusing once again on neither harming one another nor being harmed; *PD* 33). This clarifies why a 'real' law is that which agrees with what is useful in mutual associations. If the issue is seen from this perspective, Plutarch's remark that the Epicureans overthrow the polis and utterly abolish the laws cannot be reasonable; indeed, it cannot be reasonable that they withdraw themselves and their disciples from participating in politics (or rather of some 'form of government': πολιτεία; Plutarch, *Col.* 1125C). What the Epicureans urge, as did other 'political philosophers', is the reformulation of what a just legal system should be, so that it can guarantee the existence of a real justice-based state. Further, there is no political philosopher in antiquity (or in our time) who has limited himself to describing the existing state of affairs. Plutarch's remark, in short, turns out to be a mischievous rhetorical exaggeration which, strictly speaking, evinces an eloquent silence. Plutarch, like Cicero, omits the rich Epicurean themes focused on security, justice and law and does not provide any testimonies or considerations on the elements of Epicureanism's political reflection that we have discussed in the first three chapters.

3 Why was Epicurus so dangerous for christians? Lactantius and his hostility towards Epicurus and Epicureanism

Lactantius is a good representative of an apologist talking about Epicurus. The way in which he starts speaking of Epicurus, we hold, is not very promising: in fact, when discussing the problem of the origin of the world and of evil, and while attempting to show that there is good reason to endorse the view that the world is the result of divine providence's making, Lactantius calls Epicurus 'the lone lunatic' (*Div. Inst.* 2.8, 49: *unus . . . delirus*). That the world has been made by divine providence is so obvious, Lactantius contends, that everyone (including Trismegistus, the Sibylline verses, the prophets, and Greek thinkers, such as the Pythagoreans, the Stoics, the Peripatetics, and even the Seven Sages, Socrates and Plato) have taken such a view to be certain (*Div. Inst.* 2.8, 48-49). Of course, one should say that the fact that all the above-mentioned figures support the view that the world has been made by divine providence (if this is in fact the case)[26] is simply an *ex auctoritate* account that proves nothing. Epicurus and the Epicureans[27] have some reasonable arguments to defend the view that there is no providence or teleology in the world. Lactantius' argument against Epicurus is that 'it is more credible' [*credibilius . . . potius*] that matter was made by God because of his omnipotence [*quia deus potest omnia*] than that the world was not made by God, because nothing can be made without purpose, system and plan (*sine mente ratione consilio*; *Div. Inst.* 2.8, 52).

Several scholars have agreed that Lactantius was very hostile towards Epicurus and that the Epicurean school was his chief opponent.[28] At the beginning of the

1970s, Maslowski published a set of important papers focused on anti-Epicureanism; the paper devoted to Lactantius is relevant and helpful for our interests because, even granting that Lactantius' preoccupation with Epicurus and Lucretius in his apologetic works bears out the view that his chief opponents were the Epicureans, Maslowski proposes a re-examination of the notion of Lactantius' anti-Epicureanism by investigating what he calls 'secondary' opponents of Lactantius. As a result of his investigation, Maslowski holds, it is clear that the term 'anti-Epicurean' is too narrow and ought to be replaced by 'anti-atomistic'.[29] His project is appealing insofar as it shows that some labels are too limited for the proper consideration of an author from the past who, to a certain extent, has contributed to a particular kind of reading of a philosopher like Epicurus. But our purpose in this section is much more modest: we will examine in a general way how Lactantius assesses the Epicurean theses and arguments. In the limited framework of this chapter, such a procedure has the advantage of providing an overview of the Christian apologist as a reader of Epicurus and Epicureanism, which will make it possible for us to contrast his judgement of the Garden with that of Cicero and Plutarch.

Certainly, one can reasonably start by examining what the main purpose of Lactantius was when he set out to write *Divine Institutions*. Of course, as a convinced Christian, he sees himself waging an all-out battle against the pagans. He feels his mission to be to free people from the absurdities and damage arising from pagan religion and philosophy; and in his view philosophy does not play a minor role in such a struggle. Philosophers discuss religion; they argue about whether there are gods; if there are, what one should examine of their nature and what their role is in the cosmos as well as in human life. As could not be otherwise for a Christian apologist, Lactantius wishes to show that Christianity is the best doctrine (both religiously and philosophically), since it is the only one that has managed to unite wisdom with religion. Philosophers, on the other hand, have been especially concerned with trying to solve the problem of how 'to live well', that is, how to achieve happiness.[30] The fact that there are so many theories to explain the same thing, Lactantius seems to suggest (*Div. Inst.* 1.1, 5-8), shows that the multiple existing philosophies can and must be overcome by 'true religion', without which 'the supreme good of true wisdom' [*uerae sapientiae summum bonum*] is unattainable. To be sure, he is convinced that when the teachings of philosophy have been disapproved [*conuictis philosophiae disciplinis*; and of course he thinks that they will be disapproved], people will come to true religion and wisdom (*ad ueram nobis religionem sapientiamque ueniendum est*; *Div. Inst.* 3.9, 1; 3.9, 14; 3.30, 9).[31] As is obvious, he takes *all* religions (except the

Christian one) and philosophies to be false, and thus to be real sources of confusion.

Lactantius mentions Epicurus so many times in his *Divine Institutions* that it would be cumbersome and tedious to cite all the places where he quotes him; hence, we will limit ourselves to commenting on only a few representative and critical passages. A particularly relevant section is *Div. Inst.* 3.17, 1-20, where Lactantius strives to show the alleged 'errors' of Epicurus. Lactantius remarks here that he does not intend to fight philosophers since, 'they could not resist anyway' [*qui stare non possunt*]. This somewhat arrogant observation is not without surprise, since, strictly speaking, he sometimes does not argue on strictly philosophical grounds, but tries to show why his approach is better than that of the philosophers without providing truly rational arguments as to why what the philosophers say should be rejected. To be sure, we do not mean that he *never* argues (for instance, see his arguments for the sake of the existence of providence in *Div. Inst.* 3.17, 16-27). However, if you call your adversary 'lunatic', 'fool', and so on (2.8, 49; 3.20, 15), your arguments cannot be taken seriously; in that case you are not undermining someone else's reasoning, but rather attacking the person.[32]

Lactantius starts by pointing out that he will focus on Epicureanism because this is supposed to be 'the best known of all the philosophies', even though this is not for any contribution to truth but because hedonism (a central Epicurean stance) turns out to be very appealing to many. This is so since everyone is prone to vice (*Div. Inst.* 3.17, 2).[33] Once again, it is clear that such a starting point is full of biases and inaccuracies; in various ways, this determines the way he reads (and makes others read) Epicurus' hedonism, a concept which, as Lactantius himself probably knew, is much more refined than saying that a general tendency towards pleasure must be identified with a general propensity to vice or evil. Nor is it true that Epicurean hedonism recommends the lazy not to study and advises cowards against politics. This last point is particularly prejudicial and unfair. Indeed, it seems especially illegitimate to accuse the Epicurean philosophy of propagating the idea that people should be kept away from politics when Epicurus himself, who recommended 'living unnoticed', was seriously involved in developing a sophisticated theory of law and justice. Of course, Lactantius refers to 'the cowards'; but an Epicurean philosopher might reply that there is no such cowardice in those who seek to show that conventional laws (based on a common notion of justice, which rule over current forms of the state) require a profound modification to cease being laws in the formal sense of norms. At best, people obey such 'formal laws' to avoid being punished, not because they believe that such rules should be rationally internalized, activated and deployed effectively within the practical domain.

It is also interesting to note that Lactantius believes that he can explain the origin of learning and, in general, of Epicurus' philosophy. According to him, Epicurus said that good people are always liable to misery, whereas evil persons flourish with more power and influence; additionally, crimes can be committed with impunity, and so on (*Div. Inst.* 3.17, 7-8). Once one has said this in a very general fashion (in order to avoid reproducing all the details provided by Lactantius), one might suggest that the apologist's point is that all which is bad usually turns out to be successful. In contrast, the opposite is subject to misery and pain. To sum up, if the apologetic discourse was right, the view of Epicurus would have been encouraged by the unfairness of things (*Div. Inst.* 3.17, 16), an opinion that, according to Lactantius, depends on Epicurus' ignorance of the 'real reason' [*sic enim causam rationemque ignoranti uidebatur*]. This is the way, Lactantius holds, in which it can be explained that Epicurus states that there is no providence; if there is no providence, it cannot be understood how the world is organized and ordered.

Some scholars argue that when Lactantius ascribes to Epicurus the view that 'there is no order', he is drawing on what Lucretius states in a formidable passage of *On the Nature of Things* (5.195-234).[34] Nevertheless, Lucretius is not describing a disorder in nature in this section of his poem, but a particular order in which each thing seems to take its proper place. What Epicurus, Lucretius and other Epicureans intend to prove is that this immanent order of nature is not due to a providence or intelligence that plans the cosmos' order. What they wish to show is that a cosmology without teleology is possible; 'but how is that possible?', a Christian and even a pagan philosopher (such as Plato, Aristotle and the Stoics) might wonder. From the Epicurean perspective, what follows from this is a challenging question that must be answered by a teleological account of the cosmos: 'why the world-builders suddenly appeared on the scene, after sleeping for countless centuries'. (Cicero, *ND* 1.21, reporting the Epicurean Velleius' objection to Plato and the Stoics). One might argue that if the world did not exist, time did exist (which implies some difficulties, insofar as the world was created at a point of time, a view that Lactantius would endorse). Besides, the Epicurean god is taken to be an imperishable and blessed being, but this is incompatible with the strains of world administration.[35] Further, the Epicurean gods do not have any control over celestial phenomena and they are not interested in human affairs (Lucretius, *RN* 5.1182-1192); of course, this view turns out to be unacceptable to Lactantius.[36]

4 A critical balance of Epicurus' theoretical adversaries

From the passages just discussed, we can conclude that the works of the adversaries of Epicureanism contain important elements of doxography and relevant critiques. But when faced with what they call 'Epicurean hedonism', their opposition, as the historian Green points out,[37] adopts a kind of craziness or hysteria that to a great extent coloured the traditional interpretation of Epicureanism and supported interpretive procedures which would be considered unacceptable in the case of any other philosopher of whose writings only few fragments have been preserved. We refer to the reconstruction of Epicurean approaches based on the absolutization of slogans extracted from doxography without support in Epicurus' texts, or decontextualized and mutilated from their original version. Such is the case of the famous slogans such as 'live unnoticed' and 'do not participate in politics' which circulated in antiquity (Seneca, *Ep.* 90.35) and which are still present today in several contemporary descriptions of Epicurean political philosophy, despite neither appearing in the *Principal Doctrines*.[38]

Epicurus' characterizations of the final end of human life are not easy to reconcile, since they indicate that the end [τέλος] is constituted by the absence of pain [ἀπονία] in the body and of perturbation in the soul (ἀταραξία; DL 10.136; see also DL 10.132).[39] Now, 'pleasure' seems to imply that absence of pain and imperturbability constitute the pleasure sought and that, in some way, Epicureanism posits certain qualifications of pleasure that allow this formulation. According to some scholars, this is the purpose of the distinction between kinetic [κατὰ κίνησιν] and katastematic [καταστηματικαί] pleasures (DL 10.136). It is indeed a complicated task to describe a theory that makes absence of pain in the body and of perturbation in the soul the highest good from a hedonistic perspective: and this is so because it seems to be properly described, as Wolfsdorf has pointed out, as an 'analgesic hedonism'.[40]

This is partially so because we tend to identify hedonism with 'crude hedonism' (probably influenced by Plutarch and Christian writers); but even in Plato (who attacks crude hedonism), certain kinds of hedonism which should be incorporated into the good life can be envisaged.[41] The suggestion that there are different kinds of pleasure (first adumbrated by Plato in the *Gorg.* 495a1-2 and discussed later in the *Resp.* 505b-c; 561c) is clearly taken up by Plato in the *Philebus*, where the character Socrates argues that 'the moderate person takes pleasure in his very moderation [...], the fool in his own foolishness, and likewise the wise person takes pleasure in his wisdom' (*Phl.* 12d; 13b-c). What is beyond doubt is that if one considers Epicurus' (presumed) distinction between stable and dynamic pleasure (as reported by DL 10.136 = Us. 2),[42] Lactantius' remarks about Epicurean hedonism are entirely out of focus and somewhat mistaken (*Div. Inst.* 3.17, 2-5). If this is so, when Epicurus maintains that pleasure is the ultimate end of existence he cannot be thinking of mere sensual pleasure. He declares that, if he were to remove the pleasures of taste, of sex, of listening, and so on, he does not even know what he should conceive the good to be. But it is also true that such kinds of pleasures are not pursued for their own sake, but for the sake of removing both physical and psychological pain. Thus, the final end is again imperturbability and absence of pain. We suspect that Lactantius and other writers, who were concerned with discrediting Epicureanism, were aware of this simple fact. Still, their polemic reasons were stronger than a balanced and rational examination of the theory. As said above, we are not suggesting that Lactantius never worried about 'arguing'. But when he describes the requirements that the so-called 'supreme good' must fulfil (i.e. it should be a property of human beings alone and thus cannot be shared with irrational animals; *Div. Inst.* 3.8, 3), he makes his reasoning depend on his own biases and shortcomings. Lactantius' interpretation is vitiated by his reliance on his own presuppositions, insofar as he seems to hold the view that the supreme good is a human property that belongs to the spirit, not the body (3.12, 1-8). Indeed, if a real supreme good belongs only to human beings, physical pleasure, or release from pain, must be ruled out as plausible candidates for a supreme (or real) good. But for Epicurus the hallmark of what exists is corporeality, and both the soul (or 'the spirit') and the body are bodily items. Further, Lactantius also thinks that 'living according to nature' (a typical Stoic injunction that should be practiced by the rational agent to be happy) must be removed from the conditions to attain the supreme good. But, of course, while stating that release from pain and living according to nature do not belong to what is really good, Lactantius is trivializing the Epicurean view of pleasure as well as the Stoic tenet that in order to be happy a person must develop his natural capacities, which are deeply linked to his rationality.

As observed above, when describing Epicurus' theory as hedonistic and making absence of pain and imperturbability the highest good, one encounters difficulties that did not go unnoticed to the adversaries of Epicureanism in antiquity. Those adversaries highlighted these descriptions as one of the philosophy's fundamental inconsistencies. Cicero and Plutarch have the double role of being both the main sources of these controversial Epicurean formulations and, at the same time, their most famous critics, which has given rise to a broad debate about the objectivity, depth and completeness of their testimonies and the appropriateness of their critiques.[43] However, within the framework of this debate, even the most benevolent interpreters of Cicero and Plutarch acknowledge that both made use of what, in our view, constitutes another fundamental tactic of the enemies of Epicureanism: opposing the intention and theory of Epicurus to its *ultimate effect*,[44] that is, by emphasizing the hypothetical germs of danger that the philosophy encompasses and its repercussions at the level of social practice.[45]

Adversaries of Epicureanism used this strategy and the already mentioned absolutization of mere slogans to oppose Epicurean ethics, but their use is particularly virulent when they deal with the political approaches of the Epicureans, as can be seen especially in Cicero's and Plutarch's texts. Both of them are Platonic in some way, active politicians, and illustrious members of their societies, and their critiques imply a peculiar approach to Greek philosophy which can be seen in Plutarch's idealization of 'the ancients', and in the way that both integrate philosophy into the performance of real political activity. In Plutarch's view 'the ancients' stand for excellence and constitute educational and moral models. 'The ancients' are thinkers and authors prior to Hellenistic philosophy; he mentions Thales, Bias, Lycurgus, Anaxagoras, Pherecydes, Anaximenes, Parmenides, Heraclitus, Empedocles, Democritus, Melissus, Socrates, Plato, Aristotle and Stilpon.[46] It is obvious that the grouping of such heterogeneous and disparate characters and philosophical approaches under the normative figure of 'the ancients' can only be sustained at the price of its complete levelling, which Plutarch carries out from a depleted version of Plato. Such levelling is particularly clear when compared, for example, to the meaning that the figure of Socrates had for Hellenistic ethics, who, as A. A. Long observes, represented a particular vision of the task of ethics more than a doctrinal inheritance: he stood for the questioning of conventions, the elimination of fears and desires that lacked rational foundation and a radical rearrangement of priorities around the notion of the health of the soul.[47] This legacy is not recognized in the exaltation of Plutarch, directed against the Epicureans, of the contribution of Plato, his disciple Aristotle, and the Academy, which Plutarch practically presents as a school for the training of politicians to the political life of the Greek world (*Col.* 1126B-D).[48] The complex and problematic relationship between philosophical and political life (so clearly documented in comedy,[49] in the life and death of Socrates, in Isocrates' speeches,[50] in Plato's biography and work, and in Aristotle's considerations on the primacy of the contemplative life, on the true politician and the theoretical occupation of the philosopher with politics) are entirely passed over for the sake of a neat integration of philosophy into the exercise of real politics that Plutarch, like Cicero, projects onto the past of Greek philosophy.[51] C. Lévy stressed that in Cicero's case, such an integration is based on extremely vague modalities of philosophy.[52] Like Plutarch, Cicero demotes the complex and problematic relationship between philosophical life and Greek political life (see chapter 6). However, he does highlight the defence of the pre-eminence of the *vita activa* in the heterodox Peripatetic Dicaearchus, though, according to Campos Darocca's view, Cicero does not fully understand its significance.[53]

According to Cicero,[54] Epicurean hedonism implies the collapse of the entire social system and even the impossibility of society itself, for, as he repeats in *Fin.* 2, if pleasure is made the supreme good then all virtue, all decency and all glory must be abandoned, since all action will be directed solely to usefulness and self-profit, making impossible any bond of harmony among human beings (*Fin.* 2.37, 44, 58, 72, 76, 78, 80, 85, 109, 117. *Off.* 1.2).[55] For Cicero the Epicureans are responsible for the abandonment of human society, with which they do not collaborate by lending their love, industry and talents (*Off.* 1.9).

At the end of *Against Colotes* (1124D) Plutarch makes explicit his criticism of the political considerations of the Epicureans by referring to philosophical approaches that, in his judgement, bring about the destruction of laws and civilized life and the return to a primitive and bestial level of existence. Some interpreters have suggested that the target of the Colotes critique is Arcesilaus, although, as Roskam has indicated, the fact that Plutarch's reply is not mentioned, unlike numerous philosophers attacked by Colotes, seems to suggest that the critique was directed against non-Epicurean philosophers in general.[56] Plutarch tries to show, through a traditional strategy of philosophical diatribes, that it is actually the Epicureans themselves who should be accused of destroying laws and the social system and encouraging a return to a wild life. Plutarch wonders what would happen to the Epicureans and followers of other philosophers such as Heraclitus, Socrates or Plato if the laws were abolished. In his opinion, in the case of the latter, nothing would happen and there would be no return to animal life, because 'we would fear the shameful and honour[57] justice for its nobility, considering that we have good rulers in the gods [θεοὺς ἄρχοντας ἀγαθούς] and protectors of our life in the daemons' (δαίμονας ... τοῦ βίου φύλακας; *Col.* 1124E).

By contrast, in Plutarch's view, the Epicureans who do not believe in providence despise virtue if it is not related to pleasure and think that good is in the stomach; they need 'law and fear and blows and some king or ruler who has in his hand justice, so that they do not devour their neighbours because of a gluttony emboldened by atheism' (1125A). In other words, those who abide by 'the life of enjoyment' (βίος ἀπολαυστικός) cannot control themselves and therefore require laws and authorities. Without them their behaviour would be savage. The Epicurean only acts out of fear of laws and sanctions and, according to Plutarch, even the Epicurean sage will commit injustice if he is certain that his crime will remain hidden (see chapter 5). Further, Plutarch understands that the basis and cohesion of a society and of the legal order is the belief in gods, as Plato already emphasized in the *Laws*. In his view, the Epicureans destroy this basis and thus destroy every possibility of authorities, institutions and legal order. Interestingly, Lactantius repeats the same argument within the framework of Christian apologetics. For him, the Epicureans represent the synthesis of evil and pagan error. He sees in Epicurean hedonism the necessary consequence of the denial of providence, and, like Cicero and Plutarch, he maintains that it makes any community impossible except that of individuals dedicated to theft and pillaging (*Div. Inst.* 3.17 39-43).

Epicurean hedonism and atheism show, in Plutarch's opinion, the falsehood of the apology of the laws of Colotes. Plutarch also describes it as dishonest and hypocritical, since, as he holds, the Epicureans claim to defend laws and institutions but recommend abstaining from participating in politics, mock the most famous politicians and legislators of the past and cannot exhibit any feat or contribution by the members of their school to the benefit of society (*Col.* 1125C-1127C). The Epicurean, according to Plutarch, is incapable of humanity [ἀφιλάνθρωπος][58] (*Pleasant Life* 1098D) and behaves like a profiteer, a parasite [ἀσύμβολος], who benefits from the advantages of life in society without making the least contribution (*Col.* 1127A). Cicero (*On the orator* 3.64) and Epictetus (*Diss.* 2. 20, 6 20 and 17 19) repeat the same accusation.

5 Concluding remarks

Cicero, Lactantius and Plutarch (like other critics of Epicurus and Epicureanism), despite being so critical of Epicureanism, constitute valuable sources for our knowledge of the Garden and, in several cases, paradoxically offer relevant testimonies for the sophistication of certain Epicurean theses and arguments.[59] Indeed, in the comparison that can be made of their testimonies with other secondary sources (and with the few texts that have come down to us from Epicurus himself), one cannot but notice the refinement of Epicurean philosophy and, implicitly, of the reasons that its most ferocious critics had for trivializing its theories and arguments. We cannot accuse the most virulent critics of Epicurus and his school of having their own agenda (no philosopher or philosophical writer lacks one). But as philosophers as well as historians of philosophy, we must demand that these critics substantiate their objections to Epicurus and Epicureanism more precisely, so as not to contribute to the silencing of a philosophical theory that was not only of theoretical but also of practical interest and considerable impact already in antiquity. The interpretation of Epicureanism by Cicero, Plutarch and Lactantius was not historiographical but belligerent, and it turns particularly virulent when they deal with the political approaches of the Epicureans, as can be seen particularly in the texts of Cicero and Plutarch. Cicero and Plutarch both are Platonic in some way, active politicians, and illustrious members of their society. Their critiques imply a peculiar approach to Greek philosophy, which can be seen in Plutarch's idealization of 'the ancients', and in the way that they both integrate philosophy into the performance of real political activity. Both of them, though, omit the Epicurean interconnection between the study of nature and political theory. They do not set out the Epicurean theoretical framework in which Epicurean contractualism is inscribed. Consequently, its specific features and the rich Epicurean theme focused on security, justice and law are ignored.

5

The Epicurean Sage, the Issue of Justice and the Laws

The assessment of actions performed by a person without witnesses was a topic repeatedly addressed by Greek philosophers when dealing with justice and laws. Suffice it to recall the fragments of Democritus (DK 244, DK B 264, DK 68 B 264), the preserved passages of Antiphon's *On the Truth*,[1] and the well-known story of the Ring of Gyges in Plato's *Republic* (359c6-360c5; 612b). The experience of a distance between crime and punishment was likewise a fundamental element of theodicy from the Homeric poems on, to which corresponds the gradual personification of time in poetry and tragedy as a scrutinizing witness who sooner or later reveals the truth.[2] In the satirical drama *Sisyphus*, Critias (or Euripides) suggested that belief in the gods was invented precisely for deterring crime in the absence of witnesses (see Critias, DK B25). Lactantius offers a curious psychological account of the genesis of Epicurus' thought that focuses on the experience of the distance between crime and punishment. In his opinion, Epicurus was led to the denial of providence, and to all the consequent errors in his philosophy, by 'the injustice of the facts' when he observed that crimes went unpunished and bad people won, while the good and innocent were made miserable (*Div. Inst.* 3.17, 8-16). Epicurean philosophy combines views that yield an interesting approach to this old topic of actions performed without witnesses. On the one hand, the Epicurean conception of the gods rules out the idea of providence, while also denying that the gods are capable of, or interested in, punishing us. An Epicurean god is a blessed and indestructible entity that has no troubles itself and does not trouble anyone else (*PD* 1). The gods are a model for the Epicureans whose piety aspires to an assimilation to god [ὁμοίωσις θεῷ], which is reflected in living pleasantly, prudently, nobly and justly. On the other hand, Epicureanism upholds a contractualist genealogy of justice and laws that stresses, as one of the main factors of the effectiveness of laws, having internalized punishment. Suspicion, uncertainty and the fear of being discovered and condemned represent, in Epicurus' view, punishments triggered by the perpetration of an unwitnessed crime. The Epicurean sage is free from the vain desires responsible for most crimes. Thus, he is free from the disturbance represented by uncertainty and fear of discovery, just as he is free from the fear of death and the gods. Now, if the Epicurean wise person knows that he will not be discovered, will he carry out actions contrary to the laws? This was a question that Epicurus indeed asked himself in a passage from the *Puzzles* [Διαπορίαι] transmitted by Plutarch (*Col.* 1127D). Cicero also refers (in *Off.* 3.38-39) to the Epicurean position vis-à-vis the story of the Ring of Gyges, which has clear similarities with the passage from the *Puzzles* just mentioned. Naturally, Cicero and Plutarch do not miss the opportunity to discredit Epicureanism. In the present chapter we will attempt to clarify, through the analysis of these polemical considerations by Cicero and Plutarch, as well as the reconstruction of the Epicureans' answer to the question above, the Epicurean characterization of one of the fundamental aspects of the proverbial pictures of the sage in late antiquity: the relationship between the sage, justice and the laws.

The chapter proceeds thus: in section 1, we contrast the Epicurean and the Stoic sages and suggest that, contrary to the testimony of several indirect sources, the Epicurean sage was interested in maintaining a link with his polis. We begin our examination by considering the difficulties raised by the aforementioned passage from the *Puzzles*, where Epicurus wonders whether the wise Epicurean, knowing that he will not be discovered, will carry out actions contrary to the laws. In section 2 we argue that this passage from the *Puzzles* evokes the story of the Ring of Gyges in Plato's *Republic*; we present the contractualist model in which this story is embedded, and compare it with the Epicurean contractualist model to show that the advantage [πλεονεξία] of Gyges is not attributable – according to the Epicureans – to the 'presocial' human beings nor to the first human groupings subject to pacts of justice but, if anything, to later human beings who are forced to establish laws and sanctions. The figure of Gyges represents neither a challenge nor a fascination for the Epicureans. In section 3, we stress the biased reading of Cicero in *Off.* 3.38-39 of the Epicurean view regarding the story of Gyges and Plutarch's malicious interpretation of Epicurus' reply to the relevant passage from the *Puzzles*. We note that both omit the role of the study of nature [or Epicurean 'physiology': φυσιολογία] and prudence [φρόνησις] in the motivations and decisions of the Epicurean sage in their analyses of the topics mentioned. Both suggest that the reason Epicureans refrain from crime is the fear of being discovered and punished. In section 4, we focus on the theme of punishment and draw on Plato's discussion of the topic in the

Gorgias. We argue that even if Epicurus does not state (as Plato does) that punishment makes the person better, he maintains that the suspicion that one will not escape the notice of those assigned to punish bad actions works as a sort of chastisement for the offenders (thereby evoking the Platonic therapeutic feature of punishment). The Epicurean sage, we argue, does not act out of fear of punishment, but, on the contrary, disregards behaviours authorized by the law and goes beyond what is required by law in social relations. In section 5, we return to the issue of friendship and justice and show how closely friendship is related to our rational condition. We also note the importance of self-sufficiency for the Epicurean sage and state that, far from being an egoistic property of the sage, self-sufficiency involves a social dimension and thereby an engagement with law. Finally, we show how friendship and justice occupy a central place in two fundamental doctrinal resources of Epicureanism: the biographical tradition of the 'imitation of Epicurus' [*imitatio Epicurei*] and the practice of 'becoming like god'. Section 6 provides an abstract of the chapter and some concluding remarks.

1 The stoic and Epicurean sage, and the Epicurean's commitment to the city

The picture of the sage (both Epicurean and Stoic) had gained proverbial status in late antiquity. In Diogenes Laertius' summary, several explicit references point to the differences between Epicurean and Stoic sages. The fact that the Epicurean sage shouts and moans when he is tortured (DL 10.118) is strongly opposed to the heroic picture of the Stoic sage, who keeps quiet about his pain. The Epicurean, Diogenes Laertius reports, will not participate in politics; we have already extensively discussed why that view should be nuanced (and surely challenged) and to what extent it is reliable to deal with any worldly fact as decisive in moving away from imperturbability. An Epicurean sage is the one who has achieved tranquillity and detachment from worldly affairs, which can produce – at least theoretically – a blessed state for the person.[3] The Epicurean sage will not behave like a tyrant or a Cynic; surely this is once again a direct reference to Stoicism, holding that, at times, the sage may act like a Cynic. Being a Cynic is for the Stoic 'to live like a dog', i.e. rejecting the conventions of what is supposed to be a civilized life.[4]

By contrast, Epicurus rejects such a possibility; in fact, though all the formal institutions of society are no more than the result of a pact, such a pact must guarantee coexistence and avoid mutual aggression in order to facilitate a real human mode of existence. Institutions work as 'tools', as it were, for civil security (as we argue in chapter 2), which is an essential condition for the existence of a political organization. But if this is so, and if marriage can be taken to be a sort of social institution, one might wonder why the Epicurean wise person will not marry and beget children (although 'he may marry in accordance with special circumstances in his life'; DL 10.119).[5] After all, the Epicurean sage, in spite of having certain special features (i.e. 'theoretical and practical' skills that permit him to neutralize his anguish and hence to live with tranquillity and without vain fears), is a real person, not a mere utopian ideal. Indeed, as we have already shown, the integration of family relations into the practice of philosophy is a feature of Epicurus' life that is reiterated throughout the history of the school.

The same contrast can be noted between Epicurus and the Stoics when it is said that the former had a friendly attitude towards his homeland (DL 10.10-11). In contrast, the Stoics (especially the Older Stoics) have no country or, more precisely, they are 'cosmopolitan' citizens of the world who reject all conventions that have value only in a given region.[6] It is arguable, we submit, that Marcus Aurelius, the emperor who in a certain way made Stoicism the official philosophy of an empire, transformed the idea of Stoic cosmopolitanism advanced by Zeno in his *Republic* into a political reality. If Stoic cosmopolitanism can be read this way, it is no longer a pointless ideal but the political appropriation of that ideal to the real state of affairs.

Nevertheless, there is another essential disagreement (focused on the issue of desire, so important for explaining how a person performs his actions) between the Epicurean and the Stoic sage: unlike the Stoic sage (who is emotionless; DL 7.117), Epicurus, according to Plutarch, held that the wise person 'is a lover of sights and enjoys hearing and seeing Dionysiac performances as much as anyone' (*Pleasant Life* 1095C; Us. 20). Interestingly, Diogenes Laertius states that the Epicurean can be *more* delighted than others at festivals (DL 10.120; Us. 593); he can feel grief and gratitude toward his friends, present and absent alike, and can be more susceptible to emotion than other people (DL 10.117-120). However, there are some coincidences between the two models of sage: both the Epicurean and the Stoic wise person can earn money due to the exercise of their wisdom (DL 10.121). This is an interesting detail that shows that the Epicurean sage can (and eventually should) work for a living. As is clear, such activity must be carried out within a social context (which can be considered a way of participating in politics insofar as this contributes to the social community in which he lives). Further, both kinds of sage will formulate beliefs and not be sceptics: the Stoic sage gives his assent to cognitive impressions.⁷ For his part, the Epicurean wise person states that it should be believed that 'atoms bring with them none of the qualities of things which appear except shape, weight, and size' (*LH* 54). Moreover, he also recommends 'not to believe that atoms have every possible magnitude, so that one may avoid being testified against by the appearances' (*LH* 55). This suffices to show that the Epicurean wise person is not a Sceptic. Another issue relevant to the Epicurean sage is that of friendship. Indeed, friendship was also highly relevant for the Stoics, primarily because, according to them, only the wise are capable of being friends (DL 7.124); this is the case since only they are free from 'passions' or 'affective states'. This therefore guarantees that, given their self-sufficiency, the Stoic sage would act only according to virtue, unconstrained by any affective state, which technically is the same as 'perverse reason' (Plutarch, *On Moral Virtue* 441C-E; *SVF* 1.202; BS 25.3).⁸ Nonetheless, this can be challenged, since friendship, understood in the traditional sense, presupposes an affective state that at times implies a certain 'affective intimacy'. Besides, if a 'Stoic friend' must be 'a virtuous person' then the theory appears counterintuitive: although usually one is not (and is not usually considered to be) a moral model, it does not follow that one is not or cannot be a genuine friend, nor that one is incapable of developing friendships.⁹ To be sure, these are problems inherent to the Stoic idea of friendship; however, we suggest, they may help us to better understand how the Epicureans explain friendship, its role in the political community, and its function in the conceptualization of the Epicurean sage.

Epicurus explicitly links wisdom to friendship and suggests wisdom is a property of *every* human being that is neither strange, difficult nor impossible to acquire. In other words, wisdom and its benefits are accessible by all human beings willing to understand and practice Epicureanism and to appreciate the link between friendship (correctly understood according to Epicurean patterns) and wisdom. Considering the issue from such a standpoint, one might even suggest that Epicurus was challenging the Stoic idea that becoming a sage is a rare and peculiar event. Moreover, as Plutarch ironizes, Chrysippus does not show himself or any of his acquaintances and teachers to be excellent or virtuous people. If this is so, what can we expect from other people? (*Stoic. Rep.* 1048E; *SVF* 3.662, 668).¹⁰ This doctrine imposed on the ancient Stoics the bad reputation of trying to establish an entirely impracticable ethics: the Stoic sage (with his characteristics of moral infallibility – since he is unable to make false assumptions –, rational perfection – his actions are always virtuous –, absolute coherence and the disposition of doing everything well, i.e. everything that he does) is an extremely rare person. It would not be strange if Epicurus were attempting to contrast this with the image of his model of a sage, i.e. a person who, for the sake of becoming wise, must fulfil specific requirements. It is noteworthy that such Epicurean requirements are susceptible to being fulfilled by practically any human being.

In the characterization of the Epicurean sage that is drawn from his contrast with the Stoic sage, respect for laws and institutions, as well as a friendly attitude towards his homeland, play an important role. In order to deepen this characterization, it is thus of particular interest to explore an issue that Epicurus raised in his *Puzzles* (DL 10.27). After referring to Metrodorus' mockery of the wise persons who vainly claim to be legislators, Plutarch stresses that the Epicureans are in fact at war not with lawgivers but with laws, as can be seen, in his opinion, from Epicurus' own writings. Plutarch then goes on to quote a passage from Epicurus' *Puzzles*. The only version of this can be found in Plutarch:

> **T1** For in the *Puzzles* Epicurus asks himself whether the wise man will do some things which the laws forbid, if he knows that he will escape detection. And he answers: 'the plain statement [of the answer] (τὸ ἁπλοῦν ἐπικατηγόρημα)[11] is not easy (εὔοδον)'.
>
> *Col.* 1127D; transl. Inwood and Gerson

There has been significant discussion about these lines which are probably taken out of context or whose context is hard to know in detail. Boulogne, for example, underlines that Plutarch was well aware of Epicurus' *Puzzles*, a work he refers to many times, and considers that Plutarch's omissions of the context as well as the response or other possible relevant elements in Epicurus' text were not due to a deliberate purpose, but derived from the full conviction that Plutarch had regarding the doctrinal continuity between what he presents as Epicurus' response and the fundamental theses of his philosophy about the laws.[12] This is actually extremely generous to Plutarch, particularly if one considers how he interpreted Epicurus' supposed answer. After quoting the declaration 'the plain statement [of the answer] is not easy' Plutarch somewhat maliciously comments (putting words into Epicurus' mouth): 'that is, I will do it, but I do not wish to admit it' (οὐ βούλομαι δ' ὁμολογεῖν; *Col.* 1127 D; transl. Inwood and Gerson).[13] Plutarch intends us to see that Epicurus' refusal to respond fully reflects hypocrisy and shame in recognizing that he would do them, shame that implies accepting that he performs actions that he knows are bad; that is to say, they are bad regardless of whether they remain hidden or not. Plutarch, like Polus in Plato's *Gorgias* (474c), seems to appeal to shame as proof of the effective acceptance of argumentatively rejected assessments. Epictetus also appeals to the coherence between doctrine and action to attack the Epicureans. In his view there is no doubt that the coherent decision of the wise Epicurean, if he knows he will escape, is to act against the law (*Diss.* 3.7, 14).

The passage from the *Puzzles* collected by Plutarch evokes the story of the Ring of Gyges, debated by Plato in *Resp.* 359c6–360c5. Cicero (*Off.* 3.38-39) summarizes this story and comments on the interpretation of it by 'certain philosophers'. Such philosophers are easily identifiable with the Epicureans, so the passage of Cicero, although Gyges' case is not identical to that of **T1**, provides relevant elements to the analysis of this section of the *Puzzles*.[14] Thus it is worth examining the main interpretative guidelines followed by scholars when analysing **T1**, as this passage has received more attention than the Ciceronian text of *Off.* 3.38-39. However, as we will see, these are entirely relevant considerations with regard to Cicero's interpretation of the Epicureans' position vis-à-vis the story of Gyges' ring. In dealing with **T1**, interpreters have focused on the following aspects: (i) the distinction between just and unjust laws; (ii) the exceptionality of the situation concerning the satisfaction of necessary natural desires; and finally, (iii) the counterfactual character of the conditional clause 'if he knows that he will not be discovered'. We will examine these three interpretive guidelines in turn. Einarson and De Lacy advocated a reading of **T1**, advanced in some way by Philippson too, that seemed to dissolve its difficulty.[15] They argued that, since Epicurus stressed that the legal was not identified with the just, since to the extent that the legal ceased to be useful it also ceased to be just, the wise would have no problem in acting illegally in relation to laws that have ceased to be just.[16] The disadvantage of this automatic response, as Goldschmidt observed, is that it did not explain why Epicurus himself seemed to emphasize the difficulty of the matter at the time and included it among the *Puzzles*.[17] Further, one could object that this solution was nothing more than a refinement of the formulation of the problem, which could consequently be reformulated in these terms: 'whether the wise person, knowing that he will not be discovered, will do something of what is forbidden by just laws'. In dealing with the difficulty posed by this passage neither Cicero nor Plutarch consider statements such as those of Einarson and De Lacy. Nor do they suggest that Epicurus or any of his disciples did so. Moreover, one could present another two objections to Einarson and De Lacy's suggestion: (i) there is no case or situation in which it can be argued that an Epicurean sage – or indeed a sage belonging to any other school – is capable of acting illegally. If he is able to do so, and if in fact he does so, that person is not wise. (ii) Furthermore, laws that have ceased to be just due to the circumstances prevailing in any given moment do not entitle the wise man or any other citizen of the polis to act illegally.

For his part, Seel believes that it is worth wondering whether Epicurus could have taken into account the case where the sage is faced with situations in which the satisfaction of the necessary natural desires or the preservation of life implies committing injustice.[18] As is well-known, the allegation of limit situations and casuistry played an important role in Hellenistic disputes in refuting ethical formulations.[19] A famous example is the case of the two castaways who have only one float, which the adversaries of the Stoics considered as sufficient dismissal of Stoicism's foundation of justice in the theory of familiarization [οἰκείωσις].[20] In Seel's opinion, such exceptionality is what explains the presence of the word 'simple' (or 'plane': ἁπλοῦν) in the expression 'the plain statement' [τὸ ἁπλοῦν ἐπικατηγόρημα], which he translates as '*senza ulteriore precisazioni*', in Epicurus' circumspect response, or more precisely, in what Plutarch transmits, as: 'it is not feasible here [οὐκ εὔοδον] to make a categorical statement *without further precisions*' (*Col.* 1127 D). Appealing as it is, however, this interpretation would weaken the Epicurean colour of **T1** because, as Strauss stressed, the recognition (of Platonic filiation) that even natural law is subject to exception in extreme cases was a commonplace since Aristotle's meagre and marginal considerations on the subject (*EN* 1134b18-1135a5).[21] Certainly it is also true that Epicurus was not at all blind to the facts, exceptions and singularities, all details that sober prudential reasoning must take into consideration.[22]

Seel conjectures that, given his great recognition of friendship,[23] Epicurus might be thinking of the case of the wise person who, in order to save the life of a friend, has to act unjustly.[24] Vander Waerdt considers it more convincing that the conflict concerned the wise man's own preservation.[25] Additionally, he observes that since the Epicurean sage does not fear death, it is not easy for him to imagine the particular circumstances in which he would rather die than preserve his life by committing injustice. Perhaps, the possibility of this sort of exceptional case also motivated the reservation of Epicurus' answer to the question formulated by Plutarch. The fact that death poses no fear for the Epicurean sage cannot be neglected and is in fact an important point in working out the particular circumstances in which he would rather die than commit injustice to sustain his life. If you are an Epicurean sage, you are aware that death causes considerable anxiety to all those who are not willing to follow the Epicurean prescriptions for having a life of quality. Further, an Epicurean sage knows that the reasons provided by those who fear death (the concern with ingratiating themselves with the gods as they might punish them for their wrongdoings, the worry about total personal annihilation, etc.) are absurd. This is so because there is no evidence that gods are willing to punish us, and because one's soul dissipates when one dies and hence there is no sensation (Epicurus, *LH* 63). But if there is no sensation, there can be no pain either and as Epicurus argues in *LM* 126, the wise person neither rejects life nor fears death, for he is not contrary to living and he does not believe that not living is bad. However, if all this is so, the view that the wise person can be especially worried about his or her own preservation cannot be true: if 'preservation' means 'being alive', this cannot be the case since the Epicurean wise person (as Epicurus himself insists) does not see living as lamentable. Naturally, as we have shown above, the Epicurean sage, unlike irrational animals, can take precautions in anticipation of suffering ailments and provide beneficial or useful things.

Finally, Goldschmidt places the bulk of the passage on the impossibility of the conditional clause 'if he knows that he will not be discovered'. Neither the wise, paradigm of knowledge, nor the unwise can achieve certainty in this respect. In fact, Epicurus places emphasis upon the fact that there is no possibility of future certainty (*PD* 34), and thus he cannot give a simple answer because the puzzlement incorporates presuppositions that are impossible. Still, this shows that the Epicurean sage is not as strange a person as the Stoic sage:[26] being an Epicurean sage does not confer extraordinary powers that other human beings lack. There is no doubt that an Epicurean wise person is one who is endowed with 'special' skills. But no matter how wise an Epicurean may be, he cannot predict the future[27] and therefore cannot be certain about it.

2 Gyges' ring and the Epicurean origin of justice

In the classical tradition before Epicurus, the most complete and best-argued discussion on the consideration of bad actions performed by a person without witnesses is Plato and his story of the Ring of Gyges (debated in *Resp.* 359c6–360c5). In our view, it is evident that Epicurus' emphasis in **T1** on the role that the possibility of passing undetected when performing an illegal act evokes the Platonic debate on the topic. The story of Gyges' ring is framed in the debate of the contractual origin of justice, such as it is presented by the character Glaucon. Now, the Epicurean genealogy of justice and the laws differs in several respects from that of Glaucon. To be sure, Gyges, with or without a ring, is certainly not an Epicurean sage. It is worthwhile, therefore, to dwell on Plato's text in order to analyse **T1** and Plutarch's commentary, as well as Cicero's interpretation of the position of the Epicureans vis-à-vis the story of Gyges' ring.

When discussing the issue of justice in *Republic* 2, the character Glaucon does not offer a clear definition of justice. At the end of his first speech, after presenting a contractual explanation of the genealogy of justice, he says that 'this is the origin and the essence of justice' (359a5); this is incorrect, since he has only spoken of the origin [γένεσις] of justice and precisely not of its essence [οὐσία]. If he had spoken of its essence, he would have given a true definition of justice. Glaucon argues that the origin and nature of justice is the product of a kind of social pact or agreement. His interest – or the position he represents if we are willing to believe that his view is not that the life of the unjust is better than that of the just[28] – is directed towards the consequences of justice as a means of ensuring a kind of pact of mutual non-aggression among the members of society (cf. *Resp*. 358e4-359b5). Justice would be a middle term between the greatest good (which is to commit injustice with impunity) and the greatest evil (which is not to be able to take revenge for injustice). In other words, human beings take refuge in justice not because it is a good thing, but because they are forced to respect it; otherwise, they will be punished (i.e. people cannot commit a crime without paying for it). In fact, as Glaucon goes on to argue, one who can commit an injustice without having to pay for it will refrain from making an agreement or pact with anyone to prevent injustices, neither to commit injustice nor to suffer it (*Resp*. 359b).[29] The view that it is necessary to make such a pact explains why Glaucon (or rather, 'what people say about justice, i.e. that to do injustice is by nature good and to suffer injustice bad'; *Resp*. 358e3-4) thinks that justice is not inherently good, but *something necessary to avoid mutual aggression*. If this is so, it is advantageous [λυσιτελεῖν] to come to an agreement with one another neither to do injustice nor to suffer it (μήτ' ἀδικεῖν μήτ' ἀδικεῖσθαι; 359a1-2), and as a result people started to make laws and pacts [συνθῆκαι], and what such laws commend they call lawful and just.

It would be challenging (and highly questionable) to argue that Plato subscribes to a contractualist theory of justice, but it is clear from the *Republic* passages commented on above that he developed a line of reasoning that Epicurus and the Epicureans subsequently revisited and expanded in their own terms. Regarding this, Glaucon maintains as part of the strongest thesis that people are tolerant of the fact that those who practise justice do so involuntarily, not out of true goodness but out of necessity. Later in the text it is revealed that a person's opinion – *any* person, whether just or unjust – would always prefer to carry out unjust acts if he had some guarantee that injustice could go unpunished.

When Gyges turned the setting of the ring toward himself, the story goes, he became invisible to those sitting near him, and they proceed to talk as if Gyges had gone (*Resp.* 359e-360a). Thus, Gyges noted the extraordinary power he wielded, as turning the setting inward rendered him invisible and turning it outward made him visible again. The power of the ring tested Gyges' moral character and in fact revealed his awful moral disposition, as he used the powers of the ring to seduce the king's wife, attack the king with her help, commit regicide and assume possession of the kingdom.

Now if there were two rings of Gyges, Plato contends, and one was given to the unjust and the other one to the just, both would behave unjustly. The character Glaucon declares that this constitutes a 'significant proof' (μέγα τεκμήριον; 360c5) that no one is willingly just [οὐδεὶς ἑκὼν δίκαιος] unless compelled to be so. This would also show, according to the theory of justice endorsed by 'what people say', that what is truly valuable is not *being* just but simply *appearing* to be so. It is surprising that Glaucon (or the theory he claims to represent) finds this proof so significant; we believe there is reason to think that his conviction of widespread agreement that those who live a just life do so involuntarily is because he starts from the implicit assumption that there are certain things he takes to be goods (wealth and reputation, among others), which are not guaranteed during a just life but appear to be so in the case of an unjust life. Indeed, in many cases those who are just have no money, reputation, or other things conventionally recognized as goods. If we trust Glaucon and hence in good faith believe he would not dare to subscribe without further argument to the thesis that the life of the unjust is much better than that of the just, it is easy to discern the origin of his state of perplexity (ἀπορῶ; *Resp.* 358c7). This perplexity may arise from the fact that the unjust person *seems* to do well in life; to take the example of Thrasymachus, if in an association between a just and an unjust person the latter defrauds the former and gets away with it (*Resp.* 343d-e), it is at least paradoxical to admit that it is much better to be just than unjust. Plato's implicit answer to this objection is that this is only valid in an explanation presupposing that wealth or reputation are real goods. The character Adeimantus suggests that Socrates leave aside reputation [τὰς δὲ δόξας ἀφαίρει] 'as Glaucon recommended' (*Resp.* 367b6; see also 361b-c). In other words, both Adeimantus and Glaucon believe that when Socrates argues that justice should be included within the kind of goods that are valued for their own sake and for their consequences, one of those consequences may be reputation, something they consider to be a good but which Socrates might not endorse. Our hunch is that neither Adeimantus nor Glaucon understand what Socrates believes the consequences of justice to be, and that this is so because they start from a conventional conception of the good. The consequences of a just life are that the just are wiser, morally superior (σοφώτεροι καὶ ἀμείνους; 352b8) and more effective in their actions [δυνατώτεροι πράττειν], consequences that the conventional theory of good taken for granted by Glaucon and Adeimantus does not envisage as *practical*, and thereby does not see as advantages.

Of course, these details are already part of the Platonic argument endeavouring to show that the life of the just (even lacking the conventionally recognized goods) is – always and in all cases – better than that of the unjust. Additionally, when considering the Platonic passages discussed above it is important to note that, like Plato, Epicurus also leaves aside conventional goods such as wealth or reputation. Were this not the case, it would prove difficult to understand why, if one wishes to make someone wealthy, one should not give him more money but rather reduce his or her desires (Stobaeus, *Anthology* 3.17.23; Us. 153). Once more, this passage clearly illustrates the relevance of the idea that the *highest good* is a soul free of passions or appetites (Seneca, *Ep.* 9, 1; Us. 74).[30] This also makes it clear why *every* possession is wealth if (and only if) it contributes to satisfying nature, and why even the greatest wealth (i.e. conventional wealth) is poverty when it is in line with unlimited desires (Porphyry, *To Marcella* 27; Us. 202).[31] Surely this kind of redefinition of wealth can be seen as a mere *desideratum*, but it is undoubtedly a condition of the Epicurean sage, who not only cannot believe that money is a real good (Philodemus, *On Property Management* col. xv 31-xvi 18) but is also capable of applying this idea to everyday life. Indeed, this approach is helpful for better understanding why, strictly speaking, there is no difference between an extravagant meal and a bit of bread and water (Epicurus, *LM* 130-131; DL 10.11). After all, the fundamental purpose of food is to eliminate the pain of hunger; but, of course, the Epicurean sage is not a hermit who preaches a life of deprivation, and thus if hunger can be satisfied by an extravagant meal the sage will not refuse it.

Coming back to the counterpoint we were making about the contractual model of Glaucon in Plato's *Republic* and the Epicurean one, it should be stressed that the formulae by which Glaucon (Plato, *Resp.* 359a1-2) and Epicurus (*PD* 31) specify the purpose of the pact are undoubtedly similar, although, as Kahn pointed out, this may be due to their coming from a common source.[32] Both also base the pact on utility or convenience. However, Glaucon's contractualist model, despite its parsimony, allows for differences from the Epicurean model. The Epicureans divide, conceptually and temporally, the genealogy of justice from that of the laws, entailing, as we showed in the first two chapters, differentiated descriptions of the people involved in the respective pacts and, incidentally, of the hypothetical 'presocial' human beings. As should now be evident, the description offered by Hermarchus and Lucretius of the nature of the human beings composing the first human groupings subject to pacts of justice is dissimilar to that posited by Glaucon. The background of the story of Gyges' ring is Glaucon's specific contractual model, in which advantage is the essential motivation of human nature (Plato, *Resp.* 359c3-5). By contrast, in Epicureanism the advantage is framed by the emergence of vain desires and fears that necessitate the establishment of laws and sanctions. Thus, it is a phenomenon subsequent to the establishment of the first covenants of justice, which implies that it is not attributable to presocial human beings either, as can be seen in Lucretius. The background of Gyges' ring story is Glaucon's specific contractualist model, grounded on a particular understanding of human nature, which, presumably, stems from what 'people say'. In this model Gyges represents, as it were, the figure of a human being *ante pactum* living among human beings subject to a pact. Hence perhaps the fascination which Plato attributes to the common mind (*Resp.* 360b6) with the figure of one who, like Gyges, could do everything as if he were 'equal to a god [ἰσόθεον] among men' (*Resp.* 360c3). Certainly, as is well-known, Plato's theology and agenda is quite different: the human being, he argues, should as far as possible assimilate himself to god or rather become like god insofar as is possible (i.e. cultivate his immortal soul).[33] At the end of *Letter to Menoeceus* Epicurus seems once again to use Plato's expressions to condense his own philosophy as well as his view of the gods. Epicurus states that whoever practices his philosophy – not Gyges or the Platonic philosopher, one might add – will live as a god among men (*LM* 135: ζήσῃ δὲ ὡς θεὸς ἐν ἀνθρώποις).

3 Cicero on Gyges' ring and how Plutarch deals with the *Puzzles*

As already indicated, Cicero was also interested in explaining the meaning of the story of Gyges. In fact, in *On Duties* 3.38-39; 77-78, he summarizes the story, noting that certain philosophers, not bad people nor particularly subtle (obviously referring to the Epicureans: see *Fin.* 2.80, and *Tusc.* 3.46),[34] underestimate its value in that they consider the assumption illustrated by Gyges' story to be impossible in the world of human actions. The Epicureans, who apparently criticized Plato for mythologizing like a poet,[35] stubbornly resist considering the hypothesis and go no further because, according to Cicero, they do not truly understand the question.[36] In their opinion, answering such a question would put them in a real predicament: if they answer that they would act against others *knowing* that they would not be discovered, they would reveal themselves as villainous, while if they answered to the contrary, they would admit that they must avoid bad actions. This is precisely the thesis of the preceding section of *On Duties*, where Cicero introduces the story of Gyges and the Epicurean interpretation.

Goldschmidt insists on Cicero's blindness to Epicurus' position concerning what is impossible, although it seems that his peculiar solution of the puzzle sets aside – as do Cicero's rebukes – fundamental theses that the Epicureans could offer as an answer to the question contained in **T1**. By concentrating on the counterfactual conditional, as some late Epicureans ostensibly do, Goldschmidt implicitly seems to leave intact the thesis shared by Cicero and Plutarch that the only reason that Epicureans abstain from certain actions is the fear of punishment, from whose escape one can never be certain, an uncertainty that indeed already constitutes castigation (*PD* 34). To be sure, the Epicureans could begin by objecting to the expressions 'intrinsically good or bad actions' and 'actions performed by themselves or avoided by themselves', whose acceptance Cicero and Plutarch intend to force, declaring them fallacious. In fact, Torquatus does so in *On Ends* 1: Cicero, a skilful rhetorician, endeavours to embarrass him by opposing his hedonistic and utilitarian explanations of actions, the noble and heroic patriotic deeds carried out by Torquatus' own ancestors (*Fin.* 1.23-25). Unintimidated, Torquatus wonders whether they were thrown into these great feats, incidentally always performed before the viewing public, like animals without awareness of their effects and consequences. The obviously negative answer calls into doubt that the *exclusive* motivation of these patriotic heroes was the performance of intrinsically good actions (*Fin.* 1.34-36).[37] Cicero attributes irrationality and animality to Epicurean hedonism. Torquatus throws this disqualification straight back: if the patriotic feats were carried out *exclusively* for the sake of duty, they constitute irrational, animal behaviours, unsuitable for rational beings.[38]

Perhaps the best Epicurean argument would be to focus the issue on the Epicurean sage, as Plutarch (*Col.* 1127D) and Cicero (*Off.* 3.9) do, probably with the purpose of highlighting the ignominy of Epicureanism through the behaviour of its most qualified representative. The question, therefore, concerns the emblematic representative of the possession of 'physiology' and prudence that Epicureanism advocates. This qualification is decisive, since it forces us to consider if the figure of the Epicurean sage is recognized in the motivations alleged by Cicero to carry out bad actions knowing that they will not be discovered, and in the consequent way of deciding that it presents. Cicero reviews the first in these terms: 'for the sake of riches, power, despotism or lust' (*divitiarum, potentiae, dominationis, libidinis causa*; *Off.* 3.39, transl. M. Atkins).[39] Regarding the second point, Cicero tries to show, as we have indicated, that either the Epicureans are villainous (because they act badly when they know they will remain unnoticed) or they act well (because they abstain from performing bad actions even knowing their bad actions will remain unnoticed) and, consequently, they accept that bad actions should be avoided. The second point would mean that Cicero accuses the Epicureans of being inconsistent, the first point of being perverse. At the very beginning of the paragraph, he insinuates this, qualifying them 'as not bad people but not very subtle'.

As we have already suggested in passing, Plutarch wants us to see that Epicurus' refusal to respond actually reflects hypocrisy and shame in recognizing that he will commit illegal actions, shame that implies accepting that he will perform actions knowing they are bad; that is, that they are bad actions regardless of whether they remain hidden.

The considerations of Cicero and Plutarch strip the Epicurean sage of his defining characteristics: 'physiology' and prudence. One of the purposes of the former is to achieve what Epicurus calls, with an expression of his own convincingly interpreted by Erler,[40] a 'firm contemplation' (ἀπλανὴς θεωρία; *LM* 128) that discriminates and hierarchizes desires while explaining and dispelling those that have their origin in fears and vain opinions. The latter refers to all choice and avoidance of what Epicurus calls, with an expression also coined by him, a 'sober reasoning' (νήφων λογισμός; *LM* 132).[41] Cicero does not even mention the role of 'physiology' and prudence in the motivations and decisions of the Epicurean sage when analysing the Gyges passage. Nor did Plutarch do so while commenting on **T1**. Neither Cicero nor Plutarch capture the interesting conflation of theory and praxis that reflect the expressions 'firm contemplation' and 'sober reasoning', coined by Epicurus. They are obliged to do so, of course, because of their malicious identification of the Epicurean way of life with what tradition called a 'life of enjoyment' (βίος ἀπολαυστικός; see Aristotle, *EN* 1095b17).

None of the motivations that Cicero alleges for those who carry out bad actions knowing that they will not be discovered (see *Off.* 3.39, briefly commented on above)[42] are taken to be valid in the hierarchy of desires that the 'firm contemplation' of the Epicurean discriminates as fostering serenity, peace of mind and absence of pain. In other words, not only do these not constitute motivations of an Epicurean sage, but also they (especially the first three listed) are analysed by the Epicureans as vain desires aroused by fear, from which the Epicurean wise person has freed himself.⁴³ Epicurus knows that the polis establishes legal channels for its satisfaction. However, in his opinion, this in no way accredits them as constituents of *living prudently, honourably, and justly* [φρονίμως καὶ καλῶς καὶ δικαίως] on which he focuses pleasant living; that is, tranquillity (*LM* 132; *PD* 5). Hence, the actions derived from the motivations listed by Cicero, whether just or unjust, legal or illegal, hidden or in plain sight, do not correspond to those of an Epicurean sage. The honourable and just living of the Epicurean sage does not take into account the fear of the punishment of laws, as is the case with many of his fellow citizens, but rather abides by necessary natural desires that not only do not promote unjust actions but even cause actions authorized by the law to be disregarded.

Plutarch's interpretation of Epicurus' answer to the puzzle posited in **T1** assumes that the reason why the wise Epicurean does not commit crimes is the fear of being discovered and punished. Consequently, in Plutarch's view, as long as the Epicurean agent is certain that he will not be discovered, he will act illegally. As we have shown, a fundamental aspect of the malicious character of Plutarch's interpretation is the omission of the link that Epicureanism establishes between the study of nature and the actions of the sage. There is, though, another aspect that evinces his deficient interpretation of Epicurus' answer. Plutarch understands Epicurus' implicit reply in **T1** to be a rule of conduct ('whenever the Epicurean sage is certain not to be discovered, he will act unlawfully'). However, Epicurus' answer points precisely to the impossibility of giving a categorical answer such as 'yes, always' or 'no, never'. Perhaps the reason for this is that the question, despite its appearance, is too general, i.e. it does not determine the singular circumstances in which the sage must make the decision. We do not know the context of **T1**, and we also do not know whether Epicurus provided any examples. Attempts by interpreters to supply them have certainly proved controversial.⁴⁴ Epicurus, as we have shown above, stresses that unique circumstances constitute a fundamental ingredient of the Epicurean sage's decisions. In fact, none of the *Principal Doctrines* offers categorical rules of conduct and, not for nothing, Epicurus places prudence at the top of the doctrine (*LM* 132). In sum, Plutarch's interpretation of **T1** omits the two fundamental items of Epicurean ethics: 'physiology' and prudence, which clearly means leaving aside two decisive aspects of the Epicurean characterization of the sage.

4 Epicurus, Punishment and Plato

According to Plutarch, Epicurus does not think that one ought to restrain people from injustice by any means other than the fear of punishment (Plutarch, *Pleasant Life* 1104B; Us. 534). As far as we can see, it is difficult to place this remark in context from the texts of Epicurus that have come down to us. But if fear of punishment is the only means of preventing people from carrying out unjust actions or, more dramatically, criminal acts, that certainly cannot be the reason why the Epicurean sage does not commit unjust acts. First, this is because if a person is wise, he does not submit to fear. Second, it is because, even though Epicurus understands the notion of justice as a 'modality of usefulness', such usefulness cannot be understood solely in the individualistic sense of what is useful for oneself but rather always has a social dimension. The issue of punishment itself could be seen from a 'utilitarian' point of view, as long as it can be considered as a 'solitary and isolated experience', so to speak (i.e. when someone receives chastisement). Thus, punishment can be taken to be an evil by the offender due to the pain inflicted on him. By contrast, the chastisement considered as part of a social and legal system can be viewed as something useful or beneficial. Through a few punishments – the utilitarianist could argue – thousands of crimes might be avoided; thanks to the suffering of a few guilty people, the safety of many can be 'purchased'.[45] In other words, punishment is bad for the punished person but good for the social order, and if it is seen that way, there is a conflict of interest between the individual interest on the one hand and the general interest on the other. This account turns out to be helpful if considered from the perspective that it provides 'the greatest good for the greatest number of people'.[46]

Interestingly, in Plato's *Gorgias* the character Socrates maintains that punishment has an exemplary function that can help to avoid crime and is therefore valuable. The soul of the criminal – the argument runs – is full not only of disorder but also of infamy because of his license, luxury, insolence, and the intemperance of his deeds (*Gorg.* 525a3-5). It behoves the one who is 'rightly punished' [ὀρθῶς τιμωρουμένῳ] either to become better and profit from it, or to serve as an example to others (*Gorg.* 525b1-2) in order that they may fear and become better by seeing what he is suffering. Those who benefit by paying their penalty, both at the hands of the gods and of men, are those who commit crimes that admit of cure (*Gorg.* 525b6). For those who have committed curable crimes, then, the punishment is not exemplary but therapeutic. In other words, just punishment has as its goal to make the punished person better, to increase his human excellence and, therefore, his happiness or well-being (cf. 476b-477a; 478d-e).

But how helpful can this portentous Platonic passage be for understanding the function of (legal) punishment in the Epicurean society? Firstly, as we have already indicated, Epicurus does not support the idea that the gods are capable of, or interested in, punishing us. In fact, an Epicurean god is a blessed and indestructible entity having no troubles itself, nor giving trouble to anyone else. It is a self-sufficient entity that is not affected by any feeling (Epicurus, *PD* 1; this passage is paraphrased by Cicero, *ND* 1.45). Thus, if it really is a self-sustaining thing (as it is), it does not need anything else.[47] Moreover, there is nothing better than a person who has pious opinions about the gods, Epicurus claims, since if you are a pious person, you will be always fearless about death and understand that the limit of good things is both easy to achieve and to provide. Again, according to Epicurus this is a quite simple account: if one is suspicious about the matters of the myths (stories that can involve the view that the gods are perverse and powerful beings, interested in perturbing human life with threats and exhibitions of their power), one cannot remove feelings of fear and hence cannot attain peace of mind and happiness.[48]

We hold that Plato's view that punishment is suitable for the one who is *rightly* punished (either to become better and profit from it, or to serve as an example to others) could have inspired Epicurus. As Plato stresses, punishment can have a therapeutic function insofar as *just* punishment is for the sake of making the punished person better. Indeed, Epicurus does not say that punishment makes the person better, but he strongly suggests that the suspicion that one will not escape the notice of those assigned to punish bad actions works as a sort of chastisement for the offenders (*PD* 34-35). For Epicurus 'suspicion' [ὑποψία] is responsible for the fear of being caught committing an injustice (*PD* 34), but this view, we suggest, is once again trivialized and (perhaps consciously) misinterpreted by Plutarch when he states that Epicurus denies that one ought to restrain people from injustice by any means other than the fear of punishments (*Pleasant Life* 1104B; Us. 534). This is so because he takes justice to be the same for everyone (*PD* 36), but 'mere immunity from punishment gives no happiness'.[49] But the sage is the one who has already attained happiness. Thus, immunity of punishment is irrelevant for attaining happiness (which is the same as attaining wisdom, peace of mind and so on). This, we suggest, is probably a *desideratum* shared by any human being (after all, there is nothing to prevent anyone from becoming an Epicurean sage). If this is so, the burden of proof is not to be found in punishment, but in the way a person is able to get rid of his unfounded fears through Epicurean 'physiology' for the sake of achieving wisdom.

Now, can this Epicurean stance be understood in a utilitarian manner à la John Stuart Mill? We believe that the answer must be 'no', since what Epicurus and the Epicureans claim or suggest is that the interest of the individual must match with the social interest,[50] which immediately eliminates the very possibility of a conflict of interests.[51] The good of the individual *is* a social good. It is true that the study of nature creates strong and *self-sufficient* [αὐτάρκεις] people, who pride themselves on their own personal goods and not those of external circumstances (*VS* 45), but those persons live in mutual associations. Further, such self-sufficiency is clarified by Epicurus himself: when the wise person 'is brought face to face with the necessities of life, he knows how to give rather than receive – such a treasury of self-sufficiency has he found'. In other words, the sage's self-sufficiency also has a social dimension: it is self-sufficient because he can give his personal goods to those who need them more than he does (see *VS* 44).

If this is so, it follows that, given that the self-sufficiency of the wise person does not have an egoistic character but a generous social dimension, it is more understandable why the pleasant life (synonymous with a happy life) is supposed to be an 'honourable' life (*LM* 132; *PD* 5). Again, the pleasurable life of the Epicurean sage is not a life of pure personal, sensual pleasure, but a life in which living wisely and prudently is tantamount to living honourably, justly and pleasantly. In fact, the adverb 'honourably', so profusely used by Epicurus, along with the adverb 'justly' qualifies the life of the Epicurean sage in different terms from a simple attachment to the laws. Indeed, there are behaviours authorized by the law that do not correspond to the sage, such as 'being sordidly stingy' (*VS* 43) and in general the love of money (φιλοχρηματία; see Philodemus, *On Property Management* col. xvii 2-14, xxv 23-24).[52] Likewise, the expression 'living honourably' encompasses behaviours of the Epicurean sage that go beyond what is required by law in social relations, such as, giving and donating, friendship or philanthropy. This characterization of the life of the Epicurean sage does not, in our view, imply a tension between the relational imprint of the 'contractual' justice, circumscribed by the structure of mutual obligations, and the apparently intrinsic and personal scope of the expression 'living honourably and justly' in *LM* 132 and *PD* 5. We hold this is so because both cases fit, in an Epicurean view, into the purpose of human being's happiness.

Additionally, such 'fitness' has an interesting causal structure: on the one hand, the wise person living with justice requires the security [ἀσφάλεια] provided by contractual justice. It is precisely in this sense that a passage of Stobaeus (Us. 530) may be interpreted; there it is pointed out that the laws are established for the sake of the wise [χάριν τῶν σοφῶν], not so that they will not commit injustice but so that they will not suffer it.[53] On the other hand, by living honourably and justly the Epicurean sage at once strengthens his security and promotes the reduction of the causes of harm and being harmed, to the avoidance of which, as is well-known, the arrival of the pact and justice is orientated (*PD* 33). In fact, as we have already indicated, some Epicureans seem to have considered that a consequence of the universalization of Epicureanism would be the elimination of laws and penalties as unnecessary. This was so because, in an ideal but nonetheless possible scenario, if everyone became an Epicurean wise person no one would harm anyone and no one would be harmed. But while Epicurus may have considered this possibility, his 'political realism', as we argued extensively in chapter 3, led him to emphasize the need for laws to change as circumstances change (without that entailing a crude 'relativism').

5 The friendship and justice of the Epicurean sage and the gods

While examining the textual evidence that has come down to us from Epicurus' works, one can conclude that he seems to have thought of friendship as an essential condition for imperturbability (one of the stable pleasures). The benefit that it produces explains its origin, and such a benefit is produced in reciprocal relations. In fact, the existence of friendship presupposes a certain kind of reciprocal relationship, which can take place both at the individual level (in a relationship of intimate friendship between two people, for instance) and at the social level, where friendship can also be understood as the mutual respect people have for the covenants that guarantee communal life. That is probably why Epicurus goes so far as to say, in almost lyrically beautiful language and probably evoking the mysteries, that friendship 'dances around the world [οἰκουμένη], announcing to all of us that we must wake up to blessedness' (*VS* 52). Moreover, when Epicurus emphasizes that 'of the things that wisdom [σοφία] provides us for the blessedness of one's whole life by far the greatest is the possession of friendship' (*PD* 27), he is not only explicitly linking wisdom to friendship, but also suggesting that wisdom is a property of *every* human being (and that it is therefore not a strange, difficult or impossible possession to acquire). Epicurus may also be suggesting that friendship – understood as an intimate relationship of mutual trust – plays a decisive role in achieving the demands that make a person wise. Moreover, that crucial role of friendship does not occur only at the limited level of 'the community of Epicurean friends' but must be extended to the rest of society. According to Cicero, Epicurus and the Epicureans claim that friendship cannot be separated from pleasure, as is said about the virtues. This is so because a solitary life without friends is full of dangerous traps and fear. This kind of approach can help show how friendship can have an important social role in a political community.

Further, Epicurus seems to have suggested that reason itself is what advises us to make friends. Thus, friendship is closely related to our natural rational condition, the rationality that can make calculations regarding the future, and each person's expectation that pleasures will be acquired. In fact, without friendship one cannot secure a stable and long-lasting pleasantness in our life, as Cicero indicates (*Fin.* 1.67). Additionally, the wise rejoice at their friend's joys just as much as their own, while they also grieve as much for their pain. Thus, as rational people, the wise will have the same feelings for their friends as for themselves. This approach has a particular Aristotelian flavour in its conceptualization of friendship (see Aristotle, *EN* book 8), but it also explains why having a feeling of friendship based on and dependent on shared interests is crucial both for one to flourish and for the political associations we inhabit to thrive (Cicero, *Fin.* 1.66-68). In sum, friendship is an indispensable condition for happiness and, like justice, is a powerful means for achieving imperturbability. But friendship is also thought of as a sort of kinetic pleasure: the memory of a dead friend appears to Epicurus 'sweet' (Plutarch, *Pleasant Life* 1105E; Us. 213); it produces joy and ends by being a relief capable of counteracting the body's pains.

The Epicurean sage, like the Aristotelian and the Stoic wise person, is particularly concerned about self-sufficiency. However, the Epicurean sage's self-sufficiency does not impose on them a life that must be conducted in an environment devoid of law or formal political organization. If Stobaeus is to be trusted, the Epicureans maintained that the laws exist for the sake of the wise, even though laws are not there to prevent the wise from committing injustice but to prevent them from suffering it (Stobaeus, *Anthology* 4.143; Us. 530).[54] This testimony is relevant because it shows that the Epicurean sage lives within a political organization where injustice is indeed possible. In fact, the way to read Stobaeus' remark is not to assume that the wise person cannot be a victim of a crime, but that, if he does receive injustice in any way, the laws will compensate for the injustice received and 'do justice' by sanctioning the offender. As we have already pointed out in previous sections of this book, the Epicurean receptivity to legality must be understood to operate according to regional requirements. The law, or rather 'what is just' (meant to be a modality of usefulness), has a sort of 'local functionality', which explains why it is only valid locally, without this meaning a kind of crude relativism. The acknowledgement of the local functionality of 'what is just' does not at all lead the Epicurean sage to observe political reality with an attitude of hostile closure and stubborn disinterest.[55] As we will show in chapter 6, the Epicureans rather display pragmatism and a coherent adherence to the surrounding reality.

The relevance of friendship and justice, a recurring theme in some central parts of this book, can be seen with some clarity in Philodemus' cultivation of the Epicurean model of biography. He followed two such models: one, apparently of a Peripatetic sort, was neutral, informative and mainly elaborated from anecdotes; the other, typically Epicurean, aimed at highlighting the moral excellence of the person whose life is recounted, with extensive use of epistolary sources. Philodemus thus continues an Epicurean biographical tradition aimed at highlighting the exemplary behaviour of the master and his main successors, preserving their memory and safeguarding their doctrine.[56] It is a model centred on the 'imitation of Epicurus' which serves as an *exemplum* for the teaching and practice of Epicureanism.[57] It also acts as proof of the validity of Epicurean philosophy, i.e. that Epicurus, as Philodemus observes, 'obviously succeeded in imitating the blessedness of the gods in so far as mortals can' (*On Piety* 2043ff. ed. Obbink). If the 'imitation of Epicurus' and the 'becoming like god' that it conveys play a central role in Epicureanism, it is most interesting to note how in both doctrinal devices friendship and justice, the two ingredients of social life we have been discussing, are emphasized. In the preceding chapters we have shown how both in the Epicurean biographical tradition and in external sources, even hostile ones, the central role of friendship in the theory and practice of Epicurus and his successors is stressed.

Likewise, the Epicurean biographical tradition presents Epicurus and his successors as people who loved their poleis, respected their laws and institutions, their piety and worship; people, in short, who acted loyally, nobly and justly in their respective cities. This is undoubtedly an aspect of Epicureanism that, although the early and influential anti-Epicurean tradition tried to distort and ignore it, can be documented through sources outside the school, as we have tried to show in the previous chapter.

The two strands of Epicurean life mentioned above – friendship and justice – as confirmed both by the Epicurean biographical tradition and by external sources, occupy a special place in the Epicurean version of becoming like god. The reading of *PD* 1 leads one to conclude that the gods do not require help, protection or security and, consequently, friendship seems to be alien to them. Philodemus points out that this is not so: among the gods there is a form of friendship centred on relationships devoid of any element of usefulness; their friendship involves contact and takes the form of pleasant conversations and kindly gift exchanges. Philodemus points out that the gods can and should be able to converse with the gods, with whom they are friends, just as we do with friends. In his view it would be foolish to deny this; it would also mean depriving them of a source of indescribable pleasure.[58] Philodemus explains the basis of such pleasure in an illustrative and important passage in *On Frank Criticism*:

> **T2** although many fine things result from friendship, there is nothing so grand as having one to whom one will say what is in one's heart and who will listen when one speaks. For our nature strongly desires to reveal to some people what it thinks.
>
> Frag. 28, 1-12; transl. David Konstan, Diskin Clay, Clarence E. Glad, Johan C. Thorn and James Ware[59]

Epicurean theology makes room, as can be seen, for the becoming like god around friendship. Interestingly, Philodemus presents the memory of the dead friend as the expression of human friendship in which it is fully assimilated to the friendship between the gods. Any consideration of interest or utility between the deceased friend and ourselves is absent in these memories, and yet, as Philodemus observes, we experience towards him friendship in the highest degree of intimacy and affection [τῆς ἄκρας οἰκειώσεως] and, with it, great pleasure (Philodemus, *On the gods*, Frag. 83, 1-2, ed. Essler). As Armstrong observes, friendship for pure pleasure – the only one known to the gods – is exceptionally present in human beings in the memory of a deceased friend.[60] Perhaps this is why Epicurus can say that friendship is an immortal good (*VS* 78).

As in the case of friendship, *PD* 1 does not seem to leave room for justice in the Epicurean becoming like god, since '[w]hat is blessed and indestructible has no troubles itself, nor does it give trouble to anyone' (*PD* 1). Again, Philodemus clarifies the linkage insofar as in *On Piety* he points out that the happiness of the gods stems from their harmlessness [ἀβλαβία] towards everyone (*On piety* 2051-2, ed. Obbink). In this respect, too, the gods are to be emulated. As Obbink comments, Philodemus suggests human beings should endeavour as far as possible to make themselves harmless to everyone.[61] Such harmlessness is attained by piety; the pious and wise person is just and thus enjoys the greatest benefit from the gods.⁶²

As can be seen, the characterization of the Epicurean sage is derived from both the biographical tradition of the imitation of Epicurus and the becoming like god, and embraces the communal ingredient of life clearly represented by friendship and justice. It is perhaps not surprising, therefore, that the *hapax* φιλόκηπος, 'fond of a garden', does not appear in DL 10, devoted to Epicurus and the Epicureans, but in reference to Pyrrho.⁶³

6 Concluding remarks

This chapter began our discussion of the Epicurean sage by contrasting the Stoic and the Epicurean wise persons. In the characterization of the Epicurean sage that is drawn from this contrast, respect for laws and institutions, as well as a friendly attitude towards his homeland, plays an important role. Thus, in order to deepen this characterization, it turns out to be illustrative to study the Epicurean view regarding the traditional Greek topic of actions performed without witnesses. We reconstruct the Epicurean position from the study of two testimonies in the indirect tradition: a passage from the *Puzzles* of Epicurus transmitted by Plutarch (*Col.* 1127D), in which Epicurus asks himself whether the wise man will do things which the laws forbid if he knows that he will escape detection, and an important passage of Cicero (*Off.* 3.38-39) in which he presents his interpretation of the response of the Epicureans to the story of Gyges' ring. We show the difficulties raised by the interpretation of the above-mentioned passage from the *Puzzles* and then underline that the background of the story of Gyges' ring is Glaucon's specific contractual model, in which 'advantage' is the essential motivation of human nature (Plato, *Resp.* 359c3-5; Cicero stresses this link between advantage and contractualism in *On Laws* 3.13, 23). Now, in Epicureanism the issue of 'advantage' is framed by the emergence of vain desires and fears posterior to the establishment of the first covenants of justice. Next, we analyse Plutarch's and Cicero's interpretations of the position of Epicureanism vis-à-vis the ancient cliché of actions performed without witnesses, and place emphasis upon the fact that it constitutes a malicious interpretation that strips the Epicurean sage of his crucial defining traits: the study of nature and prudence. Cicero and Plutarch assume that the reason why the wise Epicurean does not commit crimes is the fear of being discovered and punished. So, in Cicero's and Plutarch's view, as long as the sage person is certain that he will not be discovered, he will act illegally; however, as we argued above, that cannot be the case. The adverb 'honourably', so profusely used by Epicurus, along with the adverb 'justly' qualifies the life of the Epicurean sage in different terms from the simple attachment to the laws. Indeed, there are behaviours authorized by the law that do not correspond to the life of the sage, such as 'being sordidly stingy' (*VS* 43) and in general the love of money. Likewise, the expression 'living honourably' [καλῶς ζῆν] encompasses behaviours of the Epicurean sage that go beyond what is required by the law in social relations, such as, giving and donating, friendship or philanthropy. We have also analysed several Platonic considerations on punishment and pointed out some affinities with the treatment of chastisement in Epicureanism, evincing again the important presence of Plato in Epicureanism (which does not mean that Epicurus or his followers agreed with Plato on everything, but rather that Plato was an important inspiration in some key themes of their political philosophy).

Finally, we have emphasized the role of friendship in achieving the demands that make a person wise and have argued that the crucial role of friendship does not occur only at the limited level of 'the community of Epicurean friends' but must be extended to the rest of society. We close the chapter by showing how two fundamental ingredients of community life – justice and friendship – are highlighted in two famous doctrinal devices of Epicureanism: the biographical tradition of the 'imitation of Epicurus' and the 'becoming like god'.

6

The Greek Poleis, Rome and Its Illustrious Epicurean Citizens

The slogans 'live unnoticed' and 'do not participate in politics', the inability to perform feats or contributions for the benefit of the community, and the mockery of great politicians of the past all clearly demonstrate the Epicurean disinterest in political communities to their philosophical adversaries. To be sure, this is a very diffuse image of Epicureanism, in which the ancient anti-Epicurean tradition converges with the philosophical historiography of the nineteenth century. As we have shown in the previous chapters, Cicero and Plutarch contributed to this critical picture by omitting central aspects of Epicurean philosophy in their writings. Indeed, none of the themes to which we have devoted the first three chapters are present in their considerations of Epicureanism. Something similar happens in the philosophical historiography of the nineteenth century, since the contemporary rehabilitation of the Epicurean political philosophy starts at the beginning of the twentieth century due to Falchi's and Philippson's works.[1]

Traditionally, the Epicureans are not only regarded as having a theoretical disinterest in political communities, but above all as having a practical disinterest in such matters which is translated into a refusal to participate in politics and a minimal interaction with society. But how reliable is this image of the Epicureans forged by their critics? If they omitted essential aspects of the Epicureans' political philosophy, it is reasonable to think that they were not interested in scrupulously reporting their lifestyle either. Exaggeration and the use of a melodramatic tone were typical rhetorical devices in the philosophical diatribes of antiquity, of which contemporary readers seem to have been fully aware. Furthermore, the opponents of the Epicureans refer only sporadically to public performances of the Epicureans to try to show that they represent a hypocritical and unimportant mode of behaviour that is inconsistent with their doctrine. This is another typical strategy of Hellenistic critical writing, which is not aimed at providing reliable information about a philosophical doctrine and the lifestyle of those who follow it but rather at repudiating it.

Although the figures of Epicurus and the founders of the Garden have maintained a strong presence throughout the history of Epicureanism, Epicurean philosophy, as Grimal rightly emphasized, was not a religion.² Grimal's observation is particularly interesting, since it seems to contrast in some ways with the advice of Epicurus himself, who, according to Hermippus' report, 'got into a bathtub filled with warm water, asked for unmixed wine, and drained the cup' (DL 10.16; transl. P. Mensch). After this, Epicurus urged his friends to remember his doctrines, and then he died. One might interpret these words of Epicurus as the recommendation of a teacher who is especially concerned with the fact that his doctrine remains intact in the sense of preserving, in a 'rigid' way, the fundamental principles of his philosophy. But it should not be forgotten that Epicurean philosophy understood as a 'way of life' places a strong emphasis upon the prudential aspect of how each person must deal with particular situations in life. Understood from this perspective, the injunction to 'not forget the doctrines of the master' does not necessarily mean that one cannot or should not adapt one's decisions in a prudential way to the concrete situation in which one finds oneself. Indeed, Epicureanism places prudence φρόνησις at the centre of its doctrine (*LM* 132); according to Epicurus, prudence is *more valuable* even than philosophy. In ancient philosophy, prudence is associated with an insightful attention to situations and the concrete circumstances of decisions and actions. The high Epicurean valuation of prudence seems to connote versatility, i.e. having the capacity to adapt if the concrete situation thus requires. In Epicurus' letters, for example, one can see how his message is tailored to specific addressees, people who are being initiated into doctrine or who are busy (ἄσχολοι; *LP* 84), such as the politicians Idomeneus and Mithras.³

Thus, a wise Epicurean person, or someone like a student or a busy person who is progressing towards wisdom, must be able to make a balanced judgement that allows for an appropriate outcome according to the vicissitudes the person is going through. It is natural to think, therefore, that the way of life of those who adhered to Epicureanism over more than five centuries, and in cultural spheres as diverse as the Greek cities and the Roman world, did not follow a single model. Social class, gender, political community and historical context must have led to different modes of belonging, adherence or proximity to Epicureanism, or so we shall argue. Also, the practice and teaching of philosophy and its social perception and assessment undoubtedly underwent changes over such a long period. To reduce the behaviour of those who cultivated Epicureanism over several centuries to a single pattern is a polemical strategy that involves much historical levity.

Our purpose in this chapter is twofold. On the one hand, we are concerned with examining various tenets by which the adversaries of the Epicureans ascribe to them a kind of apoliticism or anti-politics, and a disinterest in political communities. On the other hand, the chapter attempts to highlight various aspects of the interaction between Epicurus (and the Epicureans), and the societies in which they developed their philosophy. From both tasks, a richer, more complex, and more interesting picture of the Epicureans' political doctrine and lifestyle emerges than the one that their critics to a large extent managed to impose on later interpretations of Epicurean philosophy. The discussion proceeds as follows. In section 1 we show how Cicero, Epictetus and Plutarch base the apoliticism of the Epicureans on their refusal of the natural sociability of human beings. They derive this refusal from the egoistic hedonism they attribute to the famous Epicurean slogans 'live unnoticed' and 'do not participate in politics', as well as the maxims of conduct for the Epicurean wise person and their criticisms of great politicians of the past. However, we hold, these critiques do not deal with the context or meaning of these slogans, maxims and criticisms in the work and thought of Epicurus, and their polemical strategy involves a certain historical levity insofar as it does not include a scrupulous examination of the lifestyle of Epicurus and the Epicureans. Epictetus' objections are especially interesting in this regard, since he accuses the Epicureans of being 'antisocial' while also acknowledging that they do perform activities related to political life (thereby confirming indirectly that the Epicureans were involved in such activities).

In section 2 we highlight the interaction between Epicurus and Athens through the consideration of several testimonies dealing with his life and through the analysis of an exceptional document: Epicurus' testament. Such testimonies present Epicurus as a person who loved his city, respected its laws and institutions, participated in the worship of his city, and integrated his family relationships into the exercise of philosophy. To sum up, Epicurus acted loyally, nobly and justly in his city and recommended his friends to act in the same way.

In section 3 we provide a significant amount of evidence to show that, contrary to what Cicero, Plutarch and other ancient writers used to say about the Epicureans' disinterest in politics, there were numerous Epicureans, most of them belonging to higher class, involved in politics and in the life of their own poleis. They served as advisers of kings, distinguished diplomats, ambassadors, priests of the imperial and local cult, and even as prophets. We analyse heterogeneous documents related to different ancient cities. These include the *Vita Philonidis* (*PHerc.* 1044), recovered among the papyri of Herculaneum; brief inscriptions, both public and private, from different cities, and two exceptional epigraphic testimonies: the inscriptions on stone blocks that formed part of the great wall on which Diogenes of Oenoanda had Epicurus' doctrine engraved, and the inscriptions reproducing several letters addressed by Plotina, Trajan's widow, and perhaps also by Hadrian, to the Athenian Epicureans in the third decade of the second century AD.

Finally, section 4 is dedicated to examining some illustrious Roman Epicureans who were involved in the most important political events in Rome in the first century BC, and were also in one way or another related to Cicero. Those people have been the subject of numerous studies that make plausible their Epicureanism and the Epicurean imprint of various orientations and decisions in their lives. We shall limit ourselves to a brief presentation of three examples: Trebatius Testa, Pomponius Atticus and Cassius Longinus. We will complete our account with a brief reference to a work by Philodemus (*On the Good King According to Homer*), which is of special interest for the study of Epicureanism and politics. In section 5 we furnish some brief concluding remarks.

1 Cicero, Epictetus, Plutarch and the assumed apolitical attitude of the Epicureans

Cicero objects to the Epicureans that history remains mute in their arguments (*Fin.* 2.67). 'I have never heard,' he writes, 'Lycurgus mentioned in Epicurus' school, or Solon, Miltiades, Themistocles, or Epaminondas, all of whom receive due acknowledgement from other philosophers'. To this list, he adds a long enumeration of illustrious Romans, which practically covers the whole history of Rome. With a clear polemical purpose Cicero includes among those people the ancestors of Torquatus, the representative of Epicureanism to whom he recites the glorious past of Rome. 'Either you must denigrate their actions', says Cicero to Torquatus, 'or you must give up your advocacy of pleasure' (*Fin.* 2.67). As we have shown in the previous chapter, Torquatus replies that this is a false dilemma since he can perfectly well explain the heroic actions of his ancestors from the perspective of Epicureanism.

Epictetus and Plutarch express themselves in similar terms to Cicero. After referring to the Epicureans' denial of providence and the piety of the polis, Epictetus ironically declares that it was out of principles like these that our well-governed states have grown great, and that Sparta has become what is. Those who died at Thermopylae, Epictetus sarcastically points out, died because of doctrines like those of Epicureanism (*Diss.* 2.20. 26). Plutarch is also in the habit of opposing Epicureanism to the great contributions to Greek political life by non-Epicurean philosophers, especially by Plato and his disciples. Plutarch practically depicts the Academy as a school for the training of politicians in the political life of the Greek world (*Col.* 1126B-D). In *Live Unnoticed* he contrasts the figures of Epaminondas, Thrasybulus, Themistocles, Camillus and Plato to the uselessness of Epicurus and his followers (1128D, 1129B-C).[4]

Cicero, Epictetus and Plutarch therefore present Epicureanism as a philosophy entirely contrary to the motivations and actions based on the natural sociability of human beings who forged the history and greatness of Greece and Rome. In their view, Epicureanism is at odds with the ideals of Greece and Rome and with human nature. All of them emphasize that human beings are social by nature, something that the Epicureans deny. None of them mention evidence from the political philosophy of Epicureanism to support the idea that they challenge the natural sociability of human beings. They derive it rather from the egoistic hedonism which they attribute to the rules of conduct of the Epicurean wise, such as 'the Epicurean sage will not marry, will not have children, will not participate in politics, and will live unnoticed' (these are issues that are particularly prevalent in the indirect tradition). By omitting central elements of Epicurean political philosophy, the adversaries of the Epicureans find it easy to argue that Epicurean behaviour in fact *corroborates* the natural human sociability that their philosophy elsewhere denies. Epictetus offers the most eloquent version of this argument, which in Cicero, as we have already pointed out, adopts the figure that Lévy called 'l'éloge paradoxal'. Epictetus indicates that, just as it is impossible to remove the sexual desires of those castrated, so it is impossible to make human behaviours disappear entirely from human beings. Such, he continues, is what happens in the case of Epicurus. He, Epictetus insists, cut off everything that characterizes a man, the head of a house, and a friend, but failed in cutting off the desires of human beings. Thus, although he holds antisocial views (τὰ ἀκοινώνητα; *Diss.* 2.20, 16), Epicurus cares for others, has friends, writes, and wants his philosophy to be spread.[5] To be more precise, Epictetus rebukes Epicurus for the fact that, even though he intends to destroy the natural sense of fellowship that binds people together, he actually makes use of this sense of fellowship (see especially *Diss.* 2.20, 6). Consequently, Epicurus' own actions turn out to be the best refutation of his theory, whose universalization would entail the elimination of society (*Diss.* 3.7, 19-20). But what is especially striking in Epictetus' critique is his comment that Epicurus *does perform activities related to political life*; Epictetus would therefore not agree with the view that Epicurus and the Epicureans did not participate in politics or, in a more general way, in the real life of their cities (as claimed by the slogan 'do not participate in politics').

Cicero and Plutarch argue that the natural sociability of human beings makes dedication to politics the most fulfilling way of life. At the beginning of *On Republic*, written in a difficult political time, Cicero asserts the supremacy of the exercise of real politics over theoretical life (*De Re.* 1.2, 2-3). He addresses this remark against philosophers in general and even repeats the same expressions (*De Re.* 1.2, 2) with which the character Callicles in Plato's *Gorgias* mocked Socrates' dedication to philosophy. Nevertheless, the Epicureans are the main targets of his criticism. As Gilbert underlines, Epicureanism is the 'philosophical other' against which Cicero structured his arguments, literary *persona* and political/cultural self-representations.[6] But, according to Schofield, there is a more unsettling dimension of Cicero's position regarding Epicurean (and Academic) philosophy.[7] In Schofield's view, Cicero makes the assumption that establishing a philosophical foundation regarding the natural basis of justice that would put commonwealths on a firm footing and bring stability to cities requires pragmatism and authority, and that in this circumstance debate does not form part of the relevant methodology.[8] Cicero therefore considers that, in this context, the views of the Epicureans must be rejected *even if what they say is true*. However, he also states that the Epicureans do not know and have never wanted to know anything about the republic (*Leg.* 1.39).[9] Active involvement in political life, Plutarch writes in *Whether an old man should engage in public affairs*, 'is a way of life of a tamed social animal living in an organized society, intended by nature to live throughout its allotted time the life of a citizen and in a manner devoted to honour and the welfare of mankind' (791C; transl. North). Just as in Cicero, Epicureanism is the 'philosophical other' of Plutarch's ideal of life which he reaffirms in these writings about old age.[10] It is understandable that the contenders in philosophical diatribes are not excessively keen in presenting the adversary accurately. However, it is striking that Plutarch, an heir of Socrates and Plato, establishes a radical opposition between 'the ancients', to whom he ascribes his same ideal of life, and the attitudes he attributes to the Epicureans. Indeed, it suffices to look at the *Gorgias* –a Platonic dialogue that Dodds, following Schleimacher, described as *apologia pro vita sua* – to understand Plutarch's disproportion, as well as the facets of the figure of Socrates that Plutarch omits. In the *Gorgias* Socrates not only explicitly distinguishes himself from politicians (*Gorg.* 473e) and mocks great men of the past, such as Themistocles, Pericles and Cimon (*Gorg.* 519a), but he also defines himself as the *true* politician (521d) since, unlike these men, he seeks to transform desires and make men better through the care of the soul not in assemblies but in dialogue with each individual person (*Gorg.* 517b). Socrates' invectives against great Greek figures were continued by the Cynics and were present also in Theopompus. A central aspect of this tradition seems to have been the questioning of the moral character and motivations of great Greek characters. In Cynical literature, for example, a contrast is drawn between the figure of Heracles, their paradigm of good government, and a completely negative presentation of Alexander as a bad ruler, whom his flatterers would have ranked above even Heracles. Alexander is viewed by the Cynical tradition as a clear exponent of the vanity τῦφος of the tyrant, and is accused of being insatiable, ambitious and depraved (descriptions repeated later by Seneca).[11] Theopompus, one of the main historians of the fourth century, also seems to have delivered severe judgements on Greek politicians and figures to show the disparity between moral excellence and political and military success. He saw one example of this in Philip II of Macedon.[12]

Epicurus certainly criticized Epaminondas (Plutarch, *Col.* 1127AB), and apparently Miltiades and Themistocles (Cicero, *De Re.* 1.5; Plutarch, *Pleasant Life* 1097C). Plutarch notes, unfortunately without giving names, that Metrodorus mocked some wise men who tried to imitate Lycurgus and Solon and pretended to be legislators (*Col.* 1127B). In *On Property Management* col. 22, 10-48, Philodemus seems to refer to the rise among his Latin contemporaries of the fashionable *Exempla* and *Vitae* of great Greek and Roman militaries, politicians and men of action. Insofar as their lives reflect 'thirst for fame' (δοξοκοπία; col. xxii, 24) they produce, in Philodemus' view, a negative echo in the lives of those who read them.[13] Nevertheless, Philodemus, like Lucretius[14] and in accordance with Epicurus' views (discussed in chapter 2), in no way condemns the activity of any politician.

Plutarch was well aware of both the Cynical and Stoic literature already mentioned, as well as the work of Theopompus; but by presenting the Epicureans' criticisms of politicians of the past as an expression of their selfish apoliticism, Plutarch omits any kind of link to a tradition that could easily be traced back to Socrates, one of 'the ancients' *par excellence* in his estimation. The assessment of the motivations and ambitions of politics were, at least since Socrates, not marginal but inherent to the process of self-definition of philosophy in Greece. Cicero's and Plutarch's controversy with Epicureanism is a fundamental part of their defence of the assimilation of philosophy to the exercise of ordinary politics. Isolating Epicureanism from later Greek philosophy contributes to this purpose. There is, however, another argumentative procedure more surprising from today's methodological perspectives. Cicero and Plutarch absolutize the slogan 'do not participate in politics' as a principle of conduct of the Epicureans, but they do not dedicate a single line to the specification of which text of Epicurus it comes from and what its original context was. Diogenes Laertius (10.119) states that it was contained in the first book of *On Ways of Life* but offers no further information. The case of the slogan 'live unnoticed' is even more significant and, to some extent, more intriguing, since Plutarch devoted to it an entire treatise (*Live Unnoticed*) which does not contain the slightest information about its meaning or the text of Epicurus from which it comes. From this perspective, Plutarch's opuscule is especially disappointing, although very illustrative of how some topics in ancient thought were formed. Plutarch, in fact, not only does not provide any indication about the context of the expression 'live unnoticed' but almost makes it the appropriate motto for a hidden way of life by emphasizing to its perversity (*Live Unnoticed* 1128D-E). These are, certainly, characteristic rhetorical procedures in the philosophic diatribes of antiquity.

To do justice to Cicero and Plutarch, it must also be emphasized that both of them point out, albeit with clear polemical purposes, that the Epicureans acknowledge circumstances that imply reservations to the application of the slogan 'do not participate in politics'. Again, these pass over the context in which these ideas were inserted in Epicurus' work. The exceptions face in two directions: external circumstances and personal situations. The former (Cicero, *De Re.* 1.10. Seneca, *De otio* 3.29) perhaps encompass those exceptional circumstances in which the security of society, and with it that of the Epicurean community and the sage, are compromised, such as war or states of emergency in which law and order are threatened. In such cases, prudence and sober hedonic reasoning would advise political participation. Cicero mocks this approach, since in his opinion it falls prey to the absurdity of recommending political activity, especially in difficult situations, to those who lack any experience in it. This first type of exception could also become manifest in cases where circumstances put the Epicurean community at risk and encouraged some of its members to engage in politics to safeguard, for example, the life of one of its members or the assets and continuity of the school. Roskam favours this understanding of exceptional circumstance.[15]

According to Plutarch's testimony, the exceptions referring to personal circumstances seem to indicate that Epicurus would have advised certain people, avid due to their constitution for fame and honour, to devote themselves to politics rather than to abstain from doing so, since to abstain would mean for them greater turmoil and deterioration (Plutarch, *On peace of mind* 465F-466A;

see also *Col.* 1125C).[16] Plutarch replies that it could then be said that Epicurus recommends politics not to the most skilful, but to those who are incapable of leading a quiet life. But there is another, more specific, explanation for these kinds of exceptions. Perhaps it would not be about individuals eager due to their character for fame and honour, but people who already have fame and honour because of their lineage. In their case, not participating in politics would be more inconvenient than the opposite.[17] In addition to the exceptions mentioned above, there is another one recorded by Diogenes Laertius, who states that the Epicurean sage will pay court to a king (or rather will take care of him) when the occasion is appropriate (10.120).

The already indicated exceptions are illustrative of the weight that facts have in the Epicurean practical wisdom or prudence, as well as in the sober reasoning in which it is expressed. However, the documentary contribution of the just indicated exceptions, like that of Cicero's and Plutarch's considerations of the slogan 'do not participate in politics', is disappointing, since they do not provide information about the actions of Epicurus and the Epicureans in political communities. As mentioned above, a rarely quoted passage from Epictetus is evidence of the kind of information absent in these texts by Cicero and Plutarch. In a speech in which Epictetus attacks the Academics and the Epicureans[18] (an association that would probably have surprised the Epicureans), after referring to the antisocial opinions of the latter he writes:

> And then people who talk in this way go on to marry, and father children, and fulfil their duties as citizens, and get appointed to be priests and prophets! Priests of whom? Of gods who don't exist! And they themselves consult the Pythian priestess, to know her lies and interpret the oracles to others? Oh what colossal impudence, what imposture!.
>
> *Diss.* 2.20.27; transl. R. Hard

To be sure, the passage furnishes valuable information about striking public performances of Epicureans which, as we will show below, are confirmed by other sources. Two other discourses of Epictetus complement the information in the passage. In *Dissertations* 3.7, 1 a conversation is recounted between Epictetus and an Epicurean 'inspector' (διορθωτής).[19] *Dissertations* 1.19 contains remarks on the role of the priest of the imperial cult which, in a way, challenges the insults that Epictetus addresses to the Epicureans in the passage just quoted. One of his fellow citizens of Nicopolis, a city of special religious significance due to its imperial foundation, remarks to Epictetus that he wants to become a priest of the cult of Augustus. Epictetus asks him why he wants to incur such great expense, and he replies that he wants to wear a crown of gold and for contracts to be inscribed with his name when they are drawn up. Epictetus mocks this, and tells him that it would be preferable for him to crown himself with roses (*Diss.* 1.19.26-29). Two details are striking: on the one hand, it is evident from the conversation that the office of imperial priest required abundant resources, which presupposes that it was held by members of the upper classes. On the other hand, neither Epictetus nor his interlocutor appeal to anything resembling religious motivations for aspiring to the office of priest. The conspicuous motivation is honour, a natural aspiration of those who belonged to the upper classes of the polis. These are, as we shall see, relevant data when examining the testimonies concerning priests, prophets and other offices held by Epicureans in the poleis.

Plutarch, and especially Cicero, certainly knew more Epicurean politicians and prominent men than Epictetus. Some of these Epicureans, as is well known, were their friends. But when the authors polemically refer to Epicurean apoliticism, they remain on a rhetorical level and keep silent about the names and public actions of Epicureans whom they knew perfectly well. One could well apply a reproach that Cicero addresses to the Epicureans to Plutarch and Cicero: when they denigrate the attitude of the Epicureans towards the political communities, 'history remains mute'.

2 Epicurus and Athens: Life and testament

The way of life of those who adhered to Epicureanism over more than five centuries and in cultural spheres as diverse as the Greek cities and the Roman world did not follow a single model. Social class, gender, political community and historical context must have led to different modes of belonging, adherence or proximity to Epicureanism. In addition, the practice and teaching of philosophy, along with its social perception and valuation, undoubtedly underwent changes over such a long period.[20] To reduce the behaviour of those who cultivated Epicureanism over several centuries to a single pattern is a polemical strategy that involves historical levity.

The lives of those who called themselves 'Epicureans' and were recognized as such by their fellow citizens constitute the ostensible historical reality of Epicureanism in the Greek cities. Rather than reporting this reality, the opponents of Epicureanism were more interested in disqualifying the doctrine, and behaved in this respect somewhat like mute or malicious witnesses, especially with regard to the interaction between the Epicureans and their cities. As suggested in the previous chapters, the malicious interpretation of slogans such as 'live unnoticed' and 'do not participate in politics' practically denied such interaction. The opponents of the Epicureans only refer to it by sporadic examples when they can use them to criticize Epicurean philosophy or to show the alleged disagreement between Epicurean life and Epicurean doctrine. Obviously, no reliable picture of the interaction between the Epicureans and their cities can be derived from this interpretative approach. Fortunately, we have other more benevolent, reasonable and reliable sources at our disposal.

In *On Piety* (col. lii, 1512-1532), Philodemus notes that while some philosophers were exiled, persecuted and even condemned to death, Epicurus remained 'magnificently' [μεγαλομερῶς] in the city and was not even mocked by the comedy writers. Philodemus undoubtedly exaggerates here, since Epicurus was apparently parodied in several comedies.[21] However, he agrees with other authors (DL 10.10) on his central idea, namely that Epicurus loyally observed the cults of the city. Philodemus collects fragments of Epicurus' works and letters to show that he participated and recommended his friends to participate in Athenian worship, prayers, feasts, oaths and mystical cults. As we shall see, Epicurus' testamentary dispositions confirm his concern for maintaining familial ancestor worship. Philodemus also emphasizes that Epicurus' behaviour is based on respect for the laws of the city and on the piety implied by his own conception of the gods.[22] As Erler has shown, Epicureanism appropriates traditional religious practices and integrates them into a theology that helps those who observe them to cultivate their mortal identity.[23] In this respect, Epicurus' conception of justice and law did not alienate him from his city.

Epicurus shares in the rejection of two figures who represent contempt for the laws of the polis: the tyrant and the Cynics (DL 9.119). Indeed, love of country, concern for reputation ('insofar as this ensures that he is not despised'; DL 10.120a), care for patrimony, and concern for the future differentiate Epicurean life from the shamelessness, cosmopolitanism, mendacity and disinterest of the Cynics. It is not difficult to see that each of these Epicurean concerns entails immersion in legality and in the social relations and institutions that shape the polis. Clay highlighted a very significant example: Epicurus is the only philosopher we know who deposited his texts in the city's archive, the Metroon. Interestingly, Clay also underlines that Epicurus is the only Greek philosopher whose works are dated by the year of the eponymous archon in which they were written.[24] Diogenes Laertius (10.9-10) stresses Epicurus' love for his homeland (which he describes as 'indescribable'; ἄλεκτος) and his piety, as well as his good character and philanthropy, which earned him many friends. Even Cicero and Plutarch, fierce critics of Epicurus, support the latter views of Diogenes Laertius.

Epicurus' prolific correspondence evinces the plurality and heterogeneity of his friendships;[25] indeed, among Epicurus' friends there were influential politicians who were close (even very close) to Epicureanism, such as Idomeneus, a prominent politician of Lampsacus, and Mithras, Lysimachus' minister of finance who provided financial aid to the Garden. His homeland seems to have dedicated statues to Epicurus (DL 10.9), apparently with public funds. If Epicurus not only respected the cult of the gods, but also organized certain important aspects of his life and school according to the Athenian laws (laws regulating actions such as the legal mechanisms of inheritance), it is counter-intuitive and probably a rhetorical exaggeration to claim, as Plutarch does, that Epicurus and his disciple Metrodorus 'banished laws and forms of government', and thus consequently 'banished human life' (*Col.* 1127D).

Epicurus' will, quoted by Cicero (*Fin.* 2.101) and transmitted by Diogenes Laertius (DL 10.16-21), is a remarkable document that shows Epicurus' connection with the polis; it also provides an interesting example of the economic and legal relations between Athenian citizens and foreign residents.[26] The will links the Athenian legal system with a central theme of Epicurus' philosophy: the attitude towards death. Cicero emphasizes the fact that Epicurus is inconsistent in the act of making a will, since he maintains that death is nothing to us (Epicurus, *LM* 124-125) and what happens after it does not concern us (Cicero, *Fin.* 2.101). Warren supports Cicero and claims that Epicurus cannot justify from his philosophy the decision to leave a will. If Cicero and Warren were right (*quod non*, in our opinion), it seems that Epicurus' consistent position would be not to make a will. For his part, Warren concludes that Epicurus makes his will only to ensure the continuity of the Garden and because of his respect for the laws and customs, which he recommends observing for the sake of tranquillity.[27]

Now, Athenian law does indeed regulate the succession of property, but it does not make it compulsory to make a will; in other words, not making a will in no way entails breaking the law for an Athenian citizen. Consequently, one must ask why Epicurus prefers to make a will and not to die intestate. The analysis of the clauses of Epicurus' will allows us to glimpse some reasons and also to assess whether, as Warren claims, Epicurus' decision to make a will 'was determined not by his philosophical outlook at all'.[28] But before examining the clauses of the will, one should recall the significant facts that Epicurus had no children and that Hermarchus, Epicurus' successor, was not an Athenian and was thus unable to inherit.

The first interesting point that emerges from the will is that it does not, as Warren argues, have a single purpose. It features one of the fundamental motivations of Athenian inheritance law: to ensure the continuity of the cult of the family ancestors (DL 10.18). It also incorporates testamentary provisions to ensure the maintenance of Metrodorus' and Polyneus' children. Furthermore, it establishes provisions to ensure the dowry and the marriage of the latter's daughter and the emancipation of three slaves and a female slave (DL 10.19; 21). Additionally, Epicurus also incorporates several provisions aimed at the continuity and cohesion of the Garden, so that its members and the Garden itself are preserved in the most secure manner [ἀσφαλέστατον]. He also instructs his disciples to preserve his memory and that of Metrodorus after his death (DL 10.18), and places all his books in the hands of Hermarchus (DL 10.17; 21). Two details clearly show what we might term Epicurus' 'juridical zeal'. On the one hand, he goes to the unusual lengths of depositing a copy of the will in the city archive, the Metroon. In fact, it is the only private document deposited in the Metroon that we know of. Most likely, as Sickinger suggests,[29] the decision reflects a desire to shield the document with greater security than is provided by the usual deposit in private hands. As already noted above, Epicurus had no children and perhaps thought that succession claims might arise. On the other hand, he resorted to a legal manoeuvre to ensure that the administration and future decision on the succession of the Garden remained in the hands of Hermarchus. As the latter is not an Athenian, Epicurus appoints Aminomachus and Timocrates as universal heirs, two persons apparently unconnected with Epicurean philosophy, on condition that Hermarchus retains administration of the property and decides about the succession of the Garden.[30] The only property which is to pass to Aminomachus and Timocrates on Hermarchus' death is Epicurus' house in Melite, leading to the suspicion that the house was intended as a payment to Aminomachus and Timocrates for 'lending' their name in the will. It is not difficult to imagine that, if Epicurus had died without a will, nothing would have been in place to ensure that the purposes to which the clauses of his will pointed would have been considered by the heirs determined by law.[31]

The concern for the preservation of the Garden is not the only motive of Epicurus' will. Affection, friendship, gratitude, philanthropy, piety, to which we have referred above (and which occupied such an important place both in the Epicurean narrative and in the ideal of philosophical life), and respect for the social relations of the polis are motives acknowledged in the testament. If this is so, it seems excessive and probably erroneous to claim, as Warren does, that none of these motives can be justified philosophically at all because Epicurus holds that death is nothing to us and what happens after it is of no concern to us. It follows from this interpretation that, according to Epicurean philosophy, making a will is as incoherent as fearing death and Tartarus. However, the decision to make a will is consistent with the postulates of Epicurean philosophy concerning property and friendship;[32] and, once again, it also shows Epicurus' close attachment to his city.

The Epicurean sage, unlike the Cynic, is concerned with property and the future; he sees property and the security of the polis as a legitimate means of reinforcing tranquillity and minimizing fear (DL 10.120a; Epicurus, VS 41). In Epicurus' view, it is unnecessary to put one's property in common among friends because such an action implies distrust, and if there is distrust there is no friendship (DL 10.11). The goods of the Epicurean sage exist in the service of his security and that of those who philosophize with him. Philodemus, apparently reiterating the considerations that Metrodorus, 'with Epicurus' help', devoted to the administration of goods, points out that the Epicurean sage must be concerned with the security of friends *even* after his death. Thus, especially if he has no children, he should consider friends as children and appoint them as heirs (*On the Management of Property* col. xxvii, 5-9; *On death* col. xxiv, 10-17).[33]

To make a will is a singular act; it presupposes the acquisition and continuous possession of property. Epicurus' testament reflects the recognition his philosophy accords to the security provided by the polis and friendship and, above all, to the benefit resulting from both these things, which as we showed above is of enormous importance to Epicureans since it leads to a state of confidence [θαρρεῖν], of tranquillity [ἡσυχία], and of absence of fear [ἀφοβία] regarding the future satisfaction of needs. In making his will, Epicurus is aware that the fulfilment of his last wishes is exposed to fortune; in *LM* 131 he argues that, if one accustoms oneself to a frugal diet, one can optimise one's health, become diligent for the necessary activities of daily life, and dispose oneself in the best possible way when one relates to sumptuous things and prepares oneself to be 'free from fear before fortune'. Fortune, then, can sometimes have a devastating influence on one's life; but one way to neutralize it is to be able to eliminate fear, a crucial task in becoming an Epicurean sage and an idea that Cicero objects to in *Tusc.* 5.26. It is not the case that the Epicurean sage is completely free from the vicissitudes of fortune; strictly speaking, Epicurus claims instead that he is little favoured by it, but his reason provides him with the greatest and most valuable goods (cf. *PD* 16).

Epicurus trusts that his testamentary dispositions will be fulfilled and will have the intended consequences. The basis of his trust is the legal system of the polis, since the security of the polis has made his way of life and the Garden possible. No doubt Epicurus also relies on it to secure both the Epicurean life of his friends and successors and the dissemination of his writings and teachings, a central aspect of Epicurean philanthropy that is so amply evidenced by Epicurus' prolific epistolary activity (something which also reflects the interaction between the Epicureans and their cities). In this vein Clay[34] notes that Epicurus' preoccupation with dating his works is a symptom of his concern for his survival as a philosopher (cf. also DL 10.120).

3 Illustrious Epicurean citizens

The Thessalian Cineas represents a striking example of the interaction between the Epicureans and their cities which, as we shall show, recurs in different forms throughout the history of Epicureanism.[35] Cineas was an advisor to King Pyrrhus, who entrusted him with several diplomatic missions in Rome and Sicily. According to Plutarch, he was an excellent diplomat in peace negotiations. Plutarch records a dialogue between Cineas and Pyrrhus that had become famous, where Cineas ironizes Pyrrhus' boundless desires for power and exhorts him to abandon them and enjoy the pleasure of a quiet life (*Pyrrhus* 14). Though the texts are not entirely conclusive, this dialogue and the references to Epicureanism that Plutarch assigns to Cineas on his diplomatic missions to the Romans (*Pyrrhus* 20, 6) suggest that Cineas was an Epicurean.[36] The life of Philonides of Laodicea has similarities with that of Cineas, but in his case the attribution of Epicureanism is certain. Among the papyri recovered from Herculaneum there is a *Vita Philonidis* (*PHerc*. 1044), perhaps by Philodemus.[37] Philonides' efforts for his hometown and for the Seleucid court appear in his biography as an uncontroversial strand of his Epicurean philosophy and philanthropy. Philonides was ambassador and royal advisor to Demetrius I Soter, whom he won as a disciple and turned into a king renewed by Epicurean philosophy (apparently, Demetrius I generously supported the Epicurean community; *PHerc*. 1044, col. XII, 1-9, col. 27, 1-7). Several inscriptions at Eleusis show that Philonides belonged to an aristocratic family of Laodicea, whose piety and diplomatic activities he shared.[38]

Epicurus' life, will and letters, such as the one Batis (wife of Idomeneus and sister of Metrodorus) addressed to her niece Apia, show the integration of family relations in Epicureanism and confirm the involvement of women: Batis' prudence is compared to that of the master.[39] This letter is one of the most expressive testimonies of the presence of familial affection in the Epicurean community. The sending of letters among Epicurean friends seems to have been a common practice within Epicureanism to share and thereby neutralize the pain of those who are suffering.[40] A further example of the integration of family relations in Epicureanism can be seen in the *Vita Philonidis*;[41] the same is true of the iconographic and epigraphic testimonies relating to the Epicurean scholar Phaedrus, which also constitute eloquent proofs of the implication of Epicureanism in the life of Athens, and its links with Rome. Phaedrus belonged to a noble Athenian family: his son Lysiades was an exegete of the Delphic oracle and a magistrate [ἄρχων] of Athens. Three disciples of Phaedrus, Titus Pomponius Atticus (a friend often mentioned by Cicero in his correspondence), Appius Saufeius, and his brother Lucius Saufeius, also a friend of Cicero, dedicated statues to him in Athens. Phaedrus' daughter Chrysothemis honoured her father and his disciple Atticus, 'friend and protector', with statues in Eleusis. Inscriptions are also preserved in which the polis of Athens honours Lysiades and his sister Chrysothemis 'because of their virtue and wisdom'.[42] To these documents we must add a curious epigraphic testimony of family piety and Epicureanism. This is a funerary epigram from Orchomenus in Boeotia, from the second or first century BC, which honours an Epicurean from Sidon, Philocrates, buried next to his son. The epigram stresses the Epicurean education that Philocrates received from an early age, as well as his observance of Epicureanism and its transmission, and seems to suggest some involvement by Philocrates and the son lying next to him in the cult and festivities of the Charites in Orchomenus.[43]

The *Vita Philonidis* follows the biographical model of the *imitatio Epicurei* and focuses on the same features that are observed in Diogenes Laertius' biography of Epicurus. Philonides' love and services to the fatherland and his care [θεραπεία] for King Demetrius are organically framed in the *Vita Philonidis* by the example of Epicurean philanthropy. Philonides' biographer stresses, probably aware of his public career, that he lived philosophically, nobly and honourably, and received gratefulness and recognition from his fellow citizens and even from philosophers of rival schools (col. liii, 1-8).

There are a significant number of inscriptions from different places and centuries that attest to the political role of various Epicureans in their cities. The consideration of the epigraphic corpus mentioning philosophers in the Hellenistic period and later centuries (to which several scholars have notably contributed)[44] allows us to draw an important conclusion: the mentions of 'Epicurean philosopher' are by no means fewer in number than those of 'Stoic or Peripatetic philosopher', as might be expected from the tenets of the interpretive tradition we are questioning. Our knowledge of the services rendered by the Epicurean philosopher Apollophanes to his polis, Pergamon, does not come from Epicurean testimonies as in the case of Philonides. The source is an inscription from the gymnasium of Pergamum. What we can read in it is that the people honoured Apollophanes, the Epicurean philosopher, for his virtue and because in pressing circumstances he conducted the affairs of the city happily in Rome.[45] It is not possible to fix the exact date or the basis of the inscription, since from 133 BC Pergamum sent numerous diplomatic missions to Rome. However, as Arrayás has suggested,[46] it can be speculated that Apollophanes advised Diodorus on the mission of 85 BC. Unfortunately, we have no further news about Apollophanes' biography, although it can be assumed that, like Cineas and Philonides, he belonged to an influential family in Pergamum. The Epicurean Gaius Julius Amynas of Samos was also part of an embassy from his city. Amynas is known from three inscriptions in the Heraion of Samos. One of them reads that the council and the people honour Gaius Julius Amynas, nicknamed Isocrates, an Epicurean philosopher, for his many services to the city. The second inscription shows that he was a priest of the imperial cult and that he was part of the Samian embassy to Augustus around 6/5 BC. The third shows that he was 'a demiurge' of Samos in 6/7 AD.[47] In addition to the nickname 'Isocrates', it is striking that Amynas was a priest of the imperial cult. We know of several Epicureans who served as priests of local and imperial cults and even as 'prophets' [προφηταί]. In an inscription from Palaepaphos in Cyprus, dated between 15 BC and 14 AD, the city expresses its gratitude to one of its citizens, Plous, philosopher and archpriest of the *Theos Autokrator Kaiser Sebastos* (i.e. 'God Emperor, Venerable Caesar'). The text is damaged, but Haake suggests that Plous seems to be an Epicurean.[48] According to Athenaeus (*Deipnosophists* V 215b-c), the Epicurean philosopher Lysias of Tarsus was elected 'crown-bearer' [στεφανόφορος], i.e. priest of Heracles, a magistrate entitled to wear a crown at an official activity. At the end of his duties, he refused to leave office and became tyrant of Tarsus. Lysias probably lived in the first half of the first century BC or perhaps somewhat later. Another Epicurean, Aristion, is also believed to have become tyrant of Athens in the first century BC after having been ambassador of Mithridates VI to the Greek cities (unfortunately, the ancient historians' explanations of Aristion are confused).[49] Moreover, in an inscription from the island of Amorgos, probably from the first century BC, Theocritus, son of

Aresteias, appears as an Epicurean philosopher among the musician-dancers [μολποί] of Aigialeia. The latter make a 'votive dedication' for the health of the archpriest (a kind of 'chief priest': ἀρχιερεύς) Gaius Julius.[50] His inclusion among the μολποί clearly suggests that Theocritus belonged to the local aristocracy.

From Didyma (near Miletus, nowadays Turkey) comes an inscription, of uncertain date, in which Philidas, son of Heracleon, appears as an Epicurean philosopher and 'prophet' [προφητής]. This office was elected by lot from candidates nominated by the five *demoi* of Miletus. The office entailed duties that required heavy expenditure financed from their own resources. Philidas must have belonged to one of the leading families of Miletus, from which in Roman times most of the prophets came.[51] The case of the Epicurean Aurelius Belius Philippus caught Smith's attention: an inscription from Apamea, in the Syriac Orontes, mentions Aurelius Belius Philippus as a priest of Bel and head of the Epicureans in Apamea. In Smith's opinion, the inscription may date from Hadrian's time, although he considers a later date, perhaps in the first half of the third century AD, to be more probable.[52] The temple of Zeus Belus in Apamea was an important oracular sanctuary, so we would be dealing with another Epicurean prophet.

Heraclitus, son of Heraclitus, is mentioned in a first century AD inscription from Rhodopolis, which states that the council and people of the city honour him and thank him for his deeds and donations with an image and a statue. The inscription states that he was a priest of Asclepius and Hygieia, a physician, historian and author of philosophical poems. The inscription also reads that he was honoured by many cities and by the Epicurean philosophers of Athens, suggesting that he was an Epicurean.[53] Furthermore, through Lucian (*Alexander or the False Prophet* 25), we know of an Epicurean philosopher named Tiberius Claudius Lepidus from the time of Marcus Aurelius (second century AD), who appears on an honorific inscription from Amastris as archpriest of Pontos and president [ἐπιστατής] of the polis, a rather honorific title.[54]

Like the Epicureans mentioned above, Diogenes of Oenoanda must have belonged to the upper class of Oenoanda in the second century AD and probably held some honorary office. He certainly had the influence and resources to have Epicurus' doctrine carefully engraved on a wall of more than 250 square metres in the agora, the remains of which constitute, in Haake's words, the 'empress of Greek epigraphy'.[55] It is ironic that this honour should fall to the public exposure, precisely through one of the typical means of propaganda of the official texts of power,[56] of a philosophy whose attitude to the polis was traditionally condensed in the motto 'live unnoticed'. Diogenes records his own condition and justifies his purpose in erecting the wall: he is old, in poor health and has lost a son.[57] However, Diogenes represents the opposite image to that of the discontented old man anguished by death described by Lucretius (*RN* 3.955-63; see also 3.931-42 and 1003-1010). He is grateful for his existence and wants to say goodbye by philanthropically helping his fellow citizens, foreigners and future generations (on this specific point see the description of the old age of a 'virtuous Epicurean' in Philodemus, *De electione* col. xxi, 2-22).[58] He wants to publicly exhibit the remedies of salvation which he himself has experienced and which have enabled him to free himself from vain desires and fears. Diogenes stresses that he does not engage in politics, but seems to take into account usual accusations of inaction [ἀπραξία], futility and parasitism of the opponents of Epicureanism, and stresses that he acts (fr. 3, I, 4-7), thus suggesting that he considers his work more profitable for the polis than the actions of politicians.[59] Interestingly, Erler also points out that Diogenes' action is an example of 'true politics' and, in his view, extends the agenda of the Socrates of Plato's *Gorgias* (517b, 521d).[60]

Diogenes' action is undoubtedly unique, but it shares several characteristics with the public actions of the Epicureans we have described. He belongs, like them, to the upper class. The public activity of these Epicureans, rather than being the result of political ambition and the struggle for power, which the Epicureans rejected, seems to stem from membership of prominent families. In fact, it mainly took the form of diplomatic, advisory and consultative functions, and the holding of honorary religious offices. Nor is Diogenes' public action motivated by political ambition: as in the *Vita Philonidis*, the alleged motivation is philanthropy and utility to the polis. The paucity of the testimonies on the public actions of the rest of the Epicureans mentioned does not enable us to know their justifications, though they were presumably similar to those of Diogenes and Philonides. None of them seems to have seen any contradiction between their actions and Epicurean philosophy, nor does Epicurus seem to have perceived any such problem when making his will. The epigraphic testimonies reflect, as we have noted, the commonly accepted norms of the polis. Those that mention Epicurean philosophers suggest that such a qualification was neither demeaning nor perceived as a disqualifying condition for ambassador, royal advisor, priest or prophet.

At the beginning of the last section, we pointed out how Epicurus' testament allows us to highlight multiple aspects of his connection with Athens. To conclude this section, we will refer to several inscriptions that also concern the succession process of the Athenian Epicurean community and which are, because of the characters involved, not of minor importance.[61] In 125 AD the

Emperor Hadrian sent a letter in Greek to the Epicureans of Athens, partially preserved in a fragmentary inscription, in which he reminds them of previous concessions and responds to their latest requests. The letter, which some interpreters believe is not from Hadrian but from Trajan's widow Plotina, refers to an earlier epistolary exchange that is also preserved in inscriptions. The Epicureans of Athens had asked Plotina to intercede with Hadrian and grant them the right to make wills and to choose as their successor either a Roman citizen, as was the custom, or a Greek. Plotina petitioned Hadrian on behalf of the leader of the Athenian Epicureans, Popillius Theotimus, whose son would later become archon of Athens in 155/156 AD (curiously enough, the son of the Epicurean scholarch Phaedrus also became archon of Athens). Hadrian granted the request, and Plotina wrote to the Athenian Epicureans to tell them the good news, and she went into great detail about how they should proceed in the selection of a successor so as not to make the mistakes of the past.

The language of Plotina's letters denotes familiarity with the Epicureans of Athens and with Epicurean doctrine. The editors agree that Plotina uses clearly Epicurean terms and ways of thinking. Plotina shows a great appreciation for Epicureanism and an interest in securing the future of the school. Follet's reconstruction of the end of Hadrian's letter is extremely interesting. In his opinion, Hadrian states: 'we are as proud of our fatherland … as we are of the school of Epicurus'.[62] This proposition, like the attribution of the letter to Hadrian, is controversial. However, the correspondence, seen as a whole, reveals, in addition to Plotina's proximity to Epicureanism, the connections of the Athenian Epicureans with the core of imperial power and their effectiveness in defending the interests of the Epicurean community. Such connections were not alien to Epicurus (cf. Plutarch, *Col.* 1126C) nor Philonides (though certainly their links to political power were more modest); nor, presumably, were they alien to the Epicureans mentioned in the epigraphic testimonies of the cities to which we have referred.

4 Cives Epicurei

In the preface to *Tusculan Disputations* 4 Cicero points out that the first books of philosophy in Latin were written by the Epicurean Gaius Amafinius, and that after him many rival Epicureans wrote a multitude of works and 'have occupied all of Italy' (*Italiam totam occupaverunt*; *Tusc.* 4.6-7). According to Cicero, the Epicurean doctrine was successful among the multitude [*multitudo*] and the unlearned [*indocti*] since it was easy to learn, because they were enticed by the coaxing charms of pleasure, or even because nothing better had been offered to them (*Tusc.* 4.7). Cicero excludes Epicureanism from the category of 'true and elegant philosophy' [*verae elegantisque philosophiae*] which originated with Socrates and was preserved among the Peripatetics, the Stoics, and the Academics (*Tusc.* 4.6). He includes himself among the latter, so that in the preface to *Tusculan Disputations* 4 he promotes himself as the representative in Rome of the true and elegant Greek philosophy, as opposed to the preceding success of the clumsy works of Amafinus and his Epicurean *aemuli* (*Tusc.* 4.6; see also *Fin.* 2.12). Cicero does not exaggerate when he speaks of the early spread of Epicureanism in Italy. However, the information he gives at the beginning of *Tusc.* 4 is scanty, as he only refers to the works of Gaius Amafinius and his anonymous *aemuli*.[63] Certainly, Alcius and Philiscus already taught Epicureanism in Rome in the second half of the second century BC, as later M. Pompilius Andronicus did, both in Rome and in Campania, where Siro and Philodemus also taught.

To be sure, the best-known work of Roman Epicureanism is Lucretius' *On the Nature of Things*, but two other Epicurean authors, D. Catius Insuber and Egnatius, also wrote works with the same title. Rabirius is another Epicurean writer in Italy from the first half of the first century BC. The presence of Epicurean teachers and authors in Italy is early, and their activity continued throughout the first century BC. The same can be said of the involvement of Roman politicians with Epicureanism, the first of whom we know is Titus Albucius. Albucius, a *perfectus epicureus* according to Cicero, belonged to a senatorial family and was praetor in 107 BC. After a trial for *concussio*, i.e. an illegal exaction of taxes he was condemned to exile in Athens, where he had already travelled as a young man to study philosophy, a practice that would spread throughout the first century BC among the Roman upper classes. Cicero, Atticus and Lucius Saufeius, for example, studied in Athens with the Epicurean scholar Phaedrus. Albucius is the first of a long list of Roman politicians linked to Epicureanism. Momigliano began the prosopography of these politicians in a review of Farrington's *Science and Politics in the Ancient World*. In Farrington's view, *Tusc.* 4. 6-7 (and *Fin.* 2.44) provides evidence that Epicureanism constituted in Italy a 'mass movement of lower-class people discussing among themselves the undistinguished writings of their plebeian school of thought'.[64] Momigliano countered with the argument that Epicureanism actually spread among the upper classes of Rome, a thesis shared by most later interpreters.[65] Castner, Benferhat, Gilbert, Valachova, Volk and Roskam have continued the prosopography begun by Momigliano without reaching a unanimous list of Epicurean politicians.[66] The reasons are understandable. Firstly, we are not dealing with the cultural and social sphere of the polis, nor with philosophers or professors, but with members of Roman society immersed in specific social and political practices in which it is difficult to determine the scope, or truth, of their association with Epicureanism.[67] In fact, the traditional absolutization of the slogans ascribed to the Epicureans ('do not participate in politics', 'live unnoticed') has led some interpreters to see the adherence of the Roman politicians to Epicureanism as mere frivolity or as subject to a complete separation of life and doctrine. Secondly, it is hard to prove the dependence of Roman politicians' affiliations, decisions and justifications on their presumed Epicureanism: even if we have evidence, speculation is always necessary. As we have already underlined, Epicureanism is too general in its approach to offer unambiguous guidelines for behaviour in particular situations. Precisely by placing prudence at the centre of its doctrine (Epicurus, *LM* 132), it implies a flexibility that does not exclude the conduct of its followers in accordance with the *mos maiorum*.[68] The difficulties indicated above show that the association of Roman politicians with Epicureanism must be decided in detail on a case-by-case basis, as Gilbert has highlighted.[69] Fortunately, there is considerably more information about their political actions than there is about the Epicureans of the Greek cities. Illustrious Epicureans were involved in the most important political events in Rome in the first century BC, and were in one way or another related to Cicero. They have therefore been the subject of numerous studies. The elements gathered together make their Epicureanism and the Epicurean imprint of various orientations and decisions in their lives plausible. We shall limit ourselves to a brief presentation of three examples: Trebatius Testa, Pomponius Atticus and Cassius Longinus. We will complete our account with a brief reference to a work by Philodemus (*On the Good King According to Homer*), which is of special interest for the study of Epicureanism and politics.

Trebatius Testa was one of the most renowned jurists of his time. He began his career under the protection of Cicero, who recommended him to Caesar. Trebatius joined Caesar in Gaul in 54 BC. In a letter from February 53 Cicero tells Trebatius that he knows he has become an Epicurean, and reproaches him that being an Epicurean contradicts his status as a politician and jurist (*Fam.* 2.12 1).[70] We do not know how Trebatius replied, but several facts in his biography highlight the arguments by which an Epicurean could have responded to Cicero. Trebatius did not want to pursue a political career (in fact he refused the office of military tribune offered to him by Caesar in 54, which annoyed Cicero).

However, he was able to make the most of his talent as a jurist and became Caesar's adviser and *familiaris*. Trebatius, as Benferhat points out, got through the civil war without compromising himself or becoming a victim.[71] He was also valued as a juriconsult by Augustus. It could perhaps be said that Trebatius, without aspiring to power or office, enjoyed fame and prestige, which provided him with security until his death in his eighties. In the aforementioned letter of February 53, Cicero is particularly emphatic in questioning how an Epicurean could devote himself to law. It is one of Cicero's anti-Epicurean arguments that most clearly reveals his omission of the central tenets of Epicureanism, for, as we have shown, the Epicureans developed a sophisticated defence of justice and law. One of the testimonies of Trebatius' activity as a jurisconsult reflects just the kind of argument one would expect from an Epicurean jurist: the insistence on the *utility* of law. When Augustus consulted jurists on whether the use of codicils was in accordance with the *ratio iuris*, Trebatius convinced the emperor that it was by claiming that, in effect, the codicil was most useful and necessary for the citizens [*utilissimum et necessarium hoc civibus esse*].[72]

Titus Pomponius Atticus belonged to the ancient and illustrious *gens Pomponia* and was one of the wealthiest Romans of his time. He was a banker, landowner, publisher, and was associated with the most prominent members of the Roman elite. These are certainly not the kind of biographical traits usually associated with an Epicurean. For some interpreters they are consistent with only a superficial adherence to Epicureanism.[73] Nepos wrote a biography of Atticus, and Cicero includes him several times in his philosophical works. A large volume of letters addressed by Cicero to Atticus has also survived. From this literature no clear picture emerges of Atticus' Epicureanism. Perhaps this is because Atticus himself was involved in the elaboration of his own image, for he was not only a friend of Nepos and Cicero but also their editor.[74] The epistolary genre of antiquity also responds to particular codes that call for caution in assessing the evidence it provides.[75] As Benferhat and Gilbert have pointed out, Atticus' presence seems to be familiar in certain texts, but at the same time he remains absent, 'masked' as it were.[76] Nevertheless, Cicero's dialogues and correspondence contain elements that make Atticus' Epicureanism plausible. He studied with the Epicurean scholar Phaedrus and was closely associated with his successor Patro and the Athenian Epicurean community at large, which he supported financially. Cicero's correspondence shows that Atticus was well acquainted with Epicureanism. It also highlights how their respective philosophical convictions played a key role in the epistolary exchange around the turbulent political events of the time. Atticus' life has characteristics that can be reconciled with an Epicurean orientation: he did not opt for the *cursus honorum* and skilfully and courteously declined various offers of office. He stayed away from political involvement, but was a shrewd adviser, private *procurator* and generous benefactor of politicians and relatives of politicians belonging to distinct factions. His immense resources and the extensive networks woven by his interests, as well as an extraordinary cultivation of friendship,[77] seem to have enabled Atticus to cope with very turbulent times, preserve his security, and even increase his fortune and die an octogenarian, like Trebatius. The testimonies agree on his love of his studies, the Greek language, and culture, and emphasize his affable and simple way of life.

If Atticus represented what Benferhat calls 'neutralité vigilante', Cassius Longinus played a leading role in one of the major political events of the first century BC: the assassination of Caesar in March 44.[78] Between December 46 and January 45 Cicero and Cassius exchanged a series of letters in which they discussed political events and their respective philosophical convictions.[79] Cassius recognizes himself to be, and is treated as, an Epicurean, and Cicero does not miss the opportunity to address several anti-Epicurean arguments to him. There is one, which we have analysed above, which is of particular interest due to Cassius' response. Cicero refers to their common Epicurean friend Pansa, and says that both the latter's noble deeds and those of Cassius himself prove that they are both better than the egoistic hedonistic philosophy they subscribe to. Cassius' response is remarkable for the knowledge he depicts of Epicurean doctrine. Cassius complains about the deficient interpretations of Epicurus by Amafinius and Catius, quotes Epicurus' *PD* 5 in Greek, and makes Cicero see that his attempt to undermine the compatibility of pleasure, virtue and justice is based on a deficient and biased understanding of Epicureanism. Cassius stresses that living pleasurably and attaining tranquillity is not in contradiction with living justly and nobly, but implies living justly and nobly (*Ad Fam.* 216.19). According to Seneca (*Ep.* 83, 12), Cassius drank water throughout his life. He was a great military man, and that is probably why, after supporting Pompey, he obtained Caesar's pardon and seconded him, perhaps convinced that he represented a hope for peace and tranquillity, values dear to an Epicurean.[80]

As stated above, it is hard to prove the dependence of Roman politicians' decisions on their presumed Epicureanism. We are in the same situation, despite some famous interpretative attempts,[81] with Cassius' decision to kill Caesar, given the link between Caesarism and Epicureanism that some interpreters maintain. This link, as already noted in Momigliano's review of Farrington,[82] has played an important role in the prosopography of Roman politicians linked to Epicureanism. It has also influenced the interpretation of Philodemus' *On the Good King According to Homer*, as some scholars, such as Grimal,[83] have argued that it represents a defence of Caesarism. This work is dedicated to Piso just as Philodemus' *Rhetoric* is dedicated to Pansa, another Caesarist.

However, the purpose of *On the Good King According to Homer* is more general. This treatise of Philodemus seems properly to constitute an Epicurean contribution to the literary genre of the Hellenistic treatises on kingship [περὶ βασιλείας]. Most Hellenistic philosophical schools contributed to this literary genre. Also, among Epicurus' works, one is entitled *On Kingship* (DL 10.28).[84] The Hellenistic treatises περὶ βασιλείας do not deal with the different forms of government, nor do they try to defend monarchy as the best form of government. They expound on a good king's qualities, virtues and conduct. Philodemus uses Homer for this purpose. According to him, participating in politics [πολιτεύεσθαι] includes the following activities: leading the state, giving advice, serving as an envoy, and being experienced in such things as laws and decrees (*On Rhetoric* 3, ed. Hammerstaedt, col. xa, 1-6) and administering the state (col. xia, 17-24). It is easy to see that the activities of the Epicureans mentioned in the present chapter are included in Philodemus' enumeration. However, Philodemus insists in this same work that politics constitutes a specific domain with its own characteristic activities. Politics and philosophy move in different terrains. Politics, in his view, is based on experience and talent. Philodemus polemicizes against the Stoic Diogenes of Babylon who, according to Philodemus, does not grasp the autonomy of politics. The Stoics maintain that politics and philosophy are connected and, consequently, claim that only the Stoic sage is a good statesman.[85] The position of Philodemus and Epicureanism in general does not imply the absolute disqualification of politicians entailed by this Stoic thesis. The recognition of the autonomy of politics allows Philodemus to defend politicians from the attacks of Diogenes of Babylon.[86] The question then arises as to how the Epicurean philosopher can be useful and advise the ruler. Philodemus' *On the Good King According to Homer*, perhaps like Epicurus' *On Kingship*, appears to provide an answer to this question. Although philosophy and politics are two different fields with their own features and operating modes, philosophy can improve the moral character of the ruler and thus notably contribute to better government, which is in the interest of the ruler, the ruled and, ultimately, the Epicurean sage and the wider Epicurean community. In fact, as we have shown, the *Vita Philonidis* (*PHerc.* 1044) highlights Philonides' contribution to the good government of king Demetrius, and the latter's support for the Epicurean community. As observed by Fish, it could even be argued that the Epicureans saw in the figure of a monarch enlightened by Epicureanism an exceptional example of security, provided by the exercise of power.[87]

Philodemus points out in two parallel passages of *On Rhetoric*[88] that philosophy can represent for a politician a significant contribution to make him 'a more vividly and energetically good man' and will make a sky-high [οὐρανομήκη] difference for the better. This is not a personal opinion, for Philodemus introduces it as the opinion of 'us', i.e. the Epicureans. Moreover, as Armstrong has indicated, both passages echo approaches by Metrodorus.[89] The virtues recommended to the monarch in *On the Good King According to Homer* are practically those of the Epicurean sage. Their result is also similar: on the one hand, the stability [εὐστάθεια] of the sage (on this point see chapter 2 above); on the other, a stable monarchy that Philodemus contrasts with a despotic regime based on terror (col. xxiv, 17-18). The main quality of a good monarch is prudence. Philodemus stresses the following virtues of the ruler: mildness [πραότης], equity [ἐπιείκεια], gentleness [ἡμερότης], indulgence [συγγώμη] and benevolence [εὔνοια] (col. xxiv, 6-18, col 25, 11-19). The inclusion of equity is very significant as it is consistent with the Epicurean conception of laws. For Epicurus, as we have already shown, laws are just insofar as they are useful, and equity certainly complements the law in order to achieve justice.[90] Philodemus argues that philosophers can also be of great help to their homelands by teaching the young to obey the laws, such laws having been established for their security. As already indicated in chapter 3 (section 3), Philodemus states that it is also necessary to teach children never to touch injustice, just as they are taught never to touch fire since both injustice and fire are 'destructive by nature' (ὀλέθριοι φύσει) (*On Rhetoric*, PHerc. 1078/1080, fr. 13.9–22, 2.155, ed. Sudhaus). Philodemus' *On Rhetoric* and *On the Good King According to Homer* thus adds to the defence of positive law, pragmatism and moderation, derived from Epicurean study of nature, to paint a picture of the interaction of Epicurus and the Epicureans and their political communities that is far more complex and interesting than the one put forth by his opponents.

5 Concluding remarks

In this chapter we have tried to answer the question 'how apolitical were Epicurus and the Epicureans'. We use the term 'apolitical' in a broad sense to refer to political participation and social interaction. We first show how Cicero, Epictetus and Plutarch attribute to the Epicureans a theoretical and practical disinterest in political communities that translates, in their view, into a refusal to participate in politics and minimal social interaction. Their argumentation is highly rhetorical, as is usual in the philosophical diatribes of antiquity. Cicero, Epictetus and Plutarch base the apoliticism of the Epicureans on their refusal of the natural sociability of human beings. They derive this refusal from the egoistic hedonism which they ascribe to famous slogans ('live unnoticed', 'do not participate in politics'), from the precepts of conduct of the wise Epicurean, and their criticisms of great politicians of the past. However, they do not deal with the context or meaning of these slogans, maxims and criticisms in Epicurus' work, thought and life. The argumentation of Cicero, Epictetus and Plutarch ignores the political approaches of the Epicureans and relegates the assessment of the motivations and ambitions of politics which, at least since Socrates, was not marginal but inherent to the process of philosophical self-definition in Greece. For Cicero and Plutarch, dedication to politics constitutes the most fulfilling way of life, and so the Epicureans' conception of the exercise of politics is the antipode to their conviction. The polemical strategy of these adversaries of Epicureanism, we state, involves historical levity, since they were not interested in scrupulously reporting the Epicurean lifestyle but simply in dismissing it. In sections 2, 3 and 4 we have been concerned precisely with presenting heterogeneous testimonies of the lifestyle of Epicurus and of numerous Epicureans that refute the apoliticism that has traditionally been attributed to them. First of all, we have shown how the testimonies about Epicurus' life and his testament do not paint a picture of a person shut away in the Garden and isolated from the life of Athens, but of someone who, while refusing to participate actively in politics, respected the laws and institutions of the city, participated in its worship and piety, integrated family relationships into the exercise of philosophy, and cultivated numerous and heterogeneous friendships, including with influential politicians. Furthermore, on the basis of Epicurean texts and epigraphic documents from various Greek cities, we have shown how numerous Epicureans belonging to the upper classes served as advisers of kings, distinguished diplomats, ambassadors, priests of imperial and local cults, and even as prophets, without their status as Epicureans disqualifying them from such functions. Finally, we present several examples of illustrious Roman Epicureans who were involved in the most important political events in Rome in the first century BC and highlight that Philodemus in *On the Good King According to Homer* is concerned with showing how the

Epicurean philosopher can be useful and advise the ruler. In sum, the testimonies analysed paint a much more complex and interesting picture of the theoretical and practical relationship between Epicurus (and the Epicureans) and their political communities than the anti-Epicurean tradition has largely succeeded in imposing on later interpretations.

7

Conclusions

Friendship, Law and Justice: The Epicureans and their Interest in Interpersonal Relations

How a philosophy is passed down from antiquity depends partially on the mediations of the indirect tradition. This can be seen clearly in the case of philosophers (such as Plato and Aristotle) of whom we have a 'complete' body of work preserved; but the situation becomes dramatically complicated in the case of authors whose work has been lost, with only 'fragments' surviving. A decisive fact that must be faced when studying Epicurus and the rest of the Epicureans is how to properly reconstruct his original theories, theses and arguments from the indirect tradition, a tradition which remains the primary means by which we are informed of his sayings. The fact that Epicurus was an established figure in antiquity who was not only reviled but also praised should lead us to think that his theories and arguments convinced some – to the point of generating strong adherence – and produced repudiation in others who saw in them a threat to already established philosophical doctrines. There is no major philosophy (ancient or contemporary) that produces a 'lukewarm' reaction in those who contemplate it. The case of Epicurus and Epicureanism is a clear example of a particularly 'chastised philosophy', both by pagan and Christian writers. A central thesis of this book is that the view – already established in antiquity by the indirect tradition – that Epicurus and the Epicureans recommended not participating in politics (in the sense of not getting involved in the political and institutional life of their cities) and living apart from civic life in general is inconsistent with textual evidence referring to Epicurus' and the Epicureans' texts. Moreover, we argue that political theory was integrated into Epicurean philosophy and influenced the actions and lifestyle of Epicurus and the Epicureans. In fact, as we have proved throughout this book, the anti-Epicurean literature is mostly belligerent, and furnishes neither considerations on the political theory of Epicureanism and its connections with the way of life espoused by Epicureanism, nor reliable testimonies about the actions and lifestyle of Epicurus and the Epicureans.

Cicero, Plutarch and Epictetus, as well as Lactantius, centred their objections to Epicurus around the fact that Epicurus' philosophy rejects the view that human beings are social *by nature*. Certainly, they seem to refer to Epicurean contractualism, even though they actually derive this refusal of human sociability from the egoistic hedonism that they attribute to rules of conduct of the Epicurean wise ('the Epicurean sage will not marry, will not have children, will not participate in politics, and will live unnoticed'), an issue that we know especially from the indirect tradition. They are silent about the specificity of Epicurean contractualism. However, we have shown that the interconnection between the study of nature [φυσιολογία] and political philosophy is a crucial part of Epicurean philosophy. Such interconnection constitutes the framework of the Epicurean contractual view. The application of the Epicurean study of nature to the analysis of justice and laws is translated into a genealogical approach to these realities. Contrary to what might be expected, such an interpretative pattern does not presuppose a crude conventionalist stance of justice insofar as Epicurus and the Epicureans consider the just as a modality of the useful. As argued in chapter 1, the just is not conventional because it is constrained by conformity to the purpose established in the first pacts of human communities (said conformity always being determined by circumstances). We also stress that Epicureanism subjects the traditional opposition between the disordered and bestial primitive life and civilized life to an interesting reformulation. According to their view the pre-social primitive life is not 'Hobbesian', and the Epicureans contrast this primitive state of human beings not only with the arrival of human groups and justice but also with the subsequent stage in which it became necessary to establish laws and sanctions. Generally, neither Epicurus (*PD* 37) nor the Epicureans (Hermarchus, in Porphyry, *Abs*. 1.12, 3, and Polystratus) polemicize openly against the Platonic idea of justice. Rather, they consider those who derive their conventionality or non-existence from the geographical diversity and temporal variability of what is just. Furthermore, the Epicureans are not opposed to a view of justice that minimizes its variability, but recognize that this is inherent in the peculiar ontological status of the subject. We also prove that they maintain that the just represents conformity with a collective purpose established by human beings as a result of their evolution, as seen in the separate realms of language, family and technology.

This genealogical approach would seem to be very far from the foundation of the Epicurean way of life, and especially from the imperturbability [ἀταραξία] it advocates. We have shown that such an approach brings, contrarily, a substantial element: the category of security [ἀσφάλεια]. We emphasize the continuity that exists between the recognition that Epicureans give to the security provided by political communities and the considerations that ancient literature dedicates to security, safety [σωτηρία] and freedom from fear [ἄδεια, ἀφοβία] when dealing with topics like the origins of culture, civil war [στάσις], and good order [εὐνομία]. In the ancient literature security implies satisfaction of the necessary natural desires and a state of confidence [θαρρεῖν], or lack of fear and tranquillity [ἀφοβία, ἡσυχία], with respect to future satisfaction and to the danger of a violent death. Epicureanism assumes both ideas and emphatically vindicates the value of laws and security. Hence, Epicureans oppose those who deny the existence of justice, maintain a crude relativism, or defend the cynical way of life. As such, Epicurean philosophy recognizes the security provided by the city as a necessary condition for the *vita epicurea*. However, it also attributes to the polis the promotion of vain fears and limitless desires, which can only be dissipated through the study of nature (i.e. 'physiology', as Epicurus states in his writings). Epicureanism posits 'the purest security' (εἰλικρινεστάτη ἀσφάλεια; *PD* 14), that is, a way of life freed from irrational fears and unlimited desires that make human beings unhappy and anxious for spurious securities despite the valuable sanctuary provided by the polis. The Epicurean genealogy of justice and law is thus complemented by a genealogy of these fears and desires, as well as the security to which human beings moved by them aspire. Attention to necessary natural desires, friendship and philanthropy are, in the Epicureans' view, the main factors that provide the purest security to the Epicurean way of life. Their conflation reinforces the liberation from irrational fears and desires and establishes – in human beings – a permanent articulation of the pleasant memory of the past with the satisfactions of the present and reliable expectations regarding the future.

Epictetus ascribes antisocial opinions [τὰ ἀκοινώνητα] to Epicureanism, but, like any other political paradigm, the Epicurean model has a compelling normative or regulative character expressed in the link between justice and utility. Just as Aristotle and Cicero connect justice with the 'common advantage' [τὸ κοινῇ συμφέρον], the Epicureans equate what is just with what is useful for the sake of the pact (vividly described in the saying 'neither harming one another nor being harmed'). The Epicurean genealogical approach to justice and laws is the theoretical framework from which this normative component is derived. The normative or regulative function of the Epicurean political model is embodied in the preconception [πρόληψις] of the just, which operates as a canon of the usefulness of the laws, that is, of their suitability to the purpose of the pact ('neither harming one another nor being harmed'). Epicurus applies his epistemology to the process of validating what is just, and thereby underlines the specific characteristics of its modes of confirmation. The practical consequences of certain convictions about justice, embodied in the laws, are examined as to whether they are convenient or useful as a result of not harming each other or being harmed. We reject the interpretations that instantiate the preconception of the just in the constitution ruling over the life of a community, or which distinguish a hierarchical and historical plurality of preconceptions of the just. By reflecting on this debate, we show that the Epicureans embedded the preconception of the just in the process of language learning, an ingredient of experience that is not usually considered when dealing with the empirical genesis of Epicurean preconception.

The Epicurean genealogy of justice, irrational fears and unlimited desires, the relation between security and tranquillity, and the preconception of the just are not present in the works of Cicero and Plutarch. In chapter 4 we have shown in detail how the omissions, exaggerations and simplifications of the assessments of Epicureanism made in pagan antiquity (particularly by Cicero and Plutarch) constitute fundamental and repeated strategies of a broader anti-Epicurean polemic that reaches absurd extremes in the Christian writings of Lactantius. Cicero's and Plutarch's controversy with Epicureanism is a fundamental part of their defence of the assimilation of philosophy to the exercise of ordinary politics. Discrediting Epicureanism and isolating it from later Greek philosophy contributes to this purpose. There is, however, another argumentative procedure more surprising from the perspective of today's methodologies: while Cicero and Plutarch absolutize the slogan 'do not participate in politics' as a principle of Epicurean conduct, they do not dedicate a single line to the specification of its context or from which text of Epicurus it was derived. Both of them point out, with clear polemical intention, that the Epicureans acknowledge circumstances that imply exceptions to the slogan 'do not participate in politics'. Nevertheless, their 'documentary' contribution, like that of Cicero's and Plutarch's considerations of said slogan, is disappointing, for they do not provide information about the actions of Epicurus and the Epicureans in political communities. They refer only sporadically to public performances of the Epicureans to try to show that they represent a hypocritical and unimportant mode of behaviour that is inconsistent with their doctrine.

Since Cicero and Plutarch omit the political reflections of Epicureanism, it is entirely reasonable to wonder about the apoliticism and minimal social interaction that they attribute to Epicurus and the Epicureans. We have answered this question on two complementary levels: on the one hand, through the collection of testimonies and documents about the social interaction of Epicurus and the Epicureans, and, on the other hand, by reconstructing the model of the Epicurean sage derived from ancient literature. In this regard, we have presented heterogeneous testimonies of the lifestyle of Epicurus and of numerous Epicureans which refute the apoliticism traditionally attributed to them. We have also showed how the testimonies about Epicurus' life and his testament do not paint a picture of a person shut away in the Epicurean Garden and isolated from the life of Athens, but of someone who, while refusing to participate actively in contingent politics, respected the laws and institutions of the city, participated in its worship and piety, integrated family relationships into the exercise of philosophy, and cultivated numerous and heterogeneous friendships, including with influential politicians. Furthermore, based on several Epicurean texts and epigraphic documents from various Greek cities, we showed in chapter 6 how numerous Epicureans belonging to the upper classes served as advisers of kings, distinguished diplomats, ambassadors, priests of the imperial and local cult, and even as prophets, without their status as Epicureans being perceived to disqualify them from such functions. We have also included several examples of illustrious Roman Epicureans who were involved in the most important political events in Rome in the first century BC.

Contrary to what several indirect sources say, Epicurean sages were in fact interested in maintaining a link with their polis. An Epicurean sage lived in and contributed to the development and well-being of the political community where he was a citizen. In this characterization of the Epicurean sage, respect for laws and institutions as well as a friendly attitude towards his homeland, also play an important role. In order to deepen this characterization, we analyse an issue that Epicurus raised in his *Puzzles* [Διαπορίαι]: whether the Epicurean wise person will carry out actions contrary to the laws if he knows that he will not be discovered. We suggest that this passage evokes the story of the Ring of Gyges in Plato's *Republic*, but that the figure of Gyges represents neither a challenge nor a fascination for the Epicureans. We stress the biased reading of Cicero in *Off.* 3.38-39 of the Epicurean view regarding the story of Gyges and Plutarch's malicious interpretation of Epicurus' reply to the above-mentioned passage from the *Puzzles*. Both Cicero and Plutarch omit the role of the study of nature and prudence [φρόνησις] in the motivations and decisions of the Epicurean sage when analysing the aforementioned topics. They also suggest that the reason why Epicureans refrain from crime is the fear of being discovered and punished.

The Epicurean sage, though, does not act out of fear of punishment; on the contrary, he disregards behaviours authorized by the law and goes beyond what is required by law in social relations by cultivating friendship and philanthropy. We also note the importance of self-sufficiency for the Epicurean sage and state that, far from being an egoistic property of the sage, self-sufficiency involves a social dimension. In this vein, we show how those major communal ingredients of life, friendship and justice, occupy a central position in two fundamental doctrinal resources of the picture of the Epicurean sage: the biographical tradition of the 'imitation of Epicurus' [*imitatio Epicurei*] and 'becoming like god' [ὁμοίωσις θεῷ].

According to Epicurus, pleasant living not only implies living prudently and justly [φρονίμως καὶ δικαίως], but also honourably (καλῶς; see *LM* 132; *PD* 5). Epicurus' interaction with Athens and that of the Epicureans with their political communities in general, was not restricted to actions dictated by living prudently and justly but was also framed by the activity of living honourably, a way of life that the Epicurean doctrine advocated through friendship and philanthropy. We therefore develop a picture of Epicurus' and the Epicureans' interactions with their political communities that is far more complex, varied, and interesting than the one that the anti-Epicurean tradition has largely succeeded in imposing on later readers and interpreters of Epicureanism.

It can always be objected to our overall thesis that Epicurus himself recommends freeing oneself from the 'prison of general education and politics' (*VS* 58). But a deflationary way of reading the slogan 'don't engage in politics' is, as we have suggested throughout this book, 'don't engage in *contingent* politics of your city', in which people do everything, at all costs, to gain power without actually caring about the good of their citizens, their city and even themselves. It turns out to be relatively obvious why Epicurus and the Epicureans would recommend not engaging in contingent politics: the way in which the political practices of that time (which would probably not differ much from the political practices of today) were carried out would surely contribute nothing to the longed-for states of tranquillity and absence of pain [ἀπονία]. But that does not necessarily mean that the Epicureans recommended living in hiding in small communities of Epicurean friends. On the contrary, as we have argued in chapter 6, there is good reason to believe that Epicurus and his followers found in the legal and institutional system of their own cities the framework of security necessary to develop a reasonable human life following the basic Epicurean precepts.

The most obvious proof of this is the fact that Epicurus left a will, surely concerned with the preservation of his private and school property, carefully dated his works by the year of the eponymous archon in which they were written and deposited his texts in the city's archive, the Metroon. But the relevant point for our purposes is that these important details show that Epicurus believed that the political institutionalism of Athens provided him with the necessary security to live there as a citizen, not hidden away with a small group of Epicurean friends who abide by their own rules. Additional historical facts help to reinforce our point: Epicurus was born in Samos (341 BC) and around 322 he was banished from Samos along with all the Athenians by Perdiccas, one of Alexander the Great's generals. Epicurus is likely to have been anti-Macedonian (see Us. 101); the Peripatetic Demetrius of Phaleron ruled Athens until June 307 BC, when Epicurus most probably settled in Athens and bought the Garden. As can be seen in his will, Epicurus left precise instructions for his disciples to follow upon his death. Hermarchus, his successor, was to take care of the education of the son and daughter of Metrodorus and the son of Polyneus (DL 10.19-21). He also left instructions that the members of the Epicurean community should continue to care for the poor after his death. Epicurus ordered that Nicanor be taken care of, so that all his friends and companions in the love of philosophy should not go without support. He also requested that the practice of funeral rites be maintained, first in honour of his parents, his three brothers Neocles, Chaeredemus and Aristobulus, and his friend Polyneus, and that such rites and memorials should also be celebrated in his memory and that of Metrodorus. This feast, which was to be celebrated on the twentieth day of every month in honour of Epicurus and Metrodorus, was originally a feast of the god Apollo. Epicurus provided in advance for the expenses that these celebrations would demand, devoting some of the income from his property to finance these festivities. In an extraordinary passage – unfortunately rather corrupted – the spirit that was to reign at these festivals is detailed (Us. 190; cf. Plutarch, *Col.* 1117B).

All this, we hold, is a clear indication of Epicurus' confidence in Athenian political and legal institutions and therefore in the security that the polis of Athens inspired in him, so that, far from living unnoticed, he lived (and inspired his disciples and friends to live) as a citizen of Athens. Obviously, this is not to say that Epicurus and the Epicureans were prominent politicians or that they were interested in becoming so. As pointed out in chapter 5, the character Socrates in the *Gorgias* not only distinguishes himself from politicians (*Gorg.* 473e), but also defines himself as the *true* politician (521d). But, of course, the model of politician Socrates has in mind does not match with the politician acting in the domain of *Realpolitik*. Both Socrates and Epicurus were not professional politicians, but 'political philosophers'.

If the arguments and evidence we have supplied in this book are reasonable (and we believe that they are), there are at least some reasons to think that, like the other ancient philosophers after the fourth century BC, Epicurus and the Epicureans would not have been so interested in understanding the problems of law, justice and interpersonal relations if, at the same time, they were not interested in applying the results of their conceptualization of such problems to an actual, practical political life.

Notes

Introduction

1. Strauss 1952: 111–12.
2. See Ludwig 1998: 401–54; Paganini 2020: 963–79.
3. Nussbaum 1994: 503.

Chapter 1

1. Inwood and Gerson translate 'καθ' ὁπηλίκους . . . τόπους' 'in *whatever* places', but ὁπηλίκος refers to indeterminacy of size (see Gassendi: '*cuiusque . . . regionis amplitudine*'; Gassendi 1649: 158). The propositions contained in *PD* 33 seem to reflect a polemical intention against Plato's idea of justice. This is how Philippson understood the issue (1910: 293.); he claims that Epicurus intends to underline that justice, which Plato had considered to be a virtue of individuals, is not a property of man himself but concerns relations among people. Bignone (1920: 66–67), as well as Bailey (1926: 369), Müller (1972: 90–92), and Goldschmidt (1977: 72–73, 80–83), also insist on the anti-Platonism of *PD* 33. They do note, however, that Epicurus established an opposition between the Platonic idea of justice – something existing in its own right, everlasting and immutable – and the pacts concretized in each instance under specific geographical and historical conditions on which justice would be founded.
2. On the use of the terms συμβεβηκότα and συμπτώματα in Epicurus and Lucretius' coining of *coniuncta*, see Sedley 1988: 303–16.
3. Alberti 1995: 181–3.
4. According to Morel 2000: 403–4, there is no reason to radically dissociate the analysis of human communities from the physical explanation of bodily aggregates [συστροφαί]. He argues that while human communities do not constitute bodies themselves, they must nevertheless receive properties whose status is analogous or identical to that of bodily properties. In his opinion the status of the just in *PD* 33 corresponds to that of the permanent properties [*coniuncta*], since the just does not exist in itself but instead constitutes an inseparable and permanent property of the human groupings subject to the pact.
5. The disagreements between Alberti's and Morel's interpretations evince this difficulty, as while Alberti identifies what is just with *eventa* of individuals (their

actions), Morel assimilates what is just with *coniuncta* of human groupings that are subject to a pact.

6 See Philippson 1909: 490–1 and Adorno 1980: 155–6. Scholars disagree on the identity of the adversaries against whom Polystratus addresses his arguments. Philippson 1909: 496–9 denies that it was the Pyrrhonians because, he claims, even though they questioned the existence of natural moral values, they nevertheless proclaimed themselves to be following custom [συνήθεια] and the land norms; therefore, he suggested that the likely target was the Cynics. For Striker 1996: 130–1, Polystratus seems to be debating mainly the Sceptics, who, like the Cynics, also truly fought their master. Indelli 1978: 82, the most recent edition of the papyrus containing Polystratus' treatise, argues that it seems to be the Cynics, Stoics and Megarians who are confronted.

7 On the simplification of the list of categories in Hellenistic philosophies, see Krämer 1971: 75–107. On the Epicurean reformulation of the categories, see Krämer 1971: 84, Adorno 1980: 157–60, and Warren 2002: 142–9. In the preserved sections of Polystratus' treatise, the 'translation' of the category of the relative [πρός τι] to the vocabulary of Epicurean ontology is not explicitly tackled. Alberti 1995: 181–3 holds that all *eventa* are relatives. Warren 2002: 148, argues that Polystratus did not raise the issue of the position of these properties and, moreover, that he did not need to do so, because the argument is purely dialectical, and metaphysics is not the main subject of the treatise. However, the response of the Epicureans to the dialectical arguments, which they despised, is, as Polystratus points out, φυσιολογία. Polystratus appropriates, as we will show, the category of the relative [πρός τι] from the Epicurean study of nature to emphasize that certain instances included under such a category (whose existence is questioned) really exist, although their mode of existence differs from that of what exists in itself [καθ᾽ αὐτά, κατὰ τὴν ἰδίαν φύσιν λεγόμενα] – a category similar to the Epicurean '(existing) natures by themselves' [φύσεις καθ᾽ ἑαυτάς].

8 This is one of the central approaches of the sceptical tropes collected by Sextus Empiricus (Krämer 1971: 96–107).

9 To some extent, this evokes Aristotle's *EN* 1096a26, in which an example of the meaning of the good in the category of relation [πρός τι] is τὸ χρήσιμον. Polystratus xxv 18-19 points out that the relative predicates do not occupy the same space [χώρα] as things said in virtue of a particular nature [κατὰ τὴν ἰδίαν φύσιν λεγόμενα]. Interestingly, this metaphorical use of the term χώρα is also found in *PD* 37 in reference to what is just and useful: 'Of things considered to be just, that which is confirmed to be useful in the necessities of mutual associations has its existence in the domain of the just [ἔχει τὸ ἐν τοῦ δικαίου χώρᾳ εἶναι], whether it is the same for everyone or not'.

10 The passage provides a reminder of the contrast between preconceptions [προλήψεις] and false suppositions [ὑπολήψεις ψευδεῖς] concerning the gods (*LM*

124, 1), as Epicurus also contrasts the preconception of the just with empty assertions [φωναῖς κεναῖς] about the just (*PD* 37).
11 Sedley 1988: 305–7; Alesse 2011: 200–11.
12 Alesse 2011: 209–10.
13 Kahn 1981: 95.
14 Kahn 1981: 96.
15 Some interpreters, such as Solmsen 1936: 209–10, held that Plato's elaboration combined the theories of the Presocratics and the Sophists. More recently, Sedley 2013: 346–7 and Betegh 2016: 25–32 have suggested Archelaus; the few preserved testimonies indicate that Archelaus distanced himself from the function that his master Anaxagoras ascribed to the intelligence [νοῦς] and developed a mechanistic physics that was extended in explanations about the origin of living beings, communities, techniques and laws. Tate 1936: 53–4 had previously suggested Archelaus.
16 See Sedley 2004: 119–23.
17 The texts by Lucretius and Diogenes of Oenoanda highlight the rejection of the figure of a divine or human legislator or inventor of language. For a compilation of passages and comments, see Levine 2003: 170–81. The idea of a legislator of language is surely inspired by Plato (see *Cratylus* 388d-390a, where it is established that the name-making artisan should be a legislator; on this cf. Sedley 2004: 66–74). Plato argues that, in addition to favorable conditions and his own art, the legislator needs divine support (see *Laws* 708d-709d).
18 See Brunschwig 1994: 25–32, 37–8 and Levine 2003: 172–4.
19 In the *PD* (33; 36-38) he asserts that justice arises from pacts, but, as already indicated, also emphasizes that what is just (understood as what is useful for the pact based on the principle of 'neither harming nor being harmed') depends on the specific circumstances of each people and territory. Philippson 1910: 298–9, held that the Epicureans had defended the idea of natural law in the supposed parallelism existing between the origin and development of language and that of justice and laws. Müller 1972: 93–9 presents the most detailed critique of Philippson's thesis. For Goldschmidt 1977: 167, the genesis of right begins where the formation of language ends (see chapter 3).
20 Kahn 1981: 94.
21 Dierauer 1977: 28–30 attributes a fundamental role to Archelaus in shaping this topic. Campbell 2003: 193, 339–40, has compiled several mentions of the primitive 'bestial life' [θηριώδης βίος] in Graeco-Latin literature. The contexts are very different (tragedy, medicine, philosophy, architecture, oratory, history), although the contrast between primitive bestial life and civilized life seems to have been highlighted especially in rationalist treatments of prehistory to emphasize that, while primitive people were not divinely endowed with technology (Plato, *Prot.* 321c-e),

they gradually acquired it by their effort. There are, however, theological versions of this lack, where it is derived from the resentment of the gods or is seen as a deliberate spur of the gods to stimulate human inventiveness. Lovejoy and Boas 1935 offers a helpful compilation of ancient texts devoted to the figure of primitive man.

22 Erler 2008: 49–52, 2002 and 2020: 28.
23 On the differences between the history based on written testimonies and the rational reconstruction of prehistory, see Manuwald 1980: 6–7, 12–13. Taking these differences as his starting point, Manuwald emphasizes that Lucretius does not properly speak of 'history of culture' [*Kulturgeschichte*] but, rather, of 'theory of the origin of culture' [*Kulturentstehungslehre*]. On the diachronic analogies of Lucretius' prehistoric reconstruction see Schiesaro 1990: 91–139. Brunschwig 1994: 22, 35, stresses that the stages of the so-called rationalist 'archaeologies' of prehistory reveal the authors' understanding of the essence of the phenomenon whose genealogy they consider (for example, language or justice).
24 As Manuwald 1980: 56 n. 212 emphasizes, *mollescere* in *RN* 5.1014 combines the literal meaning 'to weaken' with the positive translational meaning 'to become sweet, friendly'. Manuwald suggests that the most appropriate translation would be 'humanization' [*Humanisierung*].
25 On the topic of man as an unarmed animal, see Dierauer 1977: 48–52.
26 See Holmes 2013: 180–91. The usefulness of children as help and security in the old age of their parents and relatives (Lucretius, *RN* 4.1256) and for the preservation of the homeland is a recurrent theme in ancient literature.
27 As it is known, in Aristotle, one can find the classic expositions of such an idea (see Nagle 2006: 177–200). Aristotle observes that the origins and sources of friendship [φιλία] are given in the family (*EE* 1242b1). He says of children the same as he indicates of friends: A friend is like 'another himself' (*EN* 1161b27-28, 1166a31-32). The φιλία toward the children consequently prolongs that of the parents toward themselves.
28 Holmes 2013: 180–91.
29 Verlinsky 2005: 86–90 has highlighted the remarkable resemblance of this Lucretian text to a passage by the ethnographer Agatharchides, where he refers to the insensitivity and impassivity of the ichthyophagoses when their wives and children are beheaded before them. Agatharchides stresses that the ichthyophagoses manifest neither anger nor pity. Agatharchides blames their extreme insensitivity on using only inarticulate sounds and gestures (cf. Diodorus Siculus, *Bibliotheca Historica* 3.18 4-6). For Verlinsky, the comparison of this observation by Agatharchides, which is accompanied by other references to Epicurean approaches, with Lucretius' verses would show that for the Epicureans the first cause of the articulation of language would be the development of emotions favored by the *mollescere* of the primitive man.

30 For Mitsis 1988: 105–6 and Armstrong 1997: 327 n. 8, the word *amicitiem* in *RN* 5.1019 cannot be translated into 'friendship' because the content of the agreement establishing *amicities* is none other than that of the contract of justice – that is, not to harm or be harmed – which does not seem to be a sufficient basis for friendship. Yet, neither Nussbaum 1994: 266 n. 33 nor Konstan 2008: 90–2 find convincing arguments to deny affective implications of friendship in the term *amicities*, such as it is used by Lucretius. It is precisely Lucretius who presents them, along with compassion for the weak, as an innovation in the history of humanity that, together with the recognition of what is useful, makes possible and founds the first pacts of human groups.

31 These interpretations are reviewed in Goldschmidt 1977: 75–6 and Konstan 2008: 89–90. For Schrijvers 1999: 102–7, the use of the verb *commendari* in *RN* 5.1021, as well as the Lucretian theory of the origin of language, show that Lucretius appropriated the Stoic theory of familiarization [οἰκείωσις] and conflated it with the Epicurean idea of the pact and the *mollire* resulting from *voluptas*. Schrijvers omits the reference to the central function of piety and compassion in the origin of justice, clearly stated in the verse *imbecillorum esse aequum miserier omnis* (*RN* 5.1023). The Stoics, as is well known, condemn piety and compassion (on this detail, see Aoiz et al. 2014: 153). Campbell 2003: 277–8, 281 takes the use of the verb *commendari* in *RN* 5.1021 to be consistent with the Epicurean approaches with which Lucretius operates. In our opinion, Algra 1997 convincingly showed that, in these verses, Lucretius reflected approaches equivalent to the Stoic theory of οἰκείωσις, which were inspired, like this one, by the convictions of the Greek tradition about the formation of communities and the different degrees of friendship and interpersonal relationships. In the postscript to his well-known paper, 'Pleasure and social utility: the virtues of being Epicurean', Long 2006: 199–201 agreed with Algra's approach. Vander Waerdt 1988 and Besnier 2001: 138–43 dealt with the presence of the term οἰκείωσις in the Hermarchus extract transmitted by Porphyry (*Abst.* 1.7, 1) from very different perspectives. Both of them emphasize their secondary contribution to the explanation of the origin of justice and the laws of Hermarchus; however, while Vander Waerdt insists that it represents a reformulation of Stoic approaches, Besnier suggests that it should be framed in Democritus' reflections on recognition among animals of the same species. Regarding Lucretius' relation to evolutionist and rationalist accounts, Campbell 2003: 1–8 compares Lucretius' view with Empedocles, Plato's *Timaeus*, and Darwin. He concludes that Lucretius can be considered an anti-evolutionist in modern terminology, as he insists on the fixation of species, and also as an evolutionist, as he accounts for the clear difference between the human race and animals with an evolutionary process. Konstan 2017 has shown how the recognition of the evolutionary process of the human race, which Lucretius expressed through the verb *mollescere*, differentiated the Epicureans from the Stoics. For the latter, human nature had always remained the same.

32 Πᾶσα φιλία δι' ἑαυτὴν αἱρετή· ἀρχὴν δὲ εἴληφεν ἀπὸ τῆς ὠφελείας. In the manuscript it is written as ἀρετή. Usener 1888: 183, proposed the correction αἱρετή. More recently, Essler 2012: 147 proposed ἀρεστή, a verbal adjective frequently employed by Philodemus.
33 Usener 1888: 183. For Brown 2002 :79, the reading proposed by Usener requires to attribute the *SV* 23 not to Epicurus but to more recent Epicureans (to whom Cicero refers in *Fin.* 2.82).
34 Ἡ φιλία περιχορεύει τὴν οἰκουμένην κηρύττουσα δὴ πᾶσιν ἡμῖν ἐγείρεσθαι ἐπὶ τὸν μακαρισμόν. Armstrong, 2011:105–9 has convincingly drawn attention to the rather metaphorical sense of this and other passages in Epicureanism that also use the language of the mystical cults.
35 See Mitsis 1988: 127–8 and Annas 1993: 240–1.
36 See O'Connor 1989: 173–7, O'Keefe 2001, and Németh 2017: 181–3.
37 See Gill 2002, 12–18, Algra 2003: 272–3, 291, Long 2006: 201, Gray 2015: 37–41. Konstan 2000: 7 has shown that even Callicles admits a concern for others (*Gorg.* 486b6-7, 492c2). Convincingly, Essler 2012 has focused on showing that the egoism–altruism disjunction is not appropriate for tackling Epicurean considerations on friendship.
38 Gill 2002: 334–55; Algra 2003: 270–3.
39 Aristotle, *EN* 1166a7-8, a27-29 and Konstan 2000: 14 n. 22.
40 Some (such as Barigazzi 1983: 84–7), maintain that *PD* 39 and 40 refer to the life of the Epicurean communities. For Philippson 1910: 304–5, they indicate stages of the development of history of the right and society. Others argue that, as in the case of *VS* 61, the frame of reference would be interpersonal relations in general, which would not necessarily rule out Philippson's interpretation.
41 Hirzel 1877: 170–2 claims that the theory of the Epicurean *timidiores* represents an adaptation of Epicureanism to Roman culture, whose authors were Philodemus and Siro. For Tsouna 2001: 161–4, the three theories of friendship expounded by Cicero do not compete with each other; instead, they complement one another. Cicero could have been inspired by Philodemus, Zeno of Sidon, or a source common to them all (Tsouna 2007: 14–15). On this issue see also Mitsis 2019: 112.
42 Goldschmidt 1977: 71 n. 3, proposes to translate συστροφαῖς by 'fréquentations'. See also the use of the expression συντροφία καὶ συνήθεια regarding the first gatherings of men in Polybius' *Histories* (6.5.9–10).
43 Mitsis 1988: 107–9.
44 Mitsis, like Cole 1990: 139 n. 29, considers it unlikely that Epicurus subscribed to the considerations on friendship that Cicero attributed to the Epicureans. Mitsis 2019 reconsiders his earlier interpretation of Cicero's testimony.
45 See Cole 1990: 22, 83–4, 87–90, 131–3, 171.
46 Aubenque 2014: 106–52.

47 Roskam 2007b: 35–6 and 2007a, 36–41. Lactantius *Div. Inst.* 3.17, 2-7 offers a caricature of this qualification of the Epicurean philosophy by pointing out that Epicurus, to please everyone, enunciated principles that are adapted to the character of each one and that generated, in him, varied and opposing customs that made him debate with himself in an immense internal struggle.
48 Fish 2011: 96–101.
49 Through a keen analysis of Lucretius' comparison of certain politicians with Sisyphus (*RN* 3.995-1003), Fish 2011 provides an illustrative example of a traditional misinterpretation of Epicureanism that relegates the flexibility of its prudential approach to the choice of ways of life.
50 In *Rhetoric* 5, col. xx 25-36, Philodemus employs a similar contrast by pointing out that while most people and Epicurean philosophers consider the same thing to be just, good and honourable, the latter achieve an ἐπιλογιστικῶς grasp of these realities, while the former's understanding is given παθητικῶς and thus often forgotten. Müller 1983: 192–5 maintains that the two levels of preconception of the just correspond to the two moments distinguished by Hermarchus in grasping what is useful for human groups. The lower or simpler degree of the preconception of the just would be the result of the irrational memory of what is useful (ἄλογος μνήμη τοῦ συμφέροντος; *Abst.* 1.10, 4); the higher degree would be reached through the 'comparative appreciation' of the useful (ἐπιλογισμὸν τοῦ χρησίμου, *Abst.* 1.8, 2). Of course, the preconception of the just mentioned in *PD* 37–38 presupposes this (on which see chapter 3).

Chapter 2

1 Hamilton 2013: 7. The Latin noun *securitas* seems to have been coined by Cicero out of the pre-existent adjective *securus*. The prefix *se-* denotes separation or negation, such as the privative α in ἀταραξία or ἀσφάλεια. For Cicero, according to Hamilton 2013: 51, *securitas* removes a *cura* that is negative and psychological, an oppressive source of anxiety, and denotes a mental state of calm. In *Fin* 5.23, Cicero uses *securitas* as a synonym for εὐθυμία. Later, the term denotes an idea of military or government protection; that is, it approaches the sense of ἀσφάλεια (on this, see Hamilton 2013: 58–9).
2 On the history of theses analogies see Brock 2013: 79–112. For discussion of the ship analogy in Plato cf. Gastaldi 2003: 187–216 and Schofield 2006: 27–30; 53–5. Plato provides a fresh version of the analogy in the *Stat.* 296e-297b; see also *Laws* 758a-b, 906d-e, and especially 961e-962a, where the idea of the 'salvation' or 'preservation' (961e4: σῴζουσιν; 962a1: σωτηρία) of the ship is associated with that of the helmsman and the sailors (in the analogy these are, respectively, the ruler and the ruled).

3 Fear also plays a central role regarding security in the internal and external politics of the Greek city, as it works as a principle of so-called 'negative associations'. These are associations that are the result of a common interest moved by a common concern, such as the 'common fear' [ὁ κοινὸς φόβος] that can exist even among enemies who, for the sake of their self-preservation, decide to join with each other (see *Pol.* 1304b23-24). Such common fear guarantees to a certain degree the cohesion of the community as well as compliance with laws and strategy in international relations. Evrigenis 2008: 22–46 has analysed the political function of fear in Thucydides and Aristotle. See also Piepenbrink 2017.
4 The terms στάσις ('civil war') and ἀσφάλεια ('security') in Archaic Greece have been dealt with by van Wees 2007. For the lexicon and theme of security in the political discourses of classical Athens, see Piepenbrink 2016.
5 Aristotle clearly seems to have this passage in mind when stating that warfare [ἡ πολεμική] will be somehow a natural part of property acquisition, as it should be used both against wild beasts and against those people who are unwilling to be ruled (see *Pol.* 1256b23-25).
6 On this point, see Miller 1995: 35–6. In *Pol.* 1315a31-35 Aristotle argues that given that a polis is composed of two parts (the poor and the rich), it is best to suppose that both of them are preserved due to the government, and such a government prevents either from being injured by the other. In 1321a5-12, he states that in some cities, where the country turns out to be suitable for cavalry, there are natural conditions for the establishment of a 'powerful oligarchy?' and, in fact, the preservation (or 'security': σωτηρία) of the inhabitants depends on this kind of power, i.e. 'horse power' (and, of course, the horse breeding is the privilege of those who have significant means). Elsewhere, Aristotle refers to the dispute over whether access to the sea is beneficial or harmful to a well-ruled city. For it is argued that, for example, the overpopulation of a multitude of traders (who use the sea for their activities involving importing and exporting merchandise) is contrary to being well governed. But if these problems are avoided, he claims, it is better for a city to have access to the sea, both for the sake of *security and for ensuring* a ready supply of necessary things (*Pol.* 1327a19: πρὸς ἀσφάλειαν καὶ πρὸς εὐπορίαν τῶν ἀναγκαίων).
7 Cohen 2000: 28.
8 Cohen 2000: 31.
9 Rashed 2002: 44–5.
10 In De Romilly's judgement 1971: 112–14, 140–3, both the *Anonymous Iamblichus* (100, 5) and the figure of Meidias himself in Demosthenes' *Against Meidias* describe a profile similar to that of Callicles in Plato's *Gorgias*. Sancho's 2011 study of the accusations from ἀσέβεια and ὕβρις in *Against Meidias* coincides with De Romilly's assessment.
11 Cf. Cohen 2005: 175, 206.

12 Goldschmidt 1977: 33.
13 See also Aristotle *Rh*. 1402b10-12; *EN* 1113b30-33.
14 Goldschmidt 1977: 51–7 held that Hermarchus departed from the position of Epicurus who, based on the recognition of current practices and customs, accepted the existence of legal relationships between human beings and domesticated animals. In Goldschmidt's opinion, the position of Epicurus reappears in Lucretius (*RN* 2.1092; 5.860-874) under the 'quasi-contract' represented by the legal figure of the *tutela* of domesticated animals. Goldschmidt's interpretation has not found a following among other interpreters.
15 Goldschmidt 1977: 70.
16 This is even clearer in the case of Aristotle, as he explicitly states that ethics is a sort of 'appendix' to politics. In fact, politics is taken to be the most architectonic science (*EN* 1094a26–27), as it is the science that 'prescribes (διατάσσει) which of the sciences need to exist in cities and which ones each group in cities should learn and up to what point' (Aristotle, *EN* 1094a28-b2).
17 Roskam 2007b: 79.
18 Hermarchus states that it is also happening *now* (καὶ νῦν συμβαῖνον; *Abs*. 1.7 4), as it had done in the origins, that some understand the advantages of abstaining from crime and abstain, while others do so out of fear of the threats of the law. This is the only reason, Hermarchus reiterates (*Abs*. 1.8 3), that *even today* ordinary people abstain from committing harmful actions in private and in public. The *present* domesticated state of men (τὴν καθεστῶσαν ἡμερότητα; *Abs*. 1.9 5), says Hermarchus, is due to the measures that legislators originally established to tame the irrational movement of appetite. The first legislators thus introduced legislation which is still in force *today* (τὰς ἔτι μενούσας καὶ νῦν κατὰ τε ἔθνη πόλεις; *Abs*. I 11 1) and which has advantages for *our* daily life, such as the laws which regulate current behaviour with wild and domestic animals (1.11 4-6). As *we* do not live in the same place, Hermarchus emphasizes (1.12 4), these laws are different. The license that *we now* have to kill animals derives, according to Hermarchus (1.12 5-6), from the fact that it is not possible for us to establish agreements with them.
19 Interestingly, the three expressions (ἀσφάλεια, ἡσυχία, θορύβων) that Colotes uses to refer to the benefits derived from the establishment of laws and magistracies belong to the standard descriptive lexicon of the Epicurean way of life.
20 Konstan 2008: 117 sees in ἀφοβία one of the factors that promote the violation of the prevailing solidarity before the necessary implementation of laws and sanctions. In our opinion, Hermarchus, on the contrary, gives ἀφοβία a totally positive sense (as is also the case in the *Anonymous Iamblichus* and Demosthenes' *Against Meidias*). In fact, Hermarchus does not attribute ἀφοβία to the disappearance of the threat of wild animals but to the fulfillment of the laws that authorize their death because of the security of the community.

21 See Neck 1964: 46–74, 82–4. To be sure, these considerations can be taken as part of the epic form and didactic character of Lucretius' poem. However, they can also be considered as an implicit argument for proving that, given that the whole of reality is in permanent change, human beings must be especially attentive if they want to constitute and preserve a real political order: Without security regarding other animals and persons there can be no political community. Lucretius' intention (in these and other similar passages) can also be read in the sense that, if indeed many things disappear and others reappear (in the everlasting process to which the whole of nature is subject), and if the human world is not exempt from that kind of process, the human effort to constitute and preserve true political communities is particularly demanding. Humans are not only subject, like the rest of living creatures, to change and eventual destruction; the fact of being in possession of a rational capacity (which places us above the rest of the living species) obliges us to make sensible plans to preserve our political communities. *PD* 37 and 38 show the permanent need to adapt the laws to the preconception of what is just due to the emergence of new circumstances or the verification of the inefficiency and uselessness of what was previously regarded to be just (see chapter 3, section 2).
22 Gardner 2020: 79–112.
23 Erler 2020: 118–20.
24 G. Müller 1977: 218. Sedley 2004: 165.
25 Diogenes Laertius (6.13) reports that, according to Diocles, Antisthenes stated *that prudence is the surest fortress*, for it neither crumbles nor gives in to betrayal [Τεῖχος ἀσφαλέστατον φρόνησιν· μήτε γὰρ καταρρεῖν μήτε προδίδοσθαι].
26 Kechagia 2011: 157–60.
27 As observed by Long 2006: 180, 186, the pre-social individuals that Lucretius conceives of in *RN* 5. 924-1010 could not have practised an Epicurean way of life, as they lacked the minimum conditions of subsistence and security. Epicurus takes it for granted that humans have reached a level of civilization and technical sophistication more than sufficient to satisfy the external conditions of happiness.
28 On this inflection of the term φύσις in Epicureanism, already present, for example, in Antiphon see Pasquali 1970: 24–5; Manuwald 1972: 85–7; Brunschwig 1994: 45–8; Pendrick 2002: 319–20.
29 Campbell 2003: 10–12 rightly observes that the terms 'primitivism' and 'progressivism' proposed by Lovejoy and Boas 1935: 1–22 do not accurately describe the views of any ancient anthropologist, and more often obfuscate rather than illuminate ancient theories. In the case of Lucretius, this is especially evident.
30 One of the inscriptions of Diogenes of Oenoanda (Smith 1993: Frag. 35) reads: 'As a matter of fact this fear is sometimes clear, sometimes not clear [ἀτρανής] – clear when we avoid something manifestly [ἐκ φανεροῦ] harmful like fire through fear that we shall meet death by it, not clear when, while the mind is occupied with something else, it

(fear) has insinuated itself into our nature and [lurks] …' (transl. Smith 1993: 385). In Warren's view (2004: 11–12), Diogenes' distinction is not Epicurean because it contradicts the thesis 'death is nothing to us' on which the possibility of eliminating the wholly irrational fear of death is based. Nevertheless, in *RN* 5.970-1010, Lucretius also suggests a distinction close to that of Diogenes. Austin 2012 argues against Warren that the fear of violent death is, for Epicurus, ineliminable and sometimes even advantageous. For Austin, the desire for security from violent death at the hand of others is natural and necessary and there is no way to remove it. Armstrong 2004: 40-3 has highlighted that, in *On death*, Philodemus refers to 'the most natural sting' [τὸ φυσικώτατον δῆγμα] that is experienced in the face of death. Armstrong establishes a parallel between the references of Philodemus to 'natural rage' [φυσικὴ ὀργή] and the 'natural stings' [φυσικὰ δήγματα] before death, which even the wise would suffer. In both cases, a distinction analogous to that of Diogenes of Oenoanda seems to be suggested. For Philodemus' analysis of φυσικὴ ὀργή, see also Armstrong 2011.

31 According to Konstan 2008: 75–6, 146–9, obsessive love should also be included in the typology of unlimited desires.
32 See Sedley 2013: 331, 337–41.
33 Gigante: 1957: 97–8.
34 See Obbink 1995: 198–9.
35 According to Piergiacomi 2016, Diogenes has the final myth of Plato's *Gorgias* in mind.
36 Obbink 1995: 206–9, has shown that, while the Epicureans' rejection of the myth is unequivocal, they nevertheless gave their approval to several pious hymns to the god. On Epicureans and prayer, see Piergiacomi 2013; Erler 2020: 88–99.
37 Fowler 2002: 80.
38 *SV* 43: 'It is impious to love money [φιλαργυρεῖν] unjustly, and shameful to do so justly; for it is indecent to be sordidly stingy even when one acts justly'.
39 On the difficulties of the expression χάριν τῶν σοφῶν, see Goldschmidt 1977: 97 n. 1, and Besnier 2001: 133 n. 11.
40 Warren 2018: 218.
41 The comparison with Zeus is especially significant in a text that refers to hope [ἐλπίζειν] of human beings, since, as is known, Greek literature emphasizes that for mortals, unlike the gods, the future is 'opaque' [ἄδηλον] and hopes are often empty (see Semonides 1.1–10). Barigazzi 1983: 73–4 underlined the importance of the confident disposition towards the future [ἐλπίς] in Epicurus' views on security, an aspect of his thinking, which, as can be seen in the recent work of Kazantzidis and Spatharas 2018: 23, frequently goes unnoticed by interpreters. On the complex semantics of ἐλπίς, see Cairns 2016.
42 Warren 2018 has shown how widespread this claim by Epicurus was in antiquity and how his adversaries used it to refute him, which seems to have moved Demetrius of Laconia to submit the fragment to his famous philological expertise.

43 Warren 2014: 204–7; Warren 2018: 220–1.
44 Plutarch (*Pleasant life* 1009E) does not fail to observe that it is an unreliable and unsafe foundation for living pleasantly. See also Origen, *Against Celsus* 3.80, 23-27.
45 Some interpreters have pointed out that the consideration of the past and the future would differentiate the Epicurean hedonism from the Cyrenean theory of pleasure which is 'uni-temporal' [μονόχρονος], as proposed by Tsouna 1998: 15–16, to translate this adjective (see also Mitsis 1988: 50–8: Warren 2014: 189–96, 201–3). For Cyrenaics, in Tsouna's opinion, pleasure has no prospective or retrospective value due to its kinetic nature. In his monograph on the Cyrenaics, Lampe 2015: 56–99 has questioned whether the anti-eudaimonism that several contemporary interpreters deduced from the supposed 'presentism' of Cyrenaics can be categorically maintained. The relegation of personal identity, the radical subjectivism or the 'a-prudentialism' on which they base this interpretation do not resist a careful analysis of the testimonies on the Cyrenaics. In fact, such testimonies allow us to glimpse their connection to the prudential tradition and their similarities with the approaches of Hellenistic ethics, especially the Stoic one (on the relevance of abiding to the present, see Goldschmidt 1953: 168–86).
46 Gigante 1993 has collected and analysed the relevant texts concerning the relationship between Cynicism and Epicureanism. Regarding the debate on begging, penury and heritage, see Müller 1972: 24–8; Asmis 2004: 148–9; Balch 2004: 192–6; Tsouna 2012: xxv–xxxiii. Woolf 2009 rightly emphasizes that Epicureans do not pursue luxury, but neither do they exhort themselves to avoid their enjoyment (see *LM* 131 and the ingenious appropriation that Plutarch (Us. 490) makes of this passage). Rider 2019: 10–14 has also convincingly argued against the ascetic image of Epicurean life. On the alleged Epicurean 'exercises' of frugality, see Avotins 1977.
47 On this point, see García 1991: 207–13.
48 See also Tsouna 2012: 100–1.
49 In *On Property Management*, Philodemus uses the expressions 'measure of wealth' [πλούτου μέτρον] (col. xii 18-19) and 'natural wealth' [φυσικὸς πλοῦτος] (col. xiv 19). See Tsouna 2012: xxvi–xxvii.
50 Yona's 2018 article on Horace (*Satires* 1.1) offers an interesting sample of this closeness. Yona refers to the 'quasi-Aristotelian doctrine of a measure of wealth' of the Epicureans and maintains that, although traditionally these verses of Horace have been related to the Aristotelian doctrine of the middle-term, they seem rather to reflect the reception and application of the approaches that his contemporary Philodemus developed in *On Property Management*.
51 This, indeed, implies the disposition of the property of the Epicurean for the sake of friends (see Philodemus, *On Property Management* xxiv 19–xxv 23).

52 This is a very condensed way of saying that 'pains which produce great distress are short in duration, and those which last for a long time in the flesh cause only mild distress' (Epicurus, *VS* 4).

53 See also the parallel passage in Cicero, *Fin*. 1.68; when he states that 'there is no eternal or even long-lasting bad thing (*aut sempiternum aut diuturnum timeret malum*) to fear', it is clear that he is reading Epicurus' *PD* 28 [μηθὲν αἰώνιον εἶναι δεινὸν μηδὲ πολυχρόνιον].

54 Armstrong 2011: 126–8; 2016: 184–91. Armstrong 2011: 105–8 has convincingly analysed the language of mystery and initiation present in various statements by Epicurus about friendship (see *VS* 52 and 78).

55 For the Stoic city as a community of friends (or of 'wise people'), see Stobaeus, *Ecl*. 2.108, 5-28, ed. Wachsmuth (which stresses the view that friendship is admitted only among the wise; this is so because only among them is there concord, which is 'the knowledge of common goods'). The Stoic point is that true friendship cannot exist without trust and psychological stability. Unlike the Stoic view, the Epicurean notion of friendship emphasizes the issue of utility, but, like the Stoics, Epicurus states that there must be confidence among friends, and that such confidence is so strong that the Epicurean wise person will have 'the same feelings for his friend as for himself' (*sapiens erit affectus erga amicum, quo in se ipsum*; Cicero, *Fin*. 1.68, reporting Epicurus' view). According to Epicurus, when there is a lack of confidence, friendship has been destroyed (*VS* 56-57). But the somehow radical Stoic stance that 'all those who are not virtuous are hateful, enemies, slaves, and strangers to each other' (DL 7.32-34; *SVF* 1.226; LS 67B) is not shared by the Epicureans. If this is so, though Epicurus and the Epicureans sometimes seem to be thinking primarily of the 'community of Epicurean friends', it is not impossible that they were also suggesting that their 'political model' was capable of being applied to the polis at large.

56 De Sanctis 2012.

57 Roskam 2007b: 139–44.

58 Erler 2020: 48–58. Arenson 2019: 132–3, following to some extent Merlan, focuses on the fact that Epicurus is counteracting his *bodily* pains rather than his mental ones, with his joy. She is right in pointing out that it is not the case that Epicurus no longer feels bodily pain thanks to his joy of mind. What is not so clear, though, is Arenson's view that, even having been unable to counteract his bodily pain (in fact, Epicurus still feels pain even recalling the past conversations with Idomeneus), Epicurus has lost absence of pain [ἀπονία], but maintains his imperturbability [ἀταραξία]. The word ἀπονία means more than the painless condition of one's body. It can also mean the absence of psychological pain; that is why freedom from anxiety (or tranquillity: ἀταραξία) and the absence of pain are stable or 'katastematic' pleasures (DL 10. 36), while joy and delight are regarded as kinetic pleasures in action. Epicurus' joy of soul in recollecting the past discussions with Idomeneus and

the other Epicurean friends does not remove his physical pain but is helpful in neutralizing and likely moderating it. This issue could even be seen from the perspective of physics and the theory of causation: since in every causal relationship what causes and what is caused must be of a bodily nature.

59 In *Fin* 2.96, Cicero refers again to the *Letter to Idomeneus*, which, according to him, was addressed to Hermarchus. Cicero understands the word 'conversations', 'discussions' [διαλογισμοί] as the theories and discoveries (*scripta et inventa*) of Epicurus (see also Us. 191) and accuses him of being inconsistent. Most contemporary translators give διαλογισμοί the meaning of 'conversations' or 'discussions'. Arrighetti 1973, however, opts for 'ragionamenti philosophici', probably from the use of διαλογισμός in *LP* 84, and from διαλογίσματα in *LP* 85 and *LH* 68. Cooper's 1999: 502 reading of διαλογισμοί also takes them as 'philosophical discussions'. Our interpretation of the *Letter to Idomeneus* concurs with the translations by Cicero, Arrighetti, and Cooper.

60 As Cooper 1999: 502 has pointed out, the pleasure of the exercise of philosophy, like the pleasure of its memory, is both physical and intellectual. See also Giovacchini 2007: 31–3. For Giovacchini 2007: 4, the 'réminiscence affective' (Salem 1989: 44–52) operates as an ability to refind the balance [σταθμός] of pleasures and pains, rationally rewarding the 'balance of the flesh' [τὸ εὐσταθὲς σαρκὸς κατάστημα].

61 See the seminal work by De Witt 1937 and the subsequent works by Görler 1997, Milanese 2003, and Rider 2019. On the meaning of the term 'gratitude' [χάρις] in Aristotle and Epicurus and of *grata*, *ingrata*, and *ingratum* in several passages of Lucretius *RN* 3, see, respectively, Konstan 2006: 157–68 and Rider 2019: 6–8.

62 Curiously, *VS* 75 points out that Solon's well-known *dictum* ('a man should not be called happy while he lives, but only when he has already reached his end'; cf. Aristotle, *EE* 1219b6-7), which he synthesizes in the expression 'look to the end of a long life', is ungrateful for past goods [εἰς τὰ παρῳχηκότα ἀγαθὰ ἀχάριστος].

63 Grilli has proposed an analysis of the disposition [διάθεσις] and stability [εὐστάθεια] of the Epicurean sage from the consideration of the movement of atoms (see Grilli 1983 and 1994). For Grilli 1994: 243, in the expression 'the stable condition of the flesh' [τὸ γὰρ εὐσταθὲς σαρκὸς κατάστημα] of the passage we have just cited above *On the end*, the adjective εὐσταθές ('stable') refers to the stability of atomic movements in the flesh. Grilli also suggests that Epicurus received from Democritus the term εὐστάθεια. On the difficulties of an atomistic interpretation of the term εὐστάθεια in Democritus, see Warren 2002: 58–72.

Chapter 3

1 The Ciceronian testimony is now widely accepted, and the lexicography seems to corroborate it, since no mention of prolepsis is recorded prior to Epicurus. We also

owe to Cicero the most extended proposals of translation (*anticipatio*; *praenotio*); indeed, he is also responsible for the innatist interpretation of the term.
2 The word 'naturalistic' can be ambiguous in so far as it can refer either to a 'political naturalism' (i.e. the theory that political communities exist 'by nature', in the sense that it is in human nature to generate such communities) or to a naturalistic (or physicalistic) conception of reality. To be sure, the Epicureans were physicalists and thus 'naturalists' in their conception of reality, but in advocating a contractual political model they were not 'naturalists'.
3 See Long 1999: 623.
4 For an updated discussion of the issue of preconception in Epicurus and the Epicureans, see Tsouna 2016.
5 The passage is printed by Masi 2006: 94–5, who also provides a brief discussion of the preconception of responsibility (124–5). For the Epicurus passage see also Long and Sedley 1987: 20C, 2–4.
6 See Epicurus, *On Nature* 28, fr, 12 col. III, 9–14, and the comments by Manuwald 1972: 87–102, and Sedley 1973: 19–23, 59–60.
7 On this, see Asmis 2004: 159 and more recently Tsouna 2012: xxv–xxvii (especially xxvii). The fact that natural wealth is one (among other things) that we naturally seek in order to satisfy natural desires and thus feel pleasure indicates that wealth cannot be completely removed from life, as the Cynics recommend. In *VS* 25 Epicurus states that wealth can be taken to be a great poverty if limits are not set for it, which implies, we think, that wealth, within its limits, is something necessary (this view is present in Philodemus' idea that wealth 'does not bring profitless difficulties – ἀλυσιτελεῖς δυσχερείας – through itself, but rather through the wickedness of those who use it'; παρὰ τὴ[ν] τῶν χρωμένων κακίαν; transl. Tsouna 2012.
8 Additionally, the Epicurean interest is always focused on removing the disturbance of the soul, as suggested by Epicurus himself in *VS* 81.
9 And let alone from the *iusnaturalistic* approach, as Phillippson argued (see his 1910: 292–5).
10 Epicurus, *LH* 45; 73–74. Lucretius, *RN* 4.823-857 ; 5.156-234, 837-877 *et passim*.
11 Dodds 1959: 268. Some commentators are used to substituting the Sophist Antiphon's periphrasis τὰ τῆς φύσεως (Pendrick 2002: fr. 44a 1, 22–3) with nouns such as 'precepts' or 'norms'. However, as Pendrick wisely suggests, that is not necessary as long as such periphrasis is nothing more than an expression equivalent to φύσις (Pendrick 2002; 323–4).
12 On this detail see Clay 2001: 28; 34–5.
13 Erler 2012: 45–55 has underlined another example of this procedure: the striking Epicurean reformulation of the Platonic wording of the *Timaeus* contained in the expression 'firm contemplation' [ἀπλανὴς θεωρία], coined by Epicurus (*LM* 128). On this issue see below chapter 6, section 3.

14 Gómez-Lobo 2017: 60–1 has conveniently suggested that Callicles' maxim 'that the stronger rule the weaker' might have been inspired by Thucydides' famous Melian Dialogue. He notes that both texts assign a special place to the terms 'law' [νόμος] and 'nature' [φύσις], and above all, in both passages, one can find a theory of power which is supposed to justify certain forms of domination.
15 On this point see chapter 2, section 2.
16 The crucial role played by the issue of 'suspicion' [ὑποψία] as responsible for fear (of the gods; of death; of being caught committing an injustice) surely cannot be overemphasized. In *PD* 11, our suspicions about heavenly phenomena and about death trouble us (which is why the study of nature – φυσιολογία – is required). Further, in *PD* 34 our suspicion that we may be discovered committing an injustice is what explains why injustice is not a bad thing in its own right (see also *PD* 13). This, as suggested by Clay 2001: 39, explains why injustice directly harms the individual, not society, and it harms the individual because injustice makes one's soul turbulent. Epicurus' idea seems to be that injustice cannot harm society because society, thanks to the pact, can neutralize the person who has committed a crime. The issue of suspicion is also helpful for understanding in what sense a psychological state can produce an emotional state (*negative* in this case), and why it is decisive to build our beliefs not upon false suppositions ('the opinions of the many') but upon preconceptions (cf. Epicurus, *LM* 123-124). Furthermore, as Erler 1994 notes, the motions of celestial bodies are not due to the gods but to atomic motions, so 'the gods preserve blessedness without complaint'. Science of nature (φυσιολογία), while investigating and explaining the causes of phenomena, contributes to leading people to blessedness (cf. Epicurus, *LH* 78).
17 Strauss 1952: 111; Goldschmidt 1977: 26.
18 Angelli 2013: 29–30.
19 We follow Dorandi's text (2013), preferring the reading ἔχει τὸ ἐν τοῦ δικαίου χώρᾳ εἶναι, instead of ἔχει τὴν τοῦ δικαίου χώραν [εἶναι] (Marcovich 1999), and ἔχειν τοῦ δικαίου χώραν <δ>εῖ (Arrighetti 1973). On this interesting metaphorical use of the term χώρα cf. chapter 1, section 2.
20 The noun *evidentia* was created by Cicero (*Acad.* 2.17) to render what 'the Greeks – Cicero recalls – call ἐνάργεια'. The Greeks to which he refers are, in fact, the Hellenistic philosophers, whose controversies and terminology he discusses in detail in this work. Cicero coined numerous Latin words to translate this terminology through the 'tracing procedure'. It is not the case of the term *evidentia*, which Cicero creates from the verb *video*; in fact, the noun ἐνάργεια does not stem from any Greek word similar to *video*, but from the adjective ἐναργής, which in turn derives from the adjective ἀργός, 'bright', 'resplendent', 'fast'.
21 Huby 1989: 107–22 has gathered and analysed the main testimonies in this regard. She argues that, from Clement's testimony (*Strom.* 2.4, 119, 20, 32, ed. Früchtel; she

also cites other passages, cf. 1989: 120–1, n. 3), one should conclude that Theophrastus understood πίστις as 'conviction' or 'certainty' (Huby 1989: 115). We fail to understand how Huby thinks that πίστις must mean 'conviction' *or* '*certainty*'. There is no doubt that 'conviction' is a reasonable interpretation of πίστις, but why 'certainty'? Maybe Huby is thinking about the use the word sometimes has (for instance, in some of Aristotle's passages), where the term means (or seems to mean) 'certainty' insofar as it is a real 'proof' of something (cf. Aristotle, *Physics* 254a35). Evidence, ἐνάργεια, and apprehension of the first principles are clearly linked in the epistemology of Alexander of Aphrodisias, Ptolemy and Galen. The first two also highlight, as a factor of such correlation, the way of awareness that both the philosophers of late antiquity (Ps. Philoponus, *In Arist. De anima* 586, 21-23; Simplicius, *In Arist. De an.* 299, 35) and of Byzantium (Michael Psellos, *Opusculum* 13, 71, 6-7, ed. O'Meara) called 'awareness' [συναίσθησις]. Several philosophers of late antiquity made use of the link between ἐνάργεια, and συναίσθησις and seem to have seen a compelling argument against the views of the sceptics.

22 Indeed, Aristotle never supports this view; it probably belongs to Theophrastus or the other Peripatetics (on this see Huby 1989: 108–11).

23 In Hellenism 'evidence' [ἐνάργεια] is initially discussed within the philosophical controversies that take place regarding the establishment of a criterion of truth for the knowledge of the world and the attainment of a happy life. Later, it will also interest those who were dedicated to history, rhetoric and poetics. The evidence that specifically interests historians, orators or critics is the artificial one, that is, the evidence raised through discussion techniques in readers and listeners about facts and objects that these do not have before them (see Zangara 2007 and Otto 2009).

24 Cf. Dumont 1982: 281–3; Bakker 2016: 14–17.

25 Sextus explains this by providing the following example: 'when Plato is approaching from a long way away [μακρόθεν], I conjecture and hold the opinion [εἰκάζω μὲν καὶ δοξάζω], given the distance, that it is Plato, but when he comes near there is an additional confirmation [προσεμαρτυρήθη] that it is Plato, now that the distance has been shortened, and there is confirmation in favour of it through the evidence itself' (transl. R. Bett, slightly modified). Both the example and the idea remind us of Plato's view that our judgements depend on memory and perception. Often a person seeing something from a distance, Plato claims, does not see it very clearly and wishes to decide what she is seeing. This person might wonder what it is that appears to be standing by the rock under a tree. This account of what a person might say to him- or herself after observing such an appearance seems plausible. The person might next make a guess, such as 'that is a man', but may mistakenly suppose that what she sees is a sculpture (Plato, *Phl.* 38c-d; see also *Resp.* 602c7-8, where Plato explicitly argues that the same object, viewed from nearby, does not appear the same size as when viewed from a distance). Nonetheless, what is interesting here is that opinion

depends on perception and memory; for Epicurus, both perception and memory (in fact, an Epicurean preconception is a sort of memory) are criteria, and thereby they are prior to opinion. Perception and appearance are always true (in the sense that they are 'real'): when one sees something from a distance, there is a something one sees, i.e. there is a certain thing in front of oneself 'that appears to be standing by the rock under the tree'. That is why what appears to madmen and to people in dreams are true, for they produce effects; by contrast, what is 'unreal' never does (cf. DL 10.31 = Us. 36). But the position that 'this something is a man or a sculpture' is the result of one's conjecture or opinion, which can be false.

26 DL 10.34 (Us. 260); Plutarch, *Col.* 1121A-C (Us. 252); Sextus Empiricus, *M* 7.208, Us. 247); this is probably a response to the Sceptics who argue that a square tower that appears round from a distance shows that one should not draw conclusions from the senses (see DL 9.107). By contrast, the Epicureans are willing to state that if something is confirmed (by new perceptual evidence), or is not counter-witnessed, it is true; but if it is not confirmed by evidence, or is counter-witnessed, it is false. Therefore, perceptual evidence can be checked on closer inspection in a new moment of perceptual experience.

27 As translated by Asmis, who preserves the notion of '*counter*-testimony' contained in ἀντιμαρτυρεῖται.

28 Epicurus claims that it is the phenomena themselves which suggest that there are several different explanations. Thus, if one view is accepted and the other is rejected, even being equally in agreement with what appears ('the phenomena': τὰ φαινόμενα), it is obvious that one has abandoned any science of nature (φυσιολογήματα) and has fallen into a mythical explanation. For discussion cf. Asmis 1984: 321–36, and Bakker 2016: 14–21.

29 Sedley 1973: 66–8.

30 Sedley 1973: 67. Sedley underlines that in *On Nature* 28, 13, 7, the fullest surviving passage on ἐπιλογισμός, this is expanded into the bold principle that the truth of any opinion must stand or fall on the advantageousness or otherwise of the behaviour to which it can be seen to lead, Sedley 1973: 28. Sedley collects a remarkable amount of Epicurean and doxographic passages in which ἐπιλογισμός is used with the sense indicated in the domain of praxis (Sedley 1973: 28–30).

31 On the Athenian legal framework and oratory practices regarding the validation of laws cf. Goldschmidt 1977: 208–23.

32 Asmis 1984: 50.

33 In his pioneering 1902 work, Falchi already noted that '*usefulness is the substance and content* of what is just and right, such as the contract is its formal element, the means by which the useful is recognised and affirmed' (Falchi 1902: 53; italics and translation are ours). What is interesting in his remark is the stress he places upon the essential function of what is useful for determining what is just and right. We do

not agree with him, though, regarding his view that the right, which is a 'signal' (σύμβολον; *PD* 31) of the useful, is the right of nature understood as the right that must be made fully 'uniform with *natural laws*' (Falchi 1902, 54). The expression 'natural laws' is potentially misleading as it can suggest an iusnaturalistic reading that we reject. We do not share the stance that positive law is outside of the Epicurean ethical-legal speculation; it is true that there is never a single positive law in Epicurus or a discussion about current or past constitutions, but this does not necessarily mean that Epicurus did not contemplate applying his political model (based on 'the just of nature') to actual political organizations.

34 The issue regarding circumstances is especially important in accounting for the sense in which, as we suggest, justice is a 'modality of usefulness'.

35 In this section we are drawing on Boeri 2013: 192–4.

36 As observed by Vigo 2006: 399–403, this is precisely an aspect of Aristotle's reflection that the later Aristotelian tradition was unable to recognize. Duke 2020: 17–39, 85–108, has stressed that Aristotle derives the rationality of law not merely from intellect [νοῦς] but also from prudence [φρόνησις]; the 'common advantage' [τὸ κοινῇ συμφέρον] is the proximate *telos* of law and serves as a criterion for assessing the correctness of constitutions and laws. The common advantage is normative reason, identifiable with political justice.

37 See De Romilly 1971: 203–25; Goldschmidt 1977: 195–7, 221–2.

38 Goldschmidt 1977: 193–5.

39 In Goldschmidt's opinion such redefinition is expressed by the verb μεταπίπτειν in *PD* 37 (see Goldschmidt 1977: 200).

40 Goldschmidt 1977: 205.

41 Atherton 2005: 132 n. 55 takes ἐπιλογισμός to mean '*empirical* reasoning' (our italics), but in addition to the fact that the expression '*empirical* reasoning' may sound strange, there is nothing in the context that should lead us to think that such ἐπιλογισμός has an empirical character. The word rather seems to mean an examination, a calculation or 'weighting' of what is useful (or 'more useful') or, as Schofield puts it, 'our *everyday procedures* of assessment and appraisal' (1996: 222). Seen from this viewpoint, Hermarchus' ἐπιλογισμός is not different from Epicurus' 'sober calculation'.

42 Müller 1983: 192–5.

43 The most detailed explanation of the origin of language is found in Lucretius (*RN* 5.1028-1090), who forcefully argues that nature has prompted human beings to utter 'the various sounds of speech' [*uarios linguae sonitus*], and that it was utility that coined the names of things (this echoes Epicurus, *LH* 75; see also Diogenes of Oenoanda, Frag. 12, ii, 11-v 14). The constraint of nature is concretized, according to Epicurus, in each case in a specific 'environment'. This causes similar natural reactions in the human groups that live in the same region and gives rise to their

particular linguistic code. Epicurus thus reverses the traditional arguments about the diversity of languages in order to defend the conventional character of language (see Brunschwig 1994: 25–32, 37–8 and Levine 2003: 172–4).

44 Verlinsky 2005: 77–83, has convincingly objected to this view and has proposed a reading both of the expression οὐ συνορώμενα πράγματα (*LH* 76) and Hermarchus' excerpt that does not agree with Müller's proposal (and does not require putting forward a third stage of language development). Konstan 2008: 96 also objects to Goldschmidt's interpretation.

45 Cf. Jürss 1991: 84.

46 Goldschmidt 1977: 166–70.

47 Isocrates' passage is so remarkable that we think that it should be fully cited: 'For in the other powers which we possess, [...] we are in no respect superior to other living creatures; nay, we are inferior to many in swiftness and in strength and in other resources; but, because there has been implanted in us the power to persuade each other and to make clear to each other whatever we desire, not only have we escaped the life of wild beasts, but we have come together and founded cities and made laws and invented arts; and, generally speaking, there is no institution devised by man which the power of speech has not helped us to establish. For this it is which has laid down laws concerning things just and unjust, and things honourable and base; and if it were not for these ordinances we should not be able to live with one another' (*Antidosis* 253-254. transl. G. Norlin). See Levine 2003: 9–11, 140–5.

48 Vlastos 1946: 52–3; Brunschwig 1994: 32–8.

49 Philippson 1910: 298–9.

50 Müller 1972: 93–9, has presented the most detailed critique of Philippson's thesis, although he later modified his position in this regard (1983). For Goldschmidt 1977: 167, the genesis of right begins at the end of the formation of language.

51 Lucretius, who in turn seems to be inspired by Epicurus' treatise *On Nature* 12, testifies to this approach; see *RN* 5.1028-1045. See also Verlinsky 2005.

52 That is, if we kept the reading ὑποτεταγμένα, even though, as Dorandi 2013 has underlined, the reading of the MSS. is ἐπιτεταγμένον (ὑποτεταγμένα being a correction by Suda, accepted by Gassendi 1649: 141).

53 Asmis 1984: 39–47.

54 Hirzel 1877: 117–26. Mourelatos 2003 and 2006: 66–76, and Jaulin 2007.

55 Jürss 1977: 225. Galen takes such ὑπογραφαί and ὑποτυπώσεις to be 'conceptual definitions' (ἐννοηματικοὶ ὅροι; *De differentia pulsum* IV, Vol. 8, 716 12, 741 12, 743 13). Kotzia-Panteli 2000: 45–6, 49–50.

56 Sextus Empiricus, *M* 9.25–6 (Us. 353).

57 Denyer 2001: 124.

58 According to Clement of Alexandria (*Strom.* 1.15, 67, 1; Us. 226), Plato thinks that some barbarians are philosophers, as well. Unlike Plato, Clement adds, Epicurus

supposes that *only the Greeks* [μόνους Ἕλληνας] are able to practice philosophy. Asmis 2001: 209, n. 2 suggests that this general position is the same as for the institution of justice: just as not every race of human beings was able to form social compacts so as to develop a system of justice (*Epicurus PD* 32), so not every race of humans is capable of philosophy.

59 For Socrates, the true 'treasure' or true wealth is virtue (Xenophon, *Memorabilia* 4.2, 9). See also the Platonic prescription regarding how unnecessary it is for the perfect guardians of his city to have the gold and silver coming from men if they already have the gold and silver coming from the gods (*Resp.* 416e-417a). Philodemus' remark against the impracticability of Socrates' suggestion can be read as a critique to the Stoics, who, very 'Socratically', also state that the true wealth is virtue and the true poverty vice (in addition to the fact that they take wealth to be an 'indifferent', insofar as it *does not* benefit any more than it harms. Cf. Stobaeus, *Ecl.* 2.101, 14-20; Cicero, *Paradoxa Stoicorum* 5. See also Musonius Rufus, Frag. 34, ed. Hense).

Chapter 4

1 Cf. Green 1990: 52–64; Price 1986: 315–38; Hammond 1993: 12–23; Lane 2011: 29; Chamoux 2002: 165–213; Roskam 2007b: 64–5.
2 Athenaeus, *Deipnosophists* 12.547A (Us. 512). But, of course, Plutarch avoids recalling that Epicurus also rejects the pleasures of extravagance, due to the difficulties which follow from them (Stobaeus, *Anthology* 3.17.33, Us. 181; we return to this point later).
3 Athenaeus, *Deipnosophists* 12.546E-F (Us. 67).
4 Lévy 1992: 489–90.
5 One of the most comprehensive books dealing with Cicero's objections to Epicurus is Maso 2008. Although Maso accepts that Cicero's anti-Epicureanism is certainly not in dispute, he persuasively suggests that an effort to better clarify Cicero's positions in some specific points must be made (especially those stances implying some philosophical perspective; cf. Maso 2008: 31–2).
6 It is worth noting that Cicero (in a very Platonic way) maintains that he wishes to find the truth, not to persuade anyone as an adversary (*Fin.* 1.13: *non . . . adversarium aliquem convincere*).
7 Cicero reiterates that he is *not* denying that Epicurus was a good person ('companionable and humane'; *bonum virum et comem et humanum . . . ipse bonus vir fuit*).
8 Maslowski 1974; Shearin 2012: 34–5. More recently, Verde, endorsing Maso's suggestion (Maso 2008: 31–63 and 301–16), considers the idea that Cicero's view on Epicureanism was a moderate anti-Epicureanism as 'fundamentally acceptable' (Verde

2016: 336). It is true that Cicero's knowledge of Epicureanism was outstanding, but the view that his anti-Epicureanism was 'moderate' is harder to accept. Cicero was aware of the sophistication of Epicurean hedonism, which reveals the refined knowledge he had of Epicurus. But precisely because of this, it is difficult to understand why he permanently refers to the Epicureans as animals and pigs (see Hanchey 2022: 44). In fact, in *Against Piso* 20 he takes Piso to be 'a barbarian Epicurus', and in order to stress that Piso is a bad Epicurean Cicero states that 'our Epicurus' (i.e. Piso) 'did not come out from the schools but from a pigsty' (*Against Piso* 37). In other words, Cicero presents the link between Epicureanism and animality (see Hanchey 2022: 44–5) as a clumsy understanding of this philosophy. This is a trope he returns to repeatedly. With this in mind, Cicero's anti-Epicureanism does not look very moderate. The Epicureans, though, were clever enough to turn the insult 'pigs' into the appropriate description of the state of tranquillity that is the final end. Warren, drawing on Sedley (1976: 127–8), suggests that the negative propaganda associated with the Epicureans stems from Timocrates (Warren 2002: 134).

9 Although, as it is sometimes acknowledged by scholars, Cicero usually chooses the 'rhetorical mode', he is interested in the general question of the proper form for philosophical discourse (Inwood 1990: 147). Moreover, since rhetoric in Cicero's view is the faculty of speech which *can* convince people, he surely thought that the rhetorical style was relevant in philosophical debate. In fact, rhetoric in the Ciceronian approach has the virtue of making the unfamiliar seem plausible (Inwood 1990: 148). Some valuable remarks in this sense can be found too in Maso 2008: 34–5. On Cicero's intellectual development and formation (where both philosophy and rhetoric were relevant) see again Maso 2008: 43–63; the presence of Epicureanism as well as Cicero's qualms about Epicurus' tenets are specially discussed at 55–63. Maso (2008: 59) also notes that the Epicurean compendium of indications (of an almost 'catechetical' nature), easy to apply at the practical level, may have been somewhat rigid and hence left no room for rhetoric, which for Cicero was renowned in philosophical discussion.

10 'What is blessed and indestructible has no troubles itself, nor does it give trouble to anyone else' (transl. Inwood and Gerson). Cicero's translation reads: *Quod beatum et inmortale est, id nec habet nec exhibit cuiquam negotium*.

11 Steel 2005: 12, 19, 49.

12 Certainly, Cicero does not confer much originality to Epicurus, whom he takes to be a 'mere pupil of Democritus', at least in physics (*Fin.* 4.13).

13 Annas 2013: 212–13.

14 Lévy 1992: 489–90.

15 Duke 2020: 17–39; 85–108.

16 Wood 1991: 128.

17 Wood 1991: 129–30.

18 Cicero notes that the cause of this gathering is not so much the weakness of the individual as a certain social spirit which nature has implanted in man, since the human race – *genus hoc* – is not made up of solitary individuals.
19 See also Epicurus' *LM* 125 and especially *PD* 2, which corresponds to the literal quotation of the passage Gellius attributes to Plutarch's reference (τὸ γὰρ διαλυθὲν τὸ δ' ἀναισθητοῦν οὐδὲν πρὸς ἡμᾶς).
20 To Cicero's *ND* 1.18, the Epicurean Velleius objects as 'no groundless and fanciful beliefs' [*non futilis commenticiasque sententias*] the view that there is a fabricator and builder of the world ('like the god from Plato's *Timaeus*', or 'that old woman, the πρόνοια of the Stoics'). According to Hippolytus (*Refutation of all Heresies*, 1.22.3; Us. 359), Epicurus rejected providence and defended chance as the factor that determined the way the cosmos is. However, in *LM* 134-135 Epicurus argues that the sage does not think that anything good or bad with respect to living blessedly is given by chance [ἐκ ταύτης, i.e. τύχη]) to human beings. Anyway, he grants that chance provides the 'starting points of great good and bad things' [ἀρχὰς μέντοι μεγάλων ἀγαθῶν ἢ κακῶν]. At this point the argument is not without problems since Epicurus states that it is better to be unlucky in a rational way [εὐλογίστως ἀτυχεῖν] than lucky in an irrational way [ἀλογίστως εὐτυχεῖν]. His reason for arguing thus is that 'it is better for a good decision not to turn out right in action than for a bad decision to turn out right because of chance'. The issue of absence of providence or any planning in the cosmos has been largely discussed in the literature. Asmis argues that Epicurus introduced the swerve to explain how there can be goal-directed action in a 'mechanical' universe. According to her, 'Epicurus removed teleology from the ordering of the physical universe, but he recognized it in the voluntary motion of animals. To prevent an animal's goal-directed striving from being a mechanical response, he posited a swerving motion at the beginning of each act of striving' (Asmis 1990: 288). Interesting and suggestive as this approach is, it has the difficulty that the animal kingdom is also part of the cosmos and thereby part of the physical universe. Lévy provides a detailed discussion of how the Academics cast doubts on the role of providence in the cosmos (Lévy 1992: 219), noting that the view that providence is incompatible with divine nature (inasmuch as it supposes a lack, a weakness) is also found in Lucretius (Lévy 1992: 564–5 and Lucretius *RN* 5.165-167). Of course, this is an idea already present in Epicurus *PD* 1, where he argues that one cannot ascribe to what is blessed and indestructible [μακάριον καὶ ἄφθαρτον] any trouble or feelings of anger or gratitude, since what is such resides in the domain of weakness [ἐν ἀσθενεῖ γὰρ πᾶν τὸ τοιοῦτον]. More recently, Essler 2011: 133–7 offers an interesting contrast between Stoic providentialism and the Epicurean denial of providence (making especial use of Philodemus, who in a very Epicurean way posits 'the gods' complete lack of interest in matters alien to their own divine nature'; Essler 2011: 135).

21 In the case of Plutarch, see his *On Superstition* 164F, where he refers to Epicurus' view that atoms and void are the principles of the universe; Plutarch takes this tenet to be false and argues that it leads to a denial of providence and hence to atheism (see 167A-168A, and *Oracles in Decline* 420B3 where he explicitly refers to the Epicureans – who describe providence as a 'myth' – and ironically adds: 'If there is any place for laughter in philosophy, we should laugh at their dumb, blind, lifeless "idols" – τὰ εἴδωλα –'; 420B6-8, transl. D. Russell).

22 Unfortunately, the text is corrupted again in these crucial lines: οὐ γὰρ οἶμαί τιν' ἐρεῖν, ὅτι † μετὰ τούτων ὡς προερρήθη συνέπεσε κατὰ τύχην.

23 On this see Sedley 2004: 76.

24 A view that is objected to by Lactantius in *De ira dei* chap. 4. Lactantius' argument is that, when suggesting that it is inconsistent for God to injure and to inflict harm (since this derives from the emotion of anger), Epicurus also took beneficence away from God, since if God has anger He must also have kindness. If Epicurus is right, Lactantius contends, God is an inactive being, *quod non* in his view. According to the textual evidence, Epicurus' gods are not inactive entities; the core of the Epicurean argument is (as it had been for Plato; see *Resp.* 365d-e; 388e-389b; 608d) that the gods, if they really are gods, cannot have human attributes (such as anger, kindness, gentleness, gratitude, etc.) and hence they do not care for human beings (more discussion on this can be found in Erler 2020: 24–5). Underlying these details is the debate regarding the nature of the Epicurean gods, whether they exist with 'real atomic existence', or whether they are just psychological projections of our mind. This last view was already argued by Cicero, who puts in Velleius' mouth the view that, according to the Epicureans, there is a kind of image of the gods [*species ut quaedam sit deorum*] which has nothing solid or dense about it (an Epicurean god is not a body: *corpus illud non est, sed simile corporis*), and therefore Epicurean gods are not a real thing [*non rem*], but semblances of real things [*similitudines . . . rerum*; on this intricate and debated topic cf. Konstan 2008: 115, n. 51].

25 More wisely, Roskam has suggested that 'Plutarch's importance as a source for Epicurean philosophy presupposes not merely a thorough familiarity with the Epicurean view, but also a careful analysis of the works and philosophy of Plutarch'. However, he recognizes that Plutarch's texts and his 'massive erudition' confronts us with a difficult dilemma: either we can pay attention to all elements in his works (to achieve an overview of Plutarch's use of Epicurean philosophy) or we can fix our attention on one specific domain of Epicurean philosophy. Roskam considers the second alternative as better, since it can lead us to more detailed conclusions and eventually new insights (see Roskam 2006/7: 69–70). Whatever the case may be, even for those who regard Plutarch's discussions of Epicureanism as unavoidably valuable, his works and assessments of Epicureanism must be taken cautiously.

26 Indeed, it is not certain that Aristotle supported a providential account of the cosmos or even that the world has been made or produced 'providentially'. Although the word πρόνοια is recorded several times in the *Corpus Aristotelicum*, it usually appears as an adverbial expression, (such as ἐκ προνοίας), meaning 'aforethought', 'intentionally', 'on purpose' (see Aristotle, *EN* 1135b25; *Pol.* 1300b25-26; *Rh.* 1375a7). It is true that in *EN* 1141a27-28 Aristotle refers to a capacity he calls δύναμις προνοητική, but what he means in context is that even some lower animals somewhat are φρόνιμα insofar as they have a power of *foresight* regarding their own life. In *On Heaven* 291a24-25 Aristotle uses the expression προνοούσης τῆς φύσεως, but this is within an analogical conclusion where he states that what happens with a mass of air or fire, motion, and the cause of noise is as though 'nature had foreseen' the result. In other words, πρόνοια for Aristotle is not a cosmic power, which intelligently foresees what will happen according to a plan.

27 See Lucretius' arguments described above.

28 For this view in the Epicurean scholarship, see Brandt 1891: 230, (quoted by Maslowski 1974a: 187, n. 1) and, more recently Roskam 2007: 30. If one retains doubts regarding this topic, one should look at *Div. Inst.* 3.17, 2-31, where the major ones of 'Epicurus' errors' are summarized. However, as Schmid 1984: 154 has indicated, even though Lactantius devotes more time and space to anti-Epicurean controversy in his writings than the rest of Patristic literature (including his Greek counterparts), and despite its 'undeniable weaknesses', that was a common concern amongst Patristic writers. Schmid helpfully notes that Lactantius reaches a 'considerable degree of intensity' due to his excellent knowledge of Lucretius. Lactantius' work not only contains Lucretian elements but very often quotes them directly (see *Div. Inst.* 1.16, 3; 1.21, 48; 2.11, 1, where Lucretius is cited verbatim).

29 Maslowski 1974a: 188.

30 A crucial ingredient (both of ancient ethics and of philosophy as an 'art of life') consists of providing tools for the sake of 'living well', where living well means having developed all the best capacities a human being has as such, i.e. his excellences or virtues [ἀρεταί]. Such an art of life turns out to be philosophy itself, a kind of knowledge and hence a technical skill [τέχνη] we require to achieve happiness insofar as such an 'art' provides us with sound arguments and reasons to plan one's life and take correct decisions (on this point see Nussbaum 1994: 5-6; 14-15; 50-1). Thus, an essential project of a rational being must be to clarify what a good life really is and what the correct manner of living is. Plato explicitly refers to this last issue in two well-known passages of his dialogues (*Gorg.* 500c3-4; *Resp.* 352d6).

31 See also *Div. Inst.* 3.16, 16, where he clearly declares 'true wisdom' [*uera sapientia*] to be the revealed truth contained in 'the sacred letters of truth' [*sacras ueritatis litteras*]. The truth, Lactantius states, was there all the time, but it was unknown to

the Greek philosophers who thus darkened it by debate. That is why philosophy is false wisdom and must be abandoned (*Div. Inst.* 3.30, 1-10).

32 Although Lactantius is mostly respectful of Plato, he also qualifies some of his theories as 'crazy' (*ego plane contenderim numquam quidquam in rebus humanis dictum esse delirius; Div. Inst.* 3.19, 18). At 3.20, 15 he refers to Socrates as a buffoon [*o hominem scurram*] for having invoked the dog and the goose in his oaths and thence, if he intended to mock religion, he was silly, but if he meant it seriously, he was a lunatic, since he was taking an animal as god. All these assertions against the Greek philosophers can be read as a rejection of *any* pagan thinker insofar as such a thinker does not follow the 'true wisdom'.

33 On this point, see Schmid 1984: 146–7, who suggests that 'the general tone' of Lactantius' controversy with Epicureanism leaves no doubt that genuine Epicurean belief was still widespread in the first decades of the fourth century AD. Thus, when Lactantius says that 'in his anxiety to please everyone, Epicurus goes to a bitterer war with himself than the world does with itself', this is a significant example of a recurrent conception according to which the Epicurean position provided a true model of thought containing the essence of the *homo carnalis* (Schmid 1984: 145–6; for St Augustine's discussion of the Epicurean pleasure as a carnal one, see Schmid 1984: 168–170).

34 See, for instance, Bowen and Garnsey 2003: 199, n. 46.

35 Long and Sedley 1987: vol. 1, 13.

36 Lactantius' objections to the Epicurean denial of providentialism are contained in *Div. Ins.* 3.17, 18-27.

37 Green 1990: 623. Reinhardt 2005: 174 talks about the irrationalism exhibited by Cicero when dealing with Epicurus and pleasure and shows how it is reflected even in theoretical contexts such as the approach to atomism. In Lledó's view 1995: 26, Latin writers performed one of the most surprising feats of intellectual manipulation in history with the thoughts of Epicurus.

38 According to Usener, the absence of these slogans in the *Principal Doctrines* proves that the compilation of those maxims was the work of an Epicurean so little versed in the doctrine that he left them out (Usener 1887: XLIV).

39 It is not trivial to note that, although the two stable pleasures are the absence of pain and imperturbability, the word ἀπονία ('absence of pain') does not appear even once in the preserved texts of Epicurus himself. The place generally cited to exemplify the stable pleasures is the one just quoted (DL 10.136 = Us. 2). Arrighetti (1973, *ad locum*) cites this passage as part of the *Deperditorum librorum reliquiae*. The lines in question would have been included in the treatise ΠΕΡΙ ΑΙΡΕΣΕΩΝ ΚΑΙ ΦΥΓΩΝ, but those lines – ὁ δ' Ἐπίκουρος ἐν τῷ Περὶ αἱρέσεων οὕτω λέγει· ἡ μὲν γὰρ ἀταραξία καὶ <ἡ> ἀπονία καταστηματικαί εἰσιν ἡδοναί – are taken from DL 10.136. The Greek source is still DL 10, so there seems to be a sort of 'hermeneutical circle'.

Both Lucretius (*RN* 2.16-19: *Nonne videre* ... *naturam latrare, nisi utqui corpore seiunctus dolor absit, mente fruatur isundu sensu cura semota metuque*?) and Cicero (*Fin.* 2.32: *Epicurus semper hoc utitur,* ... *ea voluptas, quae in motu sit,* ..., *non illa stabilis, in qua tantum inest nihil dolere*) refer to the katastematic pleasures. But they are part of the indirect tradition and they capture the idea of what ἀπονία and ἀταραξία are (they do not coin a term for these pleasures). On ἀπονία see also Plutarch, *Pleasant Life* 1089D (Us. 68), and the way in which he tries to ridicule Epicurus. This issue has been an object of dispute among Epicurean scholars; see Warren 2014: 97, n. 37.

40 Wolfsdorf, 2013: 147.
41 Plato offers several reasons for dismissing outright pleasure as the best candidate for the ultimate human good (*Phl.* 53d-54d), but he also underlines the fact that there are some mental pleasures without which human life is not a real human life (21a-c). When Plato states that there is no greater charlatan or impostor [ἀλαζονίστατον] than pleasure he must be thinking of sensual pleasure; as is clear in the context, sensual pleasures are 'impostors' (or rather 'the *greatest* impostors') because they possess a seductive character that can eventually cause harm to the one who acts following them. At *Phl.* 31c Socrates says that both pain and pleasure occur according to nature in the 'common kind'. This statement seems to contradict the thesis that pleasure belongs to the kind of the unlimited (31a7-10), but it is not necessary to understand it in this way. The kind of mixing (or 'common', as Plato prefers to call it) makes it possible that pleasure – which by nature belongs to the domain of the unlimited, i.e. 'the more', 'the less', and so on – has a certain quantity and thereby can be incorporated as a plausible ingredient of mixed life (on this point see Lisi 1995: 79).
42 See also Aulus Gellius, *Noc. Att.* 2.9, 4, who witnesses that Epicurus wrote that 'The pinnacle of pleasure is the removal of everything that pains'; this is, of course, stable pleasure, ἀταραξία and ἀπονία.
43 Wolfsdorf, 2013: 284 provides an updated bibliography on this point. Bonelli 1979: 19-44, emphatically exposes and defends Cicero's arguments aimed at highlighting the inconsistencies of the Epicurean theory of pleasure. Boulogne 2003 151-82 presents those of Plutarch. The studies of Hossenfelder 1986, Striker 1996: 196-208, and Stokes 1995 contain more consistent philosophical approaches.
44 Stokes 1995: 170.
45 Boulogne 2003: 144, 152-3, 166, 170, 181, 195, 197. Lactantius (*Div. Inst.* 3.35-43) explicitly recognizes this interpretative procedure and offers an interesting example of its use in apologetics.
46 Plutarch, *Live Unnoticed* 1128A-B; 1130A. *On Curiosity* 520A-C. *Eroticus* 751A-752A; 758C-D. *Oracles in Decline* 429C-F. On the portrait of the 'ancients' in Plutarch cf. Kechagia 2011: 25-8. Among the anti-Epicurean treatises of Plutarch,

that titled *Live Unnoticed* is the one that exhibits the greatest carelessness and disinterest in developing a philosophical approach to Epicureanism; for this reason, it is interesting to note the guideline that follows the treatise. Plutarch, as Goldschmidt 1977: 113 pointed out, practically limits himself to opposing Epicureanism with a kind of Homeric chant composed of all the exploits of national glories (we return to this below). A similar procedure can be seen in Cicero; in *Fin.* 2.114, he invokes 'the ancients' and, based on them, argues against pleasure as a supreme good (see also *ND* 3.28; 34).

47 Long 1993: 141.
48 The current literature on the political activity of Academics and Peripatetics contradicts the image provided by Plutarch. Speusippus, Xenocrates and Polemon seem to have led quiet lives in the company of their disciples and to have been personally involved in politics only exceptionally. On this detail, see Scholz 1998: 186–204. It is significant that Plutarch omits Arcesilaus when referring to the Academy. Diogenes Laertius underlines his detachment from politics (DL 4.39).
49 Scholz 1998: 11–71.
50 Scholz 1998: 47–9.
51 Roskam 2007b: 3–5, has called attention to the two competing traditions around the political participation of the seven sages and the Presocratics in general. Obviously, Cicero and Plutarch follow one and omit the other. As Jaeger 1934: 426–61 showed, both traditions actually went back to Academic and Peripatetic discussions focused on the ideals of the active and contemplative life and, in his opinion, the clearly political characterization of the first sages was the work of Dicaearchus.
52 Lévy 2012: 65.
53 Campos Daroca (1999) has convincingly emphasized that the interpretation of the figure of Dicaearchus as a defender (against Theophrastus) of the pre-eminence of the *vita activa* does not do justice to his position in the contest between *vita activa* and *vita contemplativa*; Campos Daroca 1999: 56–9; 64–6. This is so since his apology for the way of life of the first sages and of Pythagoras and Socrates is not to be understood as a vindication of the *vita activa*, specifically – as Cicero would have it – of the exercise of politics, but as an appeal to a way of life prior to the professionalization of philosophy and politics that gives rise to the *vita activa–vita contemplativa* disjunction. Moreover, it represents for Dicaearchus a degradation whose incipient 'archaeological' historiography is willing to highlight. Thus, Campos Daroca suggests that Dicaearchus is closer to the rigour of Antisthenes and the proposals of Cynics, Stoics and Epicureans regarding the concordance between word and action than to a supposed defence of the supremacy of the exercise of politics. Scholz's comments 1998: 206–11 on Dicaearchus agree with Campos Daroca's interpretation.
54 Cicero saw the Epicureans as his greatest opponents and did not cease to criticize them, although he also praised them repeatedly through the pseudo-encomium that

Lévy 2001 called 'l'éloge paradoxal'. When Cicero deals with Epicurean hedonism, it becomes particularly clear that philosophically he may be associated to the sceptical academy, but his real life, his ethical convictions and his philosophical interests and judgments are constantly influenced by his Roman identity as an orator, statesman and consistent pillar of the *mos maiorum* (on this point see Powell 1995: 22, 31. Lévy 2012: 72–4).

55 However, as we point out above, Cicero was aware of the sophistication of Epicurean hedonism, and thus knew positively that it could not be identified with crude hedonism.

56 Roskam 2013: 5.

57 As Roskam (2013: 6) has pointed out, the subject of these first-person plural verbs is ambiguous, because it is not clear whether Plutarch refers to the philosophers following Heraclitus, Socrates or Plato, or to people in general. If it is the former, the Epicureans could easily argue that nothing would prevent other individuals, not followers of such philosophers, from attacking them. If it is a question of the latter, one could equally argue that not only the Epicureans, but also Plato and Aristotle, were far from arguing that philosophical theories or beliefs alone were sufficient for all individuals to behave rationally. In reply to this, of course, the Platonists could insist that it is preferable to suffer injustice than to impose it, which, however, would not avoid having to recognize the existence of a state of collective brutality. As Goldschmidt 1977: 34–5 suggested, the Epicureans' insistence on security provided by contractual justice might also represent an implicit critique of the figure of the Stoic sage, who neither causes nor suffers any harm. The latter, the Epicureans would argue, is in any case not due to the hyperbolic faculties and sublime qualities of the sage, but simply to the existence of positive law.

58 The persistence of this anti-Epicurean topic in contemporary interpreters is striking. Konstan 2008: 29–37, though, has made a masterful analysis of an emblematic case of it: the reading of the prologue of Lucretius, *On the Nature of Things* 2. Most interpreters see these verses (*RN* 2.1-13) as proof of the cruel selfishness of the Epicureans. Konstan has stressed that a careful philological approach to the text was enough to look at the traditional resources that Lucretius used to dissipate this interpretation.

59 This is Inwood's implicit suggestion when he states that Cicero's critique of Epicurus is helpful for bringing into focus several key problems in Epicureanism (see Inwood 1990: 145).

Chapter 5

1 Cf. Pendrick 2002: 160–3, 323–4.
2 See Goldschmidt 1977: 95–6; De Romilly 1968: 33–57.

3 On this point see Long and Sedley 1987: vol 1, 146.
4 The Stoic Chrysippus maintains that armies are useless; Zeno rejects judicial institutions and says that money is not necessary for exchange (DL 7.33). The Stoics, like the Cynic Diogenes of Sinope, also defend anthropophagy. All this counts like 'behaving like a Cynic', but apparently being a Cynic can also mean being a beggar, which is why Diogenes reports that the Epicurean sage will not be a beggar (DL 10.120).
5 Seneca (*On Marriage* Frag. 45 [ed. Haase], in Jerome, *Against Jovinianus*, 1.48; Us. 19) suggests that the Epicurean sage usually avoids marrying because 'marriage entails many drawbacks' [*multa incommoda*]. Maybe those rare circumstances in which the sage need only marry are related to issues such as honours, bodily health, and other things which the Stoics call 'indifferent' (Seneca states), but for Epicurus and the Epicureans such things become good and bad according to use, so wives stand on the 'boundary of good and bad things' [*in bonorum malorumque confinio*]. Additionally, Seneca says, it can be a serious matter to ponder whether he is going to marry a good or a bad woman.
6 The Stoic conception that a person is truly just when obeying the law that exists by nature, along with Stoic cosmopolitanism, has its origin in the Cynics (for the Stoic view see DL 7.128; Cicero, *Leg.* 1.44; Clement, *Strom.* 4.26; *SVF* 3.327); for Cynic cosmopolitanism see DL 6.38, 72 and 98, and the commentaries by Schofield 1999: 141–5. The idea of cosmopolitanism can also be read in the framework of the theory of 'familiarization' (οἰκείωσις): as the animal develops, it extends its care not only to itself but to its offspring and close members of its species. In the case of human beings, the situation is much more sophisticated since, to the fact that the initial selfish interest of the living being is extended to an interest in its offspring and close relatives, one must add a rationality which allows a human to recognize another as a member of the same species (on this distinction of οἰκείωσις, see Aoiz and Deniz 2014: 25–35). For a Stoic, this explanation also plays a decisive role in the political domain, since the recognition of another person as a member of one's species makes possible, at least *ex hypothesi*, not only cosmopolitanism (all humans are members of the same order, that is, of the same κόσμος), but also the natural equality among all human beings. In Stoicism, this detail constitutes a powerful argument in favor of cosmopolitanism: as far as we can see, this is what both Epictetus and Marcus Aurelius (probably drawing on Epictetus) had in mind when they stated that they belong to the cosmos (or that 'they are part of a whole which is governed by nature') and not to a specific polis (Epictetus, *Diss.* 1.9, 1-2; Marcus Aurelius, 10.1, 10.6 *et passim*).
7 See *Pap. Herc.* 1020 (*SVF* 2.131), with Görler's discussion (1977: 85–6); cf. also Cicero, *Acad.* 2.57; Sextus Empiricus, *M* 7.151-157 (*SVF* 1.67-69; 2.90; LS 41C;).

8 On this important point, see also Epictetus, *Diss.* 1.4, 28-29; Clement of Alexandria, *Strom.* 6.9, 73.2-75.1 (BS 22.17).
9 For this detail cf. Long 2013: 219.
10 The view that the Stoic sage is a very uncommon person is also present in Seneca, *Ep.* 42, 1. See also Sextus Empiricus, *M* 7.433. The extraordinary skills of the Stoic sage are described in Stobaeus, *Ecl.* 2.100, 2: 112, 1–5.
11 The editors debate between the reading of the *hapax* ἐπικατηγόρημα of the MSS. and Estienne's conjecture ἐστι κατηγόρημα. Westman and Pohlenz Teubner edition of Plutarch's *Adversus Colotem* (1959) and that of Einarson and De Lacy 1967: 312–13, favour the former, as does Goldschmidt 1977:119–21, Besnier 2001: 136 n. 17, and Seel 1996: 343. Usener followed Estienne's proposal; it was also accepted by Arrighetti 1973: 166, 573. ἐπικατηγόρημα is usually taken to mean 'predicate', although it can also mean 'accusation' (see Vander Waerdt 1987: 407 n. 18).
12 Boulogne 2003:195.
13 We fail to understand why Morel (2000: 395) is so sure that the words 'I will do it, but I do not wish to admit it' belong to Epicurus. Morel states that 'Epicurus' response is at least enigmatic', but in the context, it is pretty clear that Plutarch, without argument, ascribes these words to Epicurus. Further, Morel himself recognizes that this answer 'seems hardly compatible' with *PD* 34 since it is hard to imagine that the wise person would choose a situation that would make him live in fear (Morel 2000: 396). This being so, the most reasonable way out is to recognize that the answer at stake is what Plutarch maliciously attributes to Epicurus.
14 In the next section of this chapter, we will examine Cicero's and Plutarch's interpretations of the above-mentioned texts.
15 Philippson 1910: 302–3.
16 Einarson and De Lacy 1967: 312–13; Goldschmidt 1977: 119; Konstan 2008: 124. Cosenza 1996: 368 n. 17 objects to Goldschmidt that the distinction between just laws and unjust laws is neither obvious nor trivial and could be relevant to the problem contained in the passage, since the transgression of unjust laws also triggers the fear and anguish of being discovered and punished by the criminal power associated with them. In Besnier's view it would be a case of the wise intervening in politics to change them.
17 On the possible meaning of these puzzlements (ἀπορίαι) in Epicurus cf. Seel 1996: 342–3.
18 Seel 1996: 367.
19 Besnier 2001: 136 n. 17, finds in **T1** a typical casuistic question concerning the conflict between two duties and considers that Epicureans were devoid of rhetorical resources to face it.
20 Cf. Pembroke 1971: 128–9.
21 Strauss 1952: 158–63.

22 Roskam 2007b: 57 suggests that perhaps Epicurus would give the same kind of response that he offers in the analysed passage from the *Puzzles* to the 'imaginary' question of whether the sage will accept unsolicited honours.
23 Seel 1996: 345–6, notes that we have no testimony that Epicurus dealt with the case where the wise person must commit injustice to save the life of a friend but draws attention to the testimony of Aulus Gelius who reminds that Stilpon, the legendary king of Sparta and one of the seven wise men, was faced with such a dilemma. Aulus Gelius also emphasizes that the question an pro utilitatibus amicorum delinquendum aliquando ('one must commit crime sometimes for the sake of the usefulness of the friends'; *Noc. Att.* 1.3) occupied many philosophers, among which were Theophrastus and Cicero. Seel does not rule out that Epicurus was also one of them, Cf. Seel 1996: 345 n. 15.
24 It is, for example, as Seel 1996: 359–60 points out, a transgression of the law that, in his judgement, Cicero himself accepts (*On Friendship* 17.61).
25 Vander Waerdt 1987: 416–18.
26 For the idea that becoming a Stoic wise person is a very hard undertaking, see Plutarch, *Stoic. Rep.* 1048E and our discussion of this topic in section 3 below.
27 By contrast, the Stoic sage can predict the future since, at least theoretically, he is able to know the whole causal sequence, order and concatenation of world events (see Cicero, *On divination* 1.127-129, witnessing a Stoic view).
28 'Socrates', Glaucon says, 'do not think that it is *I* who speak, but those who praise injustice rather than justice' (Plato, *Resp.* 361e1-3; our translation). Later, Adeimantus says that he will take up the point of view which he believes to be that of Glaucon: to praise justice and censure injustice (362e-363a).
29 This Platonic stance, *mutatis mutandis*, reappears in Epicurus' view that 'injustice is not a bad thing in its own right, but because of the fear produced by the suspicion that one will not escape the notice of those assigned to punish such actions' (*PD* 35).
30 Of course, this 'highest good' is the same as 'pleasure', but obviously such a pleasure cannot coincide with pleasure in the sense of an unlimited sensual pleasure (as Cicero, Plutarch, Lanctantius, and even Epictetus wrongly state), but with the static pleasures of absence of pain [ἀπονία] and imperturbability (ἀταραξία; DL 10.136; Us. 2). Epicurean happiness is the absence of physical pain [ἀλγεῖν κατὰ σῶμα] and mental disturbance (ταράττεσθαι κατὰ ψυχήν; Epicurus, *LM* 131-132. See also *PD* 3).
31 In fact, this is merely self-sufficiency, a crucial attribute of the Epicurean sage. Thus, 'nothing is as necessary as knowing well what is not necessary, and self-sufficiency is the greatest wealth of all' (Porphyry, *To Marcella* 28; Us. 476). See also Porphyry, *To Marcella* 28, Us. 479, stressing the view that people (i.e. people who are not wise, 'the many': πολλοί) mistakenly attain wealth believing that they will find an escape from their 'bad things', surely their states of anguish.
32 Kahn 1981: 95.

33 According to Plato himself, this means 'becoming just and pious with wisdom' (φρόνησις; *Tht.* 176b); the question of becoming godlike is a recurrent theme in Plato (see, for example, *Resp.* 383c; 500c-d; 613a-b. *Tim.* 90a. *Laws* 716c-d). For discussion, see Sedley 1997, and Erler 2002: 163–7.

34 It would seem to be another example of 'l'éloge paradoxal' (see Lévy 2001), which Cicero frequently addresses to the Epicureans. To recognize the Epicureans as 'good people' does not correspond to moral praise, but to the strategy of presenting them as living in contradiction of the theses they defend and as proof that in human beings there is disinterested probity which is innate (such probity being neither provoked by pleasures nor attracted by rewards; cf. Cicero, *Fin.* 2. 99). To sum up, the life of the Epicureans, Cicero thinks, denies their philosophy, and confirms the innate recognition of the intrinsic value of virtues (see Lévy 2001).

35 According to Macrobius' and Proclus' testimonies, Colotes criticized the use of the myth of Er at the final section of *Resp.* 10 (see Kechagia 2011: 53–71 and Corti 2014: 90–3). Woolf 2013: 807 n. 24, observes that one may trace this dialectic into the very different world of Ambrose's *De officiis*. Ambrose recounts the tale of Gyges (3.32); dismisses it as a fable which 'lacks the force of truth' (*vim non habet veritatis*, 3.36), agreeing to that extent with the grounds given by Cicero's opponents for not taking it seriously; but cites Biblical narratives to show (as he sees it) that there are real-world examples of resistance to expediency on a par with refusal to use the ring unjustly (33–5).

36 In Roskam's opinion (2012: 26–7), Cicero would be referring to the epigones of Epicurus. Roskam attributes to them an 'ossified' and intransigent position, far from the living thought of Epicurus, which prevents them from recognizing that it is Epicurus himself who in the *Puzzles* raises the aporia and underlines the difficulty of offering a categorical response.

37 Torquatus observes that, by removing the necklace of an enormous enemy Gaul, his homonymous ancestor achieved glory and esteem, which are the firmest safeguards for a life without fear. By punishing his son with death, he also managed to contain the army in the midst of a very serious war, and through fear of punishment he was providing for the security of his fellow citizens and, of course, for his own (*Fin.* 1.35).

38 That the objection affects Cicero is proven by the fact that he accepts (*Fin.* 2.61) that perhaps Torquatus performed the mentioned feat in *Fin.* 1 for his own utility, although Cicero also stresses that this account turns out to be unacceptable in the case of his colleague Publius Decius, who threw himself against enemy troops knowing that this would mean his death. Curiously, one of the arguments that Plutarch addresses against the Epicureans (in *Pleasant Life* 1098A-1100D) is that the pleasures experienced by the great men of action when performing their feats surpass the pleasures exalted by them.

39 The background of the story of Gyges' ring is Glaucon's specific contractual model, in which advantage [πλεονεξία] is the essential motivation of human nature (Plato,

Resp. 359c3-5). Cicero underlines this link between advantage and contractualism in *On Laws* 3.13. In fact, as Woolf 2013: 802, points out, Cicero's Gyges is presented more overtly than Plato's as a ruthless evildoer whom we should not want to be like.

40 Erler 2012: 45–55 sees in the expression a reformulation (of Epicurean imprint) of the Platonic approach to the 'becoming like god' (ὁμοίωσις θεῷ; cf. *Tim.* 90c., where the adjective ἀπλανής is also used). 'Theory', 'contemplation' [θεωρία] is an expression that in Plato is especially related to the intelligible domain. Epicurus takes up again the connotation of empirical knowledge that the term θεωρία possessed and adds to it the adjective ἀπλανής, which for Plato is often anchored in the intelligible world. The anti-Platonic result of the reformulation is clear: the Epicurean ἀπλανής θεωρία is aimed at the happiness of man as a mortal being on earth, where he lives as a god on earth.

41 Perhaps in this case too Epicurus was inspired by Plato, who argues that practical wisdom or prudence [φρόνησις] is like a sober [νηφαντική] source of pleasure (cf. *Phl.* 61c6 and Boeri, 2010: 365). We have developed this point in some detail in chapter 3.

42 Cicero also formulates the issue in *Fin.* 2.28, pointing out that Epicurus often approves of pleasure in the common meaning of the term, which puts him in a compromised situation insofar as this 'commits him to the view that no deed is foul enough to consider refraining from so long as it is done for the sake of pleasure *and no one is watching* [*ut hominum conscientia remota*]'.

43 Interestingly, Konstan 2008: 53–5 suggests that the Epicurean doctrine that fear or, more properly, anxiety is the cause of unlimited desires marks a notable difference from Plato's and Aristotle's approaches to immoderate passions such as greed or ambition.

44 Most interpreters refer to exceptional circumstances in which the satisfaction of the natural desires of the sage or of a friend (which would seem to constitute performing 'honourably') would involve breaking the law. There are, however, also very different hypotheses, such as the one put forward by Roskam, who argues that it cannot be ruled out that, if Epicurus were sure of not being discovered, he would put the harmful apostate Timocrates to death (Roskam 2012: 37–9).

45 Cf. Austin 1965: 40.

46 Or to put it more precisely in terms of John Stuart Mill's utilitarianism: 'The creed which accepts as the foundation of morals, Utility, or the Greatest Happiness Principle, holds that actions are right in proportion as they tend to promote happiness, wrong as they tend to produce the reverse of happiness. By happiness is intended pleasure, and the absence of pain; by unhappiness, pain, and the privation of pleasure. . . . pleasure, and freedom from pain, are the only things desirable as ends; and that all desirable things . . . are desirable either for the pleasure inherent in themselves, or as means to the promotion of pleasure and the prevention of pain' (Stuart Mill 2015: chapter II, 121). The last part of this passage from Mill sounds

somewhat Epicurean in character. However, see what we argue below toward the end of this section and in note 51.

47 Epicurus' piety to the gods is recalled in different passages (DL 10.10; Cicero, *ND* 1.45, 56). The view that a god is self-sufficient (so it has no need of human beings or of giving trouble to them) is incorporated by Philodemus into his discussion of piety and justice. See, for example, Philodemus, *On Piety* col. lxxviii, 2263-2265 (ed. Obbink) where he argues that piety and justice are virtually the same thing and two faces of the same coin. You cannot be a just person, Philodemus suggests, without being pious, or pious without being just (see also *On Piety* Col. xl, 1139-1150).

48 As noted by Obbink 1996: 310, the gods came to be thought of as subject to disturbance, insofar as the fear of death was mistakenly attributed to gods (cf. Philodemus, *On Piety* col. ix, 280-281, ed. Obbink).

49 As Armstrong 2011:115, rightly claims.

50 Epicurean justice only works within the domain of 'mutual associations' (*PD* 36 to 38).

51 Although as indicated above (note 46), some similarities between Epicurean hedonism and Mill's utilitarian hedonism may be noted, one should be very cautious. Mill coined the term 'utilitarianism' to refer to his view that a right action is that which an agent performs for 'the greatest happiness of the greatest number' (the so-called 'the greatest happiness principle'; Stuart Mill 2015: chap. I–II). But as lucidly explained by Long (2020: 1473), 'the greatest happiness principle' does not clarify what things it includes in the ideas of pain and pleasure (happiness being pleasure and the absence of pain, and unhappiness pain and the privation of pleasure). This being so, Mill presents himself as an unqualified psychological hedonist. More importantly, Mill's suggestion that there are 'higher pleasures' (such pleasures being the psychological ones) that are superior to sensual ones is not in line with what Epicurus states. Indeed, as pointed out by Long, the distinction itself between higher and lower pleasures cannot be attributed to Epicurus, since mental pleasures and pains are greater than bodily pleasures and pains, 'but not intrinsically or ethically better or worse respectively'; Long 2020: 1476–7.

52 Cf. *VS* 43 as well as the use of γενναῖος ('noble man') regarding the Epicurean sage in *VS* 78. On the use of 'honourably', 'nobly' (καλῶς) in Epicurus, see Robitzsch 2019: 6–7, who does not consider the illuminating remarks by Long 2006: 190–2.

53 On the difficulties of expression χάριν τῶν σοφῶν, cf. Goldschmidt 1977: 97 n.1, and Besnier 2001: 133 n. 11.

54 See also Porphyry, *Letter to Marcella* 27; Porphyry, surely evoking Epicurus, clarifies that those laws are 'written laws' [ἔγγραφοι νόμοι]; therefore, the laws that rule over the wise are formal, positive laws, such as those belonging to an existing polis. Seneca complains that the limits that law of nature ordains for us are as trivial as 'not to be hungry, not to be thirsty, not to be cold' (*Ep.* 4, 10; transl. Graver and Long), and ironically concludes that 'nature's needs are easily provided and ready to hand'.

Of course, Seneca must be thinking of the Stoic law of nature; but the 'law of nature' that the Epicurean sage has internalized is one that requires its adherent to satisfy the necessary desires (hunger, thirst, etc.), and to do so in the way that the *law of the political community* in which he lives allows (we provide a discussion of the Epicurean 'justice of nature' in chapter 3).

55 De Sanctis 2016: 87.
56 De Sanctis 2016: 71–7, 83.
57 Erler 2002: 177–80.
58 This is so because, for excellent or virtuous people, sharing conversations with those who are like them produces an 'ineffable pleasure' (ἄφατος ἡδονή; Philodemus, *On the gods* col. xiv, 4-6, ed. Diels).
59 See Glad 1995: 162–3; Armstrong 2011:125–7 and 2016: 190–3; Essler 2013: 97; Németh 2017: 178–81.
60 Armstrong 2016: 190.
61 Obbink 1996: 566.
62 Obbink 1996: 583.
63 Cf. DL 9.112 and Dorandi 1999: 6, 47.

Chapter 6

1 Philippson, in his pioneering 1910 paper on Epicurus' philosophy of right, highlights the ignorance existing in his time of Epicurus' political reflection and exemplifies it with appreciations taken from von Arnim, (see Philippson 1910: 289). A few years before Philippson's 1910 paper, the Italian jurist A. Falchi had published, in 1902, the book *Il pensiero giuridico d'Epicuro*. Almost three centuries earlier, Gassendi had devoted several pages to the Epicurean debates on justice, the right and law, that he reworked to incorporate such discussions into his philosophy (see Paganini 2020). In the seventeenth century Epicureanism appears in the background of the personal dialogue between Gassendi and Hobbes and their mutual influence in the years of the making of the *Leviathan*. However, Gassendi's appropriation of Epicureanism's political philosophy was not well known either in his time or the following centuries, as is proved by the fact that he is mentioned by neither Falchi nor Philippson.
2 Grimal 1969: 151–2.
3 On the recipients of *LM* cf. De Sanctis 2012: 107–9. Erbi 2015: 79–80, develops a thorough analysis of the fragments of Epicurus' letters sent to Idomeneus and Mithras, as well as of other Epicurean testimonies related to both politicians.
4 Interestingly, as De Sanctis 2009: 110 has pointed out, in the *Vita Philonidis* (*PHerc.* 1044) the concept of utility is repeatedly linked to the activity and personality of the Epicurean Philonides of Laodicea.

5 Epictetus *Diss.* 2.20, 6-20. As is relatively obvious, Epictetus is accusing Epicurus and the Epicureans of committing a sort of performative contradiction, which, in our view, helps to show that, according to Epictetus, the Epicureans did carry out political activities and lived within the framework of political organizations. Epictetus caricatures Epicurus, among other reasons, because he does not take into consideration the sophistication of Epicurean hedonism.
6 Gilbert 2015: 4.
7 See Schofield 2021: 229–42.
8 Schofield 2021: 232–8. See also Görler 1995 and Lévy 2001: 71.
9 Schofield 2021: 235–6.
10 Aalders 1982: 5–12.
11 For Seneca, see *Ep.* 59, 12; *De ira* 3.17.2. See also Eicke 1909: 69.
12 Connor 1968: 146; Pownall 2003: 175.
13 Tutrone 2018: 352–62.
14 As Fish 2011: 76–81 has shown, Lucretius' comparison of politicians with Sisyphus (3.995-1002) does not correspond to the widespread 'existentialist' interpretation. Lucretius does not intend his comparison to show the vanity and futility of *all* politics, but rather refers specifically to politicians who again and again fail in their quest for power.
15 Roskam 2007b: 55.
16 On the difficulties of this passage cf. Roskam 2007b: 52–4.
17 Fish 2011: 91–9.
18 As pointed out above, Cicero refers jointly (in *Leg.* 1. 39) to the Epicureans and the Academy of Carneades and Arcesilaus while justifying their silencing.
19 The 'inspector' was an officer, generally of senatorial rank, who was responsible for investigating and reforming the administration of the provinces; he could also have powers to intervene in the free cities.
20 As Scholz 2004 points out, a very significant change of perception took place during the third century, when philosophy was accepted as a part of higher education.
21 On this see Indelli 2014.
22 Usener 1887: 13.
23 Erler 2020: 88–90.
24 Clay 2001: x; 4, n.3, and especially 42–3.
25 On this point, see Erbi 2015.
26 For details on this point, see Leiwo and Remes 1999: 161–6. cf. also the seminal works by Bruns 1882, and Dareste 1882.
27 Warren 2004: 190–1.
28 Warren 2004: 191.
29 Sickinger 1999: 133–4.

30 Aminomachus is mentioned in an Athenian inscription reproducing a decree of the Mesogeioi, which suggests that he was a prominent citizen with whom Epicurus was connected (on this see Haake 2007: 146–8).
31 The house of Melite is mentioned in Cicero's correspondence. Patro, successor to Phaedrus as the head of the Garden, turned to Atticus to intervene against a decree of the Athenian Areopagus allowing C. Memmius, the patron of Lucretius, to build on the ruins of the house of Epicurus, presumably the house at Melite. Atticus asked Cicero to intervene and Cicero, as we read in *Fam.* XIII. 1, wrote to Memmius.
32 As Armstrong 2006: 296–7 has shown, Warren's considerations regarding Epicurus' inconsistency in making a will involve assumptions about altruism and Epicurean friendship and hedonism that several texts of Philodemus deny.
33 Tsouna 2007: 283–5. Armstrong 2006: 296–7.
34 Clay 2001: 69.
35 Benferhat 2005: 44–7.
36 On this point, see Roskam 2020: 390.
37 Cf. De Sanctis 2009: 108.
38 Koch 2005: 262–6; Haake 2007: 148–59. Assante (2011/12: 47; see also 50) interestingly notes that from the inscriptions and the papyrus, we learn that Philonides 'belonged to a prestigious family, that must have had some political clout due to his diplomatic activity'. She also underlines that Philonides came into contact with the king Antiochus IV Epiphanes and his grandson Demetrius I Soter (king from 162 to 150) during his maturity.
39 Cf. Campos and López 2010: 28–33.
40 As remarked by Clay 2001: 65.
41 De Sanctis 2016: 84–5.
42 Raubitschek 1949: 96–103; Koch 2005: 262–6 and 2009; Haake 2007: 159–66, 175–6 and 2017: 148–59.
43 Koch 2009.
44 Oliver 1938; Raubitschek 1949; Follet 1994; Smith 1996; Haake 2007, 2008, 2016, 2017; Koch 2005, and Van Bremen 2005.
45 On this see Haake 2007: 261–4.
46 Arrayás 2016: 86.
47 Cf. Benferhat 2005: 55; Haake 2007: 190–4.
48 Haake 2008:156.
49 Ferrary 1988: 477–86; Ballesteros 2005; Benferhat 2005: 51–4. According to Anglade (2021: 199–202), Aristion was really an Epicurean and tyrant of Athens. The Epicurean scholar Zeno of Sidon also collaborated with him. Phaedrus, on the other hand, was pro-Roman.
50 Haake 2007: 280.
51 Haake 2008: 157–8.

52 Smith 1996: 129–30. See also Haake 2008: 158.
53 Smith 1996: 129; Koch 2005: 261–2; Haake 2008: 159.
54 Haake 2008: 156–7.
55 Haake 2016: 292.
56 Dorandi 2005: 31.
57 Hammerstaedt and Smith 2018: 63.
58 See also Armstrong's comments in 2011: 124–5.
59 Roskam 2007b: 143–4.
60 Erler 2020: 71–3.
61 We use the transcriptions and commentaries by Oliver 1938, Temporini 1978, Follet 1994, Dorandi 2000 and Van Bremen 2005.
62 Follet 1994: 171.
63 On Amafinius and his anonymous *aemuli*, see Gilbert 2015: 41–68; Anglade 2021: 166–78.
64 Farrington 1939: 192.
65 Momigliano 1941: 149–51.
66 Castner 1988; Benferhat 2005; Gilbert 2015; Valachova 2018; Volk 2021; Roskam 2022.
67 See Volk 2022: 81–6.
68 Griffin 1989: 32–4.
69 The list, even in the most conservative versions, is not small. See Gilbert's version (2015): Titus Albucius, Lucius Calpurnius Piso, Gaius Cassius Longinus, Marcus Fadius Gallus, Lucius Manlius Torquatus, Gaius Memmius Caesoninus, Gaius Velleius, Gaius Vibius Pansa, Caetronianus Lucius Papirius, Paetus Titus Pomponius Atticus, Lucius Saufeius Gaius, Trebatius Testa.
70 Gilbert 2015: 134–45 has carefully analysed the anti-Epicurean arguments of this letter in order to show their continuation in Cicero's philosophical works. Such continuation also reflects the continuity of the omission of central Epicurean arguments that Cicero's anti-Epicurean arguments entail (as Erler 1992 rightly has emphasized). On the letter to Trebatius of April 53, see Erler 1992: 310–22; Griffin 1995: 332–4; Benferhat 2005: 274–81 and 2010. For Vesperini 2011: 166, Trebatius' adherence to Epicureanism lacks seriousness and is merely frivolous.
71 Benferhat 2005: 277.
72 On this, see Bremer 1896: 398.
73 See Benferheat 2005: 98–100.
74 Valachova 2018: 169–70.
75 White 2010: 3–29.
76 Benferhat 2005: 98; Gilbert 2015: 4–5 and 2022.
77 See the detailed account of Bianay 2014: 65–136.
78 Benferhat 2005: 98.

79 See Griffin 1995: 342–6; Benferhat 2005: 261–5; Armstrong 2011: 111–14; Gilbert 2015: 221–43; Valachova 2018: 112–31.
80 Sedley 1997: 41.
81 Sedley 1997: 46–7.
82 According to Momigliano (1941: 151–4), Farrington wrongly argued that the Roman Epicureans were inclined towards the Republic, since there were also Epicureans who opted for the monarchy. Anglade (2015: 766–8; 2021: 423–7) proposes a distinction between Latin and a Greek Epicureanism in Rome. The former, represented by authors such as Amafinius, his Epicurean *aemuli* and Lucretius, would be linked to the *Populares*; the latter, represented by figures such as Albucius, Atticus, L. Saufeius, Cassius and the circle of Philodemus, to the *Optimates*.
83 Grimal 1966. See also Anglade 2015: 741–5.
84 See Haake 2003: 89, 119–21.
85 Roskam 2007a 23–7; 2007b: 105–7.
86 Roskam 2007b: 106.
87 Fish 2011: 103–4; 2018: 154–5.
88 See *On Rhetoric* 2, col. xxxivb 34-39 and 3, col. xiva 19-col xvia 8 (ed. Hammerstaedt).
89 Armstrong 2011: 112.
90 Neither equity nor indulgence had a positive valuation in Stoic ethics; on this, see Erskine 2000: 73–4; Asmis 1991: 39; De Sanctis 2008: 175. On the 'legalism' of Diogenes of Babylon see Erskine 2000: 154–6.

References

Aalders, G. J. (1982), *Plutarch's Political Thought*, Amsterdam: North-Holland Publishing Company.

Adorno, F. (1980), 'Polistrato e il suo tempo. Termini platonici e aristotelici in nuovi significati,' *Elenchos*, 1: 151–61.

Alberti, A. (1995), 'The Epicurean Theory of Law and Justice,' in A. Laks and M. Schofield (eds), *Justice and Generosity*, 161–90, Cambridge: Cambridge University Press.

Alesse, F. (2011), 'Teknopoiia e amore parentale in Epicuro e nell'epicureismo,' *Cronache Ercolanesi*, 41: 207–15.

Algra, K. (1997), 'Lucretius and the Epicurean Other,' in K. Algra and M. Koenen (eds), *Lucretius and His Intellectual Background*, 141–50, Amsterdam: Royal Netherlands Academy of Arts and Sciences.

Algra, K. (2003), 'Social Appropriation in Hellenistic Ethics,' *Oxford Studies in Ancient Philosophy*, 25: 265–96.

Angelli, A. (2013), 'Lettere di Epicuro dall'Egitto (POxy LXXVI 5077),' *Studi di Egittologia e Papirologia*, 10: 9–32.

Anglade, L. (2015) 'Philosophie et politique à la fin de la République romaine: les exemples de Lucrèce et Atticus,' *Revue Historique*, 4 (676): 739–70.

Anglade, L. (2021), *La Ville et le Jardin: les épicurismes et la res publica d'Amafinius à Julien*, Perpignan: Diss.

Annas, J. (1989), 'Epicurean Emotions,' *Greek, Roman and Byzantine Studies*, 30: 145–64.

Annas, J. (1993), *The Morality of Happiness*, Oxford: Oxford University Press.

Annas, J. (2013), 'Plato's Laws and Cicero's de Legibus' in M. Schofield (ed.), *Aristotle, Plato and Pythagoreanism in the first century BC: new directions for philosophy*, 206–24, Cambridge: Cambridge University Press.

Aoiz, J. (2012), 'La evidencia en la filosofía antigua,' *Azafea. Revista de Filosofía Universidad de Salamanca*, 14: 167–79.

Aoiz, J., Deniz, D., and Bruni, B. eds (2014), *Elementos de Ética, Extractos de Estobeo y Glosas de la Suda de Hierocles el estoico*, Salamanca: Helmantica.

Arenson, K. (2019), *Health and Hedonism in Plato and Epicurus*, London: Bloomsbury.

Armstrong, D. (1997), 'Epicurean Justice,' *Phronesis*, 42: 324–34.

Armstrong, D. (2004), 'All Things to All Men: Philodemus' Model of Therapy and the Audience of *De Morte*,' in J. Fitzgerald and D. Obbink (eds), *Philodemus and the New Testament World*, 15–54, Leiden: Brill.

Armstrong, D. (2006), '*Facing Death: Epicurus and His Critics by James Warren* Review by: David Armstrong,' *The Philosophical Quarterly*, 56, 223: 294–97.

Armstrong, D. (2011), 'Epicurean virtues, Epicurean friendship: Cicero vs the Herculaneum papyri,' in J. Fish and K. Sanders (eds), *Epicurus and the Epicurean Tradition*, 105–28, Cambridge: Cambridge University Press.

Armstrong, D. (2016), 'Utility and Affection in Epicurean Friendship: Philodemus *On the Gods* 3, *On Property Management*, and Horace, *Sermones* 2.6,' in R. Caston and R. Kaster (eds), *Hope, Joy, and Affection in the Classical World*, 182–208, Oxford: Oxford University Press.

Arnim, von, I. (1903–5), *Stoicorum Veterum Fragmenta*, Stuttgart: Teubner, (3 volumes; cited *SVF* followed by the volume number and the text number).

Arrayás, I. (2016), 'Sobre la fluctuación en las alianzas en el marco de las Guerras Mitridáticas. Algunos casos significativos,' *Anatolia. Revue des Études Anciennes*, 118 (1): 79-98.

Arrighetti G. (1971), 'L'opera *Sulla natura* di Epicuro,' *Cronache Ercolanesi*, 1: 41–56.

Arrighetti, G. ed. (1973), *Epicuro, Opere*, Torino: Giulio Einaudi Editore.

Asmis, E. (1984), *Epicurus' Scientific Method*, London: Cornell University Press.

Asmis, E. (1990), 'Free Action and the Swerve,' *Oxford Studies in Ancient Philosophy*, 8: 275–90.

Asmis, E. (1991), 'Philodemus' Poetic Theory and *On the Good King According to Homer*,' *Classical Antiquity*, 10 (1): 1–45.

Asmis, E. (1999), 'Epicurean Epistemology,' in K, Algra, J. Barnes, J. Mansfeld and M. Schofield (eds), *The Cambridge History of Hellenistic Philosophy*, 260–94, Cambridge: Cambridge University Press.

Asmis, E. (2001), 'Basic Education in Epicureanism,' in Y. Lee Too (ed.), *Education in Greek and Roman antiquity*, 209–40, Leiden: Brill.

Asmis, E. (2001a), 'The Politician as public servant in Cicero's De re publica,' in C. Auvray-Assayas et D. Delattre (eds), *Cicéron et Philodème*, 109–29, Paris: Éd. Rue d'Ulm.

Asmis, E. (2004), 'Epicurean Economics,' in J. Fitzgerald and D. Obbink (eds), *Philodemus and the New Testament World*, 133–76, Leiden: Brill.

Assante, M. G. (2011/12), *PHerc. 1044 (Vita Philonidis; edizione, traduzione e commento)*, Udine: Diss.

Atherton, C. (2005), 'Lucretius on what language is not,' in D. Frede and B. Inwood (eds), *Language and Learning. Philosophy of Language in the Hellenistic Age*, 101–38, Cambridge: Cambridge University Press.

Atherton, C. (2009), 'Epicurean philosophy of language,' in J. Warren, *The Cambridge Companion to Epicureanism*, 197–215, Cambridge: Cambridge University Press.

Atkins, E. M. trans. (2004), *Cicero, On Duties* (Cambridge Texts in the History of Political Thought. Edited by M.T. Griffin and E.M. Atkins), Cambridge: Cambridge University Press (11th edition).

Aubenque, P. (2014), *La prudence chez Aristote*, Paris: Presses Universitaires de France.

Austin, J. (1965), *The Province of Jurisprudence Determined*, Cambridge: Cambridge University Press.

Austin, E. (2012), 'Epicurus and the Politics of Fearing Death,' *Apeiron*, 45: 109–29.

Avotins, I. (1977), 'Training in Frugality in Epicurus and Seneca,' *Phoenix*, 31 (3): 214–17.

Bailey, C. (1928), *The Greek Atomists and Epicurus*, New York: Russell and Russell.

Bakker, F. A. (2016), *Epicurean Meteorology Sources, Method, Scope and Organization*, Leiden: Brill.

Balch, D. L. (2004), 'Philodemus, *On Wealth* and *On Household Management*, Naturally Wealthy Epicureans Against Poor Cynics,' in J. Fitzgerald and D. Obbink (eds), *Philodemus and the New Testament World*, 197–220, Leiden: Brill.

Ballesteros, L. (2005), 'Atenión, tirano de Atenas,' *Studia Historica: Historia Antigua*, 23: 385–400.

Barigazzi, A. (1983), 'Sul concetto epicureo della sicurezza esterna,' in M. Gigante (ed.), Συζήτησις. *Studi sull'Epicureismo Greco e Romano*, 73–92, Napoli: Bibliopolis.

Barnes, J. (1996), 'Epicurus: Meaning and Thinking,' in G. Giannantoni and M. Gigante (eds), *Epicureismo Greco e Romano*, 197–220, Napoli: Bibliopolis.

Benferhat, Y. (2005), *Cives Epicurei Les épicuriens et l'idée de monarchie à Rome et en Italie de Sylla à Octave*, Bruxelles: Éditions Latomus.

Benferhat, Y. (2010), 'What if . . . ? La possibilité d'un anneau,' *Fundamina: A Journal of Legal History*, 16 (1): 23–8.

Besnier, B. (2001), 'Justice et utilité de la politique dans l'épicurisme. Réponse a Elizabeth Asmis,' in C. Auvray-Assayas et D. Delattre (eds), *Cicéron et Philodème*, 129–57, Paris: Rue D'Ulm.

Betegh, G. (2016), 'Archelaus on Cosmogony and the Origins of Social Institutions,' *Oxford Studies in Ancient Philosophy*, 51: 1–40.

Bianay, M. (2014), *Atticus et ses amis: étude sur une politique de l'ombre au dernier siècle de la République*, Montpellier: Diss.

Bignone, E. (1920), *Epicuro: opere, frammenti, testimonianze sulla vita*, Bari: Laterza.

Bignone, E. (1973), *L'Aristotele perduto e la formazione filosofica di Epicuro* T. I e II. 2nd Firenze: La Nuova Italia.

Boardmann, J., Griffin, J. and O. Murray eds (1986), *The Oxford History of the Ancient World*, Oxford: Oxford University Press.

Boeri, M. (2010), 'Epicurus the Platonist,' in J. Dillon and L. Brisson (eds), *Plato's Philebus Selected Papers from The Eighth Symposium Platonicum*, 363–8, Sankt Augustin: Academia Verlag.

Boeri, M. D. (2013), 'Natural Law and world order in Stoicism,' in G. Rossi (ed.), *Nature and the Best Life. Exploring the Natural Bases of Practical Normativity in Ancient Philosophy*, 183–223, Hildesheim–Zürich–New York: G. Olms.

Boeri, M. D. and Salles, R. (2014), *Los filósofos estoicos. Ontología, Lógica, Física y Ética*, Sankt Augustin: Academia Verlag (cited BS followed by the chapter number and the text number).

Bollack, J. (1996), 'Le Langage Philosophique d'Épicure,' in G. Giannantoni and M. Gigante (eds), *Epicureismo Greco e Romano*, 169–95, Napoli: Bibliopolis.
Bonelli, G. (1979), *Aporie etiche in Epicuro*, Bruxelles: Éditions Latomus.
Bouffartigue, J. (1977), *Porphyre, De l'Abstinence. Tome I*, Paris: Les Belles Lettres.
Boulogne, J. (2003), *Plutarque dans le miroir d'Épicure*, Villeneuve d'Ascq: Presses Universitaires du Septentrion.
Bowen, A. and Garnsey, P. trans. (2003), *Lactantius. Divine Institutes*, Glasgow: Liverpool University Press.
Brandt, S. (1891), 'Lactantius und Lucretius,' *Jahrbücher für classische Philologie*, 37: 225–59.
Bremer, F. P. ed. (1896), *Iurisprudentiae antehadrianae quae supersunt. Pars 1. Liberae rei publicae iuris consulti*, Leipzig: Teubner Verlag.
Brock, R. (2013), *Greek Political Imagery from Homer to Aristotle*, London: Bloomsbury.
Brown, E. (2002), 'Epicurus on the Value of Friendship (Sententia Vaticana 23),' *Classical Philology*, 97: 68–80.
Brown, E. (2009), 'Politics and society,' in J. Warren (ed.), *The Cambridge Companion to Epicureanism*, 179–96, Cambridge: Cambridge University Press.
Bruns, K. (1882), 'Die Testamente der griechischen Philosophen,' in K. Bruns, *Kleinere Schriften* I, 192–237, Weimar: H. Böhlau.
Brunschwig, J. (1994), *Papers in Hellenistic Philosophy*, Cambridge: Cambridge University Press.
Burnet, J. ed. (1900–3) *Platonis Opera* (Recognovit brevique adnotatione critica instrvxit Ioannes Burnet), Oxford: Clarendon Press (Tomus I-IV).
Bywater, I. (1894) *Aristotelis Ethica Nicomachea* (Recognovit Breviqve Adnotatione Critica instrvxit Ingemar Bywater), Oxford: Oxford University Press.
Cairns, D. (2016), 'Metaphors for Hope in Archaic and Classical Greek Poetry,' in R. Caston and R. Kaster (eds), *Hope, Joy, and Affection in the Classical World*, 13–44, New York: Oxford University Press.
Campbell, G. (2003), *Lucretius on Creation and Evolution A Commentary on De rerum Natura V 772-1104*, Oxford: Oxford University Press.
Campos, F. J. (1999), 'Formas de vida, política y filosofía en Dicearco de Mesina,' *Praesentia*, 2: 43–69.
Campos, F. J. and López, M. (2010), 'Communauté épicurienne et communication épistolaire. Lettres de femmes selon le PHerc. 176: la correspondance de Batis,' in A. Antonie and G. Arrighetti (eds), *Miscellanea Papyrologica Herculanensia Vol. I*, 21–36, Roma: Fabrizio Serra Editore.
Castner, C. J. (1988), *A Prosopography of Roman Epicureans*, Frankfurt: Peter Lang.
Chamoux, F. (2002), *Hellenistic Civilization*, Melbourne: Wiley-Blackwell.
Chilton, C. W. (1962), 'The Epicurean Theory of the Origin of Language. A Study of Diogenes of Oeonoanda,' *The American Journal of Philology*, 83 (2): 159–67.
Ciriaci, A. ed. (2013), *L'Anonimo di Giamblico. Saggio critico e analisi dei frammenti*, Napoli: Bibliopolis.

Clark, G. trans. (2000), *Porphyry: On Abstinence from Killing Animals*, Ithaca (NY): Cornell University Press.

Clay, D. (1972), 'Epicurus' Kyría Dóxa XVII,' *Greek, Roman and Byzantine Studies*, 13: 59–66.

Clay, D. (2001), *Paradosis and Survival Three Chapters in the History of Epicurean Philosophy*, Ann Arbor: University of Michigan Press.

Cohen, D. (2000), *Law, Violence, and Community in Classical Athens*, Cambridge: Cambridge University Press.

Cohen, D. (2005), 'Theories of Punishment,' in M. Gagarin and D. Cohen (eds), *The Cambridge Companion to Ancient Greek Law*, 170–90, Cambridge: Cambridge University Press.

Cole, Th. (1990), *Democritus and the Sources of Greek Anthropology*, Atlanta: Scholars Press.

Colman, J. (2012), *Lucretius as Theorist of Political Life*, New York: Palgrave Macmillan.

Connor, W. R. (1968), *Theopompus and Fifth-Century Athens*, Cambridge (MA): Harvard University Press.

Cooper, J. (1999), *Reason and Emotion. Essays on Ancient Moral Psychology and Ethical Theory*, Princeton: Princeton University Press.

Corti, A. (2014), *L'Adversus Colotem di Plutarco Storia di una polemica filosofica*, Leuven: Brill.

Cosenza, P. (1996), 'La dimostrazione della non eleggibilità dell'ingiustizia nella *Rata Sententia* XXXIV di Epicuro,' in G. Giannantoni and M. Gigante (eds), *Epicureismo Greco e Romano*, 361–76, Napoli: Bibliopolis.

Dareste, R. (1882), 'Les Testaments des Philosophes Grecs,' *Annuaire de l'Association pour l'encouragement des études grecques en France*, 16: 1–21.

Denyer, N. ed. (2001), *Plato Alcibiades*, Cambridge: Cambridge University Press.

De Romilly, J. (1968), *Time in Greek Tragedy*, Ithaca (NY): Cornell University Press.

De Romilly, J. (1971), *La loi dans la pensée grecque des origines à Aristote*, Paris: Les Belles Lettres.

De Sanctis, D. (2008), 'Il buon re di Filodemo tra Epicuro e Omero,' *Cronache Ercolanesi*, 38: 165–77.

De Sanctis, D. (2009), 'Il Filosofo e il Re: Osservazioni sulla *Vita Philonidis* (*PHerc*. 1044),' *Cronache Ercolanesi*, 39: 107–18.

De Sanctis, D. (2012), 'Utile al singolo, utile a molti: il proemio dell'Epistola a Pitocle,' *Cronache Ercolanesi*, 42: 95–110.

De Sanctis, D. (2016), 'La biografia del Kepos e il profilo esemplare del saggio epicureo,' in M. Bonazzi and St. Schorn (eds), *Bios Philosophos: Philosophy in Ancient Greek Biography*, 71–99, Turnhout: Brepols.

De Witt, N. (1937), 'The Epicurean Doctrine of Gratitude,' *The American Journal of Philology*, 58 (3): 320–8.

De Witt, N. (1954), *Epicurus and His Philosophy*, Minneapolis: University of Minnesota Press.

Dierauer, U. (1977), *Tier und Mensch im Denken der Antike*, Amsterdam: B. R. Grüner.

Dillon, J. and Brisson, L. eds (2010), *Plato's Philebus Selected Papers from The Eighth Symposium Platonicum*, Sankt Augustin: Academia Verlag.

Dodds, E. R. ed. (1959), *Plato Gorgias: A Revised Text with Introduction and Commentary*, Oxford: Clarendon Press.

Dorandi T. (1999), *Antigone de Caryste. Fragments*, Paris: Belles Lettres.

Dorandi, T. (2000), 'Plotina, Adriano e gli Epicurei di Atene,' in M. Erler (ed.), *Epikureismus in der späten Republik und der Kaiserzeit*, 137–48, Berlin: Steiner.

Dorandi, T. (2005), 'Le philosophe et le pouvoir. Un cas de propagande inversée', in A. Bresson and C. Pébarthe (eds), *L'écriture publique du povoir*, 27–34, Paris: Ausonios.

Dorandi, T. ed. (2013), *Diogenes Laertius Lives of Eminent Philosophers*, Cambridge: Cambridge University Press.

Duke, G. (2020), *Aristotle and Law. The Politics of Nomos*, Cambridge: Cambridge University Press.

Dumont, J.-P. (1982), 'Confirmation et disconfirmation,' in J. Barnes and J. Brunschwig (eds), *Science and Speculation: Studies in Hellenistic theory and practice*, 273–303, Cambridge: Cambridge University Press.

Dyson, H. (2009), *Prolepsis and Ennoia in Early Stoa*, Berlin: De Gruyter.

Eicke, L. (1909), *Veterum philosophorum qualia fuerint de Alexandro Magno iudicia*, Rostock, Prike: Diss.

Einarson, B. and De Lacy, Ph., trans. (1967) *Plutarch Moralia*, vol. 14, Cambridge, MA: Harvard University Press.

Erbi, M. (2015), 'Lettere dal Kepos: l'impegno di Epicuro per i *philoi*,' in D. de Sanctis and E. Spinelli (eds), *Questioni epicuree*, 75–94, Berlin: Academia Verlag.

Erler, M. (1992), 'Cicero und der "unorthodoxe" Epikureismus,' *Anregung*, 38: 310–22.

Erler, M. (1994) *Epikur. Die Schule Epikurs, Lukrez*. In: H. Flashar (Hrsg.): *Die hellenistische Philosophie (Die Philosophie der Antike*. Bd. 4). Teil 1, Basel: Schwabe Verlag.

Erler, M. (1996), 'Philologia *Medicans*. La Lettura delle Opere di Epicuro nella sua Scuola,' in G. Giannantoni and M. Gigante (eds), *Epicureismo Greco e Romano*, 513–26, Napoli: Bibliopolis.

Erler, M. (2002), 'Epicurus as deus mortalis: Homoiosis theoi and Epicurean Self-cultivation,' in D. Frede and A. Laks (eds), *Traditions of Theology Studies in Hellenistic Theology, Its Background, and Aftermath*, 159–81, Leiden: Brill.

Erler, M. (2008), 'Utopie und Realität. Epikureische Legitimation von Herrschaftsformen,' in Th. Baier und M. Amerise (eds), *Die Legitimation der Einzelherrschaft im Kontext der Generationenthematik*, 39–54, Berlin: De Gruyter.

Erler, M. (2011), 'Autodidact and student: on the relationship of authority and autonomy in Epicurus and the Epicurean tradition,' in J. Fish and K. Sanders (eds), *Epicurus and the Epicurean Tradition*, 9–28, Cambridge: Cambridge University Press.

Erler, M. (2012), '*Aplanes Theoria*. Einige Aspekte der epikureische Vorstellung vom Bios Theoretikos,' in Th. Bénatouïl and M. Bonazzi (eds), *Theoria, Praxis and the Contemplative Life after Plato and Aristotle*, 41–55, Leiden: Brill.

Erler, M. (2020), *Epicurus. An Introduction to his Practical Ethics and Politics*, Basel: Schwabe Verlag.
Erskine, A. (2000), *The Hellenistic Stoa: Political Thought and Action*, London: Duckworth.
Essler, H. (2011), 'Cicero's use and abuse of Epicurean theology,' in J. Fish, and K. Sanders (eds), *Epicurus and the Epicurean Tradition*, 129–51, Cambridge: Cambridge University Press.
Essler, H. (2012), 'Die Lust der Freundschaft und die Lust des Freundes von Epikur bis Cicero,' in M. Erler und W. Rother (eds), *Philosophie der Lust Studien zum Hedonismus*, 139–60, Basel: Schwabe Verlag,
Essler, H. (2013), 'Freundschat der Götter und Toten mit einer neue Edition von Phld Di III Frg. 87 und 83,' *Cronache Ercolanesi*, 43: 95–111.
Everson, S. (1994), 'Epicurus on Mind and Language,' in S. Everson (ed.), *Language A Companion to Ancient Thought*, 74–108, Cambridge: Cambridge University Press.
Evrigenis, I. D. (2008), *Fear of Enemies and Collective Action*, Cambridge: Cambridge University Press.
Falchi, A. (1902), *Il pensiero giuridico d'Epicuro*, Sassari: Tipografia U. Satta.
Farrington, B. (1939), *Science and Politics in the Ancient World*, London: Allen and Unwin.
Ferrary, J.-L. (1988), *Philhellénisme et impérialisme. Aspects idéologiques de la conquête romaine du monde hellénistique*, Rome: École française de Rome.
Fish, J. (2011), 'Not all politicians are Sisyphus,' in J. Fish and K. Sanders (eds), *Epicurus and the Epicurean Tradition*, 72–104, Cambridge: Cambridge University Press.
Fish, J. (2018), 'Some Critical Themes in Philodemus,' *On the Good King According to Homer*, in J. Klooster and B. Van den Berg (eds), *Homer and the Good Ruler in Antiquity and Beyond*, 141–56, Boston: Brill.
Follet, S. (1994), 'Lettres d'Hadrien aux Épicuriens d'Athènes (14.2- 14.3.125): SEG III 226 + IG II^2 1097,' *Revue des Études Grecques*, 107 (509): 158–71.
Fowler, D. (2002), *Lucretius on Atomic Motion A Commentary on De Rerum Natura Book Two, Lines 1-332*, Oxford: Oxford University Press.
Fowler, D. (2007), 'Lucretius and Politics,' in M. Gale (ed.), *Lucretius*, 397–431, Oxford: Oxford University Press.
García, J. (1991), 'Filodemo y el pensamiento antropológico griego: Phld. Sto. (PHerc.155E y 339), col. XXI,' *Florentia Iliberritana*, 2: 207–13.
Gardner, H. H. (2020), *Pestilence and the Body Politic in Latin Literature*, Oxford: Oxford University Press.
Gastaldi, S. (2003), 'L'allegoria della nave in Platone,' in M. Vegetti (ed.), *La Repubblica* vol. V, Libro VI-VII, 187–216, Napoli: Bibliopolis.
Gassendi, P. (1649), *Animadversiones in decimum librum Diogenis Laertii, qui est de vita, moribus, placitisque Epicurii*, Lyon: G. Barber.
Giannantoni, G. (1996), 'Epicuro e L'Ateismo Antico,' in G. Giannantoni and M. Gigante (eds), *Epicureismo Greco e Romano*, 21–63, Napoli: Bibliopolis.

Gigante, M. (1957), 'Lucretius Sisyphum Critiae est imitatus,' *Dionysio*, 20 (4): 31–2, 97–8.
Gigante, M. (1993), 'Cinismo e Epicureismo,' in M. Goulet-Cazé (ed.), *Le Cynisme Ancien*, 159–223, Paris: Vrin.
Gilbert, N. (2015), *Among Friends: Cicero and the Epicureans*, Toronto: Diss.
Gilbert, N. (2022), 'Was Atticus an Epicurean?,' in S. Yona and D. Gregson (eds), *Epicurus in Rome: Philosophical Perspectives in the Ciceronian Age*, 55–71, Cambridge: Cambridge University Press.
Gill, C. (2002), *Personality in Greek Epic, Tragedy, and Philosophy*, Oxford: Clarendon Press.
Giovacchini, J. (2007), 'Le souvenir des plaisirs: le rôle de la mémoire dans la thérapeutique épicurienne,' in L. Boulegue (ed.), *Hédonismes: Penser et dire le plaisir dans l'Antiquité et à la Renaissance*, 69–83, Villeneuve d'Ascq: Presses Universitaires du Septentrion.
Glad, Cl. (1995), *Paul and Philodemus Adaptability in Epicurean and Early Christian Psychagogy*, Leiden: Brill.
Glidden, D. K. (1985), 'Epicurean Prolepsis,' *Oxford Studies in Ancient Philosophy*, 3: 175–217.
Goldschmidt, V. (1953), *Le système stoïcien et l'idée de temps*, Paris: Vrin.
Goldschmidt, V. (1977), *La Doctrine d'Épicure et le Droit*, Paris: Vrin.
Goldschmidt, V. (1978), 'Remarques sur l'origine épicurienne de la prénotion,' in J. Brunschwig (ed.), *Les stoïciens et leur logique*, 41–60, Paris: Vrin.
Gómez-Lobo, A. (2017), 'Philosophical Remarks on Thucydides' Melian Dialogue,' in A. Gómez-Lobo, *Selected papers*, 49–67, Sankt Augustin: Academia Verlag.
Görler, W, (1977), 'Asthenes sunkatathesis. Zur stoischen Erkenntnistheorie,' *Würzburger Jahrbücher für die Altertumswissenschaft neue Folge*, 3: 83–92.
Görler, W. (1995), 'Silencing the Troublemaker: *De Legibus* I.39 and the Continuity of Cicero's Scepticism,' in J. Powell (ed.), *Cicero the Philosopher*, 85–113, Oxford: Clarendon Press.
Görler, W. (1997), 'Storing up past pleasures: The soul-vessel-metaphor in Lucretius and in his Greek models,' in K. Algra (ed.), *Lucretius and His Intellectual Background*, 193–207, Amsterdam: Royal Netherlands Academy of Arts and Sciences.
Graver, M. and Long, A. A. trans. (2015) *Seneca, Letters on Ethics to Lucillius* (Translated with and Introduction and Commentary by Margaret Graver and Anthony A. Long), Chicago and London: The University of Chicago Press.
Gray, B. (2015), *Stasis and Stability Exile, the Polis and Political Thought, c.404-146 BC*, Oxford: Oxford University Press.
Green, P. (1990), *Alexander to Actium the Historical Evolution of the Hellenistic Age*, Berkeley: University of California Press.
Griffin, M. (1989), 'Philosophy, Politics, and Politicians at Rome,' in J. Barnes and M. Griffin, *Philosophia Togata*, 1–37, Oxford: Oxford University Press.
Griffin, M. (1995), 'Philosophical Badinage in Cicero's letters to his friends,' in J. Powell (ed.), *Cicero the Philosopher*, 325–46, Oxford: Clarendon Press.

Grilli, A. (1983), 'Diathesis in Epicuro,' in G. Pugliese (ed.), Συζήτησις. *Studi sull'Epicureismo Greco e Romano*, 93–109, Napoli: Bibliopolis.
Grilli, A. (1994), 'Osservazioni su eushathes/eustatheia,' *Helmantica*, 45: 239–50.
Grimal, P. (1966), 'Le "bon roi" de Philodème et la royauté de César,' *REL*, 44: 254–85.
Grimal, P. (1969), 'L'épicurisme romain,' *Actes du VIIIe Congrès de l'Association Guillaume Budé*, 139–68, Paris: Les Belles Lettres.
Haake, M. (2003), 'Warum und zu welchem Ende schreibt man peri basileias? Überlegungen zum historischen Kontext einer literarischen Gattung im Hellenismus,' in K. Piepenbrink (Hg.), *Philosophie und Lebenswelt in der Antike*, 83–138, Darmstadt: Wissenschaftliche Buchgesellschaft.
Haake, M. (2007), *Der Philosoph in der Stadt. Untersuchungen zur öffentlichen Rede über Philosophen und Philosophie in den hellenistischen Poleis*, München: Verlag C. H. Beck.
Haake, M. (2008), 'Philosopher and Priest: The Image of the Intellectual and the Social Practice of the Elites in the Eastern Roman Empire (first to third centuries AD),' in B. Dignas and K. Trampedach (eds), *Practitioners of the Divine. Greek Priests and Religious Officials from Homer to Heliodorus*, 145–65, Washington: Center for Hellenic Studies.
Haake, M. (2016), 'Review of Hammerstaedt, J. and Smith, M. F. The Epicurean Inscription of Diogenes of Oinoanda. Ten Years of New Discoveries and Research, Bonn: Habelt, 2014,' *The Journal of Hellenic Studies*, 136: 291–3.
Haake, M. (2017), 'Brüder-Ritter-Epikureer: Lucius und Appius Saufeius aus Praeneste in Latium, Rom und Athen,' in M. Haake und Ann-Cathrin Harders (eds), *Politische Kultur und soziale Struktur der Römischen Republik*, 429–54, Stuttgart: Franz Steiner.
Hamilton, J. T. (2013), *Security. Politics, Humanity, and the Philology of Care*, Princeton: Princeton University Press.
Hammerstaedt, J. (1992), 'Der Schlussteil von Philodems Drittem Buch Über Rhetorik,' *Cronache Ercolanesi*, 22: 9–118.
Hammerstaedt, J. (1996), 'Il ruolo della Prolepsis epicurea nell'interpretazione di Epicuro, Epistula ad Herodotum 37 SG,' in G. Giannantoni and M. Gigante (eds), *Epicureismo Greco e Romano*, 217–37, Napoli: Bibliopolis.
Hammerstaedt, J. and Smith M. F. (2018), 'Diogenes of Oinoanda: the new and unexpected discoveries of 2017 (NF 214–219), with a re-edition of Fr. 70–72,' *Epigraphica Anatolica*, 51: 43–79.
Hammond, N. G. (1993), 'The Macedonian Imprint on the Hellenistic World,' in P. Green (ed.), *Hellenistic History and Culture*, 12–23, Berkeley: University of California Press.
Hanchey, D. (2022), 'Cicero's Rhetoric of Anti-Epicureanism: Anonymity as Critique,' in S. Yona and D. Gregson (eds), *Epicurus in Rome: Philosophical Perspectives in the Ciceronian Age Epicurus in Rome*, 37–54, Cambridge: Cambridge University Press.
Hard, R. trans. (2014), *Epictetus, Discourses, Fragments, Handbook*, Oxford: Oxford University Press.
Harris, E. M. trans. (2008), *Demosthenes, speeches 20–22*, Austin: University of Texas Press.

Hirzel, R. (1887), *Untersuchungen zu Cicero's Philosophie Schriften I*, Leipzig: Schwartz Charakterköpfe aus der antiker Literatur.

Holmes, B. (2013), 'The Poetic Logic of Negative Exceptionalism in Lucretius, Book Five,' in D. Lehoux and A. D. Morrison (eds), *Lucretius: Poetry, Philosophy, Science*, 153–91, Oxford: Oxford University Press.

Hossenfelder, M. (1986), 'Epicurus- hedonist malgré lui,' in M. Schofield and G. Striker (eds), *The Norms of Nature Studies in Hellenistic Ethics*, 245–63, Cambridge: Cambridge University Press.

Huby, P. (1989), 'Theophrastus and the Criterion,' in P. Huby and G. Neal (eds), *The Criterion of Truth*, 107–22, Liverpool: Liverpool University Press.

Indelli, G. ed. (1978), *Polistrato, Sul Disprezzo irrazionale delle opinioni popolari*, Napoli: Bibliopolis.

Indelli, G. (2014), 'Epicuro fondatore e maestro del Giardino,' in M. Beretta, F. Citti, and A. Iannucci (eds), *Il culto di Epicuro. Testi, iconografia e paesaggio*, 65–88, Firenze: Casa Editrice Leo S. Olschki.

Inwood, B. (1990), 'Rhetorica Disputatio: The Strategy of *de Finibus* II,' *Apeiron*, 23 (4): 143–64.

Inwood, B. and Gerson, L. P. eds and trans. (1994), *The Epicurus Reader: Selected Writings and Testimonia* (Translated and Edited by Brad Inwood and L.P. Gerson. Introduction by D. S. Hutchinson), Indianapolis/Cambridge: Hackett Publishing Company, Inc.

Irwin, T. (1985), 'Socrates the Epicurean,' *Illinois Classical Studies*, 11: 85–112.

Jaeger, W. (1934), *Aristotle Fundamentals of the History of His Development*, Oxford: Oxford University Press.

Jaulin, A. (2007), 'Democrite au Lycèe: la définition,' in A. Brancacci and Ph. Morel (eds), *Democritus*, 265–75, Leiden: Brill.

Jürss, F. (1977), 'Epikur und das Problem des Begriffes (Prolepse),' *Philologus*, 121: 211–25.

Jürss, F. (1991), *Die epikureische Erkenntnistheorie*, Berlin: Academia Verlag.

Kahn, Ch. (1981), 'The origins of social contract theory,' in G. Kerferd (ed.), *The Sophists and their Legacy*, 92–108, Wiesbaden: Franz Steiner.

Kazantzidis, G. and Spatharas, D. eds (2018), *Hope in Ancient Literature, History, and Art*, Kölhn: De Gruyter.

Kechagia, E. (2010), 'Rethinking a Professional Rivalry: Early Epicureans against the Stoa,' *Classical Quarterly*, 60 (1): 132–55.

Kechagia, E. (2011), *Plutarch Against Colotes. A Lesson in History of Philosophy*, Oxford: Oxford University Press.

Koch, R. (2005), 'Des Épicuriens entre la vie retirée et les honneurs publics,' in V. Dasen et M. Piérart (eds), *Idia kai dèmosia. Les cadres privés et publics de la religion grecque antique*, 259–72, Liége: Presses Universitaires de Liége.

Koch, R. (2009), 'Philocrates de Sidon, disciple d'Épicure (Inscriptiones Graecae VII, 3226),' in N. Belayche et S. Mimouni (eds), *Entre lignes de partage et territoires de passages. Les identités religieuses dans les mondes grec et romain*, 121–37. Paris: Peeters Publishers.

Konstan, D. (2000), 'Altruism,' *Transactions of the American Philological Association*, 130: 1–17.

Konstan, D. (2006), *The Emotions of the Ancient Greeks: Studies in Aristotle and Classical Literature*, Toronto: University of Toronto Press.

Konstan, D. (2007), 'Response to Morel,' *Proceedings of the Boston Area Colloquium in Ancient Philosophy*, 23: 27–32.

Konstan, D. (2008), *A Life Worthy of the Gods. The Materialist Psychology of Epicurus*, Las Vegas: Parmenides.

Konstan, D. (2011), 'Epicurus on the Gods,' in J. Fish, K. Sanders (eds), *Epicurus and the Epicurean Tradition*, 53–71, Cambridge: Cambridge University Press.

Konstan, D. (2017), 'Mankind's Past: Evolution or Progress?,' in C. Mussini and S. Rocchi (eds), *Imagines Antiquitatis: Representations, Concepts, Receptions of the Past in Roman Antiquity and the Early Renaissance*, Philologus, suppl. 7: 17–25.

Kotzia-Panteli, P. (2000), 'Ennoematikos and oyxiodes logos as exegetical paired concepts (Classical Greek, Galen, Porphyry),' *Philologus*, 144 (1): 45–61.

Krämer, H. J. (1971), *Platonismus und hellenistische Philosophie*, Berlin: De Gruyter.

Lampe, K. (2015), *The Birth of Hedonism The Cyrenaic Philosophers and Pleasure as a Way of Life*, Princeton: Princeton University Press.

Lane, R. (2011), 'The First Hellenistic Man,' in A. Erskine and L. Llewellyn-Jones (eds), *Creating a Hellenistic World*, 1–31, Swansea: The Classical Press of Wales.

Leiwo, M. and P. Remes (1999), 'Partnership of Citizens and Metics: The Will of Epicurus,' *The Classical Quarterly*, 49 (1): 161–6.

Levine, D. (2003), *Ancient Greek Ideas on Speech, Language, and Civilization*, Oxford: Oxford University Press.

Lévy, C. (1992), *Cicero Academicus*, Rome: École Fançaise de Rome.

Lévy, C. (2001), 'Cicéron et l'épicureisme: la problématique de l'éloge paradoxal,' in C. Auvray-Assayas et D. Delattre (eds), *Cicéron et Philodème*, 61–76, Paris: Rue D'Ulm.

Lévy, C. (2012), 'Cicéron et le problème des genres de vie: une problématique de la voluntas,' in Th. Bénatouïl and M. Bonazzi (eds), *Theoria, Praxis and the Contemplative Life after Plato and Aristotle*, 57–74, Leiden: Brill.

Lisi, F. (1995), 'Bien, norma ética y placer en el *Filebo*,' *Méthexis* VIII, 65–80.

Lledó, E. (1995), *El epicureísmo*, Madrid: Montesinos.

Long, A. and Sedley, D. (1987), *The Hellenistic philosophers Vol I and II*, Cambridge: Cambridge University Press.

Long, A. A. (1971), 'Aisthesis, Prolepsis and Linguistic Theory in Epicurus,' *Bulletin of the Institute of Classical Studies*, 18 (1): 114–33.

Long, A. A. (1993), 'Hellenistic. Ethics and Philosophical Power,' in P. Green (ed.), *Hellenistic History and Culture*, 138–56, Berkeley: University of California Press.

Long, A. A. (1999), 'The Socratic Legacy,' in K. Algra, J. Barnes, J. Mansfeld, and M. Schofield (eds), *The Cambridge History of Hellenistic Philosophy*, 617–41, Cambridge: Cambridge University Press.

Long, A. A. (2006), *From Epicurus to Epictetus Studies in Hellenistic and Roman Philosophy*, Oxford: Oxford University Press.
Long, A. A. (2013), 'Friendship and Friends in the Stoic Theory of the Good Life,' in D. Caluori (ed.), *Thinking about Friendship. Historical and Contemporary Philosophical Perspectives*, 218–39, New York: Palgrave MacMillan.
Long, A. A. (2020), 'Epicureanism and utilitarianism,' in Ph. Mitsis (ed.), *Oxford Handbook of Epicurus and Epicureanism*, 1035–59, Oxford: Oxford University Press.
Longo, F. ed. (1988), *Ermarco, Frammenti*, Napoli: Bibliopolis.
Lovejoy, A. and G. Boas (1935), *Primitivism and Related Ideas in Antiquity*, Baltimore: The Johns Hopkins University Press.
Ludwig, B. (1998), *Die Wiederentdeckung des epikureischen Naturrechts: Zu Thomas Hobbes' philosophischer Entwicklung von De cive zum Leviathan im Pariser Exil, 1640-1651*, Frankfurt am Main: Klostermann.
Mansfeld, J. (1993), 'Aspects of Epicurean Theology,' *Mnemosyne*, 46 (2): 172–211.
Manuwald, A. (1972), *Die Prolepsislehre Epikurs*, Bonn: R. Habelt.
Manuwald, B. (1980), *Der Aufbau der Lukreiszischen Kulturentstehungslehre*, Mainz: F. Steiner.
Marcovich, M. ed. (1999), *Diogenes Laertius, Vitae philosophorum*, Leipzig: Teubner Verlag.
Masi, F. G. (2006), *Epicuro e la filosofia della mente (Il XXV libro dell'opera. Sulla Natura)*, Sankt Augustin: Academia Verlag.
Maslowski, T. (1974), 'The Chronology of Cicero's Antiepicureanism,' *Eos*, 62: 55–78.
Maslowski, T. (1974a), 'The Opponents of Lactantius [Inst. VII. 7, 7-13],' *California Studies in Classical Antiquity*, 7: 187–213.
Maso, S. (2008), *Capire e dissentire. Cicerone e la filosofia di Epicuro*, Napoli: Bibliopolis.
Mensch, P. and Miller, J. eds (2018), *Diogenes Laertius Lives of the Eminent Philosophers*, Oxford: Oxford University Press.
Milanese, G. (2003), 'La felicità. Scoperta, costruzione, ritrovamento (percorsi lucreziani),' *Paideia*, 58: 235–59.
Miller, F. D. Jr. (1995), *Nature, Justice, and Rights in Aristotle's Politics*, Oxford: Oxford University Press.
Mitsis, P. (1988), *Epicurus' Ethical Theory: The pleasures of invulnerability*, Ithaca: Cornell University Press.
Mitsis, P. (2019), 'Cicero on Epicurean Friendship: A Reappraisal,' *Politeia*, 1: 109–23.
Momigliano, A. (1941), 'Science and Politics in the Ancient World by Benjamin Farrington, Review by: Arnaldo Momigliano,' *The Journal of Roman Studies*, 31: 149–57.
Morel, P.-M. (2000), 'Épicure, l'histoire et le droit,' *Revue des Études Anciennes*, 102: 393–411.
Morel, P.-M. (2007), 'Method and Evidence: Epicurean prolêpsis,' *Proceedings of the Boston Area Colloquium in Ancient Philosophy*, 23: 25–48.
Mourelatos, A. (2003), 'Democritus on the Distinction between Universals and Particulars,' in A. Bächli and K. Petrus (eds), *Monism (Festschrifts for Andreas Greaser)*, 43–56, Frankfurt: Ontos Verlag.

Mourelatos, A. (2006), 'The Concept of the Universal in Some Later Pre-Platonic Cosmologists,' in C. Gill, (ed.), *A Companion to Ancient Philosophy*, 56–76, Oxford: Wiley-Blackwell.

Müller, G. (1978) 'Die Finalia der sechs Bücher des Lucrez,' in O. Gigon (ed.), *Lucrèce, Entretiens sur l'Antiquité classique*, 197–221, Vandoeuvres-Geneva: Fondation Hardt.

Müller, R. (1972), *Die epikureische Gesellschaftstheorie*, Berlin: Akademie Verlag.

Müller, R. (1983), 'Zu einem Entwicklungsprinzip der epikureischen Anthropologie,' *Philologus*, 127: 187–206.

Nagle, D. (2006), *The Household as the Foundation of Aristotle's Polis*, Cambridge: Cambridge University Press.

Neck, G. (1964), *Das Problem der Zeit im Epikureismus*, Heidelberg: Diss.

Németh, A. (2017), *Epicurus on the Self*, London: Routledge.

Nussbaum, M. C. (1994), *The Therapy of Desire. Theory and Practice in Hellenistic Ethics*, Princeton: Princeton University Press.

Obbink, D. (1989), 'The Atheism of Epicurus,' *Greek, Roman and Byzantine Studies*, 30 (2): 187–224.

Obbink, D. (1992), "What all men believe-must be true": Common Conceptions and Consensio Omnium in Aristotle and Hellenistic Philosophy,' *Oxford Studies in Ancient Philosophy*, 10: 192–232.

Obbink, D. (1995), 'How to Read Poetry about Gods,' in D. Obbink (ed.), *Philodemus and Poetry: Poetic Theory and Practice in Lucretius, Philodemus and Horace*, 189–209, Oxford: Oxford University Press.

Obbink, D. ed. (1995), *Philodemus On Piety 1*. Oxford: Clarendon Press,

Obbink, D. (1996), 'Epicurus on the Origin of Poetry in Human History,' in G. Giannantoni and M. Gigante (eds), *Epicureismo Greco e Romano*, 683–700, Napoli: Bibliopolis.

O'Connor, D. (1989), 'The Invulnerable Pleasures of Epicurean Friendship,' *Greek, Roman, and Byzantine Studies*, 30: 165–86.

O'Keefe, T. (2001), 'Is Epicurean Friendship Altruistic?,' *Apeiron*, 34: 269–305.

Oliver, J. (1938), 'An Inscription concerning the Epicurean School at Athens,' *Transactions and Proceedings of the American Philological Association*, 69: 494–9.

Otto, N. (2009), *Enargeia Untersuchung zur Charakteristik alexandrinischer Dichtung*, Stuttgart: F. Steiner.

Paganini, G. (2020), 'Early Modern Epicureanism: Gassendi and Hobbes in Dialogue on Psychology, Ethics, and Politics,' in Ph. Mitsis (ed.), *Oxford Handbook of Epicurus and Epicureanism*, 941–94, Oxford: Oxford University Press.

Pasquali, A. (1970), *La moral de Epicuro*, Caracas: Monte Ávila.

Pembroke, S. G. (1971), 'Oikeiosis,' in A. A. Long (ed.), *Problems in Stoicism*, 114–49, London: Athlone Press.

Pendrick, G. ed. (2002), *Antiphon, The Sophist The Fragments*, Cambridge: Cambridge University Press.

Piepenbrink, K. (2016), 'Sicherheit im politischen Diskurs des klassischen Athen,' *Historische Zeitschrift*, 303 (1): 39–63.

Piepenbrink, K. (2017), 'Furcht und Politik in der griechisch-römischen Antike,' *Saeculum*, 67:167–89.

Piergiacomi, E. (2013), 'A che serve venerarlo, se dio non fa nulla? Epicuro e il piacere della preghiera,' *Bollettino della Società Filosofica Italiana*, 208: 19–28.

Piergiacomi, E. (2016), 'Sugli dèi tutori di giustizia. La critica epicurea al giudizio dell'Ade del *Gorgia* di Platone,' in F. de Luise (ed.), *Legittimazione del potere, autorità della legge: un dibattito antico*, 223–57, Trento: Università degli Studi di Trento.

Philippson, R. (1909), 'Polystratos' Schrift über die Grundlose Verachtung der Volksmeinung,' *Neue Jahrbücher* 12: 487–509.

Philippson, R. (1910), 'Die Rechtsphilosophie der Epikureer,' *Archiv für Geschichte der Philosophie*, 23: 289–337, 433–46.

Powell, J. (1995), 'Cicero's Philosophical Works and their Background,' in J. Powell (ed.), *Cicero the Philosopher*, 1–36, Oxford: Clarendon Press.

Pownall, F. (2003), *Lessons from the Past: the Moral Use of History in Fourth-Century Prose*, Michigan: University of Michigan Press.

Price, S. (1986), 'The History of the Hellenistic Period,' in J. Boardman, J, Griffin and O. Murray (eds), *The Oxford History of the Ancient World*, 315–81, Oxford: Oxford University Press.

Rackham, H. trans. (1914), *Cicero: On Ends*, Cambridge (MA): Harvard University Press.

Rashed, M. (2002), 'La préservation (σωτηρία) objet des *Parva Naturalia* et ruse de la nature,' *Revue de Philosophie Ancienne*, 20 (1): 35–59.

Raubitschek, E. (1949), 'Phaidros and his Roman Pupils,' *Hesperia: The Journal of the American School of Classical Studies at Athens*, 18, (1): 96–103.

Reeve, C. D. C. trans. (1998), *Aristotle. Politics*, Indianapolis/Cambridge: Hackett Publishing Company.

Reeve, C. D. C. trans. (2004), *Plato. Republic* (Translated from the New Standard Greek Text, with Introduction, by C. D. C. Reeve) Indianapolis/Cambridge: Hackett Publishing Company.

Reeve, C. D. C. trans. (2014), *Aristotle. Nicomachean Ethics*, Indianapolis/Cambridge: Hackett Publishing Company.

Reinhardt, K. (1912), 'Hekataios von Abdera und Demokrit,' *Hermes*, 4: 492–513.

Reinhardt, T. (2005), 'The Language of Epicureanism in Cicero: The Case of Atomism,' in T. Reinhardt and M. Lapidge (eds), *Aspects of the Language of Latin prose*, 151–77, Oxford: Oxford University Press.

Reinhardt, T. (2008), 'Epicurus and Lucretius on the origins of language,' *Classical Quarterly*, 58 (1): 127–40.

Rider, B. (2019), 'The ethical significance of gratitude in Epicureanism,' *British Journal for the History of Philosophy*, 27 (2): 1–21.

Robitzsch J. M. (2017), 'The Epicureans on Human Nature and its Social and Political Consequences,' *Polis. The Journal for Ancient Greek Political Thought*, 34: 1–19.

Robitzsch, J. M. (2019), 'The Presentation of the Epicurean Virtues,' *Apeiron*, 53 (4): 419–35.

Rosenbaum, St. (1996), 'Epicurean Moral Theory,' *History of Philosophy Quarterly*, 13 (4): 389–410.

Roskam, G. (2006/7), 'Plutarch as a Source for Epicurean Philosophy. Another Aspect of his Nachleben. Scholarly,' *Journal of the International Plutarch Society*, 4: 67–82.

Roskam, G. (2007a), *A Commentary on Plutarch's De latenter vivendo*, Leuven: Leuven University Press.

Roskam, G. (2007b), *Live unnoticed* (Λάθε βιώσας). *On the Vicissitudes of an Epicurean Doctrine*, Leiden: Brill.

Roskam, G. (2012), 'Will the Epicurean Sage Break the Law if He is Perfectly Sure that He Will Escape Detection?,' *Transactions of the American Philological Association*, 142: 23–40.

Roskam, G. (2013), 'Plutarch's polemic against Colote's view on legislation and politics. A reading of *Adversus Colotem* 30–4 (1124D-1127E),' *Aitia*, 3: 2–15.

Roskam, G. (2020), 'Providential Gods and Social Justice. An Ancient Controversy on Theonomous Ethics,' *Harvard Studies in Classical Philology*, 110: 311–40.

Roskam, G. (2020a), 'Politics and Society,' in Ph. Mitsis (ed.), *The Oxford Handbook of Epicurus and Epicureanism*, 388–425, Oxford: Oxford University Press.

Roskam, G. (2022), 'Sint Ista Graecorum: How to be an Epicurean in Late Republican Rome –Evidence from Cicero's *On Ends* 1–2,' in S. Yona and D. Gregson (eds), *Epicurus in Rome: Philosophical Perspectives in the Ciceronian Age*, 11–36, Cambridge: Cambridge University Press.

Ross, W. D. (1957), *Aristotelis Politica* (Recognovit Brevique Adnotatione Critica Instruxit), Oxford: Oxford University Press.

Salem, J. (1989), *Tel un dieu parmi les hommes. L' éthique d' Épicure*, Paris: Vrin.

Sancho, L. (2011), 'Riqueza, impiedad y ὕβρις en el *Contra Midas* de Demóstenes,' *Emerita. Revista de Lingüística y Filología Clásica*, 79: 31–54.

Schiesaro, A. (1990), *Simulacrum et imago. Gli argomenti analogici nel De rerum natura*, Pisa: Giardini.

Schmid, W. (1984), *Epicuro e l'epicureismo cristiano*, Brescia: Paideia.

Schofield, M (1996), 'Epilogismos: An Appraisal,' in M. Frede and G. Striker (eds), *Rationality in Greek Thought*, 221–37, Oxford: Oxford University Press.

Schofield, M. (1999), 'Social and political thought,' in K, Algra, J. Barnes, J. Mansfeld and M. Schofield (eds), *The Cambridge History of Hellenistic Philosophy*, 739–70, Cambridge: Cambridge University Press.

Schofield, M. (1999), *The Stoic Idea of the City*, Chicago and London: The University of Chicago Press.

Schofield, M. (2006), *Plato. Political Philosophy*, Oxford: Oxford University Press.

Schofield, M. (2021), *Cicero. Political Philosophy*, Oxford: Oxford University Press.

Scholz, P. (1998), *Der Philosoph und die Politik, Die Ausbildung der philosophischen Lebensform und die Entwicklung des Verhältnisses von Philosophie und Politik im 4. und 3. Jh. v. Chr.*, Stuttgart: F. Steiner.

Scholz, P. (2004), 'Peripatetic Philosophers as Wandering Scholars: Some Remarks on the Socio-Political Conditions of Philosophizing in the Third Century BCE,' in W. Fortenbaugh and S. White (eds), *Lyco of Troas and Hieronymus of Rhodes – Text, Translation and Discussion*, 315–53, London: Routledge.

Schrijvers, P. (1999), *Lucrèce et les sciences de la vie*. Leiden: Brill.

Sedley, D. (1973), 'Epicurus, On Nature Book XXVIII,' *Cronache Ercolanesi*, 3: 5–83.

Sedley, D. (1976), 'Epicurus and His Professional Rivals,' *Cahiers de Philologie*, 1: 121–59.

Sedley, D. (1988), 'Epicurean Anti-Reductionism,' in J. Barnes and M. Mignucci (eds,), *Matter and Metaphysics*, 295–327, Napoli: Bibliopolis.

Sedley, D. (1997), 'The Ethics of Brutus and Cassius,' *The Journal of Roman Studies*, 87: 41–53.

Sedley, D. (2004), *Lucretius and the Transformation of Greek Wisdom*. Cambridge: Cambridge University Press.

Sedley, D. (2013), 'The atheist underground,' in V. Harte and M. Lane (eds), *Politeia in Greek and Roman Philosophy*, 329–48, Cambridge: Cambridge University Press.

Seel, G. (1996), 'Farà il saggio qualcosa che le leggi vietano, sapendo che no sarà scoperto?,' in G. Giannantoni and M. Gigante (eds), *Epicureismo Greco e Romano*, 341–60, Napoli: Bibliopolis.

Shearin, W. H. (2012), 'Haunting Nepos: Atticus and the Performance of Roman Epicurean Death,' in B. Holmes and W. H. Shearin (eds), *Dynamic Reading Studies in the Reception of Epicureanism*, 30–51, Oxford: Oxford University Press.

Sickinger, J. (1999), *Public Records and Archives in Classical Athens*, Oxford: The University of North Carolina Press.

Slings, S. R. ed. (2003), *Platonis Rempvblicam* (Recognovit brevique adnotatione critica instrvxit) Oxford: Oxford University Press.

Smith, M. F. (1993), *Diogenes of Oinoanda: The Epicurean Inscription*, Naples: Bibliopolis.

Smith, M. F. (1996), 'An Epicurean Priest from Apamea in Syria,' *Zeitschrift für Papyrologie und Epigraphik*, 112: 120–30.

Smith, M. F. trans. (2001), *Lucretius, On the Nature of Things*, Indianapolis: Hackett.

Solmsen, F. (1936), 'The Background of Plato's Theology,' *Transactions of the American Philological Association*, 67: 208–18.

Steel, C. (2005), *Reading Cicero. Genre and Performance in Late Republican Rome*, London: Duckworth.

Strauss, L. (1952), *Natural Right and History*, Chicago: University of Chicago.

Stokes, M. (1995), 'Cicero on Epicurean Pleasures,' in J. Powell (ed.), *Cicero the Philosopher*, 145–70, Oxford: Clarendon Press.

Striker, G. (1996), *Essays on Hellenistic epistemology and ethics*, Cambridge: Cambridge University Press.

Stuart Mill, J. (2015), *On Liberty, Utilitarianism, and Other Essays* (Edited with an Introduction and Notes by Mark Philp and Frederik Rosen), Oxford: Oxford University Press.

Tate, J. (1936), 'On Plato: Laws X 889cd,' *Classical Quarterly*, 30: 48–54.

Temporini, H. (1978), *Die Frauen am Hofe Trajans*, Berlin: De Gruyter.
Tsouna, V. (1998), *The Epistemology of the Cyrenaic School*, Cambridge: Cambridge University Press.
Tsouna, V. (2001), 'Cicéron et Philodème: quelques considérations sur l'éthique,' in C. Auvray-Assayas et D. Delattre (eds), *Cicéron et Philodème*, 159–72, Paris: Rue D'Ulm.
Tsouna, V. (2007), *The Ethics of Philodemus*, Oxford: Oxford University Press.
Tsouna, V. (2012), *Philodemus, On Property Management*, Atlanta: Society of Biblical Literature.
Tsouna, V. (2016), 'Epicurean preconceptions,' *Phronesis*, 61: 160–221.
Tutrone, F. (2018), 'Filodemo, Cicerone, Nepote: a proposito del contesto storico-culturale di Oec. Col. XXII.9-48,' *Rheinisches Museum*, 161: 328–66.
Usener, H. (1887), *Epicurea*, Leipzig: Teubner Verlag.
Usener, H. (1888), 'Epikurische Spruchsammlung,' *Wiener Studien*, 10: 176–91.
Valachova, C. (2018), *The Political and Philosophical Strategies of Roman Epicureans in the Late Republic*, Edinburgh: Diss.
Van Bremen, R. (2005), 'Plotina to all her friends: The letter(s) of the Empress Plotina to the Epicureans in Athens,' *Chiron*, 35: 499–529.
Van Wees, H. (2007), 'Stasis Destroyer of Men. Mass, Elite, Political Violence and Security in Archaic Greek,' in C. Brelaz (ed.), *Sécurité collective et ordre public dans les sociétés anciennes*, 1–48, Vandoeuvres-Genève: Fondation Hardt.
Vander Waerdt, P. A. (1987), 'The Justice of the Epicurean Wise Man,' *Classical Quarterly*, 37: 402–22.
Vander Waerdt, P. A. (1988), 'Hermarchus and the Epicurean Genealogy of Morals,' *Transactions of the American Philological Association*, 118: 87–106.
Verde, F. (2016), 'Epicuro nella testimonianza di Cicerone: la dottrina del criterio,' in M. Tulli (ed.), *Testo e forme del testo. Ricerche di filologia filosofica*, 335–68, Pisa-Roma: Fabrizio Serra Editore.
Verlinsky, A. (2005), 'Epicurus and his predecessors on the origin of language,' in D. Frede and B. Inwood (eds), *Language and Learning. Philosophy of Language in the Hellenistic Age*, 56–100, Cambridge: Cambridge University Press.
Vesperini, P. (2011), 'Cicero, Trebatius Testa, and a crux in *Fam.* 7, 12, 1,' *Revue de philologie*, 85: 150–73.
Vlastos, G. (1946), 'On the Pre-History in Diodorus,' *AJP*, 67: 51–9.
Volk, K. (2021), *The Roman Republic of Letters: Scholarship, Philosophy, and Politics in the Age of Cicero and Caesar*, Princeton: Princeton University Press.
Volk, K. (2022), 'Caesar the Epicurean? A Matter of Life and Death,' in S. Yona and D. Gregson (eds), *Epicurus in Rome: Philosophical Perspectives in the Ciceronian Age*, 72–86, Cambridge: Cambridge University Press.
Vigo, A. (2006), *Estudios aristotélicos*, Pamplona: Eunsa.
Warren, J. (2002), *Epicurus and Democritean Ethics. An Archaeology of Ataraxia*, Cambridge: Cambridge University Press.

Warren, J, (2004), *Facing Death: Epicurus and His Critics*, Cambridge: Cambridge University Press.

Warren, J. (2006), 'Psychic Disharmony: Philoponus and Epicurus on Plato's *Phaedo*,' *Oxford Studies in Ancient Philosophy*, 30: 235–60.

Warren, J. (2014), *The Pleasures of Reason in Plato, Aristotle, and the Hellenistic Hedonists*, Cambridge: Cambridge University Press.

Warren, J. (2018), 'Demetrius of Laconia on Epicurus *On the Thelos* (Us. 68),' in J. Bryan, R. Wardy and J. Warren (eds), *Authors and Authorities in Ancient Philosophy*, 202–21, Cambridge: Cambridge University Press.

White, P. (2010), *Cicero in Letters: Epistolary Relations of the Late Republic*, New York: Oxford University Press.

Wolfsdorf, D. (2013), *Pleasure in Ancient Greek Philosophy*, Cambridge: Cambridge University Press.

Wood, N. (1991), *Cicero's Social and Political Thought*, Los Angeles: University of California Press.

Woolf, R. (2004), 'What Kind of Hedonist Was Epicurus?,' *Phronesis*, 49 (4), 303–22.

Woolf, R. trans. (2004), *Cicero, On Moral Ends* (Cambridge Texts in the History of Philosophy. Edited by Julia Annas; translated by Raphael Woolf), Cambridge: Cambridge University Press.

Woolf, R. (2009), 'Pleasure and desire,' in J. Warren (ed.), *The Cambridge Companion to Epicureanism*, 158–78, Cambridge: Cambridge University Press.

Woolf, R. (2013), 'Ciceron and Gyges,' *The Classical Quarterly*, 63, 801–12.

Yona, S. (2018), 'An Epicurean Measure of Wealth in Horace, *Satires* 1.1,' *Classical Antiquity*, 37 (2): 351–78.

Zangara, A. (2007), *Voir l'histoire. Théories anciennes du récit historique*, Paris: Vrin.

General Index

Adorno, F. 168 nn.6-7
affection (affection as a criterion of truth; see also feeling) 52-4, 61, 127, 146
agreement 6, 16, 20, 25, 39, 63, 69, 90, 93, 108, 114978135000297515, 171 n.30, 175 n.18, 184 n.28
Alberti, A. 167 n.3, 168 n.7
Albucius 151, 205, 169, 206, 182
Alcius 151
Alesse, F. 169 nn.11-12
Alexander of Aphrodisias 183 n.21
Algra, K. 27, 171 n.31, 172 nn.37-8
Aminomachus 143, 204 n.30
Amynas 147
Anaxagoras 3, 21, 87, 100, 169 n.15
Angelli, A. vi, 65, 182 n.18
Anglade, L. vi, 204 n.49, 205 n.63, 206 n.82 n.83
Annas, J. 87, 172, 135, 188 n.13
Anonymus Iamblichus 56
Antiochus IV Epiphanes 204 n.38
Aoiz, J. 171, 196 n.6
appetite 116, 175, 118
Apollophanes 147
Archelaus 3, 21, 87, 169 n.15 n.21
Arenson, K. 179 n.58
Aristion 147, 204 n.49
Aristotle 3, 9, 12, 20, 22, 27-8, 35-6, 38-9, 42, 44-5, 50-1, 55-6, 59, 66, 70, 73, 86, 88-9, 97, 100, 112, 119, 125, 161, 167 n.1, 178 n.50, 180 n.61, 183 nn.21-2, 185 n.36, 191 n.26, 195 n.57, 200 n.43
Armstrong, J. 63, 53, 127, 156, 171 n.30, 172 n.34, 177 n.30, 179 n.54, 201 n.49, 202 nn.59-60, 204 nn.32-3, 205 n.58, 206 n.79, 204 n.89-90
Arnim, von, J. 202 n.1
Arrighetti, G. vii, 180 n.59, 182 n.19, 192 n.39, 197 n.11
Asmis, E. 178 n.46, 181 n.7, 184 n.27-8, 184 n.32, 186 n.53, 187 n.58, 189 n.20, 206 n.9

Assante, M. G. 204 n.38
atheism (Epicurus as an atheist) 90, 102, 190 n.21
Atherton, C. 185 n.41
Atticus 134, 151-4, 204 n.31, 205 n.69, 206 n.82
Aubenque, P. 29, 172 n.46
Aulus Gellius 81, 89, 92, 193 n.42, 198 n.23
Austin, E. 177 n.30
Avotins, I. 178 n.46

Bailey, C. 167 n. 1
Bakker, F. A. 183 n.24, 184 n.28
Balch, D. L. 178 n.46
Ballesteros, L. 204 n.49
Barigazzi, G. 172 n.40, 177 n.41
Batis 145-6
Belius Philippus 148
Benferhat, Y. 151, 153-4, 204 n.35, 204 n.47, 204 n.49, 205 n.66, 206 n.79
Besnier, B. 171 n.31, 177 n.39
Betegh, G. 169 n.15, 197 n.11, 201 n.53
Bias 100
Bignone, E. 167 n.1
blessedness ('blessing life') 26, 31, 45, 46, 51, 52, 54, 80, 85, 107, 122, 124, 126, 182 n.16, 189 n.20
Boas, G. 170 n.21, 176 n.29
Boeri, M. D. 185 n.35, 200 n.41
Bonelli, G. 193 n.43
Brock, R. 173 n.2
Bruns, K. 203 n.26
Brunschwig, J. 169 n.18, 170 n.23, 176 n.28, 186 n.43

Caetronianus Lucius Papirius 205 n.69
Cairns, D. 177 n.41
calculation (see also 'sober calculation') 29, 31, 70, 125, 185 n.41
Callicles 63-4, 77, 136, 172 n.37, 174 n.10, 182 n.14

Campbell, G. 169 n.21, 171 n.31, 176 n.29
Campos Daroca, F. J. 101, 194 n.53, 204 n.39
Castner, C. J. 151, 205 n.66
Catius 154
Chamoux, F. 187 n.1
Cicero 1–5, 9–11, 15, 22, 28, 51–2, 54, 56, 59, 73, 79–95, 97, 99–103, 106, 111, 114, 117–20, 122, 125, 128, 131, 133–40, 142, 144, 146, 150–4, 157, 160–3, 172–3, 179–82, 187–97, 204–5
Cineas 145, 147
city 4, 11, 13, 20, 33, 50, 69–70, 107, 133, 141, 143, 147, 148, 157, 161, 163–5, 171 n.3, 179 n.55, 187 n.59
civil war 31, 33–6, 41, 45, 153, 161, 174 n.4
Clark, G. 38
Clay, D. 127, 141, 145, 181 n.12, 182 n.16, 203 n.24, 204 n.34
Clement of Alexandria 182 n.21, 186 n.5, 196 n.6, 197 n.8
Cohen, D. 35–7, 174 n.7
Cole, Th. 172 n.44–5
Colotes 40, 42–4, 101–2, 175 n.19, 199 n.35
Community (political, Epicurean community) 8–9, 12–13, 16, 20, 23, 27–8, 30, 37–9, 42, 44–5, 49, 51–2, 60–1, 69, 71, 74, 77–8, 93, 102, 108–9, 125, 129, 131–2, 138, 140, 145–6, 149–50, 153, 155–6, 162–3, 165, 174 n.3, 175 n.20, 176 n.21, 179 n.55, 202 n.54
confidence 4, 7–8, 12, 43–4, 48–9, 51, 53, 144, 161, 165, 179 n.55
confirmation (of the just) 60, 67–8, 70, 162, 183 n.25
contempt 33, 53, 79, 141
contractualism 4, 21, 70, 74, 81, 87, 89, 103, 128, 160, 200 n.39
convenient (*see also* useful, usefulness) 12, 38, 44, 60, 78, 93, 116, 162
Cooper, J. M. 180 n.59–60
covenant (*see also* pact) 4, 24, 117, 124, 128
crime 10, 30, 37–8, 45, 97, 102, 105–6, 114, 120–1, 125, 128, 163, 175 n.18, 182 n.16
Critias 45–6, 105
Cynicism 62, 168 n.46
Cynics 7, 49–50, 137, 141, 168 n.6, 181 n.7, 194 n.53, 196 n.6
Cyrenaics 178

danger (of violent death) 4, 7, 9, 12, 30, 34, 36, 43, 47, 49, 161
Dareste, R. 203 n.26
death (fear of) 4, 7, 11–12, 22, 41, 43–9, 54–5, 90–100, 106, 112–13, 122, 142–4, 149, 161, 165, 175 n.20, 177 n.30, 182 n.16, 199 n.37–8, 201 n.48
De Rommilly, J. 174 n.10, 185 n.37, 195 n.2
De Sanctis, D. vi, 54, 169 n.56, 202 n.55–6, 204 n.37, 204 n.41, 206 n.90
desire (natural and vain desire, desire for security) 4, 6, 7–8, 12, 15, 22, 29, 31–2, 34, 42–51, 53–6, 62, 88, 100, 106, 108, 111–12, 116–17, 119–20, 128, 135–6, 145, 149, 161–2, 177 n.30–1, 181 n.7, 200 n.43–4, 202 n.54
De Witt, N. 180 n.61
Demetrius of Laconia 17, 19, 63, 177 n.42
Demetrius of Phaleron 165
Demetrius I Soter 145–7, 155, 204 n.38
Democritus 11–12, 63, 75, 100, 105, 171, 180 n.63, 188 n.12
Demosthenes 36–7, 40, 56, 174 n.10, 175 n.20
Deniz, D. 196
Denyer, N. 76, 186 n.57
Diagoras 45
Dierauer, U. 169 n.21, 170 n.25
Diogenes of Babylon 155, 206 n.90
Diogenes of Oenoanda 17, 23, 45, 54, 134, 148–9, 176 n.30, 177 n.30, 185 n.43
Diogenes of Sinope 196 n.4
Diogenes Laertius 2–3, 21, 27, 54, 61, 66, 77, 107–8, 138–9, 141–2, 146, 176 n.25, 194 n.48
disturbance 13, 39, 42, 50, 98, 106, 181 n.8, 198 n.30, 201 n.48
Dorandi, T. 66, 182 n.19, 186 n.52, 202 n.63, 205 n.56, 205 n.61
Duke, G. 185 n.36, 188 n.15
Dumont, J.-P. 183 n.24

Empedocles 100, 171 n.31
enjoyment (life of) 46, 102, 119, 178 n.47
envy 36, 47, 53
Epictetus 1–2, 10, 47–8, 102, 111, 133–5, 139–40, 157, 160–1, 196 n.6, 197 n.8, 198 n.30, 203 n.5
Epicureanism 1–7, 9–10, 12, 15–16, 23–4,

26–7, 29–30, 33, 42–3, 45, 51, 55–7, 60, 64, 79–80, 83, 87–8, 92, 94–5, 98–100, 102–3, 106–7, 109, 117–18, 120, 126, 128–9, 131–2, 134–6, 140–1
Epicurus 1–3, 5–13, 15–21, 25–31, 33, 38–41, 45, 47–56, 59–80, 82–100, 102–14, 126–35, 137–46, 148–52, 154–66, 167 n.2, 169 n.10, 172 n.33, 173 n.47, 175 n.14, 176 n.27, 177 n.30, 179 n.52–5, 179 n.58, 180 n.59, 180 n.61, 181,nn.4–8, 181 n.10, 181 n.13, 182 n.16, 184 n.25, 185 n.33, 186 n.43, 187 n.58, 187 n.2, 187 n.5, 187 n.7, 188 n.8, 189 n.19–20, 190 n.21, 190 n.24, 191 n.28, 192 n.33, 193 n.39, 195 n.59, 196 n.5, 197 n.13, 196 n.5, 197 n.13, 198 n.22–3, 199 n.36, 200 n.40–2, 201 n.47, 202 n.1, 203 n.5, 204 n.30–2
Erbi, M. 202 n.3, 203 n.25
Erler, M. vi, 6, 23, 41, 54, 119, 141, 149, 170 n.22, 176 n.23, 177 n.36, 179 n.58, 181 n.13, 182 n.16, 190 n.24, 199 n.33, 200 n.40, 202 n.57, 203 n.23, 205 n.60
Essler, H. 117, 172 n.32, 189 n.20, 202 n.59
evidence (as a 'clear datum of experience') 66–7, 72, 183 n.21, 183 n.23, 184 n.26
Evrigenis, I. D. 174 n.3
expectation 34, 36, 49, 55–6, 125, 161

faction (political faction) 44
faith (in the gods) 45
Falchi, A. 131, 184 n.33, 185 n.33, 202 n.1
fame 31, 46–8, 90, 137–9, 153
familial relations (and affection) 29, 141, 146, 170 n.26, 196 n.6
fear 4, 7–10, 15, 22, 30–8, 40, 42–7, 50–3, 55–7, 84–7, 93, 100–6, 112–13, 117–23, 128, 144, 149, 161–4, 174 n.3, 175 n.18, 176 n.30, 177 n.30, 179 n.53, 182 n.16, 197 n.13, 197 n.16, 198 n.29, 199 n.37, 200 n.43, 201 n.48
fearless 40, 122
feeling (as criterion of truth; see also affection) 8, 61, 66–8, 89
Fish, J. 29, 156, 173 nn.48–9, 203 n.14, 203 n.17, 206 n.87
Follet, S. 150, 204 n.44, 205 nn.61–2
Fowler, D. 46, 177 n.3

friend, friendship 6–7, 10–11, 13, 15–16, 22–9, 32, 34, 37, 51–4, 56–7, 70–3, 107–10, 112, 123–8, 135, 140–6, 154, 157, 159, 161, 163–5, 170 n.24, 170 n.27, 171 n.30, 172 n.37, 178 n.51, 179 nn.54–5, 198 n.23, 200 n.44, 204 n.32

Gaius Amafinius 150–1, 154, 205 n.63, 206 n.82
Gaius Cassius Longinus 134, 152, 154, 205 n.69, 206 n.82
Gaius Memmius Caesoninus 205 n.69
Gaius Velleius 205 n.69
Gaius Vibius Pansa 154–5, 205 n.69
Galen 75, 183 n.21, 186 n.55
Gardner, H. H. 41, 176 n.22
Gassendi, P. 1, 167 n.1, 186 n.52, 202 n.1
Gastaldi, S. 173 n.2
genealogy (of the laws) 2, 4, 6–7, 15, 21–2, 29–30, 33–4, 38, 40, 42, 44–5, 56–7, 64, 72, 87–8, 105, 113–14, 116, 161–2, 170 n.23
Gerson, L. 16, 62, 93, 110
Gigante, M. 45, 177 n.33, 178 n.46
Gilbert, N. 151–3, 203 n.6, 205 n.63
Gill, C. 27, 172 nn.37–8
Giovacchini, J. 180 n.60
god, gods (irrational fear of; becoming like god) 4, 7, 10, 12, 22–5, 30, 35, 43, 45–6, 53, 59, 61, 70, 75–6, 84–7, 92, 94–5, 97, 101–2, 105–7, 117, 121–2, 124, 126–8, 129, 139, 142, 164, 170 n.21, 177 n.36, 182 n.16, 189 n.20, 190 n.24, 199 n.33, 200 n.40, 201 n.47
Goldschmidt, V. 38–9, 64, 71–3, 111, 113, 118, 167 n.1, 169 n.19, 171 n.31, 172 n.42, 175 n.12, 175 nn.14–15, 177 n.39, 178 n.45, 182 n.17, 184 n.31, 185 nn.37–40, 186 n.44, 186 n.46, 194 n.46, 195 n.57, 197 n.11, 197 n.16, 201 n.53
Gómez-Lobo, A. 182 n.14
Good (as 'the good of nature') 7, 43, 47, 64
Görler, W. 180 n.6, 196 n.7, 203 n.8
gratitude 8, 10, 54–6, 92, 108, 143, 147, 180 n.61, 189 n.20, 190 n.94
greed, greedy 12, 22, 31, 36, 45–8, 200 n.43
Green, P. 98, 187 n.1, 192 n.37

Griffin, M. 205 n.68, 206 n.79
Grilli, A. 180 n.63
Grimal, P. 132, 155, 202 n.2, 206 n.83
Gyges (ring of) 9–10, 105–6, 111–19, 128, 163, 199 n.35, 200 n.39

Haake, M. vi, 147–8, 204 n.30 nn.42–53, 206 n.84
Hadrian 150
Hamilton, J. T. 33, 173 n.1
Hammerstaedt, J. vi, 45, 155, 205 n.57, 206 n.88
Hammond, N. G. 187 n.1
Hanchey, D. 188 n.8
happiness 27, 49–50, 79, 95, 122–7, 176 n.27, 191 n.30, 198 n.30, 200 n.40, 200 n.46, 201 n.51
harm, harmful 3–9, 16, 20, 23, 30, 38–40, 63, 73–4, 76–7, 87, 124, 127, 175 n.18, 176 n.30, 182 n.16, 187 n.59, 190 n.24, 193 n.41, 195 n.57
harming (in the principle 'neither harming one another nor being harmed') 4–8, 16, 19–21, 23, 30, 32, 39, 44, 46, 48, 53, 62–3, 65, 68–9, 71, 73–7, 88, 93, 124, 127, 161–2, 169 n.19, 171 n.30, 174 n.6
harmlessness 127
Harris, E. M. 37
Heraclitus 100–1, 148, 195
Heraclitus (son of Heraclitus) 148
Hermarchus 2, 4, 18–22, 25, 28, 30–2, 38–40, 43–5, 63, 71–3, 88, 117, 143, 160, 165, 171, 173 n.50, 175 n.14, 180 n.59, 185 n.41, 186 n.44
Hirzel, R. 75, 172 n.41, 186 n.54
Hobbes, T. ('Hobbesian') 1, 6, 16, 22, 31–2, 160, 202 n.1
hope 45, 52, 154, 177 n.41
Holmes, B. 170 n.26
Hossenfelder, M. 193 n.43

Idomeneus 54–5, 132, 142, 145, 179 n.58, 180 n.59, 202 n.3
imitatio Epicurei 10, 107, 126, 128–9, 146, 164
imperturbability (peace of mind) 4, 15, 31, 33, 47, 49, 88, 98–9, 107, 119, 122, 124–5, 160, 179 n.58, 192 n.39, 198 n.30
indestructibility (god as an indestructible and blessed being) 46, 85, 105, 122, 127, 188 n.10, 189 n.20
indulgence 38, 80, 156, 206 n.90
injustice 38–9, 45–7, 76, 93, 102, 105
insecurity 44, 46–7
Inwood, B. 16, 82, 66, 93, 110, 167 n.1, 188 nn.9–10
Isocrates 73, 100, 147, 168 n.47

Jaulin, A. 186 n.54
Jürss, F. 186 n.45, 186 n.55
just, justice 4–10, 12–26, 30–5, 37–47, 51, 53–6, 59–79, 86–8, 93–6, 101–7, 111–12, 171 n.30, 173 n.50, 176 n.21, 177 n.38, 182 n.16, 184 n.33, 185 nn.33–4, 186 n.47, 187 n.58, 194 n.53, 195 n.57, 196 n.6, 197 n.16, 198 n.23, 199 n.33, 201 n.47, 201 n.50, 202 n.54

Kahn, Ch. 116, 169 n.20, 198 n.32
Kazantzidis, G. 177 n.41
Kechagia, E. 42, 176 n.26, 193 n.46, 199 n.35
Konstan, D. vi, 75, 127, 171 n.30, 172 n.37, 175 n.20, 177 n.31, 180 n.61, 186 n.44, 190 n.24, 195 n.58, 197 n.16, 200 n.43
Kotzia, P. 186 n.55
Krämer, H. J. 168 nn.7–8

Lactantius 5, 9, 11–12, 25–6, 79–89, 91, 93–9, 101–5, 160–2, 173 n.47, 190 n.24, 191 n.28, 192 nn.32–3, 192 n.36, 193 n.45
Lampe, K. 178 n.45
Lane, R. 187 n.1
language (as a 'natural phenomenon', as a 'collective phenomenon') 5, 8, 74, 78
law (law of nature) 2, 4–12, 63, 201 n.54
Leiwo, M. 203 n.26
Lepidus 148
Levine, D. 169 nn.17–18, 186 n.47
Lévy, C. 101, 135, 187 n.4, 188 n.14, 189 n.20, 194 n.52, 195 n.54, 199 n.34, 203 n.8
life (civilized life) 4, 6–7, 16, 21–4, 34–5, 42–4, 50, 72, 101, 107, 160, 169 n.21
Lisi, F. 193 n.41
Long, A. A. 59, 91, 100, 172 n.37, 176 n.27,

181 n.3, 192 n.35, 194 n.47, 196 n.3, 197 n.9, 201 n.51
López, M. 204 n.39
Lucius Calpurnius Piso 205 n.69
Lucius Manlius Torquatus 205 n.69
Lucius Saufeius Gaius 205 n.69
Lucretius 1–7, 11, 15–32, 40–7, 55, 61, 68–75, 79, 88, 91–2, 95, 97, 117, 137, 149, 151, 167 n.2, 168 n.17, 170 n.23, 170 n.26, 171 nn.30–1, 173 n.49, 175 n.14, 176 n.21, 177 n.30, 180 n.61, 181 n.10, 185 n.43, 186 n.51, 189 n.20, 191 nn.27–8, 193 n.39, 195 n.58, 203 n.14, 204 n.31, 206 n.82
Ludwig, B. vi
Lycophron 42
Lycurgus 100, 134, 137
Lysias of Tarsus 147

Manuwald, A. 170 nn.23–4, 176 n.28, 181 n.6
Marcus Fadius Gallus 205 n.69
Maslowski, T. 95, 187 n.8, 191 nn.28–9
Maso, S. 187 n.5, 187 n.8, 188 n.9
Melissus 100
memories (pleasant memories of the past, memories of the conversation, 'irrational memories', memories of a dead friend) 30, 34, 36, 54–6, 72, 125, 127, 161, 173 n.50
Metrodorus 50, 62–3, 93, 110, 137, 142–5, 156, 165
Milanese, G. 180 n.61
Miller, J. 174 n.6
Mithras 132, 142, 202 n.3
Mitsis, P. 29, 171 n.30, 178 n.45
Momigliano, A. 151, 154, 205 n.65, 206 n.82
Morel, P.-M. 167 n.4, 168 n.5, 197 n.13
Mourelatos, A. 186 n.54
Müller, R. 71–3, 167 n.1, 169 n.19, 173 n.50, 176 n.24, 178 n.46, 185 n.42, 186 n.44
Musonius Rufus 187 n.59

nature (*see also* law of nature, natural desire) 4, 7, 12, 15, 22, 31, 34, 43–5, 47, 49–51, 54, 56–9, 62, 111–12, 120, 161, 181 n.7, 200 n.44

Neck, G. 176 n.21
Németh, A. 172 n.36, 202 n.59
Nussbaum, M. C. 13, 167 n.3, 171 n.30, 191 n.30

Obbink, D. 45, 126–7, 177 nn.34–6, 201 nn.47–8, 202 nn.61–2
O'Connor, D. 172 n.36
O'Keefe, T. 172 n.36
Otto, N. 183 n.23

pact (*see also* covenant) 4–7, 16–32, 32–9, 42–6, 53, 60–4, 69, 73–7, 88–93, 106–7, 114–17, 124, 160–2, 169 n.19, 171 nn.30–1, 182 n.16
Paganini, G. 167 n.2, 202 n.1
pain (absence of, painful) 36, 39, 54–5, 80, 84, 89, 97–9, 107, 113, 116, 119, 121, 125, 146, 164, 179 n.52, 180 n.58, 180 n.60, 192 n.39, 193 nn.41–2, 198 n.30, 200 n.46, 201 n.51
Parmenides 100
Pasquali, A. 176 n.28
Patro 204 n.31
Pendrick, G. 176 n.28, 181 n.11, 195 n.1
Phaedrus 146, 150, 151, 153, 204 n.31
philanthropy 8, 10, 13, 34, 53–7, 123, 129, 142–6, 149, 161, 164
Philidas 148
Philippson, R. 61, 63, 74, 111, 131, 167 n.1, 168 n.6, 169 n.19, 172 n.40, 186 nn.49–50, 197 n.15, 202 n.1
Philiscus 151
Philodemus 2, 11, 45, 50, 53–4, 62, 76, 85, 116, 123, 126–7, 134, 137, 141, 144–5, 149, 151–2, 156–7, 172 n.32, 173 n.50, 177 n.30, 178 nn.49–51, 181 n.7, 187 n.59, 189 n.20, 201 nn.47–8, 202 n.58
Pherecydes 100
Philonides 2, 133, 145–7, 149–50, 202, n.4, 204 n.38
Piepenbrink, K. 174 n.3
Piergiacomi, E. 177 n.35
piety 105, 126, 128, 134, 141, 143, 145–6, 157, 163, 171, 201 nn.47–8
Piso 155, 188 n.8, 205 n.69
Pittachus 38
Plato 3–4, 9, 12, 17, 20–1, 31, 35, 39, 49–50,

56, 62–7, 70, 81–2, 86–7, 90, 94, 97–8, 100–7, 110–17, 121–2, 128–9, 135–6, 149, 159–63, 169 n.15, 169 n.17, 169 n.31, 173 n.2, 174 n.10, 177 n.35, 181 n.13, 183 n.25, 186 n.58, 187 n.59, 189 n.20, 190 n.24, 191 n.30, 193 n.41, 195 n.57, 198 nn.28–9, 199 n.33, 200 nn.39–41

pleasure (kinds of pleasure) 3, 11, 25, 28, 47, 50–5, 80–4, 89, 96, 98–101, 123–7, 134, 145, 151, 154, 171 n.31, 178 n.45, 179 n.58, 180 n.60, 181 n.7, 187 n.2, 192 n.39, 193 n.39, 193 nn.41–3, 194 n.46, 198 n.30, 198 n.34, 200 nn.41–2, 201 n.51, 202 n.58

Plotina 134, 150

Plous 147

Plutarch 1–10, 15, 22, 27, 40, 42, 45, 49, 51, 53–4, 79–82, 90–4, 98, 100–6, 108–14, 117–22, 125, 128, 131, 133–42, 145, 150, 157, 160, 162–5, 178 n.44, 184 n.26, 187 n.2, 189 n.19, 190 n.29, 193 n.39, 194 n.46, 194 n.48, 195 n.57, 197 n.11, 197 nn.13–14, 198 n.26, 199 n.38

Polanski, R. vi

Polemon 194 n.48

Polyneus 143, 165

Polystratus 2, 18–19, 31, 44, 63–4, 88, 160, 168 nn.3–7

Pompilius Andronicus 151

Porphyry 2, 12, 18–22, 25, 28, 30–1, 38–40, 44, 46, 49, 62, 68, 116, 160, 171, 198 n.31, 201 n.54

Price, S. 187 n.1

preconception (of justice, as a 'scheme' or a 'sketch') 5, 7–8, 22, 46, 59–66, 70–8, 85, 88, 92, 161–2, 168 n.10, 173 n.50, 176 n.21, 181 nn.4.5, 182 n.16, 184 n.25

Prodicus 45

property (as 'private property') 7, 50, 57, 142–4, 165, 174 n.5, 178 n.51

prudence (prudently, prudential tradition) 10, 13, 29, 44, 53, 67, 105–6, 112, 118–23, 128, 132, 138–9, 146, 152, 156, 163–4, 173 n.49, 176 n.25, 178 n.45, 185 n.36, 200 n.49

Ps. Philoponus 183 n.21

Psellos 183 n.21

punishment 10, 30–1, 37–9, 45, 53, 62, 105–7, 118, 120–2, 129, 164, 199

Pyrrho 128

Rashed, M. 36, 174 n.9

Raubitschek, E. 204 n.42

reasoning (sober, prudential reasoning) 29, 91–2, 112, 119, 138–9

relative ('category of relative') 6, 15–16, 18–19, 32, 168 n.7, 168 n.9

relativism 5–6, 12, 69, 124, 126, 161

Remes, P. 203 n.26

Rider, B. A. 178 n.46, 180 n.61

Robitzsch, J. M. 201 n.52

Roskam, G. 29, 40, 101, 138, 151, 173 n.47, 175 n.17, 179 n.57, 187 n.1, 190 n.25, 191 n.28, 194 n.51, 195 nn.56–7, 198 n.22, 199 n.36, 200 n.44, 203 nn.15–16, 204 n.36, 205 n.59, 206 nn.85–6

Salem, J. 180 n.60

Sancho, L. 174 n.10

Schiesaro, A. 170 n.23

Schmid, W. 191 n.28, 192 n.33

Schofield, M. 136, 173 n.2, 185 n.41, 196 n.6, 203 nn.7–9

Scholz, P. 194 nn.48–50, 203 n.20

Schrijvers, P. 171 n.31

security, safety (contractual security) 4–8, 12, 15, 19–20, 31, 33–54, 56–7, 64, 72, 79, 81, 87–8, 94, 103, 108, 123–4, 127, 138, 143–5, 153–4, 156, 161–5, 170 n.26, 173 n.1, 174 nn.3–4, 175 n.20, 176 n.21, 177 n.30, 195 n.57, 199 n.37

Sedley, D. 167 n.2, 169 n.11, 169 nn.15–17, 176 n.24, 177 n.32, 181 nn.5–6, 184 nn.29–30, 188 n.8, 190 n.23, 192 n.35, 193 n.3, 199 n.33, 206 nn.80–1

Seel, G. 112, 197 n.11, 198 nn.23–4

Seneca 98, 116, 137–8, 174, 196 n.5, 197 n.10, 201 n.54, 203 n.11

Sextus Empiricus 17, 45, 66–7, 75, 168, 183–4, 186, 196 n.7, 197 n.10

Shearin, W. H. 187 n.8

Sickinger, J. 143, 203 n.29

Simplicius 183 n.21

Siro 151, 172 n.41

Smith, M. F. 17, 23, 45, 148, 176 n.30, 177 n.30, 204 n.44, 205 n.52
Socrates 3, 10, 54, 73, 76–7, 94, 98, 100–1, 115, 121, 136–7, 149, 151, 157, 165, 187 n.59, 192 n.32, 193 n.41, 194 n.53, 195 n.57
Solmsen, F. 169 n.15
Solon 63, 134, 137, 180 n.62
Spatharas, D. 177 n.41
Speusipus 194 n.49
Steel, C. 86, 188 n.11
Stokes, M. 193 n.43
Stilpon 100, 198 n.23
Stobaeus 47, 116, 124–5, 179 n.55, 187 n.59, 197 n.10
Stoicism 47–8, 107–8, 112, 196 n.6
Strauss, L. 1, 64, 112, 167 n.1, 182 n.17, 197 n.21
Striker, G. 168 n.6, 193 n.43
Stuart Mill, J. 123, 200 n.46, 201 n.51
study of nature ('physiology') 3–4, 9–10, 15, 18, 21, 31, 34, 42, 47, 65, 77, 79, 81, 87, 103, 106, 118–20, 123, 156, 160–1, 163, 168 n.7, 182 n.16

Tate, J. 169 n.15
Thales 100
Theocritus (son of Aresteias) 147–8
Thuchydides 35, 41, 45, 174 n.3, 182 n.14
Timocrates 143, 188 n.8, 200 n.44
Titus Albucius 151, 205 n.69, 206 n.82
tranquillity 7, 42, 48, 50, 72, 90, 107–8, 111, 142, 144, 154, 161–4, 179, 188 n.8, 198 n.30
Trebatius Testa 134, 152–4, 205 n.69
trust (in human beings, in the future; mutual trust) 36–7, 49, 51–3, 56, 125, 144–5

Tsouna, V. 172 n.41, 178 nn.45–6, 181 n.4, 204 n.33
turmoil 40, 51, 138
Tutrone, F. 203 n.13

usefulness (justice as modality of usefulness) 5–8, 16, 19, 28–30, 32, 38–9, 44–5, 51, 53, 59–60, 62–4, 69, 72, 76, 88, 93, 101, 121, 126–7, 162, 170 n.26, 184 n.33, 185 n.34
Usener, H. 26–7, 172 nn.32–3, 192 n.38, 197 n.11, 203 n.22

Van Bremen, R. vi, 204 n.44, 205 n.61
Van Wees, H. 187 n.8
Vander Waerdt, P. A 112, 171 n.31, 197 n.11, 198 n.25
Verde, F. vi, 188 n.8
Verlinsky, A. 170 n.29, 186 n.44
Vigo, A. G. 185 n.36
Vlastos, G. 186 n.48

Warren, J. 142–4, 168 n.7, 177 n.30, 178 n.43, 180 n.63, 188 n.8, 193 n.39, 203 nn.27–8, 204 n.32
wealth (as 'wealth of nature') 50, 62, 178 n.49, 181 n.7
Wolfsdorf, D. 98, 193 n.40
Wood, N. 88, 188 n.17
Woolf, R. 178 n.46, 199 n.35, 200 n.39
worship 12, 126, 133, 141, 157, 163

Xenocrates 194 n.48

Yona, S. 178 n.50

Zangara, A. 183 n.23

Index Locorum

Anonymous Iamblichus

100, 5	174 n.10
100, 13–15	36
102, 8–17	36
103, 1–3	36
103, 20–21	36

Aristotle
Ethica Eudemia

1219b6–7	180 n.62
1242b1	170 n.27

Ethica Nicomachea

1094a26–27	175 n.16
1094a28-b2	175 n.16
1095a5–7	
1095b17	119
1096a5–7	50
1096a26	168
1109b31–32	38
1112b27–28	27
1113b30–33	175 n.13
1134b18–1135a5	112
1135b25	191 n.26
1141a27–28	191
1141b14–16	70
1159a10–13	20
1160a21–22	12
1161b27–28	170 n.27
1166a7–8	172 n.39
1166a23–29	172 n.39
1166a31–32	27, 170 n.27

On Heaven

291a24–25	191 n.26

Physics

254a35	183 n.21

Politics

1252a6–8	35
1252b16	12, 44
1253a7–18	22, 73
1256a23	39
1256b23–25	174 n.5
1256b30–31	50
1258a12–14	50
1261a10-b15	35
1274b19–23	38
1280b5–12	42
1300b25–26	191 n.26
1304b23–24	174 n.3
1315a31–35	174 n.6
1321a5–12	174 n.6
1327a19	174 n.6

Rhetoric

1375a7	191 n.26
1375b3–4	20
1383a5–8	44
1402b10–12	175 n.13

Athenaeus
Deipnosophists

12.546E-F	187 n.3
12.547A	187 n.2

Aulus Gellius
Noctes Atticae

1.3	198 n.23
2.8, 1	90
2.8, 5	90
2.8, 8	90
2.9.1–4	89
2.9, 4–5	89, 193 n.42

Cicero
Academica

1.9–10	82
1.25–27	82
2.17	182 n.20
2.57	196 n.7

Against Piso
37	188 n.8

De natura deorum
1.18	189 n.20
1.21	97
1.43–44	59
1.43–45	201 n.47
1.45	122
1.56	201 n.47
1.57–62	86
1.57–115	84
1.58–59	84
1.62	84
1.85	86
2.32	87
2.76	90
3.28	194 n.46
3.34	194 n.46

De Officiis.
1.2	101
3.9	118
3.38–39	10, 106, 111, 117, 119, 128, 163
3.77–78	117

De Repvblica
1.2, 2	136
1.2, 2–3	136
1.5	137
1.10	138
1.25, 40	22, 73
1.39	89
3.23	89

De Finibus
1.1–4	82
1.6	82
1.8	83
1.10	83
1.13	82–3, 187 n.6
1.15	82
1.17	11
1.23	89
1.23–25	118
1.25	11
1.34–36	118
1.35	199 n.37
1.61	199 n.38
1.65	51
1.67	125
1.66–68	125
1.68	179 n.52
1.69	28
2.12–13	82
2.15	83
2.27	83
2.28	200 n.42
2.32	193 n.39
2.37	101
2.44	101, 151
2.57	56
2.58	101
2.61	199 n.37
2.67	134
2.72	101
2.76	101
2.78	101
2.80	101, 117
2.82	28, 51, 172 n.33
2.83	52
2.84	52
2.88	83
2.94–95	54
2.96	180 n.59
2.99	199 n.34
2.101	142
2.109	101
2.117	101
3.67	91
4.4–6	86
4.5	86
4.11	87
4.13	188 n.12
5.7	87
5.23	173 n.1

De legibus
1.39	136, 203 n.18
1.44.	196 n.6
3.13, 23	128

Letters to Friends
2.12, 1	152
7.26, 1	80

Index Locorum 235

On divination
1.127–129   198 n.27

On Friendship
17.61   198 n.24

On the Orator
3.64   102

Paradoxa Stoicurum
5   187 n.59

Tusc.
3.46   117
4.6–7   3, 150–1
5.26   144

Clement of Alexandria
Stromateis
1.15, 67, 1   186 n.58
2.4, 119, 20–32   182 n.21
4.26   196 n.6
6.9, 73.2–75, 1   197 n.8

Critias

DK B 25   105

Democritus

DK 68 B 264   105
DK 244   105
DK B 264   105

Demosthenes
Against Meidias
210, 6   37
221   37

Diodorus Siculus
Bibliotheca Historica
3.18, 4–6   170 n.29

Diogenes of Oenoanda

Frag. 12 (ed. Smith)   185 n.43
Frag. 14 (ed. Smith)   17
Frag. 35 (ed. Smith)   176
Frag. 56 (ed. Smith)   23
Frag. 126 (ed. Smith)   45
Frag. 167 (ed. Smith)   45

Diogenes Laertius

6.13   176 n.25
7.32–34   179 n.55, 196 n.4
7.85–86   91
7.105–107   50
9.34   67
9.107   184 n.26
9.119   141
10.9–10   141
10.11   52, 144
10.12   3, 50, 87
10.16   132
10.16–21   142
10.17   143
10.18   143
10.19–21   165
10.21   143
10.22   80
10.27   110
10.28   2, 155
10.29–30   12
10.31   61, 184 n.25
10.32   75
10.33   67, 73
10.34   184 n.26
10.117   53, 108
10.118   93, 107
10.119   62, 108, 138
10.120   50, 108, 145
10.120a   141, 144
10.132   98
10.136   98–9, 192 n.39, 198 n.30

Epictetus
Dissertations
1.4, 28–29   197 n.8
1.9, 1–2   196 n.6
1.19, 26–29   140
1.23   47
2.2   47
2.20, 6   102, 135, 203 n.5
2.20, 15–16   135

2.20, 26	134	*On Nature*	
2.20, 27	139	12	21, 45, 156 n.51
3.7, 1	139	28, frag. 12, col. iii, 9–14	181 n.6
3.7, 14	111		
3.7, 19–20	135	28, 13, 7	184 n.30
		34, 26–30	61
Handbook			
Chap. 38	48	*Principal Doctrines*	
		1	64, 92, 105, 127
Epicurus		2	189 n.19
Letter to Herodotus		3	89
37–38	64, 75	5	13, 53, 120, 123, 154, 164
40	17		
45	181 n.10	6	47
50	67	7	7, 43, 47
51–52	69	8	17
54	109	12	51
55	109	13	51, 182 n.16
63	113	14	4, 7, 33, 41, 47–8, 161
68	17, 64, 180 n. 59	15	49–50, 61, 62
71	17	16	144
72	61	21	49
73	17	27	26, 51, 124
73–74	181 n.10	28	26, 51
75	21, 185 n.43	30	42
76	21, 186 n.44	31	8, 45, 50, 60, 62, 63, 65, 93, 116, 185 n.33
77	17		
127	49	32	39, 60, 62, 63, 167 n.1, 187 n.58
Letter to Menoeceus		33	16, 17, 19, 20, 28, 44, 53, 60, 69, 88, 93, 124, 169 n.19
122	55		
123–124	46, 61, 76, 85, 182 n. 16		
124–125	142, 189 n.19	34	113, 122, 197 n.13
126	113	35	122, 198 n.29
127	49	36	19, 60, 69, 122, 169 n.19, 201 n.51
128	39, 119, 181 n.13		
130	49	37	5, 8, 18, 22, 31, 52, 59, 60–1, 64, 65, 68, 70–3, 77, 88, 160, 185 n.39
131	3, 178 n.46, 198 n.31		
132	13, 29, 53, 119–20, 123, 132, 164, 198 n.31		
		38	5, 8, 19, 22, 59, 60–1, 66, 38, 70–3, 88, 169 n.19
134–135	117, 189 n.20		
		39	28
Letter to Pytocles		40	28, 33, 53, 167 n.1
84	132		
85	180 n.59	*Vatican Sayings*	
85–87	68	4	179 n.52
86–87	68	14	49
113	68	17	55

19	55	**Jerome**	
23	26, 52	*Against Jovinianus*	
27	55	1.48	196 n.5
28	53		
29	52	**Lactantius**	
31	41	*Divinae Institutiones*	
33	49	1.1, 5–8	95
43	123, 129	1.16, 3	191 n.28
45	123	1.21, 48	191 n.28
52	26–7, 124	2.8, 48–49	94, 96
55	55	2.8, 52	94
56	179 n.55	2.11, 1	191 n.28
57	179 n.55	3.8, 3	99
58	164	3.9, 1	95
61	28	3.12, 1–8	99
67	53	3.14	95
69	55	3.16, 16	191 n.31
78	26, 179 n.54	3.17, 1–20	95
81	181 n.8	3.17, 2–7	12, 95, 99, 173 n.47
		3.17, 2–31	191 n.28
Galen		3.17, 7–8	97
On Pulse Differences		3.17, 8–16	105
4. Vol. 8 716 12;	186 n.55	3.17, 18–27	192 n.36
741, 12; 743, 13		3.17, 16–27	95, 97, 192 n.36
		3.17, 39–43	102
Herculaneum Papyri		3.17, 42	25
		3.19, 18	192 n.32
1012	19, 63	3.20, 15	96, 192 n.32
(col. lxvi–lxviii)		3.30, 1–10	192 n.31
1020	196 n.7	3.30, 9	95
1044	2, 133, 145, 155	3.35–43	193 n.45
1078/1080	76, 156	5.7 1	25
		6.10 2	25
Hierocles			
Elements of Ethics		*Epitome*	
1.44–50	92	55 1	25
3.5–45	92	60, 2	25
Hippolytus		**Lucian**	
Refutation of all Heresies		*Alexander or the False Prophet*	
1.22, 3	189 n.20	25	148
Horace		**Lucretius**	
Satires		*De rerum natura*	
1.1	178 n.50	1.482	17
		1.455–456	17
Isocrates		2.1–13	195 n.58
Antidosis		2.7–8	41
253–254	186 n.47	2.16–19	193 n.39

2.1092	175 n.14	**Marcus Aurelius**	
3.17, 42	25		
3.60–71	46	10.1	196 n.6
3.67	46	10.6	196 n.6
3.931–940	55, 149		
3.955–963	55, 149	**Musonius Rufus**	
3.995–1003	173 n.49		
3.1003–1010	55	Frag. 34	187 n.59
4.823–824	91	(ed. Hense)	
4.823–857	181 n.10		
4.1256	170 n.26	**Origen**	
5.62–63	68	*Against Celsum*	
5.156–170	92	3.80, 23–27	178 n.44
5.156–234	181 n.10		
5.165–167	189 n.20	**Papyrus Oxyrincus**	
5.181	92		
5.195–200	24	5077 (col. ii,	64, 65
5.195–234	97	frag. 2, 1)	
5.218–227	24		
5.837–877	181 n.10	**Philodemus**	
5.830–831	41	*Against the Sophists*	
5.855–877	69	4.7–14	
5.857–859	43		
5.860–874	175 n.14	*On signs*	
5.924–1010	176 n.27	34.5–11	
5.931–932	22, 25, 74		
5.948	22	*On Choices and Avoidances*	
5.960–961	25	xiv, 1–4	54
5.970–1010	177 n.30	xxi, 2–22.	149
5.983	43		
5.1011–1027	23, 26	*On death*	
5.1014	170 n.24	col. xxiv, 10–17	144
5.1019–1020	29, 73, 171 n.30		
5.1020	23	*On Frank Criticism*	
5.1020–1023	22, 171 n.31	Frag. 28, 1–12	127
5.1021–1023	73–4		
5.1024–1027	25	*On the gods*	
5.1026–1027	43	Frag. 3	53
5.1028–1090	185 n.43, 186 n.51	Frag. 83, 1–2	127
5.1115	31, 45		
5.1182–1192	97	*On Piety*	
5.1447	23	519–541	45
6.1–8	11	1139–1150	201 n.47
6.1–11	41	1512–1532	141
6.1–40	79	2043	126
6.10–11	41	2051–2	127

2145–2174	45	524b	90
2263–2265	201 n.47	525a3–5	121
		525b1–2	121
On Property Management		525b6	121
xii, 18–19	178 n.48		
xii 25, xiv, 9	50	*Laws*	
xiii 36–38,	50	708d-709d	169 n.17
xxv 1–14		716c-d	199 n.33
xv 31-xvi 18	116	758a-b	173 n.2
xvii 2–14,	123	888b8	3, 21, 87
xxv 23–24		906d-e	173 n.2
xxii, 10–48	137	961e4	173 n.2
xxiv, 29–31	53	962a1	173 n.2
xxiv, 19-xxv, 23	178 n.51		
xxiv, 29–31	53	*Philebus*	
xxvii, 5–9	144	12d	98
		13b-c	98
Rhetoric		21a-c	193 n.41
2, col. xxxivb 34–9	206 n.88	31a7–10	193 n.41
3, col. xiva 19-	206 n.88	31c	193 n.41
col. xvia 8		38c-d	183 n.25
3, col.xa, 1–6	155	53d-54d	193 n.41
5, col. xx 25–36	173 n.50	61c6	200 n.41

Plato

Alcibiades I		*Phaedo*	
111a	76	67d4–10	90
Cratylus		*Protagoras*	
388d-390a	169 n.17	321c-e	169 n.21
		321c7-d5	35
Gorgias		322a-b	35
473e	136, 165	322b5	35
474c	110	322c	35
476b-477a	122		
478d-e	122	*Respublica*	
483c3–4	63	343d-e	115
483e3	63	352b8	116
484b1	63	352d6	191 n.30
486b6–7	172 n.37	358e4–359b5	114
492c2	172 n.37	358c7	115
495a1–2	98	359a1–2	20, 114, 116
500c3–4	191 n.30	359a5	114
517b	137, 149	359b6	64
519a	136	359c3–5	117, 128
521d	136, 149, 165	359c6–360c5	111, 113
		359e-360a	115

360b6	117	1127D-E	93, 106, 110, 112, 118, 128, 142
360c3	117	1128D	135, 138
361b-c	115	1129B-C	135
361e1–3	198 n.28		
362e-363a	198 n.28		
365d-e	190 n.24	*Eroticus*	
367b6	115	751A-752A	193 n.46
383c	199 n.33	758C-D	193 n.46
388e-389b	190 n.24		
416e-417a	187 n.59		
442e-443b	70	*Live Unnoticed*	
500c-d	199 n.33	1128A-B	90, 193 n.46
505b-c	98	1130A	193 n.46
561c	98	1128A-B	193 n.46
602c7–8	183 n.25	1129A- B	81
608d	190 n.24		
613a-b	199 n.33	*On Curiosity*	
		520A-C	193 n.46
Statesman			
294a7–8	70	*On Moral Virtue*	
296e-297b	173 n.2	441C-E	109
Symposium		*On Peace of Mind*	
200b-e	49	465F-466A	138
Theaetetus			
176b	199 n.33	*On Superstition*	
		164F	190 n.21
Timaeus		167A-168A	190 n.21
90a	199 n.33		
90c	200 n.40	*On the Pytian Oracles*	
		399D-E	91
Plutarch			
Against Colotes		*Oracles in Decline*	
1107D	51	420B3	190 n.21
1089D	49	429C-F	193 n.46
1111B	27		
1117B	165	*Pleasant Life*	
1121A	184 n.26	1009E	178 n.44
1124D	40, 101	1089D	193 n.39
1124E	101	1090C-D	93
1125A	102	1095C	108
1125C	93–94, 139	1098A-1100D	199 n.38
1125C-1127C	102	1098D	53, 102
1125E-F	46	1099D	54
1126B-D	100, 135	1104B	46, 121–2
1126C	150	1105B	46
1127A-B	102, 137	1105E	125

Index Locorum

Pyrrhus
14	145
20, 6	145

Stoic. Rep.
1048E	108, 198 n.26

Whether an old man should engage in public affairs
791D	136

Polybius
Histories
6.5, 9–10	25
6.6, 2–5	25

Polystratus
On the Irrational Contempt of Popular Opinions
Col. iii, 5–11	44
Col. xxii 6	19
Col. xxii 23–4	18–19, 64
Col. xxiv 3–5	19, 64
Col. xxiv 24-xxv 16	64
Col. xxv 9–10	18, 64
Col. xxv 18–9	168 n.9
Col. xxv 18–24	64
Col. xxvi 22–5	64
Col. xxvii 10	64
Col. xxviii 10	18–19,

Porphyry
Abst.
1.7, 1	171 n.31
1.7, 2	12, 44
1.7, 4	175 n.18
1.8, 1–2	30, 72, 173 n.50
1.8, 4	30
1.8, 19–20	30
1.9, 5	175 n.18
1.9, 1–16	38
1.10, 1	28, 43
1.10, 4	30, 72, 173 n.50
1.11, 1	175 n.18
1.11, 2	40
1.11, 4–6	175 n.18
1.12, 2	64
1.12, 3	31, 160
1.12, 4	175 n.18
1.12, 5–6	175 n.18
1.12, 19	88
1.12, 23–25	39

To Marcella
27	62, 201 n.54
28	198 n.31

Psellos
Opusculum
13, 71, 6–7 (ed. O'Meara)	183 n.21

Pseudo Philoponus
In Arist. De anima
586, 21–23	183 n.21

Seneca
De ira
3.17.2	203 n.11

De otio
3.29	138

Ep.
9, 1	116
59, 12	203 n.11
83, 12	154
90.35	98

On Marriage
Frag. 45	196 n.5

Sextus Empiricus
M
7.151–157	196 n.7
7.166–189	67
7.203	67
7.208	184 n.26
7.212	67
7.215	67
7.218	66
7.253–260	67
7.424–425	67
7.433	197 n.10
9.25–26	186 n.56
9.54	45
10.219–220	17

Simplicius
In Arist. De anima
299, 35   183 n.21

Stobaeus
Anthology
3.17.23   116
4.143   125

Ecl.
2.100, 2   197 n.10
2.101, 14–20   187 n.59
2.108, 5–28   179 n.55
2.112, 1–5   197 n.10

Thucydides
1, 2, 6   41
1, 6, 3   41
3.82   36

Us.
2   192 n.36
14   62
20   108
36   66
67   187 n.3
68   49
101   165
138   80
181   3, 187 n.2
190   165
202   62
213   125
226   186 n.58
240   21
252   184
247   67
353   186 n.56
396   41
464   49
466   49
470   49
476   198 n.31
478   46
490   178 n.46
491   55
512   3
530   47, 124–5
532   93
534   122
536   53
539   51
543   52
544   54

Xenophon
Memorabilia
4.2, 9   187 n.59

www.ingramcontent.com/pod-product-compliance
Lightning Source LLC
Chambersburg PA
CBHW062137300426
44115CB00012BA/1962